The Cost of Free Shipping

Wildcat: Workers' Movements and Global Capitalism

Series Editors:
Immanuel Ness (City University of New York)
Malehoko Tshoaedi (University of Johannesburg)
Peter Cole (Western Illinois University)
Raquel Varela (Instituto de História Contemporânea (IHC) of Universidade Nova de Lisboa, Lisbon New University)
Kate Alexander (University of Johannesburg)
Tim Pringle (SOAS, University of London)

Workers' movements are a common and recurring feature in contemporary capitalism. The same militancy that inspired the mass labor movements of the twentieth century continues to define worker struggles that proliferate throughout the world today.

For more than a century, labor unions have mobilized to represent the political-economic interests of workers by uncovering the abuses of capitalism, establishing wage standards, improving oppressive working conditions, and bargaining with employers and the state. Since the 1970s, organized labor has declined in size and influence as the global power and influence of capital has expanded dramatically. The world over, existing unions are in a condition of fracture and turbulence in response to neoliberalism, financialization, and the reappearance of rapacious forms of imperialism. New and modernized unions are adapting to conditions and creating class-conscious workers' movements rooted in militancy and solidarity. Ironically, while the power of organized labor contracts, working-class militancy and resistance persists and is growing in the Global South.

Wildcat publishes ambitious and innovative works on the history and political economy of workers' movements and is a forum for debate on pivotal movements and labor struggles. The series applies a broad definition of the labor movement to include workers in and out of unions, and seeks works that examine proletarianization and class formation; mass production; gender, affective and reproductive labor; imperialism and workers; syndicalism and independent unions, and labor and Leftist social and political movements.

Also available:

Choke Points:
Logistics Workers Disrupting the Global Supply Chain
Edited by Jake Alimahomed-Wilson and Immanuel Ness

Dying for an iPhone
Apple, Foxconn and the Lives of China's Workers
Jenny Chan, Mark Selden and Pun Ngai

Just Work?
Migrant Workers' Struggles Today
Edited by Aziz Choudry and Mondli Hlatshwayo

Wobblies of the World:
A Global History of the IWW
Edited by Peter Cole, David Struthers and Kenyon Zimmer

Southern Insurgency:
The Coming of the Global Working Class
Immanuel Ness

Workers' Inquiry and Global Class Struggle
Strategies, Tactics, Objectives
Edited by Robert Ovetz

The Spirit of Marikana:
The Rise of Insurgent Trade Unionism in South Africa
Luke Sinwell with Siphiwe Mbatha

Solidarity
Latin America and the US Left in the Era of Human Rights
Steve Striffler

Working the Phones:
Control and Resistance in Call Centres
Jamie Woodcock

The Cost of Free Shipping

Amazon in the Global Economy

Edited by Jake Alimahomed-Wilson
and Ellen Reese

First published 2020 by Pluto Press
345 Archway Road, London N6 5AA

www.plutobooks.com

Copyright © Jake Alimahomed-Wilson and Ellen Reese 2020
The right of the individual contributors to be identified as the authors of this work has been asserted in accordance with the Copyright, Designs and Patents Act 1988.

British Library Cataloguing in Publication Data
A catalogue record for this book is available from the British Library

ISBN 978 0 7453 4147 7   Hardback
ISBN 978 0 7453 4148 4   Paperback
ISBN 978 1 7868 0751 9   PDF eBook
ISBN 978 1 7868 0753 3   Kindle eBook
ISBN 978 1 7868 0752 6   EPUB eBook

This book is printed on paper suitable for recycling and made from fully managed and sustained forest sources. Logging, pulping and manufacturing processes are expected to conform to the environmental standards of the country of origin.

Typeset by Stanford DTP Services, Northampton, England

Simultaneously printed in the United Kingdom and United States of America

Contents

List of Figures and Tables	viii
Dedication	ix
Acknowledgments	x
Preface: Amazon and the Future of Work in the Global Economy Ruth Milkman	xi
Introduction: Amazon Capitalism Jake Alimahomed-Wilson, Juliann Allison, and Ellen Reese	1

PART I AMAZON'S RISE IN GLOBAL POWER

1 Amazon: Context, Structure, and Vulnerability Kim Moody	21
2 Power Accrues to the Powerful: Amazon's Market Share, Customer Surveillance, and Internet Dominance Dana M. Williams	35
3 Transnational Amazon: Labor Exploitation and the Rise of E-Commerce in South Asia Jeb Sprague and Sreerekha Sathi	50

PART II EXPLOITATION AND RESISTANCE ACROSS AMAZON'S GLOBAL EMPIRE

4 The Amazonification of Logistics: E-Commerce, Labor, and Exploitation in the Last Mile Jake Alimahomed-Wilson	69
5 Automation and the Surveillance-Driven Warehouse in Inland Southern California Jason Struna and Ellen Reese	85
6 Gender, Race, and Amazon Warehouse Labor in the United States Ellen Reese	102

The Cost of Free Shipping

7   A New Industrial Working Class? Challenges in Disrupting
    Amazon's Fulfillment Process in Germany   116
    Nantina Vgontzas
8   A Struggle for Bodies and Souls: Amazon Management and
    Union Strategies in France and Italy   129
    Francesco Massimo

PART III   COMMUNITIES CONFRONTING THE E-COMMERCE GIANT

9   Company Town: What Happens to a City and its Democracy
    when Amazon Dominates?   147
    Katie Wilson
10 Lessons from New York City's Struggle Against Amazon HQ2
    in Long Island City   161
    Steve Lang and Filip Stabrowski
11 What Happens When Amazon Comes to Town? Environmental
    Impacts, Local Economies, and Resistance in Inland Southern
    California   176
    Juliann Emmons Allison
12 Worker and Community Organizing to Challenge Amazon's
    Algorithmic Threat   194
    Sheheryar Kaoosji

PART IV   STRUGGLING TO WIN AGAINST AMAZON

13 Amazon Strikes in Europe: Seven Years of Industrial Action,
    Challenges, and Strategies   209
    Jörn Boewe and Johannes Schulten
14 Bursting the Bubble: The Emerging Tech Worker Movement at
    Amazon   225
    Spencer Cox
15 The CEO Has No Clothes: Worker Leadership and Amazon's
    Failures During COVID-19   238
    Dania Rajendra

Contents

16 Think Big: Organizing a Successful Amazon Workers' Movement in the United States by Combining the Strengths of the Left and Organized Labor   250
Peter Olney and Rand Wilson

17 Amazonians United! An Interview with DCH1 (Chicago) Amazonians United   265
DCH1 Amazonians United

Conclusion: Resisting Amazon Capitalism   275
Jake Alimahomed-Wilson and Ellen Reese

About the Authors   285
Index   290

List of Figures and Tables

FIGURES

11.1	Slowing growth in warehousing, distribution, and transportation in Inland Southern California	183

TABLES

1.1	Amazon global facilities as of June 2019	26
5.1	Employment and job characteristics of interview sample	88
5.2	Social characteristics of interview sample	89
8.1	General data on Amazon Fulfillment Centers in France and Italy	142
11.1	Amazon facilities in Inland Southern California	177
11.2	Spatial inequality in Southern California	179
13.1	Trade union density in European countries, 2018 (percentage of employed workers belonging to a union)	211

We dedicate this book to all the workers and communities impacted by Amazon capitalism.

Acknowledgments

The editors wish to acknowledge and thank our families for their support in making this book possible, especially given the many challenges of juggling work, home schooling our kids, and family life amidst the COVID-19 crisis.

First and foremost, Jake is grateful for all the love, support, motivation, and inspiration he received from his partner, Sabrina Alimahomed-Wilson and their two kids, Shanti and Séamus, during this entire book project. Jake is also thankful for his parents, Jay and Mary, for their positive encouragement every step of the way. Finally, Jake thanks his wonderful colleagues and amazing students at California State University, Long Beach.

First and foremost, Ellen wishes to thank her partner, Ernest Savage and her son Xavier for their support. Ellen is also grateful for the encouragement she received from her parents, Bill and Emmy, and her colleagues at the University of California Riverside, especially Juliann Allison. Ellen also thanks her UCR undergraduate Sociology 197 student research team who provided valuable research assistance, especially for Chapters 5 and 6, as well as other UCR students who helped to inform and shape ideas for this project.

We also want to thank all of the contributors for their amazing chapters and the many workers and activists who shared their stories and insights for this project. Without them, this volume would not have been possible. In addition, we want to thank David Shulman and the entire staff at Pluto Press—it is a privilege to work with all of you. To our anonymous reviewers, and our contributors, Jason Struna, Juliann Allison, and Kim Moody, and Soc 232 graduate students at UCR, we appreciate the feedback you all provided on individual chapters. We're thankful for the support we received from Carolina Bank Muñoz, Edna Bonacich, James McKeever, Rebecca Romo, Mike Chavez, Carlotta Benvegnù, Haude Rivoal, Niccolò Cuppini, David Gaborieau, Kirsty Newsome, Chima Anyadike-Danes, Kent Wong, Stephanie Luce, Bill Fletcher Jr., Peter Cole, Robert Ovetz, Spencer Potiker, and Immanuel Ness. Finally, we also thank Shaafi Farooqi for her wonderful copy-editing assistance.

Preface

Amazon and the Future of Work in the Global Economy

Ruth Milkman

Jeff Bezos, now the world's richest individual, launched Amazon as an online bookstore in 1995. Over the next quarter-century it grew into an e-commerce behemoth, offering rapid home delivery of an ever-expanding range of products and services—from A to Z, as its logo promises; its 2017 acquisition of Whole Foods made it a major player in food delivery as well. Critical to Amazon's business model are its massive warehousing and logistics operations; its cloud computing division is also a key profit center. The COVID-19 pandemic accelerated the spectacular growth of what this book's editors call "Amazon capitalism," as demand for home delivery surged while countless brick-and-mortar retailers were forced to close.

Even before the unexpected pandemic bonanza, Amazon's market value exceeded that of any other corporation on earth, displacing Walmart (still the world's largest private-sector employer) as the icon of corporate domination and labor exploitation. The two giant firms have much in common: massive market power predicated on streamlined supply chains, which in turn provides leverage to extract lower prices from manufacturers and vendors, and to deploy predatory pricing to undercut competition from other retailers. And like Walmart, Amazon is intransigently anti-union.

Amazon pays hourly workers a bit better than Walmart does, in part because Amazon needs fewer of them. It runs only a few retail outlets and makes extensive use of robotics and other forms of automation in its "fulfillment centers." Yet, as this book chronicles in rich detail, Amazon's warehouses in many respects resemble the factories of the past: workers are subject to the daily indignities, productivity pressures, and health and safety hazards long associated with manufacturing. The company also relies on an army of "last mile" delivery workers, often hired by subcontractors, who rush goods to customers' homes a day or two after online orders are placed, or sometimes within hours. In these sweatshops on wheels, as in the warehouses, old-style labor exploitation is intensified by high-tech worker surveillance, algorithmic management, gamification, and automation.

The chapters that follow document Amazon's impact outside the workplace as well as inside it. One focus is the systematic surveillance of customers, not only monetizing data from their online purchases but also tracking more intimate behavior through in-home devices like Alexa. Another theme is the destructive environmental impact of Amazon warehouses, which sharply increase truck traffic, air pollution, and respiratory illnesses in the areas where they are located. Yet cities and states compete fiercely to lure Amazon facilities to their jurisdictions, offering tax breaks and other incentives—unaware that, as Juliann Allison suggests in this volume, such concessions tend to neutralize any economic development benefits.

In the United States, where a stunning 60 percent of households are Amazon Prime members, the company has amassed a vast base of loyal customers, and it is increasingly replicating that success in other countries. Most customers relate to Amazon simply as a convenient and affordable place to shop, oblivious or indifferent to the catalogue of ills this book reveals. They are even less likely to be aware of the labor and community organizing efforts that aim to challenge Amazon's vast power on multiple fronts, also chronicled here.

The most successful struggles to date have unfolded in Western Europe, where labor unions have made significant inroads. Amazon workers in Germany, Poland, France, Italy, and Spain launched a series of strikes in the 2010s, winning significant concessions; an international "Amazon Alliance" of unions involved in these efforts has grown to include 15 countries. In the United States, where obstacles to unionism are especially formidable, such efforts have been more elusive. Once again, there is a Walmart echo: after spending millions of dollars on a decades-long series of campaigns to organize Walmart workers, the United Food and Commercial Workers accepted defeat in 2015. That bruising experience, along with other setbacks for U.S. organized labor in recent years, help explain the lack of any major union resource commitments to Amazon organizing in the company's home country.

Nevertheless, a few notable efforts have emerged. The first breakthrough was a 2018 work stoppage at an Amazon warehouse in Minneapolis, led by Somali workers demanding Muslim prayer rights. Its success helped stimulate the formation of Athena, a national coalition coordinating Amazon-focused organizing across the nation. Separately, New York City unionists' insistence that Amazon maintain neutrality vis-à-vis future union organizing efforts in that city contributed to the collapse of the controversial plan to locate an Amazon "HQ2" in Long Island City in 2019. That same year, Amazon's tech workers, led by progressive Millennials, staged a walkout demanding that the company aggressively combat climate change and stop providing services facilitating federal immigration enforcement. Finally, against the background of the COVID-19 pandemic, workers protested the lack of personal protective equipment at Amazon warehouses in walkouts across the U.S. in the spring of 2020.

So far, these efforts have had little impact on the Amazon juggernaut, which continues to gain momentum in the United States and worldwide. But for those who hope to change that, the probing studies by labor and urban scholars collected in this book provide an invaluable resource.

Introduction: Amazon Capitalism

Jake Alimahomed-Wilson, Juliann Allison, and Ellen Reese

Among the world's most powerful corporations, Amazon's recent growth has been unparalleled. Initially founded in 1995 as an electronic book vendor, Amazon became the world's second "trillion-dollar corporation" (after Apple) in 2018, a feat underscoring its immense size and economic influence.[1] The following year, Amazon overtook Google and Apple to become the world's most valuable corporation on the planet in terms of market value.[2] By April 2020, the corporation's market cap increased even further, to $1.14 trillion as demand for its services surged amid the global COVID-19 pandemic.[3] That same month, as COVID-19 cases were spreading across its global workforce and the first U.S. warehouse worker death from the disease was reported, the personal wealth of the company's Chief Executive Officer, Jeff Bezos, the richest person in world history, climbed to $138 billion.[4] Amazon would emerge from the global pandemic even stronger. The meteoric rise of this corporation represents a significant shift in the global political economy, that we identify as *Amazon capitalism*. By naming this phenomenon, we seek to draw attention to the concentration of corporate power manifest in the scale and magnitude of Amazon's influence in the world's economy and to highlight the true costs of its "free shipping" for workers, communities, and the environment.

Amazon's rise illuminates a pivotal moment in global capitalism that demands naming, interrogating, and *resisting*. Amazon, the corporation, is not simply a "bad apple," nor is its peculiar business and labor practices the product of the individual greed and maniacal impulses of its founder, Jeff Bezos, and other top executives. All corporations share one fundamental objective: to maximize profit. Indeed, the problems associated with Amazon capitalism are systemic within our global capitalist system, which is embedded and interacts with other social and political relations of domination that operate at multiple scales, from the local to the global. Amazon's rise in power reflects, and makes visible, the larger global trend of the increasing influence of finance capitalism, neoliberal politics and policies, and corporate power. Indeed, the world's leading transnational corporations today continue to accrue revenues far ahead of most nation states. Of the world's top 200 economic entities, 157 are corporations and 43 are governments.[5] Even back in 2019, Amazon's market capitalization was slightly more than the combined GDP of nine Latin American countries combined.[6]

Together, the chapters in this volume provide empirically grounded and critical case studies of the dynamic and multiscalar development of the Amazon corporation, and the emerging networks of community and labor activists that are resisting its practices. Our contributors thus deepen our understanding of what Jamie Peck and Nik Theodor call the "*variegated*" nature of capitalism; variegated capitalism takes plural forms over time and across multiple spaces, places, and geographic scales.[7] Extending these insights, we argue that there are distinct types of capitalism that are emblematic of, and promoted by, the world's largest transnational corporations, such as Amazon, that are of enormous significance and worthy of investigation; their scope and influence are multifaceted, dynamic, and extend far beyond the workplace, leaving their footprints on our communities, politics, and environment. Just as the operations of Amazon, and other large transnational corporations, occur at multiple scales and sites—transnational, regional, national, and local—so do our investigations cover multiple scales, from global and regional patterns to differences across local and national contexts.

This introductory chapter provides an overview of some of the key features of Amazon capitalism. First, we review the significance of Amazon in terms of its rising but uneven influence globally and its role in promoting both one-click consumerism and surveillance capitalism.[8] After describing the increasingly diverse nature of goods and services Amazon produces and sells, we discuss its rising monopoly power and exploitation of third-party sellers. We then examine how the rise of Amazon has reshaped logistics and retail, and negatively affected workers, communities, and the environment.

THE RISE AND SIGNIFICANCE OF AMAZON CAPITALISM

Amazon's influence in the global economy is uneven, reflecting regional patterns of global trade and global inequities that characterize the imperialist and capitalist world economy. Although many of the consumer goods bought and sold through Amazon's shopping platform are manufactured in the Global South, they are mostly consumed in the Global North, particularly North America and Europe, where much of the world's relatively affluent consumers reside. Amazon's growing market dominance has been especially pronounced in the United States, where it has become the nation's second largest seller of clothing.[9] In addition, Amazon is the fastest growing logistics provider; the biggest seller of toys, books, shoes, and countless other consumer products; and, since its acquisition of Whole Foods in 2017, the fifth largest grocery retailer in the United States.[10] Meanwhile, "Over the past decade, Amazon has paid less than three percent of its US$27 billion in profits for federal income tax."[11]

Amazon's reach extends well beyond the U.S.,[12] especially with respect to cloud computing, provision of Kindle content, and management of fulfillment centers that service cross-border shopping.[13] Despite challenges by Microsoft, Google, and Alibaba,[14] Amazon made headlines in summer 2019 for owning fully half of the world's public cloud infrastructure market, valued at more than US$32 billion.[15] In terms of retail sales, Amazon has invested heavily in shipping lines and warehouses that facilitate sales and services in Europe, Latin America, Asia, and Australia. Revenue from Amazon's businesses abroad represented 28 percent of its total for 2018.[16] Yet it remains unclear that Amazon's success in the U.S. will be duplicated abroad.[17] Amazon's retail market share in Western Europe was 8 percent in 2018, according to Eurobarometer, compared to 35 percent in the United States.[18] Despite Amazon's significant e-commerce inroads in Europe, European consumers' demands for products that are difficult to market online and increasing preference for "experiences" rather than "things" has been challenging for the corporation.[19] Amazon has also found increasing government scrutiny of, and organized resistance to, its negative impacts, including reducing brick-and-mortar retail—the "Amazon effect"— and air pollution, and bad working conditions.[20]

Amazon's economic influence elsewhere outside the U.S. is weaker than in Europe. In China, Japan, and South East Asia, Amazon has so far yielded to regional e-commerce leaders, such as Rakuten in Japan and Alibaba in China.[21] In 2019, Amazon formally closed its retail business in China,[22] and strengthened its efforts in Latin America, Australia, and India. The established Argentinian online retailer, Mercado Libre, has kept Amazon at bay in Latin America.[23] Still, Amazon's Latin American operations include logistics centers in Mexico and Brazil, multiple call centers in Colombia, and corporate offices as well as call centers in Costa Rica—Amazon's biggest Latin American location.[24] Direct competition from multi-service e-commerce companies remains less consequential in Australia and India. It took two years for Amazon to double its sales in Australia, where the company's retail market share was 3 percent in 2019, just ahead of Melbourne-based Kogan.com's 3 percent retail market share, though both were eclipsed by eBay's 22 percent share.[25] Though e-commerce in India is an emerging market—3 percent of the nation's total consumption—the nation's 1.3-billion customer base represents "one of the world's fastest-growing retail markets."[26]

Although not omnipresent around the globe, Amazon capitalism remains important not only due to its sheer size and value, but also because it has propelled many novel features that currently animate the world's economy. Amazon capitalism pioneered and helped to spread "one-click" instant consumerism at the expense of workers, communities, and the ecological balance of our planet. Amazon's 440 million-metric-ton carbon footprint rivals that of competitors, such as Walmart, and even the world's largest energy companies.[27] Indeed, the speed-up of consumerism, including expedited (free) shipping of consumer products, represents a tidal shift in the global economy, driven largely by finance capitalism. Each month, approximately 200 million unique users visit Amazon.com to purchase consumer products.[28] Along with Amazon products, they purchase goods sold by third-party sellers, who have been using Amazon's shopping platform since it became public in 2000. By 2016, as many as 2 million sellers across the globe sold their goods through Amazon.com, although most were individuals selling a few items.[29]

Along with other high-tech companies, such as Google, Amazon has also been on the forefront of a phenomenon that Shoshana Zuboff calls "surveillance capitalism." Surveillance capitalism refers to "a new economic order that claims human experience as free raw material for hidden commercial practices of extraction, prediction, and sales."[30] Amazon employs a collaborative filtering engine to surveil consumers using its electronic shopping platform in order to promote its own commercial interests. Each time customers purchase products through Amazon's online shopping platform, they turn over their private information and buying habits to the corporation.[31] Amazon executives use this data to decide which products to manufacture and sell, and at what price, as well as what products to suggest to customers, and in what order. Although Amazon claims this strategy is designed to serve customers by "anticipating" their needs, critics highlight how Amazon's use of surveillance technology manipulates consumers to further the corporation's own commercial interests.[32] Likewise, Amazon uses electronic technology to surveil its fleet of workers, including warehouse workers, delivery drivers, ghost writers, and other high-tech workers, in order to extract valuable information about their work flow that is used to further exploit, discipline, and control workers, increase labor efficiency, and inform the development of workplace automation and other business investments.[33]

Amazon's surveillance technologies pose serious privacy and civil liberty threats in the context of the company's operations and relationships to governments and municipal police. Along with providing cloud data storage for the U.S. Pentagon and the Central Intelligence Agency, Amazon has pioneered and sold new surveillance technologies. Amazon's 2018 acquisition of the Ring home surveillance system has also fueled the rapid penetration of the state-corporate nexus of surveillance of everyday life.[34] In addition to Ring, police departments in several U.S. states are already using Amazon Rekognition, a new face-recognition computer system and database, and the system has been offered to the U.S. Homeland Security Immigration and Customs Enforcement (ICE) agency. Civil rights organizations have raised concerns about the use of this new surveillance technology, which tends to misidentify people of color more commonly than white people, and which could be used to better identify protesters. Likewise, hundreds of anonymous Amazon employees sent a letter to Jeff Bezos, declaring that "We refuse to build the platform that powers ICE, and we refuse to contribute to tools that violate human rights."[35] Moreover, contrary to Amazon's pseudo-liberal image, the corporation has given massive sums of money to right-wing politicians in its attempt to garner influence and buy elections.[36]

AN INCREASINGLY COMPLEX AND MULTIFACETED CORPORATION

Amazon is far more than simply a major online retailer. Indeed, "no other tech company does as many unrelated things, on such a scale, as Amazon," Duhigg reported in *The New Yorker* in 2019.[37] Overall, in 2018, Amazon "collected" US$122 billion directly from online retail sales, and another US$42 billion by "helping other firms sell and ship their own goods."[38] In addition, during that same year, Amazon earned US$26 billion from its Web-services (AWS) division[39] that sells cloud computing services—i.e., storage space, bandwidth for website hosting, and processing power—to individuals, and companies such as Netflix and Instagram,[40] and Amazon itself.[41] Although AWS supplies 10 percent of Amazon's revenues, the company's operating income, or the funds remaining after expenses are accounted for, "dwarfs any other sector," pulling in US$606 million more than Amazon made in North American sales in 2016.[42] Moreover, Amazon took in US$14 billion in Amazon Prime and other subscription services, "hundreds of millions of dollars from selling the Echo," US$17 billion from sales at more traditional (off-line) brick-and-mortar stores, including Whole Foods, and the fully automated Amazon Go stores, along with US$10 billion in advertising sales and other activities.[43] Analysts reported in 2019 that banks and credit unions were bracing for the coming Amazon "invasion" of banking.[44] At that time, Amazon was already funding small-business loans, reducing fees for merchants who use Amazon Pay,[45] and seeking to compete with prepaid wireless providers.[46]

Business analysts diverge over the reasons for Amazon's rapid growth, with some pointing to its use of a business school strategy known as the "flywheel," "loosely defined as a sort of self-reinforcing loop. Where possible, projects [are] to be structured to bolster other initiatives underway at the company."[47] More critical analyses, including our own, highlight the role of neoliberal policies and politics, such as the weak enforcement of antitrust laws, corporate welfare, and weak labor laws in the United States and other countries, which have facilitated the rise of Amazon's monopoly power and its exploitative labor and business practices.[48]

AMAZON'S GROWING MONOPOLY POWER AND CORPORATE DOMINANCE

LaVecchia and Mitchell also rightly point to the growing monopoly power the corporation has gained through dominating "the underlying infrastructure—the online shopping platform, the shipping system, the cloud computing backbone—that competing firms depend on to transact business."[49] The rapid growth in Amazon's online shopping platform, and the company's use of this platform to both sell its own goods and those of other sellers, helps to illustrate their concerns.

As of 2020, there were over 150 million Amazon Prime members, making it the world's second largest paid subscription program. Indeed, about 60 percent of American households are Amazon Prime members. Among the affluent, the numbers are even higher. A staggering 82 percent of households making more than US$112,000 per year are Amazon Prime members.[50] Prime members pay an annual subscription fee in order to utilize Amazon's platform and receive perks such as free, expedited shipping on millions of items purchased through Amazon. Amazon Prime membership is also growing rapidly among U.S. households earning less than US$50,000 annually,[51] partly due to fee discounts of 50 percent or more for college students and very low-income households.[52] To further reach the college student market, the "Amazon Campus" program created countless brick-and-mortar Amazon pick-up locations on university and college campuses throughout the United States, further exacerbating the privatization of public higher education. Although the company has lost money in the short term by offering its customers various perks and discounts, it helped the company to gain customer loyalty and market dominance. Amazon claimed nearly one of every two dollars in U.S. consumer purchases online.[53]

In this context, many sellers perceive few options other than to use Amazon.com to sell their goods. Amazon's exploitative practices extend to third-party sellers who are charged a commission on their sales (usually 15 percent) made through Amazon.com as well as rising fees for using Amazon's fulfillment, advertising, and other services.[54] It also requires third-party sellers using Amazon's platform to share information about their transactions, which the corporation uses to compete against them on popular items. The company has a long history of "predatory pricing," or selling products below market cost in order to crush, outcompete, and sometimes even acquire other companies, such as Diaper.com and Zappos.[55]

Amazon uses transaction and consumer information from its online shopping platform to decide which products should be given the "buy box"—the eye-catching and convenient one-click "buy now" or "add to cart" buttons—that show up during online shopping searches. Amazon claims its mysterious algorithm that selects a default seller for the buy box is a neutral formula designed to maximize customer satisfaction. Yet, evidence suggests that Amazon gives itself a perfect score on measures of customer experience, giving it an unfair advantage over other sellers whose measures are affected by negative online customer reviews. The company also gives its Fulfillment By Amazon (FBA) warehouse and shipping service a perfect score for measures related to fulfilling orders, which both encourages sellers to use their delivery service and reduces accountability for problems with FBA's deliveries.[56] Other research finds that "about three-quarters of the time, Amazon placed its own products and those of companies that pay for its services in that position even when there were substantially cheaper offers available from others."[57] Likewise, Amazon's voice assistant, Alexa, only chooses Amazon items when asked to purchase something. No wonder a 2016 survey of independent retailers in the U.S. identified competition from internet retailers such as Amazon as the number one threat to their business,[58] and critics are linking the growth of Amazon to a decline in small businesses.[59]

AMAZON'S GLOBAL LOGISTICS EMPIRE AND ITS IMPACT ON WORKERS, COMMUNITIES, AND THE ENVIRONMENT

Along with becoming the world's largest e-commerce company, Amazon has quickly become one of the largest logistics companies in the world.[60] Prior to Amazon, brick-and-mortar retail corporations such as Walmart dominated the global logistics industry. Amazon is currently disrupting the model that Walmart perfected. Much as Amazon handles its own warehousing, distribution, and fulfillment services, the company today increasingly manages delivery as well.

In the United States, although Amazon continues to use the U.S. Postal Service and private delivery companies, its packages, particularly Amazon Prime packages, are increasingly delivered by two main contingent groups of third-party Amazon workers: Amazon Flex drivers and Amazon's Delivery Service Partners (DSPs).[61] Amazon Flex drivers are gig workers, legally classified as independent contractors, who are paid per completion of a delivery route, or "block," by the hour. Amazon Flex drivers use their own personal vehicles (or rented vans) to make deliveries. Similar to other gig-economy platform jobs, such as Lyft, Uber, Postmates, and Doordash, Flex drivers must pay for all expenses related to their vehicle, road tolls, parking, insurance, vehicle maintenance, among other expenses; in addition, these workers receive no overtime pay, benefits, union representation, or minimum wages.

Introduction: Amazon Capitalism

DSPs are small subcontracted "independent" parcel delivery firms with approximately 20–40 delivery vans that exclusively deliver packages for Amazon, mostly Prime. DSP fleets are limited to 40 vans to avoid unionization efforts and to increase Amazon's flexibility and power over the price paid per delivery. By 2019, Amazon's own delivery network surpassed the U.S. Postal Service as the carrier delivering the plurality of its packages.[62]

As Amazon's promise of one-day shipping expanded, the company invested in its air cargo division: Amazon Air. These subcontracted pilots complain of being overworked and are among the lowest paid in the air cargo industry.[63] Other skilled workers employed by Amazon also express concerns about their labor conditions. Among software engineers at Amazon, turnover rates remain very high, with the average duration lasting one year.[64] Online outsourcing services, manifest in crowd or "ghost" work, arguably represent the worst-case scenario in this sense.[65] Amazon's Mechanical Turk crowd-sourcing marketplace connects employers with a global pool of independent workers willing to do specialized or repetitive tasks for competitively low wages.[66] Amazon employs vulnerable workers like these to augment the information available digitally, via Alexa Voice Services, to its Alexa personal virtual assistant.[67]

Other research shows how Amazon and other online service providers have contributed to the decimation of shopping centers and other retail markets.[68] Grocery stores, many of which are unionized and offer decent salaries and benefits to its commercial workers in the Global North, are also closing up shop as they face growing competition from Amazon. As small businesses and brick-and-mortar retailers close in response to the rapid growth in e-commerce,[69] many panicked cities and governments are losing tax revenue and turning increasingly to logistics and warehousing to attract jobs, which are far from ideal.

Today's massive logistics and warehousing complexes are mostly located on the outskirts of major urban metropolitan areas and depend on large concentrations of low-paid labor, particularly workers of color.[70] Typical e-commerce warehouse employees in the United States, disproportionately black and Latinx,[71] toil long hours (often 10 hours or more per day among full-time workers and more than 40 hours per week) for low pay. In 2020, entry-level wages for Amazon warehouse workers were $15 per hour, or about $31,000 annually for workers employed full-time all year.[72] Many of these non-supervisory blue-collar warehouse workers, known as "warehouse associates," are precariously employed, either as temporary or seasonal workers.[73] Amazon associates' work is grueling. They quickly pick, pack, and load and unload goods in large warehouses, sometimes the size of 17 football fields. Full-time pickers, who store and retrieve items, sometimes walk for miles, while packers must stand on their feet for long hours and engage in highly repetitive motions that leave their muscles sore and injured. Workers' motions are closely monitored through electronic scanning devices. Managers and supervisors pressure them to "make rate," in order to locate, pack, and move items quickly, while minimizing their errors and "time off task." Pressure to work fast and "make rate" increases the risk of workplace injury in an industry already known to be injury-prone. An investigation of Amazon's injury records from 23 of its 110 fulfillment centers in the United States showed their rate of serious injuries (9.6 per 100 full-time workers) was about double the national industry average.[74] Research on Amazon's warehouse workers in other nations suggests that they share similar concerns regarding their low pay, employment security, pressure to work too fast, and lack of regard for workplace safety.[75] Workers' concerns about the corporation's failure to protect their health and safety intensified during the COVID-19 outbreak, especially as the corporation failed to report potential cases, close facilities, and provide paid time out to its workers in a timely fashion.[76]

Seeking to minimize its labor costs and improve workplace speed and accuracy, Amazon has been on the forefront of warehouse automation, investing heavily in research and development of robots, digital scanners, automated conveyor belts, labeling machines, and other machinery. Reliance on subcontractors, sunk costs in traditional warehouses not suited for robotic equipment and other forms of mechanization, as well as difficulties in automating particular kinds of warehouse tasks could constrain the pace of warehouse automation.[77] Nevertheless, in 2019 Amazon boasted that it had placed more than 200,000 robotic drives worldwide.[78] Although warehouse automation could reduce some of the physical strains associated with the job, it increases the pressure on workers to work even more quickly, further increasing the risk of injury.[79] Over the long run, automation also threatens to displace workers and weaken labor unions.[80] Even so, human beings are found at every key point across Amazon's logistics network, keeping it vulnerable to worker actions. Of course, many of Amazon's various profit-maximizing techniques and strategies were not invented by

Introduction: Amazon Capitalism

this corporation, but simply more effectively implemented and combined. In the context of neoliberal global capitalism and the rise of finance capitalism, Amazon combines and intensifies various borrowed techniques of labor exploitation and market expansion with "one-click" consumerism and "surveillance capitalism"[81] in a distinct way that has contributed to its rapid rise in power, and made the company a trend-setter for other corporations around the world. As the contributors to this edited volume make clear, Amazon's "free shipping" and other practices are *not* free; they create enormous costs for workers, communities, and the environment.

OVERVIEW OF THIS BOOK

This volume provides a rich and interdisciplinary collection of critical essays by scholars, workers, journalists, and labor and community organizers that interrogate the global significance of Amazon's rise and the growing popular resistance to it across the United States, Europe, and India. Other books on Amazon—such as Brandt's *One Click*,[82] Jameson's *Amazon's Dirty Little Secret*, and Marcus's *Amazonia*,[83] Spector's *Get Big Fast*,[84]—have either focused uncritically on Jeff Bezos's and his company's financial success, or critiqued it from a narrow business, managerial, and marketing perspective. In contrast, this volume seeks to assess the true costs of free shipping and Amazon's business model on labor and communities. In the spirit of Stone's *The Everything Store: Jeff Bezos and the Age of Amazon*,[85] this book offers thoroughly researched, critical examinations of Amazon's strategic expansion and everyday operations but goes beyond a mere critique of Amazon's business model. It explores the broader economic, political and ecological significance of the rise of, and growing popular resistance to, Amazon capitalism, and does so with a global perspective.

Part I (Amazon's Rise in Global Power) examines the factors that have contributed to the rapid rise of Amazon and explores how it has reshaped the global economy, especially in terms of retail, logistics, and the internet, with particular attention to the United States, Europe, and South Asia. Part II (Exploitation and Resistance Across Amazon's Global Empire) examines what Amazon means for the future of work. It reveals how the Amazonification of the global economy exploits workers in the United States and Europe, adapting to different labor relations systems and laws, and documents its particular impacts on women workers, immigrants, and people of color. It also shows how Amazon's labor relations and practices vary across nations and regions around the world, as well as how Amazon employees—especially warehouse workers—are organizing to improve their working conditions. Part III (Communities Confronting the E-Commerce Giant) examines how the rise of Amazon has worsened traffic congestion, increased air pollution, has cost state and local government millions of dollars worth of public subsidies as well as significant losses in public tax revenues. It provides case studies of how social justice and environmental activists in Southern California, Long Island, and Seattle are fighting back to protect the environment, their communities, and local politics from corporate influence. Part IV (Struggling to Win Against Amazon) explores strategies—both actual and possible—for further resisting and transforming Amazon capitalism in the global economy.

Amazon capitalism is representative of many of the destructive forces inherent in capitalism, including: the exploitation and dehumanization of workers; corporate welfare and tax avoidance; extreme wealth inequality; nativism, racism, and sexism; an obsessive mass-consumer culture; surveillance; the erosion of privacy; monopolistic practices; neoliberalism and the public subsidization of corporations; and the assault on the ecological integrity of the earth. While the power and influence of Amazon capitalism grows, so too does popular discontent with it. The rise of Amazon capitalism sows the seeds for new waves of popular rebellion; it provides a strategic new target that could inspire activists to further collaborate across movements, cities, and nations. Transnational links between anti-Amazon activists, in particular, have so far mostly been concentrated within Europe, but they are beginning to grow between the U.S. and Europe,[86] as are national links among activists in the United States through Amazonians United and the Athena network.[87] As activists around the world are demonstrating, Amazon provides a key site for building alliances among activists not only across space, but also across different types of movements, including movements for economic and social justice, democracy, and environmental justice.

NOTES

1. David Streitfeld, "Amazon Hits $1,000,000.00 in Value, Following Apple," *New York Times*, September 4, 2018, www.nytimes.com/2018/09/04/technology/amazon-stock-price-1-trillion-value.html. Accessed October 15, 2019.

2. Mary Hanbury, "Amazon Overtakes Google and Apple to Become the World's Most Valuable Brand," *Business Insider*, June 11, 2019, www.businessinsider.com/amazon-overtakes-google-apple-worlds-most-valuable-brand-2019-6. Accessed January 14, 2020. See also, Paul La Monica, "Amazon is Now the Most Valuable Company on the Planet," *CNN*, January 8, 2019, www.cnn.com/2019/01/08/investing/amazon-most-valuable-company-microsoft-google-apple/index.html. Accessed December 20, 2019.
3. Lauren Feiner, "Amazon Stock Hits A New All-Time High As It Sees Unprecedented Demand," CNBC.com, April 14, www.cnbc.com/2020/04/14/amazon-stock-hits-a-new-all-time-high.html?__source=sharebar|twitter&par=sharebar. Accessed April 20, 2020.
4. Isobel Asher Hamilton, "Jeff Bezos is Wealthier by $24 billion in 2020, as Amazon Reports at least 74 COVID-19 Cases and its First Death," *Business Insider*, April 15, www.businessinsider.com/jeff-bezos-net-worth-jumps-23-billion-during-coronavirus-crisis-2020-4. Accessed April 20, 2020.
5. Global Justice Now, "69 of the Richest 100 Entities on the Planet are Corporations, Not Governments, Figures Show," *Global Justice Now*, October 17, 2018, www.globaljustice.org.uk/news/2018/oct/17/69-richest-100-entities-planet-are-corporations-not-governments-figures-show. Accessed December 20, 2019.
6. Howmuch.net. 2019, "Who is More Powerful-Countries or Companies?" https://howmuch.net/articles/putting-companies-power-into-perspective. Accessed April 15, 2020.
7. Jamie Peck and Nik Theodor, "Variegated Capitalism," *Progress in Human Geography* 31(6) (2007): 731–772.
8. Shoshana Zuboff, *The Age of Surveillance Capitalism: The Fight for a Human at the New Frontier of Power* (New York: Hachette Book Group, 2019).
9. Matt Day and Jackie Gu, "The Enormous Numbers Behind Amazon's Market Research," *Bloomberg*, March 27, 2019, www.bloomberg.com/graphics/2019-amazon-reach-across-markets/. Accessed October 15, 2019.
10. Ibid.
11. Daniel Flaming and Patrick Burns, *Too Big To Govern: Public Balance Sheet for the World's Largest Store. Los Angeles: Economic Roundtable*, 2019. Available at: https://economicrt.org/publication/too-big-to-govern/. Accessed April 20, 2020.
12. Shannon Liao, "Amazon Admits Defeat Against Chinese E-commerce Rivals like Alibaba and JD.com," *The Verge*, April 18, 2019, www.theverge.com/2019/4/18/18485578/amazon-china-marketplace-alibaba-jd-e-commerce-compete. Accessed April 20, 2020.
13. Caixia Liu and Jinhwan Hong, "Strategies and Service Innovations of Haitao Business in the Chinese Market: A Comparative Case Study of Amazon.cn vs Gmarket.co.kr," *Asia Pacific Journal of Innovation and Entrepreneurship*, 10(1) (2016): 101–121.

14. Adam Rogers, "Amazon Leads Market, Loses Cloud Shares," *Market Realist*, September 8, 2019, https://articles2.marketrealist.com/2019/09/amazon-leads-market-loses-cloud-shares/. Accessed October 16, 2019.
15. Jeb Su, "Amazon Owns ½ of World's Public Cloud Infrastructure Market Worth Over $32 Billion," *Forbes*, August 2, 2019, www.forbes.com/sites/jeanbaptiste/2019/08/02/amazon-owns-nearly-half-of-the-public-cloud-infrastructure-market-worth-over-32-billion-report/#6dafdd7829e0. Accessed April 20, 2020.
16. Rachel Siegel and Joanna Slater, "International Pushback Disrupts Amazon's Momentum to Expand Its Empire Worldwide," *Washington Post*, May 10, 2019, www.washingtonpost.com/business/economy/international-pushback-disrupts-amazons-momentum-to-expand-its-empire-worldwide/2019/05/10/76bd5d26-6507-11e9-82ba-fcfeff232e8f_story.html. Accessed April 20, 2020.
17. Natalie Berg and Miya Knights, *Amazon: How the World's Most Relentless Retailer will Continue to Revolutionize Commerce* (London: Kogan, 2019).
18. Victoria Pavlova, "The Amazon Effect: How Amazon Is Disrupting European E-commerce," *Forbes*, February 9, 2019, www.forbes.com/sites/victoriapavlova/2019/02/09/the-amazon-effect-how-amazon-is-disrupting-european-e-commerce/#19ceb60c5e7b. Accessed April 20, 2020.
19. Berg and Knights, *Amazon*.
20. Ibid.
21. Jane A Peterson, "A Showdown Brews between Amazon and Alibaba, Far from Home," *New York Times*, October 22, 2017, www.nytimes.com/2017/10/22/business/alibaba-amazon-southeast-asia-lazada.html. Accessed April 20, 2020.
22. Karen Weise, "Amazon Gives Up on Chinese Domestic Shopping Business," *New York Times*, April 18, 2019. www.nytimes.com/2019/04/18/technology/amazon-china.html. Accessed April 20, 2020.
23. Jörn Boewe and Johannes Schulten. "The Long Struggle of the Amazon Employees (second edition)." *Rosa Luxemburg Stiftung*, December 10, 2019, www.rosalux.eu/en/article/1557.the-long-struggle-of-the-amazon-employees.html. Accessed April 20, 2020.
24. Ibid.
25. Stacy Mitchell, "Amazon Doesn't Just Want to Dominate the Market, It Wants to Become the Market," *The Nation*, February 15, 2018, www.thenation.com/article/amazon-doesnt-just-want-to-dominate-the-market-it-wants-to-become-the-market/. Accessed April 20, 2020.
26. Saritha Rai, "Amazon Opens Its Largest Campus Yet," *Bloomberg*, August 21, 2019, www.bloomberg.com/news/articles/2019-08-21/amazon-opens-india-campus-its-largest-in-the-world
27. Matt Day and Eric Roston, "Amazon's Emission Bigger Than Some Rivals, Trails Walmart," *Bloomberg*, September 20, 2019, www.bloomberg.com/news/

articles/2019-09-20/amazon-s-emissions-bigger-than-some-rivals-trail-walmart. Accessed April 20, 2020.
28. Day and Gu, "The Enormous Numbers Behind Amazon's Market Research."
29. Olivia LaVecchia and Stacy Mitchell, "Amazon's Stranglehold: How the Company's Tightening Grip Is Stifling Competition, Eroding Jobs, and Threatening Communities," *Institute for Local Self Reliance (ILSR)*, 2016, https://ilsr.org/wp-content/uploads/2016/11/ILSR_AmazonReport_final.pdf. Accessed April 20, 2020.
30. Zuboff, *The Age of Surveillance Capitalism*, p. 1.
31. See Dana Williams' Chapter 2 in this volume.
32. Julia Angwin and Surya Matta, "Amazon Says It Puts Customers First. But Its Pricing Algorithm Doesn't," *Propublica*, September 20, 2016, www.propublica.org/article/amazon-says-it-puts-customers-first-but-its-pricing-algorithm-doesnt. Accessed April 20, 2020.
33. Beth Gutelis and Nik Theodore, "The Future of Warehouse Work: Technological Change in the U.S. Logistics Industry," *UC Berkeley Labor Center and Working Partnerships USA*, 2019, http://laborcenter.berkeley.edu/pdf/2019/Future-of-Warehouse-Work.pdf. Accessed April 20, 2020.
34. Alfred Ng, "Ring Let Police View Map of Video Doorbell Installations for Over a Year," *CNET*, December 3, 2019, www.cnet.com/news/ring-gave-police-a-street-level-view-of-where-video-doorbells-were-for-over-a-year/. Accessed April 20, 2020.
35. Drew Harwell, "Amazon Met With ICE-officials Over Facial Recognition System That Could Identify Immigrants," *Washington Post*, October 23, 2018, www.washingtonpost.com/technology/2018/10/23/amazon-met-with-ice-officials-over-facial-recognition-system-that-could-identify-immigrants/. Accessed April 20, 2020.
36. Reid Wilson, "Amazon Dumps $1 Million Into Seattle Elections," *The Hill*, October 16, 2019, https://thehill.com/homenews/state-watch/466213-amazon-dumps-1-million-into-seattle-elections. Accessed April 20, 2020.
37. Charles Duhigg, "Is Amazon Unstoppable?" *The New Yorker*, October 10, 2019, www.newyorker.com/magazine/2019/10/21/is-amazon-unstoppable. Accessed April 20, 2020.
38. Ibid.
39. Ibid.
40. Robinson Meyer, "The Unbelievable Power of Amazon's Cloud," *The Atlantic*, April 23, 2015, www.theatlantic.com/technology/archive/2015/04/the-unbelievable-power-of-amazon-web-services/391281/. Accessed April 20, 2020.
41. Alex Hern, "Amazon Web Services: The Secret to the Online Retailer's Future Success," *The Guardian*, February 2, 2017, www.theguardian.com/technology/2017/feb/02/amazon-web-services-the-secret-to-the-online-retailers-future-success. Accessed April 20, 2020.
42. Ibid.

43. Duhigg, "Is Amazon Unstoppable?"
44. Ron Shevlin, "Amazon's Impending Invasion of Banking," *Forbes*, July 8, 2019, www.forbes.com/sites/ronshevlin/2019/07/08/amazon-invasion/#708760847921. Accessed April 20, 2020.
45. Kevin Wack, "How Amazon is Shaking Up Financial Services," *American Banker*, March 18, 2018, www.americanbanker.com/slideshow/how-amazon-is-shaking-up-financial-services. Accessed April 20, 2020.
46. Jay Greene, "No Smoke Without Fire: After Amazon's Smartphone Failure, It Looks For A Way Back Into Mobile," *Washington Post*, June 7, 2019, www.washingtonpost.com/technology/2019/06/07/is-amazon-looking-get-back-into-mobile-phone-business/. Accessed April 20, 2020.
47. Day and Gu, "The Enormous Numbers Behind Amazon's Market Research."
48. LaVecchia and Mitchell, "Amazon's Stranglehold."
49. Ibid.
50. Rani Molla, "For the Wealthiest Americans, Amazon Prime has Become the Norm," *Vox*, June 8, 2017, www.vox.com/2017/6/8/15759354/amazon-prime-low-income-discount-piper-jaffray-demographics. Accessed April 20, 2020.
51. Jason DelRey, "What Amazon Prime's 100-Million Milestone Doesn't Show: The Battle to Keep Growing in the U.S.," *Vox Recode*, April 19, 2018, www.vox.com/2018/4/19/17256410/amazon-prime-100-million-members-us-penetration-low-income-households-jeff-bezos. Accessed April 20, 2020.
52. Doreen McCallister, "Amazon Lowers Prime Membership Rate for Low Income Customers," *NPR*, June 7, 2017. www.npr.org/sections/thetwo-way/2017/06/07/531856069/amazon-lowers-prime-membership-rate-for-low-income-customers. Accessed April 20, 2020.
53. Stacy Mitchell, "Amazon Doesn't Just Want to Dominate the Market."
54. Stacy Mitchell and Shaoul Sussman, "How Amazon Rigs Its Shopping Algorithm," *Pro-market: The blog of the Stigler Center at the University of Chicago Booth School of Business*, November 6, 2019, https://promarket.org/how-amazon-rigs-its-shopping-algorithm/. Accessed April 20, 2020.
55. Mitchell, "Amazon Doesn't Just Want to Dominate the Market."
56. Ibid.
57. Julia Angwin and Surya Matta, "Amazon Says It Puts Customers First. But Its Pricing Algorithm Doesn't," *Propublica*, September 20, 2016, www.propublica.org/article/amazon-says-it-puts-customers-first-but-its-pricing-algorithm-doesnt. Accessed April 20, 2020.
58. Mitchell, "Amazon Doesn't Just Want to Dominate the Market."
59. LaVecchia and Mitchell, "Amazon's Stranglehold."
60. See Kim Moody's Chapter 1 and see Jake Alimahomed-Wilson's Chapter 4 in this volume.
61. See Jake Alimahomed-Wilson's Chapter 4 in this volume.

Introduction: Amazon Capitalism

62. Matt Leonard, "These 4 Charts Explain Amazon's Fulfillment Speed," *Supply Chain Dive*, November 25, 2019, www.supplychaindive.com/news/4-charts-that-explain-amazons-fulfilment-speed/568016/. Accessed April 20, 2020.
63. Amrita Khalid, "Amazon is Struggling to Hold On to the Pilots Who Ship Your Packages," *Quartz*, December 7, 2019, https://qz.com/1763226/amazon-air-is-struggling-to-hold-on-to-into-pilots/. Accessed April 20, 2020.
64. See Spencer Cox's Chapter 14 in this volume.
65. Mary Gray and Siddarth Suri, *Ghost Work: How to Stop Silicon Valley from Building a New Global Underclass*. (Boston, MA: Eamon Dolan Books, 2019).
66. Joel Ross, Lilly Irani, M. Silberman, Andrew Zaldivar, and Bill Tomlinson. "Who are the Crowdworkers?: Shifting Demographics in Mechanical Turk." In *alt CHI 10 extended abstracts on Human factors in computing systems*, 2010. pp. 2863–2872. DOI: https://dl.acm.org/doi/10.1145/1753846.1753873.
67. Bernard Marr, "Machine Learning In Practice: How Does Amazon's Alexa Really Work?" *Forbes*, October 5, 2018, www.forbes.com/sites/bernardmarr/2018/10/05/how-does-amazons-alexa-really-work/#6cdb8c8c1937
68. Ali Modarres, "Amazon, Apple, Google and the Late Capitalism Blues," *New Geography*, January 11, 2019, www.newgeography.com/content/006191-amazon-google-apple-and-late-capitalism-blues
69. Sudheer Chava, Alexander Oettl, Manpreet Singh, and Linghang Zeng, "The Dark Side of Technological Progress? Impact of Ecommerce on Employees at Brick-and-mortar Retailers," *Georgia Tech Scheller College of Business Research Paper*, 2018, pp. 18–23. 29th Annual Conference on Financial Economics & Accounting. https://papers.ssrn.com/sol3/papers.cfm?abstract_id=3197326. Accessed April 20, 2020.
70. Kim Moody, *On New Terrain: How Capital is Reshaping the Battleground of Class War*. (Chicago, IL: Haymarket Books, 2017).
71. Beth Gutelius and Nik Theodore, "The Future of Warehouse Work: Technological Change in the U.S. Logistics Industry," *UC Berkeley Labor Center*, 2019, http://laborcenter.berkeley.edu/future-of-warehouse-work/. Accessed April 20, 2020.
72. Some workers might earn more if they work overtime while others might earn less if employed part-time or only part of the year.
73. Daniel Flaming and Patrick Burns. *Too Big To Govern: Public Balance Sheet for the World's Largest Store*. Los Angeles: Economic Roundtable, 2019. Available at: https://economicrt.org/publication/too-big-to-govern/; This is consistent with larger patterns in warehouse employment (see Jason Struna, 2015, "Handling Globalization: Labor, Capital, and Class in the Globalized Warehouse and Distribution Center, " Doctoral Dissertation, University of California, Riverside. https://escholarship.org/uc/item/3c35641d#main).
74. Will Evans, "Behind the Smiles: Amazon's Internal Injury Records Expose the True Toll of its Relentless Drive for Speed," *Reveal: The Center for Investigative Reporting*, November 25, 2019, www.revealnews.org/article/behind-the-smiles/. Accessed April 20, 2020.

75. See Chapters 4, 7, 8, 13, and 15 in this volume.
76. See DCH1 Amazonian United's Chapter 17 in this volume.
77. Gutelius and Theodore, "The Future of Warehouse Work."
78. Brian Heater, "Amazon Says It Has Deployed More Than 200,000 Robotic Drives Globally," *TechCrunch*, June 5 2019. https://techcrunch.com/2019/06/05/amazon-says-it-has-deployed-more-than-200000-robotic-drives-globally/. Accessed April 20, 2020.
79. Will Evans, "Behind the Smiles: Amazon's Internal Injury Records Expose the True Toll of its Relentless Drive For Speed," *Reveal: The Center for Investigative Reporting*, 25 November 2019, www.revealnews.org/article/behind-the-smiles/
80. Gutelius and Theodore, "The Future of Warehouse Work."
81. Zuboff, *The Age of Surveillance Capitalism*.
82. Richard L. Brandt, *One Click: Jeff Bezos and the Rise of Amazon.com* (London: Portfolio, 2012).
83. Greg Jameson, *Amazon's Dirty Little Secrets: How to Use the Power of Others to Market and Sell for You* (New York: Morgan James Publishing, 2014).
84. Robert Spector, *Amazon.com: Get Big Fast* (New York: Harper Business, 2002); Nick Statt "Amazon Warehouse Workers are Striking Across Europe on Prime Day." *The Verge*, July 16, 2018, www.theverge.com/2018/7/16/17577348/amazon-warehouse-worker-strike-europe-prime-day.
85. Brad Stone, *The Everything Store: Jeff Bezos and the Rise of Amazon* (Boston, MA: Little, Brown and Company, 2013). www.bloomberg.com/news/features/2018-10-18/amazon-battles-walmart-in-indian-e-commerce-market-it-created. Accessed April 20, 2020.
86. Transnational Social Strike Platform, "Strike the Giant! Transnational Organization Against Amazon," *TSS Journal*, 2019, www.transnational-strike.info/2019/11/29/pdf-strike-the-giant-transnational-organization-against-amazon-tss-journal/?fbclid=IwAR2g9ALU7LIhcAw-I9qUITcslN4NqGCmz1ChjSNlniMglCTXNA7XkfDxrzc. Accessed April 20, 2020.
87. Athena, 2019. *Athena Coalition*, https://athenaforall.org/#s2.

PART I

Amazon's Rise in Global Power

1
Amazon: Context, Structure and Vulnerability

Kim Moody

Amazon the corporate chameleon claims to be the world's largest online retailer. According to CEO and founder Jeff Bezos, it is actually a tech company.[1] While it is both of these, New York University business school analyst Scott Galloway notes that "Amazon is building the most robust logistics infrastructure in history."[2] Two business consultants in their analysis of Amazon concluded that as it entered its third decade, "Amazon is already a major global logistics player."[3] The U.S. trucking industry journal *Transport Topics* more recently asked "Should Amazon.com be considered one of the largest logistics companies in North America? The answer, according to most industry observers," the journal replied, "is yes."[4]

Including its technological capabilities, it is this logistics infrastructure that has propelled Amazon into its leading position in a highly competitive industry. And it is this efficiency and the costs of moving goods at high speeds in the maelstrom of global competition that has brought enormous pressures on the workers in its expanding network of sortation and fulfillment centers, Prime Now hubs, delivery stations, and data centers, as well as those working in the many forms of transportation that connect these and the ultimate customers. This chapter focuses on the expanding configuration of Amazon's logistics infrastructure, its place in the emerging global network of transportation and forces of competition in a world of shifting economic power, their impact on Amazon's workforce, and the vulnerability of Amazon to worker resistance.

Contrary to much mythology surrounding Amazon's success, Jeff Bezos and his crew of techies and quants simply did what robber barons have always done: raise, spend, and sometimes lose other people's money, dodge taxes, swindle suppliers, and avoid unions. Amazon had the good fortune to be born in the midst of the great dot.com boom of the 1990s when venture capital was cheap and investors were searching for innovative start-ups. In the heat of the boom, Amazon pulled in $2.1 billion in other people's money by 2001, far more than the $50 million typically raised by other tech start-ups in that period, according to Galloway.[5] For years, it avoided paying U.S. sales taxes because it had no brick-and-mortar stores and as a low-margin earner it paid only $2.3 billion in U.S. corporate income taxes from 2002 to 2017, comparted to Walmart's $103 billion.[6]

Amazon put its borrowings and earnings into the heartbeat of logistics infrastructure, the modern warehouse, on the one hand, and the big data operation that would become Amazon Web Services (AWS), on the other. Amazon's annual investment in property and equipment rose from $979 million in 2010 to $13.4 billion in 2018—more than Walmart invested in 2018 and, unlike Walmart, almost all of it in logistics facilities.[7] And not just any property and equipment: Amazon borrowed innovations from Walmart and others who led the "logistics revolution" and created the modern warehouse with its emphasis on moving goods rather than storing them. In addition, they applied the manufacturing practices of lean production and just-in-time delivery to warehouse configuration and its internal supply chain.[8] In the process Amazon became a capital-intensive mover of goods and a participant in the "logistics revolution," disguised as a retailer.

THE LOGISTICS REVOLUTION, COMPETITION, AND TIME

As global trade took off in the 1980s, the infrastructure needed to move the growing volume of goods expanded and the logistics revolution transformed the way goods were moved.[9] According to World Bank figures, the number of twenty-foot equivalent units (TEUs) (measured as shipping containers) entering the world's ports grew from 224.8 million in 2000 to 752.7 million in 2017, while freight carried by airlines around the world increased from 118.3 million ton-kilometers to 213.6 million over that period. The World Bank figures for rail movement are incomplete, but these rose from 2.3 million ton-kilometers in 2000 to 5.8 million in 2007.[10] And this was before the shift of the center of world economic activity eastward and the escalating density of rail traffic in Asia and China's 10,000-mile-long Silk

Road freight railway from China to Europe, all part of China's "One Belt, One Road" development initiative.[11]

In the U.S., the dollar value of all freight doubled from 1998 to 2017, while the newest form of rapid movement, intermodal truck/rail freight rose by 6½ times, from a value of $70 billion in 2002 to $460 billion in 2017.[12] The number of warehouses grew by nearly 2¾ times, from 1998 to mid-2019 to over 18,000, while their size increased dramatically and the warehouse workforce nearly doubled to just over a million production and nonsupervisory workers.[13] As logistics guru Yossi Sheffi put it, "Physical infrastructure dominates logistics investment."[14] This infrastructure has become, as LeCavalier put it, "the connective tissues and the circulatory systems of modernity."[15] Or at least, of modern capitalism.

While there are countless Third Party Logistics (3PL) firms globally and in the U.S. that help move things around this circulatory system, there are a few that dominate the industry in the U.S. and to some extent internationally, such as UPS, FedEx, XPO, DHL, Ryder, J.B. Hunt, and Schneider. UPS operates 1,000 package handling facilities, while FedEx has 1,200.[16] FedEx and UPS also command large fleets of aircraft and huge airport facilities. Most of these were formerly trucking or package delivery firms that transformed themselves into massive full-service logistics operations in the early twenty-first century. All of these appear in both *Transport Topics*' "Top 100 For-Hire-Carriers" ranking of trucking firms and its "Top 50 Logistics" companies for the U.S.[17]

Sheffi also reminds us that "an information supply chain parallels each physical supply chain."[18] In addition to the expansion of transportation infrastructure, new technology in the form of bar codes, Radio Frequency Identification (RFID), Electronic Data Interchange (EDI), GPS, "data Warehouses," "big data," and the "cloud" enabled new levels of prediction, tracking, coordination, movement, and work intensification.[19] Information technology links all aspects of logistics from the movement of goods over roads, rail, air, and sea, to the various distribution and fulfillment facilities and their internal functioning. Huge data warehouses or centers are a key part of this physical supply chain infrastructure and central to the effort to speed up and smooth out the movement of goods and money. By 2019, there were about 2,500 data centers in the U.S.—a part of logistical infrastructure that barely existed twenty years earlier.[20]

In retail, it was first and foremost Walmart that pulled together all these strands in contemporary logistics, including the massing of data about the behavior of consumers and the movement of goods from producer to distribution center to big box store. It was Walmart that pioneered the cross-dock warehouse in which goods move in one door and out another without being racked or stored.[21] Yet, a difference in the centrality of logistics between Walmart and Amazon can be seen in the fact that as of 2019 Walmart had only 114 distribution centers in the U.S., while Amazon had some 477.[22] Thus, it would be Amazon that applied the lessons of logistics infrastructure and technology to the movement of other people's goods to its own customers, without the costly stores.

The growth of global logistics has intensified both competition and the speed at which things are produced and moved to market. Beginning with the introduction of lean production and just-in-time (JIT) inventory into the West from Japan in the 1980s, the speed at which goods moved through production and along supply chains accelerated. By the twenty-first century, time itself became a leading factor in competition as "lead-time"—that is, the time from production to the market—was shortened as much as possible in order to gain advantage over rivals. Hence "Time-Based Competition" increased demands on the methods, technology, infrastructure, and workforce of logistics.[23]

By building its logistics and digital capacity and infrastructure, Amazon would become the master of what Marx called, "the annihilation of space by time."[24] By the time Amazon had moved beyond just books and its first few warehouses to see its sales soar from $6.9 billion in 2004 to $232.9 billion in 2018,[25] much of the groundwork for a new type of retail, tech, and logistics operation had been laid. In the process, while until recently bypassing brick-and-mortar stores, Amazon has become a deeply embedded capital-intensive company whose gross global property and equipment almost reached the $100 billion ($95.8 billion) mark by 2018.[26]

AMAZON'S STRUCTURE, THE MOVEMENT OF GOODS, AND THE PRESSURES ON THE WORKFORCE

First, it is important to establish just where Amazon and its workforce fit into the capitalist system today. Is Amazon really just a retailer or a tech outfit? The argument here, as suggested in the beginning of this chapter, is that given the nature of Amazon's physical infrastructure and the movement of goods from manufacturers to its own internal system of movement as well as directly to consumers, it is primarily a logistics, that is, a strategically oriented transportation operation and, hence, part of the total production process. From a Marxist perspective, the movement of materials from raw materials through the manufacturing process and on to the market are all part of production. As Marx wrote in the *Grundrisse*, "Economically considered, the spatial condition, the bringing the product to the market belongs to the production process."[27] Very few products are made in one location or plant, hence the capital employed in the spatial movement of materials is part of production. In Volume II of *Capital*, Marx stated, "The productive capital invested in this industry [transportation] thus adds value to the products transported, partly through the value added by the work of transport."[28] Thus, the vast majority of workers laboring in Amazon's global internal logistics systems and its $100 billion material facilities are producers of value; that is, they (not its consumers) are the source of the incredible wealth of this capitalist giant and its multi-billionaire boss Jeff Bezos. And it is, of course, the interaction of Amazon's infrastructure, the speed at which goods move through it, and the rate at which these workers produce this value (their rate of exploitation) that are at the heart of this company's efforts to constantly increase the intensity of work and lower the cost of this labor.

Much has been written about the evolution of Amazon, its customer focus, and the brilliance and persistence of Jeff Bezos. Here our concern is with its current structure, operations, and their impact on the 647,500 full-time and part-time workers employed globally by Amazon by the end of 2018.[29] For this reason, we will look at Amazon's global structure, investments, expenses, and employment. Virtually all of Amazon's international and even most of its U.S. facilities have been built within the last few years. With some notable exceptions such as its Whole Foods stores acquired in 2017 and its new brick-and-mortar stores, Amazon's properties are all part of its logistics system. Amazon's expanding global empire, in short, is brand new, despite its founding as an online book distributor in 1994. As the table below shows, while almost half of all of its 1093 facilities are still located in the U.S., more than half are now scattered across Asia (where India accounts for 331 facilities), Europe, and the Middle East, along with Canada and Australia. Furthermore, recently about a third of its revenues comes from outside the U.S.[30]

Table 1.1 Amazon's global facilities as of June 2019*

Global	1093
United States	477
Asia	358
Europe	230
Middle East	5
Latin America	4
Canada	14
Australia	5

*Brick-and-mortar stores not included.

Source: MWPVL International, *Amazon Global Fulfillment Center Network*, January 2020, www.mwpvl.com/html/amazon_com.html.

Looking more closely at Amazon's U.S. operations, we see that as of mid-2019 it had 10 inbound sortation centers, 166 fulfillment and return centers, 47 outbound sortation centers, 53 Prime Now hubs, 12 Whole Foods distribution centers, 21 Pantry Fresh Food fulfillment centers, 162 delivery stations, and 6 airport hubs.[31] By mid-2019, Amazon employed a highly diverse and racialized workforce of 350,000 in their U.S. facilities, not including the 100,000 or so temporary workers taken on at the peak holiday season.[32] The sortation centers are a new development in which goods are moved from fulfillment centers to the outbound sortation centers where they are organized by zip code and sent to the U.S. Postal Service (USPS) to be forwarded to customers. The Whole Foods distribution centers and Fresh Food fulfillment centers are also new since Amazon's 2017 acquisition of Whole Foods was its first major entry into brick-and-mortar stores.[33]

Missing from the MWPVL tally are Amazon's data centers (or data warehouses) about which the company is highly secretive. They are nevertheless the operational centers of Amazon Web Services, which both provides "cloud" services for other business customers and the artificial intelligence that drives its Alexa "voice assistant", as well as for its own massive "number-crunching capacity and standardized, automated computing infrastructure."[34] While Amazon does not provide detailed information on their number or location, *Datacenters.com* puts those in the US at 36, with 29 concentrated in northern Virginia, three in Ohio, three in eastern Oregon, and just one in Amazon's hometown of Seattle. According to this count, these data centers employ some 10,000 people in the 36 U.S. facilities and three in

Ireland.[35] As an article about Amazon's data centers in *The Atlantic* points out, northern Virginia is the birthplace and "heart of the internet," but also of "spook country"— that is, the epicenter of the national security state's data and surveillance operations. Amazon's lines to the national security state are also direct. The CIA is reported to have a $600 million contract with AWS.[36] Finally, along with the miles of fiber-optic cable, these data centers are just as material as its fulfillment centers and are run and maintained by workers.

It is also humans in trucks, vans, and now airplanes that connect Amazon's facilities along its supply chains to the final consumer. In logistics industry jargon, this involves the "first mile" (from manufacturer or third-party merchant to an Amazon facility), the middle (between Amazon facilities), and the "last mile" (delivery to customers). As Amazon stated in its 2018 U.S. Securities and Exchange Commission (SEC) Form 10-K report, "We rely on a limited number of shipping companies to deliver inventory to us and completed orders to our customers."[37] For the "first mile," these are a small number of well-known trucking firms, while UPS, FedEx, and the U.S. Post Office cover the "last mile." More recently, however, Amazon has begun to build last-mile capacity to eventually replace or minimize dependence on UPS and FedEx. Amazon Logistics now owns 20,000 Mercedes-Benz vans which are leased to contractors ("partners") who are tied to Amazon via its Amazon Flex, Uber-style app. This allows Amazon to maintain a high degree of control over these drivers, while avoiding the costs and responsibilities of calling them employees.[38]

In addition, as Berg and Knights note, "Amazon and its rivals ... are increasingly going after the middle and first mile of the fulfillment supply chain." For example, Amazon has established "Fulfillment By Amazon" to move goods the "first mile" from third-party merchants to Amazon facilities. Fulfillment By Amazon (FBA) controls its transportation contractors by requiring them "to meet their strict shipping and delivery timelines." Amazon also deploys a fleet of 32 Boeing 767s from its own U.S. airfields to move goods to and from its logistics system.[39]

The picture is more or less completed by its internal, middle, movement of goods between cross-dock and other sortation centers, fulfillment centers, and Prime Now hubs, on to delivery stations, and its new self-service lockers. To accomplish this, over the years in the U.S., Amazon has purchased thousands of truck-trailers, though only about 300 "power units" or tractor cabs that pull the trailers. Once again, Amazon relies on contract drivers to haul these trailers; the company uses an Amazon app to direct and supervise the drivers, so that, while some may work for small trucking firms, most are Amazon employees in all but name—or cost.[40] Given the importance of these drivers to the Amazon supply chain, it is worth noting that their situation is similar to the Los Angeles port truckers who have been organizing through the Teamsters and fighting, with some successes, to be recognized as employees rather contractors.[41] This is a possible example for Amazon's many truck and van drivers who move around within the company's logistics system and can potentially play an important role in organizing Amazon's as yet almost totally non-union workforce.

Amazon's relentless efforts to tighten, speed up and cheapen its "just-in-time" transportation systems, of course, mean more pressure on the workers in its facilities to pick, prepare, pack, and/or sort the incoming and outgoing traffic at each facility in "real time." Whether this pace is driven by algorithms, handheld computers and radio frequency identification (RFID) tags, Kiva robots, conveyor belts, or close supervision in Amazon's facilities, it is the entire system of goods movement and external competition that ultimately pushes work intensification. One result is a culture of injury. Warehousing in general has a higher rate of injuries and illness at 5.1 incidents per 100 full-time employees (FTEs), while trucking also has a high rate at 4.2, compared to construction at 3.1, and manufacturing at 3.5.[42] While we don't have comparable figures for all Amazon facilities, the Center for Investigative Reporting's *Reveal* website shows injury rates well above the national average for warehousing, ranging from 6.07 to 25.87 per 100 employees for Amazon warehouses across the U.S.[43] Furthermore, exposés by *The Guardian* and *Mother Jones* reveal both high levels of accidents and a culture of cover-up and unreported injuries that leads to personal tragedies for those affected and fear for those lucky enough to avoid injury.[44]

THE GIANT IS VULNERABLE

The irony in this seemingly bleak situation is that the tighter the supply chain, and the faster goods move into, through, and out of Amazon's capital-intensive facilities, the more vulnerable is its logistics system to disruption. This is true of the logistics industry as a whole. Indeed, since the turn of the twenty-first century, a whole new discipline of supply-chain risk management (SCRM) has supplemented the older field of supply-chain management

(SCM) to deal with the mostly unpredictable disruptions at any one of many points in the supply chain.[45] As one SCRM expert puts it, "JIT removes slack from operations and makes them vulnerable to the slightest hiccup. If there is even a small delay, breakdown, accident, surge in demand, new product or any other change, there is no cushion and the whole supply chain comes to a halt."[46] As an industry practitioner put it more modestly, "Because supply chain risks arise from the interaction between organizations, they are likely to affect several organizations through rippling effects."[47]

Amazon executives and managers are, of course, aware of the vulnerability of the company's logistics system. In its SEC 10-K report, Amazon management speaks of its "high inventory," but also mentions that "our ability to receive inbound inventory efficiently and ship completed orders to customers also may be negatively affected by inclement weather, fire, flood, power loss, earthquakes, labor disputes, acts of war or terrorism, acts of God, and similar factors."[48] Labor disputes are fairly low on its list, though just above terrorism and divine intervention, largely because so far collective workers' direct actions are relatively new to Amazon. Bearing in mind the newness of most Amazon facilities, the lack of collective action should not surprise us. As the workforce becomes aware of its shared situation, its interlocking sources of power and leverage, and the first successful acts of worker resistance become widely known, this is certain to change.

It is worth noting as well that even Amazon's high-powered data centers are not safe from disruption, which can have more than a mere ripple effect whatever the cause. In 2011, Sheffi tells us, "a minor outage in Amazon's East Coast data center cascaded when systems designed to ensure Amazon's reliability actually clogged the network with what Amazon described as a 're-mirroring storm.'"[49] Indeed, such disruptions are relatively common. A 2018 survey of nearly 900 data center personnel across many industries found that 31 percent had experienced outages in the last year and that over the previous five years almost half of those surveyed reported outages or IT failures. Thus, in addition to IT and software employees, maintenance workers of various types are crucial to the operation of data centers.[50]

The second source of vulnerability is the fact that despite its increasing dominance in online retail and computer services, Amazon faces competitors in most of the countries in which it has planted its flag. Google, Walmart, Target, and others remain competitors in the U.S., while it faces giants such as Carrefour in Europe, and the new and even more threatening giants Alibaba and JD.com in China.[51] That Amazon appears to be winning in the West is almost entirely due to its superior logistics infrastructure. But in order to justify its huge fixed investments, Amazon must stay ahead of the crowd. That, of course, is the nature of capitalist competition: to stay ahead, a firm must invest to increase productivity and control prices to expand its market.[52] And that is another reason why almost any significant disruption of Amazon's time-bound logistics system can cost it market share, as well as immediate monetary losses.

There is an even more fundamental reason why Amazon workers possess a high level of potential power: the company's deeply embedded capital-intensive facilities. The fixed nature and recent construction of its global logistics system means that despite its international presence, its facilities in any one place are not about to move "overseas." They are costly sunk investments that serve a specific, resident, mostly affluent consumer base. Its annual investments in these embedded facilities have continued to grow faster than Walmart's and are spent almost entirely on its logistics framework. In 2018, for example, Amazon spent $13.4 billion on fixed property and equipment, while Walmart spent only $5.2 billion on these, in spite of the fact that its global sales are over twice those of Amazon.[53]

As political economist Anwar Shaikh argues, "Capital-intensive industries will also tend to have high levels of fixed costs which will make them more susceptible to the effects of slowdowns and strikes."[54] Amazon's Form 10-K, for example, tells us that in 2018 its global leasing and other regular annual obligations ran to $131 billion, which is a huge portion of its total expenses, much of it for leasing land and warehouse facilities.[55] These are financial obligations that must be met during a strike or job action. This increases what economist Howard Botwinick has called the employer's "cost of obstruction"—that is, the cost to employers who attempt to block or defeat workers' actions. Clearly, high fixed costs raise this "cost of obstruction" significantly for Amazon, strengthening the hand of workers who dare to take full-scale action.[56]

Finally, Amazon is not an island unto itself. Its workers are part of the broader logistics workforce in the U.S. and internationally. Like other warehouses and centers of transportation, Amazon facilities in the U.S. are often located within the nation's 60 or so giant "logistics clusters" of warehouses and transportation networks in which thousands and tens of thousands of workers facing similar conditions are geographically concentrated. Altogether about 4 million workers are employed in this sector.[57] As Amazon workers begin to act and organize, they will be part of a broader movement in which solidarity can and must extend across company lines. At the same time, the ruthless exploitation and oppression of its workforce are producing the sparks that can ignite worker resistance throughout its system that, ironically, just might make Amazon's own slogan "Work Hard, Make History" a reality with which Jeff Bezos had not reckoned.

NOTES

1. Brad Stone, *The Everything Store: Jeff Bezos and the Age of Amazon* (London: Corgi Books, 2013), p. 243.
2. Scott Galloway, *The Four: The Hidden DNA of Amazon, Apple, Facebook, and Google* (London: Corgi Books, 2017), p. 41.
3. Natalie Berg and Miya Knights, *Amazon: How the World's Most Relentless Retailer Will Continue to Revolutionize Commerce* (London: Kogan Page, 2019), p. 232.
4. Daniel P. Bearth, "Is Amazon a Logistics Company?" *Transport Topics*, April 8, 2019, www.ttnews.com/articles/amazon-logistics-company-all-signs-point. Accessed April 19, 2020.
5. Galloway, *The Four*, p. 31.
6. Berg and Knights, *Amazon*, pp. 14–15.
7. U.S. Securities and Exchange Commission, Form 10-K AMAZON.COM INC. For fiscal year ended December 31, 2018, p. 36; U.S. Securities and Exchange Commission, Form 10-K AMAZON.COM INC. For fiscal year ended December 31, 2010, p. 37; U.S. Securities and Exchange Commission, form 10-K, WALMART INC., For the fiscal year ending January 31, 2019, p. 32.
8. Jesse LeCavalier, *The Rule of Logistics: Walmart and the Architecture of Fulfillment* (Minneapolis: University of Minnesota Press, 2016), *passim*; Stone, *Everything Store*, p. 207.
9. Edna Bonachich and Jake B. Wilson, *Getting the Goods: Ports, Labor, and the Logistics Revolution* (Ithaca, NY: Cornell University Press, 2008), pp. 96–101; Marc Levinson, *The Box: How the Shipping Container Made the World Smaller and the World Economy Bigger* (Princeton, NJ: Princeton University Press, 2006), pp. 266–267; LeCavalier, *Rule of Logistics*, p. 4.
10. World Bank, Container port traffic (TEU: 20 foot equivalent units). https://data.worldbank.org/indicator/IS.SHP.GOOD.TU?view=chart; World Bank, Air transport, freight (million ton-km), https://data.worldbank.org/indicator/IS.AIR.GOOD.MT.K1?view=chart; World Bank, Railways, goods transported (million ton-km), https://data.worldbank.org/indicator/IS.RRS.GOOD.MT.K6?view=chart. Accessed April 20, 2020.

11. Peter Frankopan, *The New Silk Roads: The Present and the Future of the World* (London: Bloomsbury Publishing, 2018), pp. 89–100.
12. U.S. Department of Transportation, Bureau of Transportation Statistics, *Freight Activity in the United States,* Table 1-58, *1993, 1997, 2002, 2007, 2012 and 2017,* www.bts.gov/content/freight-activity-united-states-1993-1997-2002-and 2012. Accessed April 20, 2020.
13. Bureau of Labor Statistics, "Warehousing and Storage: NAICS 493," *Industries at a Glance*, June 21, 2019, https://data.bls.gov/cgi-bin/print.pl/iag/tgs/iag493.htm. For a summary of this growth, see Kim Moody, "Labour and the Contradictory Logic of Logistics," *Work Organisation, Labour & Globalisation* 13(1) (Spring 2019): 79–95.
14. Yossi Sheffi, *Logistics Clusters: Delivering Value and Driving Growth* (Cambridge, MA: MIT Press, 2012), p. 147.
15. LeCavalier, *Rule of Logistics*, p. 50.
16. Bearth, "Is Amazon a Logistics Company?"
17. *Transport Topics*, "Top 100 For-Hire Carriers," 2018, www.ttnews.com/top100/for-hire/2018; *Transport Topics*, "Top 50 Logistics," 2019, www.ttnews.com/top50/logistics/2019. Accessed April 20, 2020.
18. Sheffi, *Logistics Clusters*, p. 159.
19. Moody, "Labour," p. 80.
20. *Datacenter.com*, "locations," 2019, www.datacenter.com/locations; *Cloudscene*, "Data Centers in the United States 2019," https://cloudscene.com/market/data-centers-in-united-states/all. Accessed April 20, 2020.
21. LeCavalier, *Rule of Logistics*, pp. 98–100, *passim*.
22. MWPVL International, *Amazon Global Fulfillment Center Network*, January 2020, www.mwpvl.com/html/amazon_com.html Accessed April 20, 2020. U.S. Securities and Exchange Commission, Form 10-K, WALMART INC, Year ending January 31, 2019, p. 25.
23. Martin Christopher, *Logistics and Supply Chain Management*, 5th edition (Harlow, UK: Pearson, 2016), pp. 135–153; Sheffi, *Logistics Clusters*, pp. 108–111.
24. Karl Marx, *Grundrisse: Introduction to the Critique of Political Economy* (Harmondsworth, UK: Penguin Books 1973), p. 524.
25. Statista Research Department, "Annual Net Revenue of Amazon from 2004 to 2018," *Statista*, May 7, 2019, www.statista.com/statistics/266282/annual-net-revenue-of-amazoncom/. Accessed April 20, 2020.
26. U.S. Securities and Exchange Commission, AMAZON.COM, 2018, p. 51.
27. Marx, *Grundrisse*, pp. 533–534.
28. Karl Marx, *Capital*, Volume II (Harmondsworth, UK: Penguin Books, 1978), pp. 226–227.
29. U.S. Securities and Exchange Commission, AMAZON.COM, 2018, p. 4. This figure does not include temporary workers employed at seasonal peaks who in the U.S. number about 100,000.

30. Galloway, *The Four*, p. 183; U.S. Securities and Exchange Commission, AMAZON.COM, 2018, p. 67.
31. MWPVL International, *Amazon Global*, January 2020.
32. Terri Cullen, "Amazon Plans to Spend $700 Million to Retrain a Third of its US Workforce in New Skills," *CNBC*, July 11, 2019, www.cnbc.com/2019/07/11/amazon-plans-to-spend-700-million-to-retrain-a-third-of-its-workforce-in-new-skills-wsj.html. Accessed April 20, 2020; Amazon, "Our Workforce Data," December 31, 2018, www.aboutamazon.com/working-at-amazon/diversity-and-inclusion/our-workforce-data. Accessed April 20, 2020; For the racialization of the workforce, see Jake Alimahomed-Wilson, "Unfree shipping: The racialization of logistics labour," *Work Organisation, Labour & Globalisation* 13(1) (Spring 2019): 96–113.
33. MWPVL International, *Amazon Global*, January 2020; Sara Salinas, "Amazon Raises Minimum Wage to $15 for All US Employees," *CNBC*, October 2, 2018, www.cnbc.com/2018/10/02/amazon-raises-minimum-wage-to-15-for-all-us-employees.html. Accessed April 20, 2020; Nat Levy, "Amazon Tops 600K Worldwide Employees for the 1st Time, a 13% Jump from a Year Ago," *Geekwire*, October 25, 2018, www.geekwire.com/2018/amazon-tops-600k-worldwide-employees-1st-time-13-jump-year-ago/. Accessed April 20, 2020.
34. Berg and Knights, *Amazon*, p. 135; U.S. Securities and Exchange Commission, AMAZON.COM, 2018, p. 25.
35. Datacenters.com, Amazon AWS, map and photos, www.datacenters.com/providers/amazon-aws. Accessed April 20, 2020.
36. Ingrid Burrington, "Why Amazon's Data Centers Are Hidden in Spy Country," *The Atlantic*, January 8, 2016, www.theatlantic.com/technology/archive/2016/01/amazon-web-services-data-center/423147/ 1/. Accessed April 20, 2020.
37. U.S. Securities and Exchange Commission, AMAZON.COM, 2018, p. 8.
38. Andy Geldman, "Amazon Logistics: Innovation of Exploitation?" *WebRetailer*, October 5, 2018, www.webretailer.com/lean-commerce/amazon-logistics/#/ Accessed April 20, 2020; Berg and Knights, *Amazon*, pp. 223–224.
39. Berg and Knights, *Amazon*, pp. 230–233.
40. Ibid., p. 231; Eylan Buchman, "The Rise of Amazon Logistics," *Transport Topics*, August 20, 2018, www.ttnews.com/articles/rise-amazon-logistics. Accessed April 20, 2020.
41. David Jaffe and David Bensman, "Draying and Picking: Precarious Work and Labor Action in the Logistics Sector," *Working USA: Journal of Labor and Society* 19 (2016): 67–71; Alimahomed-Wilson, "Unfree Shipping," pp. 106–109.
42. Bureau of Labor Statistics, *Injuries, Illness, and Fatalities*, Table 1, Incident rates of nonfatal injuries and illnesses by industry and case types, 2017, www.bls.gov/iif/oshwc/osh/os/summ1_00_2017.htm. Accessed April 20, 2020.
43. Reveal staff, "Find Out What Injuries Are Like at the Amazon Warehouse That Handled Your Packages," *Reveal*, November 25, 2019, The Center for Instigative

Reporting, www.revealnews.org/article/find-out-what-injuries-are-like-at-the-amazon-warehouse-that-handled-your-packages/. Accessed April 20, 2020.

44. Michael Sainato, "Accidents at Amazon: Workers Left to Suffer After Warehouse Injuries," *The Guardian*, July 30, 2018, www.theguardian.com/technology/2018jul/30/accidents-at-amazon-workers-left-to-suffer-after-warehouse-injuries. Accessed April 20, 2020; Tonya Riley, "She Injured Herself Working at Amazon: Then The Real Nightmare Began," *Mother Jones*, March 19, 2019, www.motherjones.com/politics/2019/03/amazon-workers-compensation-amcare-clinic-warehouse/. Accessed April 20, 2020.

45. Alina Stanczyk, Zelal Cataldo, Constantin Blome, and Christian Busse, "The Dark Side of Global Sourcing: A Systematic Literature Revue and Research Agenda," *International Journal of Physical Distribution & Logistics* 47(1) (2017): 41–45; Donald Waters, *Supply Chain Risk Management: Vulnerability and Resilience in Logistics* (London: Kogan Page, 2011), pp. 4–6.

46. Waters, *Supply Chain Risk Management*, pp. 62–63.

47. Uta Jüttner, "Supply Chain Risk Management: Understanding the Business Requirements from a Practitioner Perspective," *International Journal of Logistics Management* 16(1) (2005): 127.

48. U.S. Securities and Exchange Commission, AMAZON.COM, pp. 8, 19.

49. Sheffi, *The Power*, p. 221.

50. Burrington, "Amazon's Data Centers"; Uptime Institute, *Uptime Institute Global Data Center Survey* (Seattle, WA: Uptime Institute, 2018, 2018), p. 2.

51. Berg and Knights, *Amazon*, pp. 62–66, 225–226, 234–235.

52. For a thorough analysis of "real capitalist competition," see Anwar Shaikh, *Capitalism: Competition, Conflict, Crises* (New York: Oxford University Press, 2016), pp. 259–326.

53. U.S. Securities and Exchange Commission, Form 10-K, WALMART INC., Fiscal year ending January 31, 2019, pp. 29, 32; U.S. Securities and Exchange Commission, AMAZON.COM, 2018, pp. 36, 66.

54. Shaikh, *Capitalism*, p. 751.

55. U.S. Securities and Exchange Commission, AMAZON.COM, 2018, p. 57.

56. Howard Botwinick, *Persistent Inequalities: Wage Disparity Under Capitalist Competition* (Chicago, IL: Haymarket Books, 2017), pp. 224–251.

57. Kim Moody, *On New Terrain: How Capital is Reshaping the Battleground of Class War* (Chicago, IL: Haymarket Books, 2017), pp. 59–69.

2
Power Accrues to the Powerful: Amazon's Market Share, Customer Surveillance, and Internet Dominance

Dana M. Williams

Amazon's corporate logo depicts a smile. Like other corporate brands, it is both wishful thinking and record-sanitizing. Google's famous slogan "Don't be evil" sought similar revisionism. In fact, tech giants like Amazon are not benevolent, smiling parts of our lives, but are central players in a state-corporate nexus. Such companies want to sell to us (and to profit from re-selling elements from our personal lives) and to enable governments to influence our lives. This state-corporate nexus is not new, but the modern era has seen its power taken to its logical, ominous conclusion. This chapter explores this by emphasizing an often-neglected side of Amazon: its incredible corporate power, web dominance, and surveillance of customers.

Amazon has accomplished much during its relatively short existence. Unfortunately, some of Amazon's influence has been detrimental to workers, consumers, communities, and the environment. For example, by creating a "click consumerism" culture, Amazon has further facilitated the addictive lure of shopping, especially online. Thus, just as giant "big box" retail stores became the one-stop-shopping location that supplanted hardware, grocery, clothing, and electronics stores, Amazon.com makes it possible to do it all online. Amazon also has pioneered the mass collection of consumer data. While such data collection may seem innocent, it allows individuals to be unconsciously manipulated, exploited, and even preyed upon by the powerful actors who control the data. Every search and purchase by millions of users and customers is recorded by Amazon. The company uses this data to determine how to better market additional items. As an Amazon executive has stated, "In general, we collect as much information as possible."[1] An additional use of this user data is as a commodity itself to be sold to Amazon's business clients. Amazon's "Friends and Favorites" community requires validated profiles—replete with ample personal information, preferences, and behaviors—in order to be sold to other businesses for data-mining purposes.[2] Amazon's live-streaming platform Twitch is wholly about surveillance, which has been monetized in a political-economy of culture.[3] All of this user-provided data is a valuable commodity. Shoshana Zuboff calls this "surveillance capitalism," where consumers provide the raw materials: their own data, experiences, and preferences for the profit of tech corporations.[4] Such "big data" could also be employed by governmental actors seeking to control democratic participation or protest. However, few customers likely read the fine print of Amazon user agreements and therefore remain ignorant of how their curiosities, preferences, and profiles are being used. Customers often presume corporate neutrality and simply don't understand the power corporations like Amazon receive from user data.

This chapter explores how Amazon enriches itself through incredible corporate power, how Amazon has developed an impressive online data apparatus and made it available to corporate America and the government, and how Amazon has proliferated tools of mass self-surveillance among millions of customers. First, Amazon's primary objective—making lots of profit—is pursued through strategies like monopolistic practices and increasing its market share, through political lobbying, tax avoidance, and vertical integration. Second, through Amazon's pursuit of massive data collection, it created an impressive web-service infrastructure called Amazon Web Services (AWS), which is used by large portions of corporate America and state agencies (e.g., the CIA and ICE). This empowers such hierarchical organizations to wield incredible control over people. Finally, Amazon sells consumer tools that presumably offer conveniences, but in fact involve considerable compromises in security. These products expose people to privacy violations and other risks that the average customer does not understand.[5]

LIMITLESS CORPORATE POWER?

Corporations in modern America possess what legal scholars call "corporate personhood."[6] This means they are "legal fictions" that court decisions have defined as the equivalent of flesh-and-blood humans. This is greatly concerning, since corporations do not feel pain, require air, or die—they can outlast all of us and have more financial resources than nearly any other group, such as unions or consumer advocacy organizations, that challenge their power. Amazon embodies corporate personhood more than nearly any corporation in world history. Even its name is prophetic. The Amazon is the world's largest river—it dominates the ecosystem of an entire continent. In Western parlance, "Amazons" are the larger-than-life figures that physically dominate other "average" humans—in a clear reference to this, Amazon refers to its employees as "Amazonians." The association of the Amazon corporation with its historical namesakes are not accidental.

Amazon grew to prominence initially as a books-only webstore in 1994 and is widely credited with undercutting real-world bookstore sales. Since the 1990s, B. Dalton's, Borders, Media Play, and Waldenbooks have all gone bankrupt or out of business. Such bookstores were physical—albeit still market-based—sites of free inquiry and dialogue, where readers could meet with others and discuss literature, ideas, and books. Over two decades later, and with no subtle irony, Amazon has set out to create their own physical bookstores (called Amazon Books) now that some of its biggest competitors—like Borders, which operated thousands of stores—no longer exist. Capitalist investors understand and applaud Amazon's monopolistic practices. According to Mitchell, Amazon aims to *become* the marketplace, not simply dominate it.[7] In other words, its goal is not simply vertical integration, wherein all aspects of production, distribution, and sale are influenced, if not controlled, by a single economic actor. While Amazon is pursuing vertical integration, it also seeks control over the very fabric of commerce, to become the one-stop-shop for all online trade. Additionally, Amazon has branched into video content creation and streaming with Amazon Studio and Prime Video, and even healthcare products and delivery with PillPack and Basic Care. Amazon owns its own book publishing operation, Amazon Publishing, and delivers e-books through its Kindle e-reader device. Finally, Amazon Pay functions as an online payment and processing subsidiary. European Union antitrust authorities have begun investigating Amazon and the U.S. Federal Trade Commission may be beginning to watch Amazon more closely, but the U.S.'s weak antitrust laws have largely facilitated Amazon's expansion into more numerous markets and economic niches.[8] Ironically, the lack of antitrust control on Amazon has fueled the company's celestial profits, which CEO Bezos has used to invest in his Blue Origin rocket company to position himself as an early settler and colonizer in space.[9]

Power derives from political sources, too. Consequently, Amazon has nurtured sympathetic allies within the top echelons of American government. The non-partisan Center for Responsive Politics notes that Amazon employed at least 17 major lobbying firms in 2018—spending over $14 million—to influence policies that benefit Amazon.[10] Amazon's founder and CEO Jeff Bezos purchased the major newspaper *The Washington Post*—which thoroughly covers national news in the American capitol—due to its institutional importance.[11] Like many major corporations, Amazon has established a revolving door in politics, notably hiring Barack Obama's former press secretary Jay Carney in 2015.[12] Of the 115 Amazon lobbyists in 2018, 75 percent previously held government jobs.[13] Amazon was also a corporate member of the influential conservative policy group, the American Legislative Exchange Council (ALEC) until social justice advocates, like Color of Change, and unionists pressured Amazon. ALEC is the notorious organization that spawns sample legislation adopted across U.S. states advocating deregulation, voter ID laws, "stand your ground" gun laws, and curtailing union rights.[14]

The Amazon political action committee (PAC) gave $1.2 million in the 2018 election cycle to federal candidates.[15] The company, like much of the Fortune 500, knows how to ride the fence and spread its money around: the top donations went to the Democratic and Republican Congressional committees ($30k each), followed by the two parties' senatorial committees at $15k a piece.[16] From 1998 to the 2020 cycle, Amazon PAC had given $17.7 million.[17] While critics argue that these contributions are negligible in size, the money actually goes quite far in electoral campaigns. And, if such donations did not garner favorable results, corporations simply wouldn't make them. It's also worth noting that Amazon's investment in Congress doesn't stop with campaign donations—the relationship goes the other direction, too. Eighteen Congressional representatives themselves own Amazon shares and thus have a personal stake in Amazon's financial success.[18]

Like other large corporations, Amazon aims to avoid paying taxes. While it doubled its profits in one year to $11.16 billion in 2018, it paid zero dollars in federal taxes and even received a $129 million tax rebate from the government, partly due to tax credits and deductions, loopholes that exempted almost half of Amazon's profits from taxation, as well as a lowering of the corporate tax rate, stemming from the 2017 Tax Cuts and Jobs Act.[19] While it did pay local and state taxes, Amazon denied the federal government considerable resources that would likely have been paid by smaller brick-and-mortar stores. From 2008 to 2015, Amazon's effective federal income tax rate was 10.8 percent.[20] In comparison, the average American's was 13.5 percent,[21] illustrating that if Amazon is a "corporate person," it pays a far smaller portion than its poorer flesh-and-blood brethren. Individually, Amazon CEO Jeff Bezos's personal wealth has mushroomed—during the first half of 2018, he accumulated $40 billion, an amount more than the entire yearly pay of Amazon's estimated 566,000 employee workforce.[22]

AMAZON WEB SERVICES: HANDMAIDEN TO POWER

Much of Amazon's profits derive from sources beyond its e-commerce operations, through its other business ventures. It has purchased other technology companies and products, such as Ring and Twitch, which it has adapted to its central business model. But, its most profitable—and power-building—product is Amazon Web Services (AWS). Managing the world's largest online retail store required incredible computing power and storage capacity. Amazon extended this expertise to become a third-party provider of web-hosting services to other clients, primarily corporate and government. Major corporate clients, which constitute a very small sampling of all AWS clients, include 3M, Airbnb, Bristol-Myers Squibb, British Petroleum, C-SPAN, Canon, Capital One, Carlyle Group, Comcast, Condé Nast, Dow Jones, Gannett, General Electric, Johnson & Johnson, Kaplan, Kellogg's, Lexis-Nexis, Lockheed Martin, Lyft, McDonald's, Monsanto, Netflix, Novartis, Pacific Gas & Electric, Realtor.com, Royal Dutch Shell, Scholastic, Siemens, SoundCloud, Suncorp Bank, Ticketmaster, T-Mobile, and Yelp. AWS also provides financial and banking cloud services for companies and organizations like Aon, Bloomberg, Capital One, FICO, Liberty Mutual, Moody, and PricewaterhouseCoopers. Given this extensive list of clients from corporate America, it is unsurprising that AWS controls nearly half, 47.8 percent as of 2019, of the public-cloud infrastructure, worth over $32 billion.[23] AWS's cloud dominance comes from cost efficiency and "incessant rollout of new and evolving services".[24]

To illustrate some of the consequences resulting from AWS's massive cloud infrastructure—and primarily how its ability to accumulate "big data" aids in surveillance and corporate domination—consider the AWS contract with the National Football League. The NFL is a multi-billion dollar "not-for-profit" corporation that enjoys incredible popularity in the United States. The NFL uses AWS to gather terabytes of data each week, including via RFID chips placed in footballs. The partnership normalizes sports fans' interaction with big data, which has a sinister effect upon privacy. Big data involves an incredible asymmetry of power; it benefits those who control and analyze it. However, it also creates an arms race of sorts, as those who actively use it gain an advantage, while those who don't get "left behind by those who do."[25]

In addition to corporate clients, AWS also provides essential infrastructure for various governmental agencies, too. These resources allow state actors to extend their surveillance powers and social control capacity even wider across the world's population. For example, in 2013 Amazon received a $600 million cloud contract with the U.S. Central Intelligence Agency (CIA). While this contract's purpose is not completely understood, it takes little imagination to speculate on the resources AWS is providing the world's largest spying and foreign subversion organization. The CIA has a long, scandalous history of international meddling, disruption, coups, and assassination.[26]

Another major governmental contract that AWS has bid for is the Joint Enterprise Defense Infrastructure (JEDI) for the U.S. military. Potentially a $10 billion contract, AWS and Microsoft were the two finalist bidders.[27] The tech industry and the U.S.'s military-industrial complex have always been close bedfellows, especially in the recent decades of the U.S.'s "forever wars."[28] Unsurprisingly, Amazon PAC's favourite target of donations are the members of the U.S. House of Representative's Armed Service Committee, who received over a quarter-million dollars.[29] In October 2019, the Pentagon announced Microsoft had won the contract, a decision that Amazon immediately responded to by filing a lawsuit, protesting that this decision was the outcome of U.S. President Donald Trump's personal animosity against Amazon CEO Bezos, owner of the *Washington Post*, which has been critical of Trump's presidency.[30]

Amazon has explicitly claimed that it supports immigrants. The U.S. government is in the middle of its most recent immigration crackdown, with deportations and detentions of undocumented immigrants on the rise since 2002 (peaking in 2013).[31] Amazon is *not* serving as an ally to immigrants, nor is it playing a neutral role. Instead, Immigration Control and Enforcement (ICE) is an AWS client. Amazon provides essential resources in ICE's detention and deportation regime. The AWS cloud hosts digital immigration case files (including all sorts of relevant familial and residential data) as well as biometric data on 230 million humans. This biometric data includes fingerprints and some face photos. Due to Amazon's active assistance to ICE, immigrant rights activists, such as Never Again Action, have targeted Amazon. Among other actions, activists and Amazon workers protested on "Amazon Prime Day" (July 15, 2019) in multiple U.S. cities, including San Francisco, Seattle, New York City, and Shakopee, Minnesota, demanding Amazon stop doing business with ICE.[32]

As the examples from the CIA, the military, and ICE illustrate, AWS facilitates a state-corporate surveillance nexus.[33] This nexus has incorporated technologies previously unavailable to government, via powerful and reliable computer networks. For disadvantaged groups, this surveillance capitalism not only makes their lives increasingly insecure, but poses a direct threat to their safety and freedom.

THE TOOLS OF CONTROL

Amazon's 2018 annual report does not state any concerns over customer or user "privacy." In fact, the only part of the report to address privacy pertains to how Amazon's endangering of individual users' privacy poses a risk to the company through increased governmental regulation and potential lawsuits and criminal penalties.[34] In other words, violations of privacy threaten Amazon's bottom-line first. This indifference to customer privacy is telling. Amazon's many, widely used products (e.g., Echo, Rekognition, and Ring) place the corporation at the center of intense debates about individuals' privacy. Amazon stands accused of both violating the privacy of its users and customers (including minors), of facilitating such violations, and expressing only mild concern over such violations.[35]

For example, Amazon sells a popular line of speakers called Echo. The many Echo models have a special feature: a voice-activated personal assistant. This assistant is personified as "Alexa" and answers any questions and requests that are made of it. If someone audibly utters the Echo's "wake word"—by default "Alexa"—then it will respond to commands verbalized afterward. In order to do this, Echo is "always-on," awaiting any activation request. Echo also records audio after the wake word is uttered and gathers information on the user's location, sending this information to Amazon for review. According to Amazon, "Alexa should remember context and past interactions,"[36] to help its artificial intelligence (AI) to self-improve. Additionally, Amazon employees manually review these recordings for the purpose of improving Alexa, too.

The Echo introduces a variety of privacy concerns that neither Amazon nor society at large has been able to successfully answer. Users do not choose whether Amazon records their instructions to Alexa—as this recording is automated, there may be people present in a room with an Echo device that are unaware they are being recorded by Echo. Consequently, Amazon controls an incredible cache of audio, constituting a potentially huge database of customer desires ripe for economic exploitation by the highest bidder. Problematically, users have discovered a surprising number of false-positive activations from non-wake words. In other words, Alexa may activate itself without actually being summoned by a user and then proceeded to record conversations and other speech that was never intended to be recorded. In the summer of 2019, it was revealed that Apple's AI "Siri" had recorded people having sex and engaging in drug deals, all without the individuals' knowledge; similar things have occurred with Echo. Echo's AI can identify a user's mood or emotions from their voice, and thus respond in kind. Since the Alexa assistant helps users to connect to other smart devices (which involve additional purchases), interactions with these devices are also recorded. Typically, a purchase request made to Alexa results in the assistant purchasing a product from Amazon.com, thus seamlessly integrating Amazon into consumption patterns. Thus, Echo facilitates a corporate marketer's dream—having direct access to the unconscious and often only vaguely articulated desires of customers. This requires massive surveillance. When individuals share aspects of their personal lives—characteristics, preferences, interests, and aspirations—such data is easily commodified and sold to marketers and other corporations seeking to sell individuals additional products and services. This is what communication scholar Emily West refers to as "surveillance as a service," and the Electronic Privacy Information Center argued before the Federal Trade Commission that Echo constituted "unlawful surveillance under federal wiretap law."[37]

Power Accrues to the Powerful

Amazon has developed a facial recognition platform called Rekognition. Unsurprisingly, some of the most interested and enthusiastic customers are governments. The potency of technology able to compare video-recorded individuals to information stored in state-based databases opens up a panorama of potential abuses. In addition to being able to recognize and identify individual's faces, Rekognition can also identify clothing and discern gender. The platform can track many people (perhaps hundreds consecutively) through crowds, identify what individuals are doing, discern their emotional state (e.g., happy, sad, or fearful), identify non-human objects, and read words (e.g., on signs, license plates). Most concerning of all, is that Rekognition also can be used to flag "unsafe" or "inappropriate" things. Amazon has marketed Rekognition to local U.S. police forces; since AWS already hosts the body-camera and surveillance camera footage from many police departments, Rekognition can be an "add-on" feature for a mere $6–12 a month extra. Such robust and integrated facial recognition platforms are obviously able to assist authoritarian states, but "democratic" states are equally able to exploit Rekognition for their own unchallengeable advantage. Many obvious concerns have been articulated by civil liberties and privacy organizations like the American Civil Liberties Union and the Electronic Frontier Foundation. These advocates fear that Rekognition raises the risks for already over-policed populations (especially the poor and people of color), can invasively track and manipulate immigrants, and be used to identify and arrest protesters and activists.

Amazon deflects such criticisms by instead pointing to Rekognition's allegedly "positive" uses, such as finding lost children. The selective highlighting of an invasive technology's "social good" is an old, established strategy, just as states seek to negatively frame privacy-protecting technologies that limit state power. For example, public-key encryption protocols have been regularly critiqued by governments for fears that it *could* empower pedophiles, drug-dealers, or terrorists. Instead, governments advocate flawed encryption platforms for which they hold "backdoor keys," that they proclaim will only be used when absolutely necessary (e.g., with a court-signed warrant). The problem with these arguments is that backdoored encryption is known to be flawed and will be avoided by those seeking to avoid state surveillance. Robust, well-functioning encryption empowers people against state power. But, Rekognition and other facial recognition tools give a clear political advantage to states, and suppress free expression and existence in public.

Ring is a technology that integrates a doorbell with a microphone and video camera, allowing homeowners to view their front doors and be alerted—even from afar—when someone rings the doorbell. It can be activated upon ringing and detect motion; upon activation, the camera footage is recorded to Amazon's cloud, as well as sent to individuals' smartphones. Problematically, Ring can stoke or enhance homeowners' paranoia about safety and security, thus provoking the purchase of more Amazon cameras. Many people pass by or approach front doors on a daily basis—to deliver mail or packages, visit residents, drop off fliers, or ask for directions. Additionally, people soliciting donations or selling products come to front doors, often (but not always) ringing doorbells. Most homeowners are unaware of how often this occurs and Ring can generate suspicions that all the above individuals could be potential criminals seeking to break in, assault, or rob those in the house. Owners can use Ring's "neighborhood watch" app to post messages about "suspicious" people they witness on their Ring cameras. Disproportionately, Ring owners post such messages about people of color, upon whom racist stereotypes are focused. As Ring CEO Jamie Siminoff put their mission: to "declare war" on "dirtbag criminals."[38]

Because Ring generates fears related to crime, police are drawn to this technology, too. Amazon has partnered with over 400 local law enforcement agencies in the U.S.[39] Police can use their Amazon-provided portals to see maps of neighborhood Ring users and request video footage from homeowners. Some of these Ring cameras also capture activity taking place in public space, not just an owner's private property. Consequently, the Electronic Frontier Foundation calls Ring a "perfect storm of privacy threats."[40] It helps to create a wider surveillance network for police, controlled by paranoid (and biased) homeowners, with infrastructure owned by Amazon. If homeowners cannot be convinced by police—who are trained to strategically apply such pressure—to hand over their Ring's camera footage, police can simply subpoena Amazon directly for footage.

A hegemonic threat to privacy may emerge if all the "smart devices" consumers have placed in their homes can become networked and then integrated into state surveillance systems. Unfortunately, something like this may be on the horizon, with Amazon, Google, and Apple beginning to collaborate on connecting their respective products together, under the name "Project Connected Home over IP." At present, it is unclear whether this will make it easier or harder for unpermitted access to users' systems, but it absolutely invites further corporate intervention in users' homes—and all the considerable risks that involves.[41]

THE WIDER CONTEXT

Increasingly sophisticated information technologies and networks have assisted capitalist growth and domination. Behind the expansion and popularization of the World Wide Web was global capital, which stood to benefit greatly from improved access to, and connection between, markets and consumers. Thus, capitalism helped to birth the digital world that enables Amazon and other corporations in the modern era. Digital technology companies are the robber barons of the age—huge, muscular, and almost hegemonic. It is difficult to avoid interacting with them, especially after they have gutted local businesses that were previously sources for consumer products.

Amazon encourages people to be zealous consumers while it empowers states to monitor and control entire populations. If Amazon's power and influence continues to grow, we will become consumers and state subjects only. Where is our free will when Amazon knows what we "want" (perhaps even before we do)? Or when the state can monitor all of our movements, with Amazon's help? The incredible asymmetries of knowledge and power between corporations and citizens that exist under surveillance capitalism is not accidental or inevitable but reflects corporate interests in maximizing profits and social control, and the growing power and influence of large corporations.

The market position Amazon now occupies, its tremendous cache of personal user data, and the alarming human expectations it has created are troubling. It has empowered incredible corporations and governmental agencies, put everyday people at risk of manipulation and exploitation, and encouraged millions to take ongoing surveillance for granted. Presumably, if Amazon wasn't doing all this, it would be just another corporation. The problem is not so much this one, singular bad actor, as it is an unregulated economic system that facilitates monopolies, crushes workers, and addicts and spies on consumers generally. Such a corporation is all but predictable under late capitalism's neoliberal political economy. Amazon has become the dominant actor in e-commerce and its current edge is all but guaranteed by surveillance technologies, other corporations' reliance upon AWS, and fang-less antitrust legislation. These trends will likely continue unless government intervention, civil society pressure, tactical obstruction from digital denizens and hacktivists, internal resistance by workers, or some combination of all, prevent Amazon's advance. Instead, grassroots-led resistance involving citizens, labor, and social movements offer the best chances to create a more equitable and liberatory outcome.

Despite the formidable challenges to everyday people and workers and their privacy, there are avenues of resistance. To select one small example, when the Canonical corporation—which distributes the world's most popular Linux operating system Ubuntu—pre-installed an app that would direct all internal searches (and thus personal information) to Amazon.com, an uproar occurred in the tech world. Canonical quickly created a way for Ubuntu users to disable the app (which users called "spyware") and the controversy was the primary factor that led software privacy advocates to "fork" Ubuntu and create an Amazon-free Ubuntu operating system called Mint. Such small as well as substantial acts of resistance continue to occur, creating challenges in the face of Amazon's march toward greater and greater profits and power.

In the future, transnational alliances to challenge the power of corporations like Amazon will be crucial. As an entity with international reach, Amazon not only has a wide capacity to cause harm, but is also open to attack everywhere, too. Coordinated actions—whether consumer boycotts or worker strikes, hactivist actions and online campaigns, or the creation of alternative technologies for a more cooperative economy or for computer-user privacy—offer great opportunity to resist surveillance capitalism and Amazon.[42]

NOTES

1. Walter M. Brasch, "Fool's Gold in the Nation's Data-mining Programs," *Social Science Computer Review* 23(4) (2005): 401–428.
2. Jan Fernback, "Selling Ourselves? Profitable Surveillance and Online Communities," *Critical Discourse Studies* 4(3) (2007): 311–330.
3. William Clyde Partin, "Watch Me Pay: Twitch and the Cultural Economy of Surveillance," *Surveillance & Society* 17(1/2) (2019): 153–160.

4. Shoshana Zuboff, *The Age of Surveillance Capitalism: The Fight for a Human Future at the New Frontier of Power* (New York: PublicAffairs, 2019).
5. It should be noted upfront that this chapter will not cover controversies that have stalked Amazon's selling of offensive content through their e-store, such as things that advocate antisemitism, pedophilia, animal cruelty, homophobia and transphobia, and other bigoted works. Instead, the chapter focuses on how Amazon accrues and wields its power in pursuit of profit.
6. Dean Ritz, *Defying Corporations, Defining Democracy: A Book of History and Strategies* (Lanham, MD: Rowman & Littlefield, 2001).
7. Stacy Mitchell, "The Empire of Everything," *Nation*, March 12, 2018.
8. Tony Romm, "Amazon Could Face Heightened Antitrust Scrutiny Under a New Agreement Between U.S. Regulators," *Washington Post*, June 1, 2019, www.washingtonpost.com/technology/2019/06/02/amazon-could-face-heightened-antitrust-scrutiny-under-new-agreement-between-us-regulators/. Accessed April 19, 2020.
9. Kenneth Chang, "Jeff Bezos Unveils Blue Origin's Vision for Space, and a Moon Lander," *New York Times*, May 9, 2019, www.nytimes.com/2019/05/09/science/jeff-bezos-moon.html.
10. Center for Responsive Politics, "Lobbying Spending Database—Amazon, 2018," (2018), www.opensecrets.org/lobby/clientsum.php?id=D000023883&year=2018. Accessed April 19, 2020.
11. Stephanie Denning, "Why Jeff Bezos Bought the Washington Post," *Forbes*, September 19, 2018, www.forbes.com/sites/stephaniedenning/2018/09/19/why-jeff-bezos-bought-the-washington-post/. Accessed April 19, 2020.
12. Carlotta Alfonsi, "Taming Tech Giants Requires Fixing the Revolving Door," *Kennedy School Review* 19 (2018): 166–170.
13. Center for Responsive Politics (CRP), "Amazon.com: Summary," (2018), www.opensecrets.org/orgs/summary.php?id=D000023883&cycle=2018. Accessed April 19, 2020.
14. Timothy K. Rusch, "Amazon Announces it Will Stop Funding American Legislative Exchange Council," (2012), https://colorofchange.org/press_release/amazon-announces-it-will-no-longer-fund-alec/. Accessed April 19, 2020.
15. Ibid.
16. Center for Responsive Politics (CRP), "Amazon.com Expenditures," (2018), www.opensecrets.org/pacs/expenditures.php?cycle=2018&cmte=C00360354. Accessed April 19, 2020.
17. Center for Responsive Politics (CRP), "Amazon.com: Total Contributions," (2018), www.opensecrets.org/orgs/totals.php?id=D000023883&cycle=2018. Accessed April 19, 2020.
18. CRP, "Amazon.com: Summary."
19. Tom Huddleston, "Amazon Will Pay $0 in Federal Taxes This Year—and It's Partially Thanks to Trump," *CNBC News*, February 15, 2019, www.cnbc.

com/2019/02/15/amazon-will-pay-0-in-federal-taxes-this-year.html. Accessed April 19, 2020.
20. Rey Mashayekhi, "Why Amazon May Pay No Federal Income Taxes This Year," *Fortune*, March 1, 2019, http://fortune.com/2019/03/01/amazon-federal-corporate-income-tax/.
21. Matthew Frankel, "What's the Average Americans Tax Rate?". *USA Today*, March 10, 2017, www.usatoday.com/story/money/personalfinance/2017/03/10/whats-the-average-americans-tax-rate/98734396/. Accessed April 19, 2020.
22. Brad Tuttle, "Jeff Bezos is Already $40 Billion Richer This Year—While the Typical Amazon Worker Has Made Just $12,000," *CNN Money*, June 5, 2018, http://money.com/money/5301812/jeff-bezos-net-worth-2018-amazon-worker-salary/.
23. Jeb Su, "Amazon Owns Nearly Half of The Public-Cloud Infrastructure Market Worth Over $32 Billion: A Report," *Forbes*, August 2, 2019, www.forbes.com/sites/jeanbaptiste/2019/08/02/amazon-owns-nearly-half-of-the-public-cloud-infrastructure-market-worth-over-32-billion-report/#3c2a85c329e0. Accessed April 19, 2020.
24. eWeek, "Amazon Web Services Cloud Business Showing No Signs of Slowing Down," *eWeek*, May 2, 2018, www.eweek.com/cloud/amazon-web-services-cloud-business-showing-no-signs-of-slowing-down. Accessed April 19, 2020.
25. Justin Grandinetti, "Welcome to a New Generation of Entertainment: Amazon Web Services and the Normalization of Big Data Analytics and RFID Tracking," *Surveillance & Society* 17(1/2) (2019): 169–175. See p. 173.
26. William Blum, *Killing Hope: US Military and CIA Interventions Since World War II* (Monroe, ME: Common Courage Press, 1995).
27. Karen Weise, "Amazon and Microsoft Are 2 Finalists for $10 Billion Pentagon Contract," *New York Times*, April 10, 2019, www.nytimes.com/2019/04/10/technology/amazon-microsoft-jedi-pentagon.html. Accessed April 19, 2020.
28. Jacob Silverman, "Tech's Military Dilemma," *The New Republic*, July/August (2018): 14–15.
29. Karl Evers-Hillstrom, "Following Recent Spike in Lobbying, Amazon Makes Move to DC Metro Area," November 13, 2018, www.opensecrets.org/news/2018/11/amazon-makes-move-to-dc-metro-area/. Accessed April 19, 2020.
30. Annie Palmer, "Amazon Blames Trump for Losing $10 Billion JEDI Cloud Contract to Microsoft," *CNBC*, December 9, 2019, www.cnbc.com/2019/12/09/amazon-blames-trump-for-losing-jedi-cloud-contract.html. Accessed April 19, 2020.
31. Jynnah Radford, "Key Findings About U.S. Immigrants," *Pew Research Center*, 17 June 2019, www.pewresearch.org/fact-tank/2019/06/17/key-findings-about-u-s-immigrants/. Accessed April 19, 2020.
32. Ben Fox Rubin, "Prime Day Brings Out Anti-Amazon Wave of Protests and Activism," July 15, 2019, www.cnet.com/news/prime-day-brings-out-anti-amazon-wave-of-protests-and-activism/. Accessed April 19, 2020.

33. Benjamin Fleury-Steiner, "Deportation Platforms: The AWS-ICE Alliance and the Fallacy of Explicit Agendas," *Surveillance & Society* 17(1/2) (2019): 105–110.
34. Amazon, *Amazon 2018 Annual Report*, (2018), www.annualreports.com/HostedData/AnnualReports/PDF/NASDAQ_AMZN_2018.pdf. Accessed April 19, 2020.
35. Betsy Morris, "Amazon is Accused of Violating Kids' Privacy with Smart Speakers," *Wall Street Journal*, May 9, 2019, www.wsj.com/articles/amazon-is-accused-of-violating-kids-privacy-with-smart-speakers-11557374460. Accessed April 19, 2020.
36. Emily West, "Amazon: Surveillance as a Service," *Surveillance & Society* 17(1/2) (2019): 27–33. See p. 29.
37. West 2019. EPIC, "EPIC Letter to FTC AG: Always On," July 10, 2015, https://epic.org/privacy/internet/ftc/EPIC-Letter-FTC-AG-Always-On.pdf. Accessed April 19, 2020.
38. Sam Biddle, "Amazon's Home Surveillance Chief Declared War on 'Dirtbag Criminals' as Company Got Closer to Police," *The Intercept*, February 14, 2019, https://theintercept.com/2019/02/14/amazon-ring-police-surveillance/
39. Drew Harwell, "Doorbell-camera Firm Ring Has Partnered with 400 Police Forces, Extending Surveillance Concerns," *Washington Post*, August 28, 2019, www.washingtonpost.com/technology/2019/08/28/doorbell-camera-firm-ring-has-partnered-with-police-forces-extending-surveillance-reach/.
40. Matthew Guariglia, "Amazon's Ring is a Perfect Storm of Privacy Threats," August 8, 2019, www.eff.org/deeplinks/2019/08/amazons-ring-perfect-storm-privacy-threats. Accessed April 19, 2020.
41. Todd Haselton, "Apple, Google and Amazon are Cooperating to Make Your Home Gadgets Talk to Each Other," *CNBC News*, December 18, 2019, www.cnbc.com/2019/12/18/apple-google-amazon-zigbee-partner-on-smart-home.html. Accessed April 19, 2020.
42. While dated in certain details, Brian Martin's excellent book *Information Liberation* has many thought-provoking, theoretical contributions to make in regards to resisting surveillance capitalism. Brian Martin, *Information Liberation* (London: Freedom Press, 1998).

3
Transnational Amazon: Labor Exploitation and the Rise of E-Commerce in South Asia

Jeb Sprague and Sreerekha Sathi

The e-commerce phenomenon is quickly spreading across consuming strata worldwide, a new form of distribution facilitating the consumption side of the "second machine age."[1] Amazon, Walmart, Alibaba, and other transnational corporations (TNCs) are expanding across the Global South and regions with high levels of informal employment. In India, a country of 1.35 billion people, Amazon is the fastest growing company.[2] The rapid rise of transnational e-commerce is altering market relations and how people consume, rooted in how people produce their existence in global capitalism, and in ways that are often not clearly visible. This chapter examines the political economy of e-commerce, with regard to South Asia in general, and India in particular.

Jeff Bezos, the founder of Amazon and wealthiest person on the planet, visited India in 2020.[3] His visit signaled the growing importance of India for Amazon's global portfolio. In New Delhi, small-scale traders from roadside and retail shops, many in the Confederation of All India Traders (CAIT), protested Bezos' visit. Amazon's e-commerce model presents a major crisis for India's small vendors and businesses. Protests in India seem to match protests in the U.S. and beyond by small business owners opposing, for instance, the expansion of Walmart into rural and urban communities, or in China and other countries where taxicab drivers have protested the rising role of smartphone ride-hailing companies.

Rather than selling goods through storefronts and street vendors (with distribution networks that supply these outlets), e-commerce sales function through the consumer's click of a mouse over the Internet. Various companies and distribution networks move products from warehouses to people's homes in ways that increasingly involve the use of hi-tech automation at the point of sale. To remain competitive, businesses that utilize e-commerce as a sales platform are compelled to find new ways to squeeze labor. By 2018, Amazon had 67 fulfillment centers across India, where it is beginning to take advantage of economies of scale to sort and ship its consumer products to India's growing middle class. Ultimately, e-commerce creates innumerable new pressures for small businesses and an increasingly flexibilized workforce in India's widely informalized and gendered economy.

Workers continue to be exploited but under shifting conditions, as labor power becomes more thoroughly inserted into transnationalized forms of accumulation. While the major e-commerce warehouses in India remain relatively small in comparison to their Western counterparts,[4] the future of India's logistics sector will integrate more automation and new machine technologies which will increase the rate of exploitation via the production of relative surplus value. Because labor costs in South Asian warehouses remain cheaper than robots to employ, much of the South Asian e-commerce distribution system has not yet caught up to the cutting-edge technologies used in warehouses in the U.S. and Europe.

In this chapter, we will look at how neoliberal politics, corporate power, labor exploitation, and amplified consumerism undergird the rise of e-commerce in India. We show how a diversification of ownership alongside the corporate control of strategic assets drives the Amazon model. Ultimately, Amazon's entry into India is part of the deepening of the globalization of the transnational capitalist process.

NEOLIBERAL POLITICS AND E-COMMERCE IN INDIA

In the early 1990s, the Congress Prime Minister Narasimha Rao opened up the Indian economy for liberalization and structural adjustment policy (SAP) by inviting foreign direct investment, deregulating the domestic market, and reforming the trade regime. This was followed by the privatization of many of India's public-sector enterprises.[5] These policies were pursued with great rigor in 2004 under Dr. Manmohan Singh's government, further liberalizing India's economy. As an extension of neoliberal policies, public-sector expenditures fell and government support, through subsidies and other measures, for agriculture was withdrawn.[6] The country entered a period of major crop failures and farmer suicides, negatively impacting a huge section of the population that remained dependent on agriculture.[7] This coincided with the introduction of a large number of Special Economic Zones (SEZs), providing low-wage employment opportunities to unemployed and unskilled workers in the informal sector, especially women.[8]

The centrist policies followed by the Congress Party in India talked of "inclusive neoliberalism," with global market-oriented strategies coupled with social policy interventions towards protecting the marginalized.[9] India's neoliberal policies were consolidated under the far-right government of Narendra Modi and his Bharatiya Janata Party (BJP), backed by fascist organizations and taking advantage of already existing conservative cultural tendencies. This helped facilitate a massive corporatization of the country's business arena and the rise of huge monopolies; enriching India's top corporate elite families, many of whom aligned with the nationalist Hindutva agenda. Top three among the largest TNCs include Reliance Ltd., the Adani Group, and the Tata Group, with business interests that span the globe. The Tata Group, for example, which partners with Amazon, is linked into an array of transnational capitalist accumulation networks.[10] India's slide into authoritarianism under Modi has provided new space and powers for transnational elites in alliance with a sectarian and casteist Brahmanical elite.[11]

India's political economic restructuring has taken place concomitant with the rise of transnational capital. For those businesses who have successfully made the transition into the digital marketplace, they are able to circumvent significant rents and labor costs. The accessible consumer-friendly platform of e-commerce is easily reworked to target different populations. For companies to remain competitive, they have no choice but to sell their goods through these portals, linking them into more advanced distribution networks.

E-commerce TNCs have made tremendous profits, as companies such as Amazon and Flipkart violate India's government policies through predatory pricing, deep discounting, and by breaking Foreign Direct Investment (FDI) norms.[12] CAIT has mounted strikes by small vendors and carried out other forms of protest against Amazon's lack of accountability.[13] Yet, how can the old norms that guided FDI survive in this transnationalization process? Such norms are not fixed but rather are subject to change as the imperatives of capital accumulation change and as uneven development gathers momentum.[14]

E-commerce subsumes many consumers in new ways within a highly advanced and segmented capitalist society that socially alienates them. It does so in part through an additional and abstracted layer in the capitalist market. In many ways, one is now even more unable to conceive of the true character of the product. When purchasing through online retailers such as Amazon, a consumer temporarily interacts with digital platforms, enjoying a greatly advanced form of consumption. How can an Amazon customer, for example, understand the social, economic, political, and ecological implications of their consumption? This has particular implications in a society such as India, where more than 90 percent of the working population are in the informal sector and many major rural areas lack vital infrastructure.[15] E-commerce continues to expand in this uneven environment in India, adding to the significant problems faced by labor and creating an existential crisis for many small vendors and businesses. Not all consumers have a "hi-tech" existence, but we are speaking here of a massively growing segment of Indian society.

TRANSNATIONAL CORPORATIONS AND THE TRANSNATIONAL CAPITALIST CLASS

The business model of the TNC is based on functional cross-border diversity in market capitalization, ownership, administration, and production, and is seen as less identifiable with a single home country.[16] In recent decades, the TNC model has emerged as the standard form of top corporate organizations (from Microsoft to Toyota). Key to the process of transnational capitalist globalization is "time-space compression" where many forms of transportation, communication, and economic processes overcome long-standing spatial limitations and barriers.[17] The very qualities and relationship between space and time are altered. The ongoing transformation of the time-space dynamics of accumulation and the apparatuses and arrangements through which they take place is fundamental to new global forms of accumulation and corporate strategy. E-commerce as we understand it would hardly be possible without the technologies of the "second machine age" (artificial intelligence, information technology, robotics, hi-tech communication technology) and the new forms of innovation that permeate the full spectrum of the political economy. Importantly, this helps to serve as a "temporary fix" to the crisis of overaccumulation that transnational capital faces.

The restructuring of capitalist relations in the global era has been driven by the rise of a transnational capitalist class (TCC). The TCC is a social class that is tied together as a self-conscious class, a class in and for itself whose material basis is in TNCs and the accumulation of global capital.[18] The role and emergence of a TCC, with its different factions and allies, can be seen globally, and, for example, across regions of Asia and Oceania.[19] Studies on the TCC have examined the rise of Indian and Indian diasporic transnational capitalists, showing, for example, the emergence of an early TCC faction rooted among entrepreneurs in the software outsourcing industry.[20] Capitalists from South Asia and around the world have become caught up in a globally integrative process, as cross-border capital investments grow.[21] It is in this ruthlessly competitive climate that transnational capitalists compete for profits worldwide and over India's giant consumer market. India is therefore best seen as an integral part of this very contradictory process, from the vantage point of its transnational capitalist segments and the neoliberal state managers and their technocrats.

E-COMMERCE TNCS IN SOUTH ASIA

Transnational capitalists are in a race to dominate the e-commerce sector. A recent World Bank report documents how mergers and acquisitions within e-commerce in South Asia have been driven by large TNCs based primarily in China, Europe, and the United States.[22] Amazon and its competitor Alibaba are rapidly expanding across the region. The China-based Alibaba purchased a leading Bangladesh-based e-commerce company Daraz Group in 2018, and soon after Amazon began holding meetings with government officials in Dhaka, announcing plans to enter the country in 2020. By 2017, Amazon had entered Vietnam and Singapore, where it has faced competition from Alibaba, JD.com, and Tencent. In Sri Lanka, a company known as Kapruka is among the biggest e-commerce firms. In Pakistan, there are sites such as ShoppingBag.pk and ShoppingExpress.pk.

Amazon India, a subsidiary of Amazon, has become entwined with India's corporate landscape, partnering with India's largest retail group.[23] Its biggest competitor, Flipkart, is India's largest homegrown e-commerce giant. In 2018, Walmart, the biggest corporation on the planet, purchased Flipkart for $16 billion.[24] Walmart also partnered with Tata, one of India's largest corporate conglomerates.[25] The China-based TNCs Alibaba and Tencent also became increasingly active in India over these years.[26]

India, and South Asia generally, is a site where the world's largest corporation (Walmart) and the second Asian company to break the US$500 billion valuation mark (Alibaba) are challenging the world's largest online retailer (Amazon) for market power. As this happens, wealthy elites from India and many other parts of the Global South now hold investments and partnerships with these TNCs. India's newspaper *The Economic Times* explains how Amazon India's total revenue in the Financial Year 2018–19 reached IR112,316 billion (US$1.579 billion).[27] E-commerce companies and other TNCs, such as Amazon, have worked internationally to undermine consumer protections and state regulations promoting large-scale tax avoidance, along with squeezing labor by suppliers and distributors.[28]

In India, as in many parts of the Global South, formal employment in shipping and distribution is less common than in the Global North. This reflects how capitalism is a form of production that is heterogenous, where labor faces drastically different conditions and contexts around the world. As development economist Jayati Ghosh explains, "Amazon adapts to the local business and labor conditions, so they exploit the fact that India already has a very low margin distribution network and they are using that, and the fact they have deep pockets that can drive out the alternatives."[29] This is a fact that reflects the reality of uneven development as a defining characteristic of the capitalist process.[30] Reflecting shifting global political economic dynamics, capitalists in India, in order to remain competitive in the global economy, must integrate with transnational capital. Let us turn now to a case study on Amazon India.

AMAZON INDIA

In recent times, e-commerce corporations like Amazon have unleashed a raft of mass marketing propaganda campaigns. Amazon began an online marketing campaign, dubbed the "Great India Festival," in October 2018, to reach millions of new customers in India. As a population with many cultures and religions, Indians are familiar with diverse festivals and celebrations. Amazon's online virtual "festival" showcased a variety of consumer products, replacing many traditional, homemade, or locally produced goods. Amazon's corporate planners in India also see such strategies as a way to reach out to different local vendors, encouraging them to sell their products during the festival. Amazon's marketing strategy for this festival fits well with pro-market rhetoric by using expressions like "Great India" along with the use of the term "Bharat,"—the traditional name for India, regularly used by the country's right-wing movement.

In six days, during September 2019, Amazon and its main competitor in India, Flipkart, together achieved a record US$3 billion (nearly 19,000 crore[31]) of Gross Merchandise Value (GMV) in the festive sale, dominating 90 percent of the market share, and generating up to $6 billion (39,000 crore) in just one month of Amazon and Flipkart's total online sales.[32] The festival also led to a 50 percent growth in the number of new customers compared to the prior year, with 70 billion views over the six days of the sale.[33] It is estimated that Amazon will soon have around half a million online vendors, along with 200 million new customers in India. Amazon's festival slogan—"Your current budget won't stop you from celebrating"— a strategic marketing ploy in the context of India's recession. Promotional "affordability programs" function to promote credit cards and different kinds of installment schemes.[34] It also signals a way to stimulate sales to expand the accumulation of money by Amazon. This is both cultural and ideological, as many of India's businesses, middle-strata workers, and technocrats see themselves as benefiting from greater and more immediate access to readily available commodities from global commodity chains.

Often small businesspeople that lack the means to build what Amazon has achieved look to transnational alliances to build strategic connections to advance their own interests and expand the cycle for capital accumulation. One local seller in Kochi, utilizing Amazon's platform, claims to have made a growth equivalent to 1,350 percent over the past year, a "success story" that Amazon tweeted out.[35] According to Amazon India officials, the festival included a million unique products from small and medium businesses (SMBs) and over 55,000 artisan products across more than 270 unique arts and crafts from 20 states.

The company is also working on integrating multiple regional languages through its Alexa AI, expanding its built-in capabilities in English, Hindi, Kannada, Tamil, and Telugu. In addition, Echo Dot (a voice-controlled smart speaker) was amongst the highest selling products. Thus, Amazon helps to increase the commodification of production across India's diverse cultural spaces: this has to do with the broadening of the spatial and scalar processes within an expanding capitalist market process inside the country—that is, part of transnationalization.

The 48 million "bankables," those utilizing credit cards, are also a major target market, but so too are the nearly 800 million using debit cards.[36] Amazon seeks to integrate both segments of the population into e-commerce, by expanding the number of people using credit cards thereby expanding the growth of personal debt. Amazon Prime, which provides customers with free and speedy scheduled delivery of goods and an easy exchange policy, had a 50 percent increase in India subscribers within 18 months in 2018–19.[37] Amazon Prime's unlimited free music and video streaming service is a major attraction for India's movie lovers, being much cheaper than Netflix. While Amazon Prime costs $115 annually in the U.S., in India, it costs just $15. Amazon Prime has become the central revenue generator for the company, and in fact, is a key driving factor in the increase in the mass of money and Bezos's new wealth.[38] E-commerce is part of global capitalist expansion after all.

Amazon and other TNCs also work closely with the Indian state. One interesting example of this is Amazon's launch of an effort to employ India's military veterans at its sorting and delivery centers.[39] Amazon partners with military-related government offices and other army welfare organizations, which the corporation portrays as a positive contribution to "national interests." Employing military veterans in India also helps to strengthen the company's safety and security profile, without having to invest in training its own security employees out of pocket. The point is that the veterans come already trained and with certain skills and knowledge of the social scenes; the state has provided the veterans at the taxpayers' expense which enables them to anticipate and prepare for any possible emergencies at hardly any additional cost to Amazon.

Different state governments provide various corporate benefits. Amazon and many other TNCs engage in base erosion, profit shifting, and transfer shifting, where the company strategically uses tax rules and argues that it must pay its corporate branch abroad for royalties for intellectual property, technical fees, and so on, resulting in its making small profits in India, thereby avoiding paying taxes.[40]

E-companies have to bear a certain amount of the regular costs while they can provide a variety of incentives. Niche and various online markets are tapped into by a wide array of businesses, while for many of the larger volumes where the economies of scale make a difference Amazon warehouse centers are dominant. The critical point is that this business model is one that fundamentally relies upon squeezing the small suppliers who then squeeze the workers, a model that greatly profits Amazon while lowering corporate risk.

Typical of transnational capital and its integration with the local, rural, and indigenous heartlands of the Global South, Amazon has developed many initiatives with both indigenous and local businesswomen, functioning to more thoroughly marketize and financialize the day-to-day lives of their communities. In 2017, Amazon announced a new initiative aiming at providing a marketplace for products made by indigenous communities in India, with entrepreneurs from 500 indigenous groups, connecting 60,000 families.[41] Thus, transnational capital seeks to expand into every crevice of society, seeking to integrate even lower-income and marginalized populations into its networks of production and accumulation.

Promoting the rhetoric of global competitiveness, Amazon India's "Global Selling Program" has partnerships with various trade bodies, like the Federation of Indian Chambers of Commerce and Industry (FICCI), which is an association of business organizations in India, public-sector enterprises like the Central Cottage Industries Emporium (CCIE), and export associations for small and medium enterprises; these groups claim to focus on the so-called "ethnic products of India," while "selling India to the world." Meanwhile "Amazon Care" has been the company's public face for showcasing corporate social responsibility, such as with its "local development initiatives" in the neighborhoods of its fulfillment centers or warehouses.

Amazon has also entered the food delivery industry, aiming to compete with companies like Swiggy and Zomato.[42] These are online app companies that allow customers to purchase food that is then delivered to customers' homes (similar to the gig-company GrubHub). With Amazon's significant financial resources and capabilities, it is well positioned to take over the online food delivery market, by, for example, using delivery agents and organizational advancements that can lower costs and reduce the time it takes to deliver food. It will provide additional employment opportunities, but in a sector that is built on exploiting low-wage and contingent workers. It is reported that the food delivery industry in India is set to be worth US$17 billion by 2023, with an annual growth rate of 16 percent.[43] Many more businesses and malls will fall under the e-commerce onslaught, with state revenues and taxes under threat as well.

WAREHOUSE, DELIVERY, AND CONTINGENT LABOR

In 2019, Amazon India launched four new sorting centers, primarily located in commercial hubs, which are way stations between fulfillment centers and the customers in Vijayawada, Ranchi, Goa, and Siliguri, in order to respond to increased customer demand. According to Amazon, its largest delivery center in Hyderabad covers over 68 acres of land and has more than 15,000 employees. The total number of Amazon fulfillment centers in India as of 2018, was 67 across 13 states, compared to Flipkart's 34–35 warehouses, and the number has gone up with additional centers being added in the past two years.[44]

Amazon India's warehouse workers, as of 2019, received an average salary of IR12,112 (US$173) per month, 17 percent below the national average.[45] A few years earlier, in 2017, the monthly wage of Amazon India warehouse workers was around $233. A comparison of these wages suggests that the wages of each position from packer to manager, or supervisor seem to have declined or stagnated. The company though has grown significantly. On a single day during February 2020, Amazon India was hiring for 1,430 jobs in Bangalore.[46] The company also has a growing professional strata in its workforce: in 2017, for example, the company hired a thousand tech workers, mostly software programmers.[47]

While there are obvious class and wage differences between the managerial sector and the workers doing sorting, transportation, and delivery, there is not much research yet on the caste and gender composition of its India workforce. The gendered nature of Amazon India's labor force is all the more important, knowing the informal sector in the country consists of more than 90 percent women workers.[48] As some companies are employing more women warehouse workers in India,[49] feminization could be a tendency, although this could be counteracted by job losses related to further automation in female-oriented sectors within warehousing.[50]

Meanwhile, the delivery of Amazon products is made possible through a multitude of informal channels. On average, workers receive IR120–140 (approximately US$1.70–2.00) per hour for delivering Amazon packages. For a country with disastrous levels of unemployment and the vast majority of its workers informally employed, the corporate strategy of e-commerce companies aims to fish in troubled waters. This informal delivery network is highly flexibilized, with an approximate 3 million delivery workers needed to deliver Amazon and Flipkart e-commerce packages during India's Diwali festival. There are also around 1 million workers in the "fulfillment network" called "seasonal associates." Through these precarious and flexibilized workforces, e-commerce deliveries have been sped up in an unprecedented manner.

Amazon's labor policies and practices are highly exploitative because they seek to reach customers in the shortest time frame possible and in the least expensive way. Amazon operates on an extended day, its warehouses functioning around the clock, with different shifts and tightly organized practices. Workers, whether in fulfillment centers or at delivery centers, need to work intensively in a high-stress environment in order to achieve this goal. As in the U.S. and elsewhere, Indian workers complain about extreme work pressure.[51]

CONCLUSION: THE CONTRADICTIONS OF E-COMMERCE IN INDIA

Under today's globalizing form of capitalist production, e-commerce functions as a mass digital market platform, one that will continue to grow as digital literacy increases, and as governments encourage digital transactions. What makes South Asia particularly attractive is the presence of so many desperate workers and marginalized people, along with a large and growing pool of consumers.

While fundamental forces of inequality are in motion, the global e-commerce model only intensifies this process, particularly in the Global South. India's large section of marginalized workers, which includes women, Dalits, Muslims and other poorer groups who work in the corporate global chains, will be paying a price for the new consolidated distribution processes that are highly exploitative. This needs to be seen in light of an increasingly marketized and surveillance-driven society, where big data, Big Brother, and big capital merge within a highly sectarian political scene. India has few consumer protection and data privacy laws and employment conditions are worsening, alongside the rise of twenty-first-century religious-casteist fascism (with the cultural scene already cultivated as a precursor), and the targeting of marginalized and minority populations alongside the consolidation of the economy by transnational capital. Knowing that a handful of elites in India own more than half of its wealth, players like Amazon will lead to further consolidation of the country's capital and exploitation of its cheap workforce. E-commerce is a dynamic avenue for integrating consumers into lines of financial credit (and personal debt). Yet it facilitates an enhanced commodification of social life, disrupts retail and many formal jobs, and ultimately enriches only a small handful of transnational capitalists.

NOTES

1. Erik Brynjolfsson and Andrew McAfee, *The Second Machine Age: Work, Progress and Prosperity in a Time of Brilliant Technologies* (New York: W.W. Norton & Company, 2014).
2. Jitendra Singh, "With 10 Mn Prime Subscribers, India Turns Out to be the Biggest Market for Amazon," *Entrackr*, April 19, 2018, https://entrackr.com/2018/04/10-mn-prime-subscribers-india-amazon/. Accessed February 1, 2020.
3. Avery Hartmans, "Jeff Bezos Just Turned 56. Here's How He Built Amazon into a Nearly $1 Trillion Company and Became the World's Richest Man," *Business Insider*, January 12, 2020, www.businessinsider.nl/amazon-ceo-jeff-bezos-richest-man-world-career-life-story-2017-7?international=true&r=US/. Accessed February 1, 2020.
4. Malavika Velayanikal, "No Robots, Please, We Are Indian—The Lowdown on Amazon's Localisation Strategy," *TechInAsia*, November 6, 2017, www.techinasia.com/amazon-no-robots-ecommerce-strategy Accessed March 1, 2020.
5. Jayati Ghosh and C. P. Chandrasekhar, *The Market That Failed: Neoliberal Economic Reforms in India* (New Delhi, India: LeftWorld Books, 2017).
6. M.S. Sreerekha, *State Without Honour: Women Workers in India's Anganwadis* (New Delhi, India: Oxford University Press, 2017).
7. Ranjana Padhi, *Those Who Did Not Die: Impact of the Agrarian Crisis on the women in Punjab* (New Delhi, India: Sage, 2012).
8. Preethi Sampat, "Special Economic Zones in India," *Economic and Political Weekly* 43(28) (2008).
9. Jan Breman, *Capitalism, Inequality and Labour in India*. (Cambridge: Cambridge University Press, 2019).
10. J. Chesters, "The Rise of China and India and the Formation of a Transnational Capitalist Class in the Asia/Oceania Region,", in J. Sprague (ed.), *Globalization and Transnational Capitalism in Asia and Oceania* (London: Routledge, 2016) pp. 56–72; Chinmay Tumbe, "Transnational Indian Business in the Twentieth Century", *Business History Review* 91(4) (2017): 651–679.

11. Achin Vanaik, *The Rise of Hindu Authoritarianism: Secular Claims, Communal Realities* 2017 (London: Verso, 2017).
12. Aman Rawat. "Here's What Forced CAIT To Go On Hunger Strike Against Amazon, Flipkart," *Inc42*, December 27, 2019, https://inc42.com/buzz/heres-what-forced-cait-to-go-on-hunger-strike-against-amazon-flipkart/. Accessed February 1, 2020.
13. "CAIT Alleges Violation of FDI Policy by Flipkart, Amazon; Companies Reject," *Economic Times*, October 11, 2019, https://economictimes.indiatimes.com/small-biz/startups/newsbuzz/cait-alleges-violation-of-fdi-policy-by-flipkart-amazon-companies-reject/articleshow/71545578.cms/. Accessed February 1, 2020.
14. Michael Roberts, *The Long Depression: Marxism and the Global Crisis of Capitalism* (Chicago, IL: Haymarket Books, 2016); Jeb Sprague and Hilbourne Watson. "Development and Global Capitalism," *Sectors: Newsletter of the American Sociological Association's Sociology of Development Section* 6(2) (2019): 17–18.
15. S. Bhattacharya, and J. Lucassen. *Workers in the Informal Sector: Studies in Labour History 1800–2000* (New Delhi, India: Macmillan, 2005).
16. P. Dicken, *Global Shift: Mapping the Changing Contours of the World Economy* (New York: The Guilford Press, 2011).
17. David Harvey, *The Condition of Postmodernism: An Enquiry into the Origins of Cultural Change* (London: Wiley-Blackwell, 1991).
18. William I. Robinson, *Global Capitalism and the Crisis of Humanity* (Cambridge: Cambridge University Press, 2014).
19. Jeb Sprague (Eds), *Globalization and Transnational Capitalism in Asia and Oceania* (Abingdon: Routledge, 2016); Jeb Sprague, "The Transnational Capitalist Class and Relations of Production in Asia and Oceania," *Research in Political Economy* 32 (2017): 133–158.
20. Carroll Upadhya and A. R. Vasavi (eds.), *In an Outpost of the Global Economy: Work and Workers in India's Information Technology Industry* (New Delhi, India: Routledge India, 2013); M. R. Biradavolu, *Indian Entrepreneurs in Silicon Valley: The Making of a Transnational Techno-capitalist Class* (Amherst, MA: Cambria Press, 2008).
21. Carroll Upadhya, 'A New Transnational Class? Capital Flows, Business Networks and Entrepreneurs in the Indian Software Industry', *Economic and Political Weekly* 39(48) (2004): 5141–5143, 5145–5151.
22. Kathuri Kathuria, Arti Grover, Viviana Maria Eugenia Perego, Aaditya Mattoo, and Pritam Benerjee, "Unleashing E-Commerce for South Asian Integration," *World Bank Group* (2020), https://openknowledge.worldbank.org/bitstream/handle/10986/32718/9781464815195.pdf?sequence=4&isAllowed=y/. Accessed February 1, 2020.
23. Chloe Taylor "Amazon Partners with Future Retail to Further its Push into the Indian Market," *CNBC*, January 7, 2020, www.cnbc.com/2020/01/07/amazon-

partners-with-future-retail-to-further-push-into-indian-market.html/. Accessed February 1, 2020.

24. Saritha Rai, (2019). "Walmart Got a $10 Billion Surprise After Buying Flipkart," *Bloomberg*, July 10, 2019, www.bloomberg.com/news/articles/2019-07-09/walmart-payment-unit-is-raising-funds-at-up-to-10-billion-value. Accessed February 1, 2020.

25. Reeba Zachariah, "Walmart may Team up with Tata Group to Fight Amazon," *TNN*, August 21, 2019, www.gadgetsnow.com/tech-news/walmart-may-team-up-with-tata-group-to-fight-amazon/articleshow/70770971.cms/. Accessed February 1, 2020.

26. Jane Li, "How China's Alibaba and Tencent are Divvying Up India's Unicorns" *Quartz India*, December 16, 2019, https://qz.com/india/1767741/how-chinas-alibaba-and-tencent-are-divvying-up-indias-unicorns/. Accessed February 1, 2020.

27. "Amazon Wholesale India Revenue Declines 8% to Rs 11,232 Crore in FY19," *Economic Times*, October 29, 2019, https://economictimes.indiatimes.com/small-biz/startups/newsbuzz/amazon-indias-e-comm-arm-narrows-fy19-loss-to-rs-5685-crore/articleshow/71796214.cms/. Accessed February 1, 2020.

28. Rounak Jain, "Jeff Bezos may have a Laundry List of Requests for Narendra Modi when he Visits India Next Week," *Business Insider*, January 7, 2020, www.businessinsider.in/tech/article/jeff-bezos-may-have-a-laundry-list-of-requests-for-narendra-modi-when-he-visits-india-next-week/articleshow/73138271.cms/. Accessed February 1, 2020.

29. Interview with Jayati Ghosh by Sreekhah Sathi in New Delhi, January, 2020.

30. Alexander Anievas and Kerem Nisancioglu, *How the West Came to Rule: The Geopolitical Origins of Capitalism* (London: Pluto Press, 2015).

31. In India, a crore is equivalent to the sum of 10 million Indian rupees (IR).

32. "Amazon India Generate Rs 19,000 Crore During 6 Days Festive Season Sale, Flipkart," *BGR India*, October 9, 2019, www.bgr.in/news/flipkart-amazon-india-generate-rs-19000-crore-during-6-days-festive-season-sale/. Accessed February 1, 2020.

33. "Flipkart Registers 50% Growth in New Customers during Big Billion Days Sale," *BGR India*, October 4, 2019, www.bgr.in/news/flipkart-registers-50-percent-growth-in-new-customers-during-big-billion-days-sale/. Accessed February 1, 2020.

34. "36 hours of Amazon Great Indian Festival Sees Record Participation from Digital Bharat," *Amazon*, 2019, www.amazon.in/b/ref=amb_link_1?ie=UTF8&node=18978364031&pf_rd_m=A1VBAL9TL5WCBF. Accessed February 1, 2020.

35. See, for example, this post on social media: https://twitter.com/AmazonNews_IN/status/1183027784752361472/. Accessed February 1, 2020.

36. Pratik Bhakta, "Credit Card Usage Rides on Digital Push, Grows 27%," *Economic Times*, August 8, 2019, https://economictimes.indiatimes.com/industry/

banking/finance/banking/credit-card-usage-rides-on-digital-push-grows-27/articleshow/70580357.cms/. Accessed February 1, 2020.
37. Aditi Shrivastava, "Amazon Prime Doubles India Subscribers in 18 Months, 50% New Members From Smaller Cities," *Economic Times*, June 25, 2019, https://tech.economictimes.indiatimes.com/news/internet/amazon-prime-doubles-india-subscribers-in-18-months-50-new-members-from-smaller-cities/69937471. Accessed February 1, 2020.
38. Harish Jonnalagadda, "Amazon's $15 Annual Prime Membership Continues to be its Differentiator in India," *Android Central*, January 16, 2019 www.androidcentral.com/amazons-15-annual-prime-membership-continues-be-its-differentiator-india. Accessed February 1, 2020.
39. "Amazon Launches Military Veterans Employment Program in India," *Amazon*, August 26, 2019, www.amazon.in/b/ref=amb_link_6?ie=UTF8&node=17773610031. Accessed February 1, 2020.
40. Interview with Jayati Ghosh by Sreekhah Sathi in New Delhi, January, 2020.
41. "TRIFED Goes Global with Amazon," *Amazon*, June 28, 2019, www.amazon.in/b/ref=amb_link_13?ie=UTF8&node=17371478031. Accessed February 1, 2020.
42. "Amazon all set to take on Swiggy and Zomato in India: Report," *BGR* India, October 10, 2019, www.bgr.in/news/amazon-all-set-to-take-on-swiggy-and-zomato-in-india-report/. Accessed February 1, 2020.
43. "Indian Online Food Ordering Market set to Grow at 16.2%, to Touch $17.02 Billion by 2023," *Business Today*, March 26, 2019, www.businesstoday.in/current/economy-politics/indian-online-food-ordering-market-set-to-grow-at-162-to-touch-1702-billion-by-2023/story/331156.html. Accessed February 1, 2020.
44. Mugdha Variyar, "Amazon India Adds 5 More Fulfillment Centres," *Economic Times*, April 26, 2018, https://economictimes.indiatimes.com/small-biz/startups/newsbuzz/amazon-india-adds-5-more-fulfillment-centres/articleshow/63926609.cms/. Accessed February 1, 2020.
45. See, for example, www.indeed.co.in/cmp/Amazon.com/salaries/warehouse-worker.
46. Benjamin Romano, "Amazon has 37,000 Job Listings—Maybe Its Most Ever," *Seattle Times*, February 16, 2020, www.seattletimes.com/business/amazon/amazon-has-around-37000-job-listings-maybe-its-most-ever/. Accessed February 1, 2020.
47. J. Anand and Shlipa Phadnis, "In Big Research and Development Push, Amazon to Hire Over 1,000 in India," *The Times of India*, August 10, 2017, http://timesofindia.indiatimes.com/articleshow/59996195.cms. Accessed February 1, 2020.
48. Indrani Majumdar, *Women Workers and Globalization: Emergent Contradictions in India* (New Delhi, India: Bhatkal & Sen, 2007).

49. "Women Employees in Warehouses Increase Productivity at Grofers," *HRK News Bureau*, November 19, 2019, www.hrkatha.com/news/diversity/women-employees-in-warehouses-increase-productivity-at-grofers/. Accessed March 1, 2020.
50. Suneera Tandon, "Up to 12 Mn Indian Women May Lose Their Jobs to Automation By 2030: Study," *LiveMint*, June 4, 2019, www.livemint.com/news/india/up-to-12-mn-indian-women-may-lose-their-jobs-to-automation-by-2030-study-1559669338838.html. Accessed March 1, 2020.
51. Michael Sainato, "'I'm not a robot': Amazon Workers Condemn Unsafe, Gruelling Conditions at Warehouse," *The Guardian*, February 5, 2020, www.theguardian.com/technology/2020/feb/05/amazon-workers-protest-unsafe-grueling-conditions-warehouse. Accessed March 1, 2020.

PART II

Exploitation and Resistance Across Amazon's Global Empire

4
The Amazonification of Logistics: E-Commerce, Labor, and Exploitation in the Last Mile

Jake Alimahomed-Wilson

Amazon's dominance in online retailing is due to the corporation's mastery of logistics. A key aspect behind Amazon's supply chain management strategy has been its investment in building the world's largest contingent and subcontracted last mile logistics delivery network. Last mile logistics workers, including Amazon's contingent package delivery drivers, complete the final steps of goods delivery, ensuring Amazon Prime packages are delivered on time to a consumer's place of residence (or increasingly a neighborhood Amazon locker). Amazon's expanding market power in the last mile sector, namely, through its Amazon Flex program and Amazon Delivery Service Provider (DSP) program, have contributed to the weakening of existing unions in the last mile sector and has introduced new levels of exploitation, contingency, racialization, and precarity for thousands of package delivery drivers. Therefore, Amazon's growth in power in the last mile sector presents important challenges for workers and unions.

This chapter first provides an overview of some of the general structural changes in the global logistics industry resulting from Amazon's industry-leading supply chain management strategies, with a special focus on the conditions that gave rise to last mile logistics. I argue that Amazon's agenda-setting supply chain management practices have resulted in a paradigm shift in global logistics and supply chain management that previously defined the big-box retail era. I describe these structural changes as the "Amazonification of logistics," which have produced the following outcomes in the movement of consumer goods. First, e-commerce has driven the extension of retail supply chains, away from big-box retail stores and toward the new end point: a consumer's home. Logistics workers across the global supply chain face increased pressure from Amazon to deliver goods at an increasingly rapid pace. In order to do that, dominating the last touch logistics sector has emerged as a key aspect in Amazon's global supply chain management strategy. Instead of building its last mile infrastructure in-house (which would be more difficult and costly to scale at a rapid pace), Amazon expanded its supply chain delivery network by investing in contingent subcontracted last mile workers (i.e., Amazon Flex and Amazon's Delivery Service Partners). This has further amplified the racialization of labor across this sector while simultaneously weakening existing unions in the parcel delivery sector. Finally, these changes have coincided with a deeper integration of real-time technologies of worker surveillance and control. Combined, the Amazonification of logistics has detrimentally impacted workers by contributing to the further erosion of labor standards, while simultaneously increasing competitive pressure on existing unionized parcel delivery firms in the U.S. to deliver on weekends.

Next, I provide a case study of how the Amazonification of logistics has impacted Amazon's contingent last mile delivery workers in the greater Los Angeles region. Drawing on a case study of Amazon's subcontracted, last mile package delivery drivers in the greater Los Angeles region, one of Amazon's largest consumer markets, I identify some of the ways that Amazon has contributed to the deterioration of working conditions and wages across this sector. This case study is based upon a combination of qualitative data analysis of existing reports on the last mile sector, along with my own in-depth interview data with Amazon's subcontracted delivery drivers. In addition, I draw upon approximately 50 hours of ethnographic observation, in which I accompanied Amazon's subcontracted DSP delivery drivers on their Amazon Prime delivery routes throughout the greater Los Angeles region. I shadowed the drivers on their shifts where I learned the job by observing the delivery of Amazon Prime packages to consumers throughout Los Angeles. Finally, I conducted a content analysis of online job forums of 25 former (non-union) third-party subcontracted delivery drivers who previously worked for small delivery companies, Amazon's Delivery Service Partners (DSPs) in the greater Los Angeles area from December 2017 to December 2018.

THE AMAZONIFICATION OF LOGISTICS

The logistics revolution transformed the way goods are produced and transported around the world.[1] Walmart became the world's largest corporation by adapting its business practices to this system: it developed a sophisticated logistics management program, which reduced inefficiencies in the movement of consumer goods across thousands of miles.[2] However, the supply chain management approach that Walmart perfected during the peak of the big-box retail era did not necessarily adapt well to the rapid changes in logistics brought on by the growth of e-commerce and Amazon.[3] Since the global supply chain infrastructure was built to accommodate long-distance shipping, big-box retailers like Walmart struggled to compete in the e-commerce surge, which depends upon a more localized and fragmented distribution and delivery system.

As e-commerce grew, consumers demanded increasingly faster delivery of goods to their homes. Amazon's business model, particularly its Amazon Prime program, has further driven consumer demand for expedited, free shipping.[4] Amazon's logistics practices have thus created a work "speed-up," or pressure to work more quickly, for workers in both warehousing and last mile delivery. Connected to this work speed-up has been a more thorough integration of technologies of worker surveillance and control that track the movements (and speed) of workers in real time. Amazon has been the industry leader in the increasing use of worker surveillance across the global supply chain. These broad changes to logistics have further intensified time demands of labor and created more pressure for last mile delivery drivers to meet their tight delivery routes.

In 2018, Amazon captured nearly 50 percent of all online sales.[5] In addition, Amazon collected US$26 billion by helping other companies ship their own goods.[6] This has meant that Amazon has single-handedly impacted and acquired influence over the economics of the world's freight market. Amazon's increasing scale in last mile operations have also increased demand for last mile (delivery) warehouses in urban Los Angeles in order to satisfy consumer demand for same or next day shipping; shorter delivery times requires delivery centers to be as close to consumers as possible.[7] Competition by e-commerce firms over the last mile has increased demand for last mile real estate located in dense urban consumer markets.[8] Since 2016, last mile logistics and warehousing has experienced double-digit growth across urban Los Angeles, even outpacing the (suburban, or exurban) Inland Empire region's warehouse growth.

In 2018, approximately 2.2 billion online retail transactions came from consumers' smartphones—marking a year-over-year increase of over 55 percent.[9] Not only is smartphone consumerism linked to the increased corporate surveillance of Amazon's customers, but it has also led to Amazon's customers actively tracking, monitoring, and surveilling the shipment of their packages by last mile workers. In other words, Amazon's subcontracted delivery drivers remain one of the only groups of logistics workers that are simultaneously surveilled by their formal employers (DSPs), the parent company (Amazon), and Amazon's Prime customers, who increasingly keep track of the location of their package via GPS monitoring. This heavy surveillance remains an ongoing source of stress and anxiety for last mile workers.

Currently, the U.S. package delivery market delivers 44 million packages per day. Most of these packages are delivered by the big four parcel delivery firms in the U.S.: UPS, FedEx, DHL, and the United States Parcel Service (USPS). By 2025, the number of daily package deliveries is projected to increase to over 100 million packages per day, with about one-quarter of all packages being local deliveries.[10] Worldwide, Amazon shipped over 5 billion Amazon Prime items in 2018.[11] Most projections predict that Amazon will continue to grow up to 20% per year, which means the volume of shipment of small packages will also continue to grow at this pace. The COVID-19 pandemic further solidified Amazon's growth and power in the global economy, as record numbers of Amazon packages were shipped during the pandemic, leading to record profits for Amazon. Therefore, the scale of Amazon's increasing global influence has in turn impacted numerous logistics related sectors, including ocean and air freight, along with trucking and warehousing.

AMAZON'S IMPACT ON THE LAST MILE PARCEL DELIVERY SECTOR

In contrast to big-box retailers that built their warehousing operations by relying heavily on contingent, temporary agency warehouse workers,[12] Amazon has mostly taken a different approach by directly employing thousands of warehouse workers around the world, although temps are still regularly hired by Amazon during peak periods in the U.S. and elsewhere. However, in the last mile package delivery sector, Amazon has invested heavily in expanding its own network of contingent and subcontracted last mile drivers. Notably, the last mile is one of the costliest and most labor-intensive components of the e-commerce supply chain. In fact, nearly one-third of the total cost of shipping goods occurs in the final leg of the supply chain. A primary reason for the high costs in last mile delivery is the inefficiencies involved in home package delivery. Logistics experts have described the challenges facing e-commerce firms as "the last mile problem," since the final leg of delivery usually involves multiple stops with low drop sizes; in other words, the last mile is a very time-intensive component of the delivery chain.[13]

In order to decrease its dependence on unionized delivery operations such as UPS and USPS, or other large firms such as FedEx, Amazon has invested in growing its market share in the parcel delivery market. By 2019, approximately half of Amazon Prime packages were delivered by Amazon-affiliated subcontractors/contingent workers in the United States.[14] According to Cox (2019):

> Amazon has seemingly been bringing shipping services in-house as rapidly as it can as the company ramps up efforts to get packages to Prime members in just one day. But although those ubiquitous gray-blue vans and uniformed drivers all have Amazon branding on them, at least 250 subcontracted companies around the country actually do all the heavy lifting—a system that allows Amazon to skirt liability when heavy pressure on drivers means disaster strikes, according to a new report.[15]

Thus, Amazon's strategy to build market power in the last mile delivery market was to *not* hire drivers (employees); instead, Amazon hired companies (subcontractors) that employ their own drivers to work exclusively for Amazon (using leased Amazon branded delivery vans), or through its reliance on contingent Amazon Flex drivers.

By 2019, half of all Amazon Prime packages were delivered by two main groups of non-union contingent Amazon delivery drivers: Amazon Flex drivers and Amazon Delivery Service Partners (DSPs). Amazon Flex drivers are gig workers who are legally classified as independent contractors (similar to Uber drivers) and are paid per completion of a delivery route (not by the hour). Flex drivers must provide their own vehicles (or rented delivery van). Amazon's use of independent contractors in the last mile sector also makes it more difficult to unionize, enforce minimum wage protections, and complicates labor laws. Not surprisingly then, in 2019, a group of Amazon Flex Drivers based in California sued Amazon for their misclassified employment status. They claim that Amazon intentionally misclassified Flex drivers to avoid paying overtime and employee benefits.[16] In addition to Amazon Flex, Amazon is increasingly moving toward its reliance on Amazon Delivery Service Partners (DSPs). DSPs are small subcontracted "independent" parcel delivery firms with approximately 20-40 delivery vans that exclusively deliver packages for Amazon Prime customers. Despite their appearance to Amazon Prime members, Amazon's subcontracted delivery drivers do not formally work for Amazon. Amazon's Delivery Service Partner program was rolled out in 2018, and has since become a fixture in the industry. DSP fleets are limited to 40 vans to complicate unionization efforts and to increase Amazon's flexibility and power over the price paid per delivery.[17] Limiting the size of DSPs makes it difficult for these small firms to gain leveraging power against Amazon, while giving Amazon flexibility.

For years, it was most common to see white, unmarked delivery vans with workers wearing reflective vests hustling Amazon Prime packages throughout the streets of Southern California. However, today, most DSPs now lease grey-blue Amazon-branded delivery vans along with Amazon delivery uniforms for their drivers. The majority of these drivers work 8-10-hour delivery shifts and earn about US$15 per hour in Southern California; many of these workers do not receive health insurance benefits. DSPs manage between 40 and 100 employees and small fleets of about 20 vans, and primarily deliver Amazon Prime packages 7 days a week, 365 days a year. These workers face extreme pressure to meet the demands of Amazon's tight delivery terms. During peak holiday periods, the number of daily deliveries can reach as high as 400 deliveries per shift.[18] These drivers continually complain of unpaid overtime (which are violations in existing wage and hour laws), and poor working conditions, which include unrealistic expectations and pressures set by Amazon. Overall, DSPs and Amazon Flex give Amazon increased leverage over its shipping and delivery network throughout the last mile. Amazon's use of an additional layer of labor subcontractors helps to increase its profit in delivery and help the corporation avoid unionization campaigns among delivery drivers.

In addition to Amazon Flex and DSPs, Amazon has also invested in Los Angeles' last mile sector in other ways. In 2018, Amazon chose Los Angeles as the site to roll out its new pilot shipping service called "Shipping with Amazon." This program relied on contingent, non-union subcontracted delivery drivers in order to undercut established parcel delivery companies such as FedEx, DHL, and UPS. The Shipping with Amazon program involved Amazon taking control over the movement of small package shipments between Amazon's third-party merchants and Amazon's warehouses across the Los Angeles region, although the program has not yet included final delivery to customers' homes.[19] Shipping with Amazon was launched to serve warehouses located near the Los Angeles International Airport.[20] According to Ray Berman, an Amazon seller who was recruited by Amazon to participate in the pilot program in Los Angeles, the prices offered by Amazon's non-union delivery services were far cheaper compared to UPS.[21] For example, "a shipment of 600 pounds of boxes from his warehouse to Amazon's fulfillment center, Amazon charged only $80 – much lower than UPS' $160 and FedEx's $104."[22]

In order to compete with Amazon's entrance into delivery services, FedEx has begun to tap into the e-commerce market by working with hybrid (big-box stores that combine offline and online) retailers that utilize in-store pickup delivery options. According to FedEx, approximately half of all online purchases occur after 4 p.m.[23] This prompted FedEx to roll out a new late-night shipping option for Amazon's competitors, giving retailers the opportunity to offer next-day shipping on orders placed as late as midnight. Under this program, FedEx Express drivers pick up packages as late as 2 a.m. from retailers and take them to sorting hubs.[24] Deliveries then can occur as soon as the next day within the local market, and two days for destinations outside of the local market. FedEx's late-night shipping option first began in late 2017 as a pilot program in the Los Angeles market. Since then, this program has entered into approximately a hundred other local markets. Using the physical infrastructure of big-box retail outlets as a point of competitive advantage, this FedEx program signifies an increase in speed from fulfillment centers to delivery in less than a 24-hour cycle.[25]

Competition between Amazon and hybrid retail firms has fueled a race to capture the last mile market in other ways. Amazon's acquisition of Whole Foods, at a price of US$13.7 billion, had less to do with groceries and more to do with increasing Amazon's last mile market share. By acquiring

Whole Foods, Amazon instantly expanded its delivery network by adding an additional 440 refrigerated warehouses within 10 miles of 80 percent of the population. Since the acquisition, Amazon Flex drivers routinely utilize Whole Foods stores to drop off and pick up packages at Amazon lockers. In addition, the Whole Foods acquisition improved Amazon's last mile market position in relation to its hybrid retail competitors, including Walmart and Target.

EXPLOITATION IN AMAZON'S LAST MILE: A CASE STUDY OF LOS ANGELES' CONTINGENT PACKAGE DELIVERY SECTOR

When an Amazon Prime member orders an item, the first step in the delivery process begins at an Amazon Fulfillment Center, where the item is picked by a worker and put into a box; an address label is created during this step. From there, the package is typically sent to an Amazon Sortation Center, where the package is sorted and once again sent to either the post office, or increasingly, to an Amazon Delivery Center where Amazon's subcontracted DSP drivers pick up their delivery route. Each Amazon Delivery Center typically contracts with 12–20 DSPs, where hundreds of drivers pick up their racks, or bundles of packages that need delivery that day. These last mile delivery centers are key in ensuring Amazon Prime packages arrive on time that day; any package that arrives at a delivery center must be delivered that day. Delivery centers are where Amazon's DSP drivers start their workday. For most of the DSP drivers I spoke with, they usually have the same daily route.

So, how have Amazon's supply chain management practices impacted workers, specifically those in Los Angeles' (subcontracted, non-union) package delivery sector? Miguel is a 30-year-old DSP delivery driver who I first met near a major Amazon Delivery Center in the Los Angeles region.[26] I accompanied Miguel on some of his shifts throughout the Los Angeles region. Miguel later introduced me to other contingent Amazon DSP drivers in the Los Angeles region and informally trained me so I could assist him with delivering Prime packages on his route.

Prior to working for his DSP, Miguel had no previous driving experience. Upon his hiring, his driver training consisted of an "easy" online training course. While Amazon is not technically his formal employer, Miguel exclusively delivers Amazon Prime packages. Miguel's formal employer is a small parcel delivery company (Amazon DSP), which employs about 50 drivers. Miguel is an undocumented immigrant. He was born in Mexico and migrated to the United States as a baby in the early 1990s. He grew up in Los Angeles and worked in the fast food industry for over ten years before becoming a delivery driver. Miguel typically works four 10-hour shifts each week, with an occasional opportunity for an extra day of overtime work. He earns $15.50 per hour and receives no health benefits. I asked Miguel about the demographics of the workers at his DSP. He estimates that 40 out of the 50 drivers are Latinx men, and there are only two women (both Latinx) drivers at his firm. Miguel estimates there are only two white drivers, three Black drivers, and five Filipino drivers. Miguel's DSP is located in the same location as the Amazon Delivery Center.

Miguel's shift starts at 7:30 a.m. and begins when he picks up his "bag." A driver's bag contains the keys to the delivery van along with an Amazon "Rabbit." A Rabbit is Amazon's delivery device (i.e., an Android smartphone), which tracks a driver's movements in real time and dictates each step of the delivery route. The Rabbit also provides information on each package delivery, access codes to enter apartment buildings, or notes on where to leave packages. The Rabbit also gives the driver information about the Prime customer (i.e., name, address, phone number) along with the size of each of his Amazon Prime packages. "The Rabbit stresses me out," Miguel complains, "I'm constantly staring at it and thinking someone at Amazon is constantly watching me drive." Once a package is delivered, a driver must take a picture of the delivered package to prove it was delivered.

Once Miguel finds his van in the parking lot, he proceeds to the Amazon Delivery Center and waits for his "rack." There is a long line of other DSP drivers also waiting; there doesn't seem to be much order in the process in terms of how daily assignments are distributed according to Miguel. A rack is a pallet containing the total number of Prime packages that a driver must deliver on their route. The racks are distributed according to different waves of drivers, e.g. the first-wave drivers get their racks first; followed by the second wave, and so on. Each rack typically has between 225 and 350 packages. On this particular day, Miguel was in the third wave of drivers; his rack contains 227 packages, amounting to about 161 stops on his route. Once a driver receives their rack, they typically put all the small envelopes and packages up front in the cab of the van and leave the large boxes in the rear of the van. Since I was driving in the front seat of the van, I had to hold dozens of small packages on my lap.

If a driver finishes their shift early, they may be assigned as a "rescue driver" by their DSP in order to assist other drivers who have fallen behind on their delivery route. I asked Miguel what he likes and dislikes about his job as subcontracted DSP driver. He described some of the stressful aspects of the job:

> One thing that can be stressful is that my boss always knows exactly where I am because of the Rabbit. So if I am behind on my route they tell me about it ... They call me on the radio and tell me to hurry up. I'm constantly rushing and on most days, I don't even have time to take a full lunch break so I just go to a drive-thru. And if I'm lucky I'll just eat in the van as I am working ... So the thing about this job is that it is very stressful and you are constantly rushing. You can't find parking, or the Rabbit gets screwed up, it can be really hard ... I've also been accused of stealing packages, especially in rich white neighborhoods. They see a Hispanic driving around and think I am a package thief. My [company] will soon be giving us Amazon-branded uniforms and blue Amazon vans, which I'm happy about because that will help people realize that I am not a porch pirate ... Also, I wish we got paid more. I think we deserve it. I work really hard and I don't have health benefits, so if I get sick or hurt, I have to pay out of pocket ... I think Amazon should pay us more.[27]

Miguel emphasized his belief that Amazon (the parent company), *not* his formal DSP, should pay better wages. This was a common sentiment expressed by many of DSP drivers I interviewed.

During my observations, it became evident that DSP workers rarely had any time to slow down on the job; this even includes finding time for bathroom breaks. Traffic and congestion also played a role in stressing out DSP drivers, and on days where traffic is heavy, breaks for the restroom became even more limited. "I lost over 30 pounds since I started this job," Rogelio, a 26-year-old Latinx driver explained. "This job takes a lot of running ... I twisted my ankle stepping off a curb a couple months ago ... it really slowed me down. I had to keep working though, but it was really swollen." Rogelio told me that he only stops to go use the bathroom once per shift. He usually goes to the same public toilet near a park along his route. "During Prime week," Rogelio notes, "I was way behind on my route … [and] all I ate that day was a granola bar and an apple … for almost 11 hours! … I hate Prime Day."[28]

Amazon's DSP drivers regularly complained about the frantic pace they must maintain in order to meet their tight delivery schedule imposed by Amazon. When a DSP driver fails to deliver a package on their daily delivery route, or even say when a package is stolen from the doorstep of a customer's home, Amazon contacts the DSP with what drivers call a "concession." Concessions occur when Amazon Prime members submit a complaint to Amazon over a missed delivery. When a concession is issued, individual drivers are reprimanded by a superior at their DSP. Alex is a 37-year-old Latinx Amazon DSP driver and has been working for his DSP for the past ten months. I asked Alex if he ever received a concession from Amazon for missing a delivery. He responded;

> Yep… Amazon put a concession on me a few months after I started. My boss called me in, and he asked why I didn't take a picture of the package that disappeared. I told him that I did, but for some reason it didn't get logged by the Rabbit. I was written up [by my boss] and he took away one of my shifts that week as punishment. That one package cost me $150 bucks. For the next few weeks, my boss tightened the screws on me … He was always on me, calling and texting me to hurry up … but it wasn't fair … when an item gets stolen, they blame the drivers.[29]

DSP drivers also complained about low wages. For example, Justin, a 42-year-old DSP Filipino driver, told me:

> Here's the thing, I'm 42 years old. I have four kids and I make $15.00 an hour. I get about [US]$1,250 every two weeks. That's not enough to make it out here in LA. If I didn't have a family, I'd leave this area … Amazon asks a lot from us, and my boss just keeps pressuring us to work faster to make Amazon happy … I bust my ass though, and I'm good at my job, but it's really tiring … By the end of the week, I'm physically and mentally exhausted … I basically do the same work as a UPS driver but those guys get paid double what I earn, at least … We don't have representation with any union … So that's why I take as much overtime as possible, my boss knows I'll take any extra work … but it's a really tiring job at times.[30]

My interviews with subcontracted DSP drivers had similar findings that Peterson found, with drivers regularly complaining of a variety of workplace abuses, including lack of overtime pay, safety violations, wage theft, intimidation, and favoritism.[31] Drivers also described a physically demanding work environment in which, under strict time constraints, they felt pressured to drive at dangerously high speeds, blow stop signs, and even skip bathroom breaks and meals in order to meet the tight delivery deadlines.

My content analysis of subcontracted courier job postings in Los Angeles also found similar patterns.[32] One former third-party driver described what it is like to work as a package delivery driver for Amazon on a job-posting forum:

> The problem is you deliver packages for Amazon. There are several other courier companies in the same location, all fighting for parking, company vans and employee vehicles ... Then trying to log into their dinosaur of a device called a Rabbit that uses the Amazon flex app to get your route so you can get going. Most of the time you have to wait until Amazon uploads the routes, [so] you leave late. Then you [are] making your deliveries, and you come to a huge gated security apartment complex ... and you don't have access. You call support to help get you access [which] takes 20 minutes of your delivery time. Then you have 15 packages for 15 different [addresses ... which takes] you 30–40 minutes to find them all ... Then you have 185 more packages to go, with 150 more stops ... Just not worth it. Amazon don't care at all about the drivers. All they care about is getting their stuff delivered. To be honest, I don't think I will be ordering anymore from Amazon.[33]

The Amazonification of logistics has created a new group of highly exploited contingent workers: delivery drivers. The working conditions facing Amazon's last mile drivers are defined by a frantic pace of work, low wages, and relentless pressure to meet tight delivery deadlines established by Amazon. These jobs are also increasingly becoming defined as racialized-gendered jobs in the Los Angeles region, as workers of color, mostly men of color of Latinx descent, are overrepresented across the last mile sector.[34] Racialized-gendered workers can be subjected to excessively exploitative labor regimes and processes, often with little public outcry.[35] Corporations such as Amazon benefit from the racialization of labor since higher profit margins can be extracted from low-wage racialized workers, who have limited recourse for defending themselves due to a lack of access to citizenship (and workers') rights. The exploitation of racialized-gendered workforces across Amazon's last mile delivery network allow the company to avoid social, moral, legal, and financial responsibility from the oppressive conditions under which their workers labor.

CONCLUSION

As a case study, Southern California's last mile delivery sector provides insight into the ways Amazon has detrimentally impacted logistics workers. Amazon's increasing dominance over the last mile has not only reshaped the courier industry, but also created new challenges for existing unionized parcel delivery firms, along with an overall deterioration of labor standards due to the rise of contingent and subcontracted drivers across the sector, who face onerous working conditions and pressures from Amazon. The rise in contingent employment relations, the weakening of unions, and the racialization and gendering of large and growing segments of the workforce, has contributed to the lowering of labor standards. Today, workers of color and immigrant workers remain over-represented in the lowest-paying, non-union, precarious, contingent, and subcontracted sectors of the last mile logistics sector, and continue to struggle for fair wages, dignity, and safe working conditions.[36] That is, the shift towards contingent relations has been accompanied by the employment of workers with fewer rights and less power in society, leading to an over-representation of people of color and immigrants in the most exploitive jobs throughout Amazon's supply chain.[37]

Just as corporations have adapted to the changes in supply chain management in context of the growth of e-commerce, so must workers' resistance strategies adapt. Central to the success of Amazon's Prime program is the corporation's ability to move goods at a rapid pace. This also means that time is a major vulnerability in the system that workers can disrupt in order to build worker power. While Amazon's Fulfillment Center workers have received some attention, one of the most vulnerable aspects in Amazon's supply chain are its last mile delivery centers, since all packages leaving must be delivered on that day. Therefore, DSP workers picking up racks at Amazon's Delivery Centers have enormous *potential* power, should they choose to collectively organize for better wages and working conditions.

Finally, Amazon Prime customers are disproportionately affluent consumers. In fact, a staggering 82 percent of U.S. households with incomes over US$150,000 are Prime members.[38] Thus, organizing last mile workers near affluent areas of major metropolitan regions where Prime membership rates are high could prove strategic for those seeking to improve working conditions for Amazon's growing number of exploited contingent workers. Organizing efforts could also work on building labor-community-consumer alliances between Amazon's DSP drivers, Flex drivers, and warehouse workers with Amazon's Prime Members. Finally, Amazon's Whole Foods workers remain a group of workers with high visibility in the last mile logistics chain. Whole Foods workers who also tend to lean left politically are in closest contact with Amazon's Flex drivers and may therefore be sympathetic to efforts aimed at holding Amazon accountable for the working conditions across its supply chain.

ACKNOWLEDGMENTS

This chapter is dedicated to Amazon's subcontracted last mile delivery drivers in Los Angeles.

NOTES

1. Edna Bonacich and Jake B. Wilson, *Getting the Goods: Ports, Labor, and the Logistics Revolution* (New York: Cornell University Press, 2008).
2. Jake Alimahomed-Wilson and Immanuel Ness, *Choke Points: Logistics Workers Disrupting the Global Supply Chain* (London: Pluto Books, 2018).
3. Nelson Lichtenstein, *Wal-Mart: The Face of Twenty-First-Century Capitalism* (New York: The New Press, 2005).
4. Jake Alimahomed-Wilson, "The E-Logistics Revolution: E-Commerce, Labor, and the Retransformation of the Southern California Supply Chain," *Travail et Emploi* (forthcoming).
5. Lauren Thomas, "Watch Out, Retailers. This is how big Amazon is Becoming," *CNBC*, July 13, 2018, www.cnbc.com/2018/07/12/amazon-to-take-almost-50-percent-of-us-e-commerce-market-by-years-end.html. Accessed January 22, 2019.
6. Charles Duhigg, "Is Amazon Unstoppable?" *The New Yorker*, October 10, 2019, www.newyorker.com/magazine/2019/10/21/is-amazon-unstoppable?subId1=x id:fr1570756717159gjf. Accessed October 18, 2019.
7. Mark Brohan, "Old Warehouses Can't Keep Up With E-commerce Growth," *DigitalCommerce360*, September 5, 2018, www.digitalcommerce360.com/

2018/09/05/old-warehouses-cant-keep-up-with-e-commerce-growth/. Accessed January 3, 2019.
8. Bill Mongelluzzo, "E-commerce Drives Double-Digit Warehouse Rent Hikes in Top Markets," *Journal of Commerce*, April 19, 2018, www.joc.com/port-news/us-ports/e-commerce-drives-double-digit-warehouse-rent-hikes-top-markets_20180419.html. Accessed February 2, 2019.
9. Ingrid Lunden, "Cyber Monday Hits $7.9B in Online Sales, $2.2B Spent Via Smartphones," *Tech Crunch*, November 28, 2018, https://techcrunch.com/2018/11/26/cyber-monday-2018/. Accessed June 1, 2019.
10. Thomas Black, "FedEx to Start Next-Day Delivery for Orders as Late as Midnight," *Bloomberg News*, January 29, 2019, www.bloomberg.com/news/articles/2019-01-29/fedex-sees-biggest-growth-in-helping-customers-out-do-amazon. Accessed January 29, 2019.
11. Harry McCracken, "Amazon Wants its Delivery Network to Include Hundreds of Startups," *Fast Company*, June 28, 2018, www.fastcompany.com/40590799/amazon-wants-hundreds-of-startups-to-help-deliver-its-packages. Accessed February 2, 2019.
12. Juliann Emmons Allison, Joel S. Hererra, Jason Struna, and Ellen Reese, "The Matrix of Exploitation and Temporary Employment: Earnings Inequality Among Inland Southern California's Blue-Collar Warehouse Workers," *Journal of Labor and Society* 21(4) (2018): 533–560.
13. Shelagh Dolan, "The Challenges of Last Mile Delivery Logistics & the Technology Solutions Cutting Costs," *Business Insider*, May 10, 2018, www.businessinsider.com/last-mile-delivery-shipping-explained. Accessed January 7, 2020.
14. Kate Cox, "Amazon Delivery Contractors Operate With Little Oversight, Report Finds," *ARStechnica*, August 3, 2019, https://arstechnica.com/tech-policy/2019/09/amazon-delivery-contractors-operates-with-little-oversight-report-finds/. Accessed January 6, 2020.
15. Ibid.
16. For more information on this class action lawsuit, see: www.classlawgroup.com/amazon-flex-lawsuit/.
17. Todd Bishop, "Owning an Amazon Delivery Business: The Risks, Rewards and Economic Realities of the Tech Giant's New Program for Entrepreneurs," *Geek Wire*, July 15, 2018, www.geekwire.com/2018/owning-amazon-delivery-business-risks-rewards-economic-realities-tech-giants-new-program-entrepreneurs/. Accessed February 2, 2019.
18. Hayley Peterson, "Missing Wages, Grueling Shifts, and Bottles of Urine: The Disturbing Accounts of Amazon may Reveal the True Human Costs of 'Free' Shipping," *Business Insider*, September 11, 2018, www.businessinsider.com/amazon-delivery-drivers-reveal-claims-of-disturbing-work-conditions-2018-8. Accessed February 2, 2019.

19. Eugene Kim, "Amazon is Offering 50 Percent Cheaper Shipping than UPS for Some Sellers," *CNBC*, November 9, 2018, www.cnbc.com/2018/11/09/amazon-offering-50-percent-cheaper-shipping-than-ups-to-some-sellers.html. Accessed January 20, 2019.
20. David Pierson, "Amazon Reportedly Launching a Delivery Service for Businesses," *Los Angeles Times*, February 9, 2018, www.latimes.com/business/technology/la-fi-tn-amazon-delivery-20180209-story.html. Accessed January 20, 2019.
21. Kim, "Amazon is Offering 50 percent Cheaper Shipping."
22. Ibid.
23. Black, "FedEx to Start Next-Day Delivery for Orders as Late as Midnight."
24. Ibid.
25. Ibid.
26. All names of workers featured in this chapter are pseudonyms.
27. Interview with author. July, 2019.
28. Interview with author. July, 2019.
29. Interview with author. August, 2019.
30. Interview with author. July, 2019.
31. Peterson, "Missing Wages, Grueling Shifts, and Bottles of Urine."
32. Ibid.
33. Anonymous former employee of Xtreme Xpress, "Job Review Post: Not worth it! Don't do it! You will regret it," *Indeed*, 2017, www.indeed.com/cmp/Xtreme-Xpress,-Inc/reviews?fjobtitle=Driver&fcountry=US&floc=Hawthorne%2C+CA. Accessed December 15, 2019.
34. Jake Alimahomed, "Unfree Shipping: The Racialization of Logistics Labor," *Work Organisation, Labor, & Globalisation*, 13(1) (2019): 96–113.
35. Edna Bonacich, Sabrina Alimahomed, and Jake B. Wilson. 2008. "The Racialization of Global Labor," *American Behavioral Scientist*, 52 (3) (2008): 342–355.
36. According to Novello and Stettner's (2019) analysis of recent Bureau of Labor Statistics data, the representation of workers of color, particularly Latinx and Black workers, "has increased from 2005 to 2017, by 12 percent and 41 percent respectively for black workers, and 10 percent and 46 percent respectively for Hispanic workers, while representation among whites has declined." See Amanda Novello and Andrew Stettner, "New Data on Contingent and Alternative Employment Hides Mounting Job Quality Issues," *The Century Foundation*, June 19, 2018, https://tcf.org/content/commentary/new-data-contingent-alternative-employment-hides-mounting-job-quality-issues/?agreed=1 Accessed January 9, 2020.
37. Alimahomed-Wilson. "Unfree Shipping."
38. Rani Molla, "For the Wealthiest Americans, Amazon Prime has Become the Norm," *Vox*, June 8, 2017, www.vox.com/2017/6/8/15759354/amazon-prime-low-income-discount-piper-jaffray-demographics. Accessed October 21, 2019

5
Automation and the Surveillance-Driven Warehouse in Inland Southern California

Jason Struna and Ellen Reese

To maximize profits, minimize labor costs, and capture ever-growing market share, Amazon has become a key driver of automation within warehouses—quickly changing the nature of warehouse work. This chapter explores the use of automation and digital technology within Amazon warehouses generally, and how this has shaped the work experiences of Amazon's blue-collar warehouse workforce in Inland Southern California in particular. Inland Southern California, comprised of Riverside and San Bernardino Counties and located about 60 miles east of the largest ports in the U.S., has quickly become one of the main logistics hubs and centers of Amazon employment in the nation. As of June 2019, at least 16 Amazon fulfillment centers were in place or opening soon in Inland Southern California.[1] Regionally, more than 13,600 warehouse workers, most of whom are blue-collar, non-supervisory employees, were expected to be employed by the corporation. Most of these Amazon warehouse workers, much like other blue-collar warehouse workers in the region, are Latinx, male, and without college degrees.[2]

The labor economist Richard Edwards convincingly argues that every social system of production requires coordination to operate in an organized manner, but capitalist enterprises require additional managerial controls that allow for direction, evaluation, and discipline in the labor process.[3] Since the advent of the modern factory, firms have used some mixture of direct interpersonal control, machine pacing through assembly lines, and bureaucratic rule making. Workers have almost always participated in various managerial schemes designed to extract the most effort and output for the least amount of cost—and in that sense, Amazon's deployment of machines, robots, and computer technology represents continuity in capitalist practice. Yet, the ubiquitous deployment of algorithms—computer codes based on mathematical operations that solve problems in specified ways—that direct, evaluate, and discipline workers in Amazon facilities has created conditions that analysts of other industries have deemed "algocratic" modes of organization, or "rule by algorithm."[4] The combination of such algocratic control with automation, robotics, and artificial intelligence (AI) is rapidly transforming work in warehousing, although its spread is uneven across and within facilities. This kind of electronic control thus provides a workplace analogue to the kinds of "surveillance capitalism" observed by others in consumer markets.[5]

In this chapter, we argue that electronic surveillance of workers enables Amazon to control and discipline workers who do not work quickly or steadily enough and provides useful information to further automate work tasks. Although workers appreciated various aspects of Amazon's workplace technology, most informants found the close monitoring of their work flow through electronic devices to be highly stressful. Workers also raised other concerns regarding the use of workplace technology in Amazon warehouses, including dangers that it posed to their physical health, and feelings of alienation that it engendered. Our research is mainly based on an analysis of responses to 47 in-depth interviews among current and former Amazon workers employed in Inland Southern California collected by our research team, as well as other recent research on automation within Amazon. Before discussing our findings and their implications, we briefly describe our data and methods.

DATA AND METHODS

Our main source of data includes in-depth interviews with 47 current and former Amazon employees in Riverside and San Bernardino Counties. The first author also had previous employment experiences as warehouse workers in the Inland Empire, which helped inform our analysis of our interviews and various terms used by our informants.[6] In addition, we compared interviewees' responses to public research on the impacts of workplace automation, both in relationship to Amazon and more generally, that was available in newspaper articles, research reports, and other online sources. The second author also observed and took notes during a public tour of an Amazon fulfillment center in San Bernardino, which allowed her to observe the shop-floor and various machines used within that facility. The tour guide occasionally described how the labor process at that facility, one of the first Amazon warehouses in the region, compared to that found in more automated facilities in the region. Interviews were collected in several waves between July 2018 and July 2019 by a team of student researchers enrolled at the University of California, Riverside (UCR) and supervised by the second author. Given the difficulties of recruiting low-wage workers that are vulnerable to employment retaliation by current or future employers, we relied heavily upon personal networks to recruit workers in our sample.[7]

Interviews collected basic demographic information about the respondents as well as basic information regarding the jobs and tasks that they performed. Most interview questions focused on interviewees' views and experiences in terms of their working conditions and employment. In the most recent wave of interviews (including 27 out of the 47 interviews conducted), respondents were explicitly asked a series of questions regarding their views and experiences with workplace automation. Our analysis below mainly focuses on interviewees' descriptions of their experiences with and views on workplace technology and automation. However, we briefly put this analysis into context by describing the demographic and employment characteristics of our sample as well as their common workplace concerns.

Most of the interviews were audiotaped and later transcribed, but some interviews were summarized through notes (mostly at the request of the respondent, but occasionally due to technical problems with audiotaping). Pseudonyms were assigned to keep informants' identities confidential. Basic information regarding respondents' employment history with Amazon (e.g., their job titles, when and where they were employed, etc.), their social characteristics, as well as their responses to simple "yes/no" questions were coded and entered into an Excel spreadsheet. Specific themes regarding the labor process that emerged in the analysis of interview transcripts were coded in the spirit of "dwelling in theory."[8] That is, we identified interview data relating to particular themes, such as automation, scanning, surveillance, workplace control, etc., and then examined patterns in those responses.

Demographic and employment characteristics of our sample of respondents are provided in Tables 5.1 and 5.2. Table 5.1 shows the broad occupational categories of our sample in terms of their most recent position

Table 5.1 Employment and job characteristics of interview sample

	Total sample	Blue-collar employees
Start year		
2012–15	19 (48.7%)	17 (45.9%)
2016–19	20 (51.3%)	20 (54.1%)
Job titles		
Warehouse associate	42 (91.3%)	
Management/HR	3 (6.5%)	
Technician	1 (2.2%)	
Part/full-time		
Part-time	13 (29.6%)	12 (28.6%)
Median hours worked	25 hours	25 hours
Full-time	31 (70.5%)	30 (71.4%)
Median hours worked	40.0 hours	40 hours
Temp agency hire		
No	35 (77.8%)	33 (76.7%)
Yes	10 (22.2%)	10 (23.3%)
Former employee		
Yes	33 (70.2%)	31 (72.1%)
No	14 (29.8%)	12 (27.9%)
County employed		
Riverside County	28 (60.9%)	27 (62.8%)
San Bernardino County	18 (39.1%)	16 (37.2%)
Median months employed		
At Amazon	10	9.5
In warehouse	24	24

Note: Statistics shown are for valid responses only (omitting unclear or missing responses)

Table 5.2 Social characteristics of interview sample

		Total sample	Blue-collar employees
Gender	Male	21 (44.7%)	19 (43.2%)
	Female	25 (53.2%)	24 (54.6%)
	Genderqueer/Non-Binary	1 (2.1%)	1 (2.3%)
Latinx (all races)		31 (67.4%)	28 (65.1%)
Race/ethnicity	Non-Hispanic White	7 (15.2%)	7 (16.3%)
	Latinx	27 (58.7%)	24 (55.8%)
	Black	2 (4.3%)	2 (4.7%)
	Native American	0 (0.0%)	0 (0.0%)
	Asian/Pacific Islander	3 (6.5%)	3 (7.0%)
	Mixed Race	7 (15.2%)	7 (16.3%)
Foreign-born	Foreign-born	6 (13.0%)	5 (11.6%)
Estimated age at time of hire	19–24	25 (61.0%)	24 (60.0%)
	25–29	11 (26.8%)	11 (27.5%)
	30–39	5 (12.2%)	5 (12.5%)
	40 and older	0 (0.0%)	0 (0.0%)
Education	High school or GED	8 (17.4%)	8 (18.6%)
	Some college	26 (56.5%)	24 (55.8%)
	Bachelor's and up	8 (17.4%)	7 (16.3%)
	Technical degree or certificate	4 (8.7%)	4 (9.3%)
Marital status	Single, never married	38 (82.6%)	35 (81.4%)
	Married or domestic partnership	7 (15.2%)	7 (16.3%)
	Divorced	1 (2.2%)	1 (2.3%)
% of parents with minor child(ren)		15 (34.1%)	14 (31.8%)

Note: Statistics shown are for valid responses only (omitting unclear or missing responses) within Amazon. Of the 47 workers interviewed, 44 of those interviewed were most recently employed within blue-collar occupations.[9] These workers, nearly all "warehouse associates," were employed in a variety of specific jobs or tasks including product picking, packing, inventory and quality control, auditing task completion by others, building storage units, stowing goods, outbound shipping, inbound receipt, and other stocking tasks. Three interviewees were most recently employed in managerial occupations, only one of whom (a manager) lacked experience working as an Amazon warehouse associate. Other aspects of these workers' job characteristics and employment histories are shown in Table 5.1.

As shown in Table 5.2, about 67 percent of our sample was Latinx, which is reflective of the predominance of Latinxs in the region's labor force generally and among blue-collar warehouse workers in particular.[10] In other ways, our sample is somewhat peculiar and may reflect the biases of our recruitment methods. Recruited among UCR students and their personal networks, it is not surprising that most of our informants were young (mostly in their 20s) and had some college education; men, workers over the age of 30, and those without any college education were under-represented in our sample compared to the social composition of Amazon warehouse workers in Southern California.[11] Our student research team was also mostly women, which probably contributed to the relatively high percentage of women found in our sample. Although our sample is not a "representative sample" of Amazon's blue-collar warehouse workforce, our interviews are revealing and help to capture the views and experiences of actual workers.

FINDINGS: AMAZON WORKERS' EXPERIENCES WITH AUTOMATION

In order to choreograph the brutal ballet that ensues once a consumer clicks "place your order," for next-day delivery on Amazon Prime, the company leverages its algorithmic and technical prowess within its massive network of communication and digital technology, warehouse facilities, and machinery, as it numerically "flexes" its workforce up or down in sync with fluctuating consumer demands. Workers report that even hiring and scheduling is increasingly occurring online. Many respondents report that their first contact with Amazon occurred through online ads and candidate exams that one respondent referred to as a "trust test." Further, Amazon warehouses are becoming progressively capital-intensive work environments,[12] with large and increasing amounts of automation and computer technology,[13] as well as direct and digital surveillance over many aspects of the labor process. However, the deployment of automation and digital surveillance technology varies significantly across Amazon facilities, and varies across departments within them, consistent with other firms in warehousing and logistics.

Scanners are among the primary tools that management uses to direct, evaluate, and discipline workers in the labor process. As our interviewees report, the devices at the time of writing are hand-held, mounted to workstations, or carts, and are used to electronically read various kinds of barcodes, worker IDs, or other labels tracking goods and their routes from receipt to storage and shipping. In some tasks, scanners direct workers through digital displays and monitors, and track output digitally to allow management to ensure that workers carry out their designated tasks at a profitable speed, regardless of the distances required to walk, or the volume of goods passing through their hands.

Additionally, miles of conveyors and skates (long tables with rollers at the end of conveyors) move goods to and from workers at various points in the facility from inbound positions at docks in the back of trailers, to various pick-and-pack functions and beyond. Although they do not exist in every Amazon facility, automated guided vehicles (robots) that originate in "human exclusion zones"[14] or move goods from place to place also interact with workers in stationary positions who further manipulate (pick, pack, wrap, etc.) the objects that these robots bring before the workers place the goods on yet another conveyor to be whisked away again. Of course, in addition to armies of Kiva robots in Amazon's state-of-the-art fulfillment center facilities, workers also navigate various kinds of forklifts and other "powered industrial trucks" (PIT) from receiving to outbound docks in "sortation centers"—the facilities that organize the goods to get delivered for the last mile (to our homes and offices).

In addition to various printers, tape machines, and computer terminals, workers also report interacting with Human Resources (HR) and management via online applications. Workers can check their remaining paid or unpaid time off, make requests for schedule changes, and report problems to HR digitally without direct person-to-person contact. They can also monitor the points or strikes against their employment record in terms of violations related to absenteeism, tardiness, or failure to make work rates or meet quotas. The details and enforcement of points systems and work rules and standards seem to vary across facilities, departments, positions, and individual managers and supervisors and over time. Nevertheless, our respondents indicate that too many failures to work at speed, stay on task, or show up on time leads to discipline—including termination.

ELECTRONIC SURVEILLANCE AND THE PRESSURE TO "MAKE RATE"

Workers in packing, picking, and stowing are monitored in terms of their work rates, their error rates, and their time spent off task. Work-rate standards varied somewhat across interviews, reflecting the different expectations tied to their position and when and whether or not they were employed in a more or less automated facility. Work-rate standards also changed over time. As one worker put it, "They expected a lot of raised numbers and for it to constantly be going up" (Maria).

Fulfilling these work-rate expectations was not easy, especially given the pressure to simultaneously minimize errors and "time off task" (which included any time spent not making rate, including fixing or reporting problems, unless it was excused): "[E]very week you were given 30 minutes of time off task, so if you got over 30 minutes per week you were given a write-up so ... every six minutes they start counting time against you. So if you like, even use up two minutes ... they count you as two minutes off task" (Fernando).

Disciplining workers required both monitoring their work and error rates electronically, as well as in-person interactions with the workers, which was often carried out by more experienced workers known as "ambassadors." Leads and process assistants were also involved in ensuring the work flow among workers, and that packages would be delivered on time. If workers failed to "make rate," they were supposed to receive verbal warnings and after the third warning, they would get a "write up." After three write-ups, workers faced termination. As one worker put it, "They would just come to us maybe twice a day and update us individually on how we were doing in our percentages. We would be told, 'you are at this percentage, you are on rate, or you are not on rate'" (Paola).

Formal procedures were not always followed however. Some workers claimed that they were unfairly given write-ups without warnings and that HR was unresponsive to their complaints about such problems. One former worker claimed, "I got terminated supposedly because my rate was too low, even though I was told by a supervisor … my rate was fine" (Samantha). Many informants also noted how breakdowns in machinery or bad barcodes slowed them down and complained about continued pressure to make rate even in the midst of technological failures. Since workers could be fired for not "making rate," the pressure to make rate was seen as more important than workplace safety. As one worker put it, "They had a concern for safety but were more concerned with speed first" (Jimmy). Other workers reported that they sometimes skirted various safety procedures in order to "make rate."

Among the blue-collar workers interviewed, 82 percent expressed some sort of concern about Amazon's productivity and/or error rate standards, while 75 percent worried about their personal ability to meet those standards. When directly asked, 56 percent agreed that they had concerns about the "pressure to work fast." As Benjamin put it, "I was always scared every day, because I wasn't meeting rate." Describing managers' and supervisors' efforts to pressure her to "make rate," Paola reported that "I was getting made fun of because my rate was very low compared to everyone else."

Those carrying out tasks like stowing found that they could "make rate" more easily with tote boxes with more items to be stowed inside of them. According to Elizabeth, "I made friends in Amazon and when they would get a good box, they were so kind with me, and they would give me a small portion of it." Paola recalled that, "People would fight for the bigger boxes." If people got the boxes with a lot of items, they were at an advantage over the other workers stuck with the boxes with fewer ones. In pack, as Samuel put it, "Whereas one person can pack like a really high rate and then another person there kinda like is stuck at a low rate because that other person is kinda manipulating the system to achieve a higher rate than normal." Commenting on such practices, Andrea lamented, "I thought that was really, really unfair because, everybody had to make their rate … We all have families to feed." Meanwhile, Jimmy resented workers who would only choose light envelopes to scan and were "not pulling their weight physically."

Managers used various carrots as well as sticks to discipline workers. Highly productive workers were praised during stand-up meetings and sometimes given small rewards or "giveaways," especially during peak season. The best work rates would also be publicly posted before and after work breaks. Workers unable to "make rate" faced termination, contributing to high levels of turnover and stress among workers.

WORKPLACE TECHNOLOGY AND EXPERIENCE OF THE LABOR PROCESS

Although most workers complained about electronic monitoring, many workers noted the benefits associated with other aspects of their workplace technology. As Elizabeth put it, "I feel like they [machines] were all very useful and they just make the Associates' job easier." Workers described how their jobs would be more laborious or physically taxing if they lacked particular types of machinery, including conveyor belts, scanners, and forklifts, and favorably compared the quality of Amazon's technology compared to that found at other workplaces. Other workers viewed the automated scheduling system as convenient to use, and less prone to favoritism and discrimination compared to HR staff.

Yet, workers also noted the dangers associated with various machines, including injuries and accidents involving forklifts or conveyor belts. Several workers interviewed complained about hearing loss due to working for long periods in close proximity to noisy machines and understocked ear plugs. Samuel noted how stressful and difficult it was to work when forklift drivers "are honking their horns all the time." Other workers mentioned that they had difficulty getting the lights and sounds of the workplace out of their heads after leaving work that day.

Workplace technology is linked to the scale of production: Amazon's warehouses are *massive* in size: about the size of "four big-box stores" combined, as Jimmy put it. One consequence of this was the sheer physical pain and exhaustion associated with walking great distances throughout the workday, a complaint that was especially common among pickers. As Kelly, who usually worked 10 hours per day, explained, "When I worked there as a picker, I lost 20 pounds from walking so much." Jimmy recalled that "I typically walked four to seven miles within my four-hour shift." Twenty-one-year-old Jorge described the physical toll of working in the warehouse in this way: "I was exhausted ... Like, every day I would come home, and I could barely walk. That was the very first time I ever had to ice my feet."

Meanwhile, packers described the pain and exhaustion associated with standing still and engaging in highly repetitive motions at their automated packing stations, sometimes for 10 hours or more per day.

Many workers noted that although they were given a 15-minute break every 3½ hours spent working, the actual time spent resting was sometimes only 5 minutes, due to how long it took to walk to and from break rooms. Moreover, in an effort to prevent workers from stealing products, workers were required to go through metal detectors before going to break rooms. Getting to break rooms took even longer during peak seasons when there were many workers in security lines. Remembering a time when the metal detector accidently went off and he had to wait to be searched by security staff, Samuel recounts: "I was so pissed. I was starving and at the time, all I wanted to do was eat my snacks."

The scale of the facility, coupled with tight surveillance of work rates and time spent off task meant many workers found it difficult to use the restroom during the workday. As one worker described:

> Probably like once a week you'd be passing through an aisle and ... then out of nowhere a bad smell hits, and there's only one thing, and it's like you'd have to call someone and be like, "Yo' someone did some shit." It's like, instead of going to the bathroom, they'd piss in the trash can cause they didn't want to take the time to go. (Ana)

Other workers described "holding it" when they needed to use the restroom during their shifts in order to "make rate."

ALIENATION, AUTOMATION, AND WORKPLACE SCALE

The size of the facility, combined with the lack of social interaction among workers who scan or move goods all day, often left workers feeling lonely and isolated. As Alejandro described it, "Most of the time you're by yourself in one station and they're about 18 feet apart." Moreover, "It's, like, five managers and there's, like, four floors ... When you wanna talk to your managers it's so hard to find them." As Ana put it: "Honestly, you can just be there and legit [sic] cry and no one would notice, or you could just hate your life and no one would notice. It was just so big and lonely sometimes. It was the most isolating feeling every single day."

Some tasks, like outbound dock work, where work rates were less dependent on electronic surveillance and worker-to-worker interactions were more direct, were seen as desirable by many workers because of the gregarious nature of the work itself. However, other common tasks like picking—whether in conventional stacks, or at workstations where robots bring goods to workers—were viewed by many respondents as isolating and problematic:

> In pick you are just at the station by yourself. Sometimes there's someone on the other side, but it's so far that, what conversation can you really hold with someone? And it's loud ... there's still conveyor belts above ... and the pods [robots] make noise ... You are all by yourself. It's depressing and lonely. (Adriana)

Frequently, workers are in proximity to one another, but cannot talk for fear of breaking concentration. Stress-inducing work rates also have the effect of quashing social interaction in addition to the other stresses speed-ups cause. Thus, estrangement in the Amazon labor process can stem from interaction with technology, the cavernous spaces, the need to make rate, or the repetitive tasks workers execute in the face of constant electronic observation.

AUTOMATION AND WORKER DISPLACEMENT

The company often emphasized the importance of workplace efficiency, automation being just one means to that end. Yet, as Jimmy pointed out, "They want to make it as efficient as possible, which means fewer people doing more work." Some of the workers interviewed expressed fears of displacement through automation, especially after observing the efficiency of Amazon's Kiva robots. As Elizabeth remarked:

> I remember that the robots would take the totes and at the same time that it is moving it, it is also scanning it. I noticed it was doing it so quickly and I was thinking "Dammit they're going to replace us one day with robots." And the people ain't going [to] get paid ... These machines are expensive but, if they're going to pay money for them then it's like a one-time thing versus constantly paying an employee and the benefits and the services ... I would just say that props to them for affording all that, but not to take jobs away from people.

Most workers expressed long-term rather than immediate fears of displacement through automation. Many workers also expressed the idea that there were limits to automation that would help to protect jobs at Amazon. For example, Maria said: "There are certain things that robots can't do. For example, quality control and packing boxes still need a human eye for those details."

While that sentiment is shared by many—warehouse associates, managers, and some researchers alike—it must be tempered with the reality that Amazon is currently deploying automated machinery to replace some of the most common packing tasks.[15] These machines can pack between 600 and 1,000 objects per hour—far more than a human can under the best conditions.[16] Still, the industry goal of creating a "'lights-out'" facility[17] is likely to be unevenly implemented and it may be "at least 10 years away from fully automating the processing of a single order [now] picked by a worker inside a warehouse," according to director of Amazon Robotics Fulfillment, Scott Anderson.[18]

CONCLUSION

Analysis of our interviews indicates that workers' experience with automation ranges from relatively minimal digital surveillance and control in some tasks that are manually executed, to minute observations of work rates and output in combination with machinery and robotics in others. Direction, evaluation, and discipline increasingly involves electronic surveillance and algorithmic techniques for workers using scanners in various picking and packing functions, but is also combined with direct, interpersonal controls as workers are frequently verbally reminded of the need to make rate or face sanctions, including termination. Some Amazon workers report satisfaction with labor-saving technologies, especially in comparison to previous warehouse jobs. Others report injuries like hearing loss due to exposure to loud machines or repetitive motion injuries and strains from using automated equipment. Workers also describe the constant electronic monitoring of their work as very stressful. While some workers fear dislocation and potential unemployment owing to automation, others remain skeptical that particular kinds of human tasks can be executed by robots. Most interviewees report concerns about work speed-ups, under-staffing, and pressure to achieve output goals that are very difficult to meet. Some also report that some tasks induce a deep sense of alienation related to repetition, isolation, and heavy reliance on electronic monitoring and communication.

Overall, automation and surveillance at Amazon need to be understood relative to time and space. Work rates and scale of facility combine to require management to use specific tools to efficiently exploit workers through direction, evaluation, and discipline in their drive for profits. Labor intensification must be understood as a problem that exists alongside the specter of technological unemployment. Further, while we must consider the spectrum of legitimate concerns about automation displacing workers in the near future,[19] or the possibility that we will treat "robots as co-workers" without massive transformations in the total employment picture,[20] our research suggests that existing automation, algorithmic control, and scale of facilities creates highly stressful and insecure work environments for the majority of workers employed in Amazon warehouses and distribution centers. The work environment that Amazon has consciously constructed reflects Shoshanna Zuboff's assertion that "Surveillance capitalism is immune to the traditional reciprocities in which populations and capitalists needed one another for employment and consumption."[21] From retraining initiatives,[22] and plans to buy out marginal or disaffected workers with "The Offer,"[23] to other schemes to convert workers into contractors,[24] Amazon's strategy seems to suggest movement toward a "lights-out" world populated by a few technicians monitoring legions of autonomous machines. Yet, the current reality may be as bleak:

> It was very depressing on those 11-hour work days to go in when it was dark and to leave when it was already getting dark again … There were no windows, only bright lights and big boxes, and everyone was in these orange vests … It felt really wrong to know that there is a workplace like this where people are putting so much work of their lives and getting so little back. It was like seeing an episode of the "Black Mirror," … it felt wrong and terrible. (Paola)[25]

For workers like Paola, the contemporary world of warehouse work already resembles our science-fiction fears.

ACKNOWLEDGMENTS

We thank all of the former and current Amazon workers who provided interviews and all of the members of our UC-Riverside student research team that collected and transcribed their interviews. Special thanks to Veronica Alvarado and Deogracia Cornelio for helping to construct the interview guide for this study.

NOTES

1. J. Katzanek, "Here's How to Apply for 2000 New Amazon Jobs," *Daily Bulletin*, June 4, 2019, www.dailybulletin.com/2019/06/04/heres-how-to-apply-for-2000-new-amazon-jobs/. Accessed April 19, 2020.
2. Table 11.1 in Allison (Chapter 11, this volume) indicates that warehouses located in Riverside and San Bernardino Counties employed at least 13,600 employees in 2018–19, but these figures could include various occupations, while there were 18,600 warehouse workers in the four-county region of Los Angeles, Orange, Riverside, and San Bernardino as of 2018; D. Flaming and P. Burns, "Too Big to Govern: Public Balance Sheet for the World's Largest Store," *Economic Roundtable*, pp. 1–82 (2019). Available at: https://economicrt.org/publication/too-big-to-govern/. Accessed April 19, 2020.
3. R. Edwards, *Contested Terrain: The Transformation of the Workplace in the Twentieth Century* (New York: Basic Books, 1979), pp. 1–261.
4. A. Aneesh, "Global Labor: Algocratic Modes of Organization," *Sociological Theory* 27 (4) (2009): 347–370.
5. S. Zuboff, "Big Other: Surveillance Capitalism and the Prospects of an Information Civilization," *Journal of Information Technology* 30(1) (2015): 75–89.
6. The first author was employed for two months as a blue-collar warehouse worker.
7. Nearly all of the student researchers recruited current and former Amazon workers who were friends, family members, co-workers, or other personal acquaintances. We also recruited some informants by informing UC-Riverside sociology majors through an email list-serve about the opportunity to participate in the study. Informants were offered a $20 gift card to compensate them for the time they spent doing the interview, most of which lasted about 25–40 minutes, but were sometimes as long as 2 hours.
8. M. Burawoy, "The Extended Case Method," *Sociological Theory* 16(1) (1998): 28, 4–33.
9. We included three workers in this category who were employed as assistant managers because they were only paid a few dollars more per hour than warehouse associates, have low levels of supervisory control over workers, and

carry out various blue-collar tasks on the warehouse floor as needed. We also included one "technician" involved in building storage units, as well as picking who was given minimal training and paid entry-level wages.

10. J. Emmons Allison, J.S. Herrera, J. Struna, and E. Reese, "The Matrix of Exploitation and Temporary Employment: Earnings Inequality among Inland Southern California's Blue-Collar Warehouse Workers," *Journal of Labor and Society* 21(4) (2018): 533–60. doi: 10.1111/wusa.12366.
11. Flaming and Burns, "Too Big to Govern."
12. J. Struna, "Transnationally Implicated Labor Processes as Transnational Social Relations: Workplaces and Global Class Formation", in I. Wallerstein, C. Chase-Dunn and C. Suter (eds.), *Overcoming Global Inequalities, Political Economy of the World-System Annuals* (Boulder, CO: Paradigm, 2015), pp. 71–86.
13. R. Blake, "Amazon's Push to Augment Workforce with Automation Is Pig in Industrial Robotics Python," *Forbes*, February 24, 2019, www.forbes.com/sites/richblake1/2019/02/24/amazons-push-to-augment-workforce-with-automation-is-pig-in-industrial-robotics-python/#14f4ef9342ea. Accessed April 19, 2020.
14. Wired, "High-Speed Robots Part 1: Meet Bettybot in 'Human Exclusion Zone,'" *Wired: The Window*: Conde Nast (2019). Available at: www.youtube.com/watch?v=8gy5tYVR-28. Accessed April 19, 2020.
15. J. Dastin, "Exclusive: Amazon Rolls out Machines That Pack Orders and Replace Jobs," *Thomson Reuters*, May 13, 2019, www.reuters.com/article/us-amazon-com-automation-exclusive/exclusive-amazon-rolls-out-machines-that-pack-orders-and-replace-jobs-idUSKCN1SJ0X1. Accessed April 19, 2020.
16. Ibid.
17. A "lights out" facility can operate in the dark because it is fully automated and no human workers are needed.
18. N. Bose, "Amazon Dismisses Idea Automation Will Eliminate All Its Warehouse Jobs Soon," *Thomson Reuters*, May 1, 2019, www.reuters.com/article/amazoncom-warehouse/amazon-dismisses-idea-automation-will-eliminate-all-its-warehouse-jobs-soon-idUSL1N22D0NK?feedType=RSS&feedName=companyNews. Accessed April 19, 2020.
19. C.B. Frey and M.A. Osborne, "The Future of Employment: How Susceptible Are Jobs to Computerisation?" *Technological Forecasting and Social Change* (114) (2017): 254–280.
20. C. Copley, "Robots Will Be Your Colleagues Not Your Replacement: Manpower," *Thomson Reuters*, January 18, 2019, www.reuters.com/article/us-automation-jobs/robots-will-be-your-colleagues-not-your-replacement-manpower-idUSKCN1PC20A. Accessed April 19, 2020. R. Boyd, and R.J. Holton, "Technology, Innovation, Employment and Power: Does Robotics and Artificial Intelligence Really Mean Social Transformation?", *Journal of Sociology* 54(3) (2018): 331–345.
21. Zuboff, "Big Other."

22. B. Casselman and A. Satariano. "Amazon's Latest Experiment: Retraining Its Work Force," *New York Times*, July 11, 2019, www.nytimes.com/2019/07/11/technology/amazon-workers-retraining-automation.html. Accessed April 19, 2020.
23. A. Semuels, "Why Amazon Pays Some of Its Workers to Quit," *The Atlantic*, February 14, 2018, www.theatlantic.com/business/archive/2018/02/amazon-offer-pay-quit/553202/. Accessed April 19, 2020.
24. J. Novet, "Amazon Will Pay Employees $10,000 to Quit and Start Their Own Package-Delivery Companies," *CNBC*, May 13, 2019, www.cnbc.com/2019/05/13/amazon-will-pay-workers-10000-to-quit-form-delivery-companies.html. Accessed April 19, 2020.
25. *Black Mirror* is a Netflix "sci-fi anthology series [which] explores a twisted, high-tech near-future where humanity's greatest innovations and darkest instincts collide" (2011). Available at: https://www.netflix.com/title/70264888. Accessed April 1, 2020.

6
Gender, Race, and Amazon Warehouse Labor in the United States

Ellen Reese

As intersectional feminist theory suggests, class domination interacts with patriarchy and white supremacy in significant ways.[1] Building on those insights, this chapter analyzes how Amazon and other warehouse employers exploit gendered and racialized labor in the United States with a particular focus on Inland Southern California. This region, comprised of Riverside and San Bernardino Counties and located just east of the Los Angeles-Long Beach port, has quickly become one of the largest logistics hubs in the world. It also employs one of the largest (if not the largest) concentrations of Amazon warehouse workers in the world, with 16 Amazon fulfillment and distribution centers currently in place or under development in the region as of June 2019.[2] Altogether, Inland Southern California claimed about 14.2 million square feet of Amazon warehouse space in 2019, more than half of which was located in just four cities (San Bernardino, Rialto, Eastvale, and Moreno Valley).[3]

Globally, Jeff Bezos and most other warehouse executives—disproportionately white men—amass their profits and wealth by exploiting warehouse workers through low-wage and precarious jobs, taking advantage of the limits of national labor laws and social inequalities that divide workers and render them vulnerable to highly exploitative working conditions.[4] In the United States, Amazon and other warehouse executives disproportionately rely on workers of color, including immigrants of color, to carry out the most grueling tasks of loading, unloading, storing, tracking, sorting, and packing goods within warehouses. Nationally, non-supervisory blue-collar (or frontline) warehouse workers are mostly, and disproportionately, Latinx or African American workers that commonly face racial discrimination and live in areas of concentrated poverty and unemployment. Although most blue-collar warehouse workers are men, about 28 percent of those employed within traditional warehouses, and 44 percent of those employed in the rapidly growing e-commerce sector are women.[5] Across regions, the specific racial composition of frontline warehouse workers varies. For example, Latinx warehouse workers outnumber African Americans in the logistic hubs in Southern California and New Jersey, but the reverse is true in the logistics hubs surrounding Chicago and other Midwestern cities. Warehouse workers are mostly native-born, but many are immigrants. Warehouse workers of color commonly experience racism and nativism on the job, and female warehouse workers, mostly women of color, also commonly confront sexism.[6]

To examine the gender and racial dynamics within Amazon and other warehouses in the United States, especially within Inland Southern California, I analyze interviews with current and former Amazon warehouse workers employed in Inland Southern California along with observations from a public tour of an Amazon warehouse in San Bernardino. Altogether 47 former and current Amazon workers participated in interviews for this study, all except one of which had been employed within blue-collar occupations.[7] Participants were mainly recruited through personal contacts of a team of undergraduate researchers at the University of California, Riverside (UCR), as well as email messages sent to all sociology majors informing them of the study. Given the method of recruiting workers, it is not surprising that the vast majority of those interviewed were under the age of 30 and had some college education. Fifty-three percent of interviewees were women, perhaps related to the largely female composition of my research team, one person identified as "very gender neutral," while the remaining respondents were male. Sixty-seven percent of interviewees were Latinx (any race), while 59 percent reported that Latinx was their only race; this is consistent with the largely Latinx make-up of the region's population and warehouse workforce.[8] About 15 percent of the sample was non-Hispanic white, 15 percent was mixed race, 7 percent was Asian-American, and another 4 percent was African-American.[9] I put these interview findings into the context of relevant news reports and other research on U.S. warehouse workers, especially those employed by Amazon.

Consistent with patterns found in U.S. warehouses more generally, research participants described a racialized division of warehouse labor, with white men disproportionately employed as managers, and people of color employed as warehouse associates. While most of those employed as forklift drivers and in positions involving heavy lifting were men, women were commonly employed in packing and packaging jobs. Various workers reported instances of gender and/or race discrimination as well as racial, sexual and/or gender harassment, consistent with previous research findings and legal complaints. Parents, including single mothers, do not find Amazon to be family friendly in terms of its long work shifts and the high cost of its health benefits. My chapter concludes by considering warehouse workers' resistance to racist and sexist practices within Amazon, evident in both legal complaints and collective action; as these workers demonstrate, resisting Amazon is a matter of gender and racial as well as economic justice.

GENDERED AND RACIALIZED DIVISIONS OF WAREHOUSE LABOR

Many of those interviewed for this study appreciated the racial diversity of their co-workers in Amazon's warehouses. As Alejandro put it, "You see all types of races there. Hispanic, Latino, White, Indian, Asians … You see everything." Fernando noted that, "I think probably one of the pluses of working there was probably the diversity … There's a lot of immigrants working there." He personally enjoyed getting to know immigrant workers from different countries around the world and learning about their cultures. Various workers also perceived that Amazon's process of initially hiring warehouse workers as fair.

Nevertheless, various workers in the interview sample reported a distinct racial and gender hierarchy in terms of who was employed to do what within Amazon's warehouses. As Paola put it, "It was mainly black and brown bodies and the only white people were managers." Similarly, Josh noted that "There's not that many white people … If there are, they're usually higher ups." He also noted that "A lot of the managers are men … Lately, they started hiring more females and people of color [as managers] recently … but for a while, when I first started, it was like all white guys." Such observations are consistent with Amazon's data on its managerial workforce for 2018, which reveals that 74.2 percent of its managers worldwide were men, while 61.7 percent of its U.S. managers were white.[10] Moreover, only one of the 18 members of Amazon's top executive "S-team" was a woman.[11] In contrast, most non-supervisory warehouse workers were described by interviewees as people of color, mostly Latinx, a pattern consistent with regional workforce data,[12] as well as my own observations during a public tour of an Amazon warehouse in San Bernardino.

A gender division of labor within the warehouse was also apparent during my tour. Most of the workers unloading trucks were men and the only forklift driver in sight was a man. In contrast, I observed many women picking and packing. Worker interviews described similar patterns in terms of the division of warehouse labor. According to Clara, who was employed for years at Amazon, some of the supervisors were women, but managers were mostly men. As Jimmy, employed in 2013, put it: "I think women were asked to do the inbound and the guys got shoved to do the trucks. Women were tasked to do more of the scanning or problem control ... I saw more women being hired as temps."

These observations are similar to findings from legal filings and previous research on blue-collar warehouse workers.[13] For example, research finds that among blue-collar warehouse workers in Inland Southern California, women, especially Latinx immigrant women, are concentrated within low-wage packing and packaging occupations, while a significantly greater number of Latinx immigrant women are employed through temporary agencies compared to their male counterparts.[14] Meanwhile, legal research provides evidence that temporary agencies commonly steer women and men into gender-typed warehouse jobs by referring to women as "lights" and "small hands," and men as "heavies" and "big hands." Surveys collected among temporary warehouse workers in Will County, Illinois by the Warehouse Workers for Justice, also reveal that temporary agencies are more likely to offer forklift-driving jobs to men than women, even when women are trained for or express interest in those jobs. Likewise, interviews with temporary warehouse workers (all women of color) reveal that male warehouse workers avoid packing jobs because they view them as paying too little for the work involved compared to relatively higher paying jobs as forklift drivers or laborers. Meanwhile, women warehouse workers describe various examples of gender-based and sexual harassment by male coworkers as well as gender discrimination by employers. Similar to other blue-collar workplaces such as the docks, heavy machinery was associated with men and masculinity, and male co-workers commonly harassed their female counterparts who dared to used it.[15] Often viewed as "bad drivers" or physically weaker than men, women warehouse workers report being excluded from opportunities to be trained as forklift drivers, and overlooked for laborer jobs.[16]

Consistent with such findings, interviewees for this study claimed that women employed as forklift drivers or leads experienced gender harassment or felt distinct performance pressures as token women. For example, Jimmy claimed that "They trained a few women for forklift, but it is unusual to train women to do that task. Women were always being stereotyped as bad drivers or unable to perform that task." Elizabeth, another former employee, a Mexican American woman in her early 20s, recalled that:

> The forklift drivers were mainly guys. So, I did get extremely discriminated on [sic] because I was a female forklift driver. I would come home pissed because guys would hit on me. They would harass me and say things like, "Oh you grabbed the wrong fork, go put it back and grab the right one," like they're trying to put me in my place.

Another Latinx, Maria recalled that "For a female, you had to prove yourself. You had to prove yourself that you were a good worker, you could lead a department, and you weren't being a bitch. If you could lead a department and not be a little hoe. Before I came along, there were only males leading."

Other workers recounted frustrations among women in terms of being overlooked for male-stereotyped warehouse positions. For example, Samantha expressed frustrations in seeking to become a dockworker despite filling out paperwork and consulting with a manager about this. Josh shared a similar story:

> One of my friends ... She's been wanting to transfer to ship dock ... There's mostly men that are back there so she, she noticed that they never call her when they need to labor share [sic]. They stopped calling her after she addressed that it was like mostly men ... I told her just go straight to the general manager and she ended up talking to him ... and then I'm not really sure if it got resolved 'cus she's still in the same department. I think she just lost interest in that 'cus of all the trouble. She just kinda got frustrated like, "Whatever if they're not gonna call me. They don't want me" ... They did offer her a spot, but it was nightshift and she wasn't interested in nightshift.

In contrast, Fernando noted how older female workers tended to be assigned to be "pickers," a position that was commonly perceived to be the most difficult and least favorite position in Amazon warehouses:

> There's also like a lot of genderism [sic] of the workplace. If they want women out then … women, older women, they would send them off as pickers. So the first day that you're there they designate you, okay you're going to be on the dock, you're going to be a packer, you're going to be a picker. So a lot of the ladies they would send them as pickers. So I realized that if they want people out right away they're going to send them as pickers and I realized it was a lot of older ladies.

There were, of course, exceptions to the overall gender division of labor. For example, Maria expressed appreciation for Amazon for giving her the opportunity to prove herself within a traditionally male-stereotyped job:

> I get to go home and just feel accomplished. Especially when I feel that people underestimate me based on my looks because I'm small and I'm a girl. They wouldn't expect me, in a million years, to be packing thirty-pound boxes at a fast pace for ten hours. This job has given me the opportunity to prove myself. So I think that's another reason why I appreciate the job.

Yet, even this quote reveals how gender stereotypes shape employment experiences within Amazon warehouses.

When asked if there were problems such as racism or sexism at Amazon, 27 percent of the interview sample said "yes." About 26 percent also agreed that divisions among workers based on gender existed and 9 percent reported divisions among workers based on race. Interviewees also varied in their opinions in terms of whether Amazon's female workers, mostly women of color, were subject to employment fairness, discrimination, or favoritism. While such variation may reflect differences in workers' gender and racial consciousness, it is also likely that problems of racism and sexism were more extensive among some supervisors and managers compared to others. One man, Anong, claimed that "Women of Amazon do tend to be pushed aside." Similarly, Jorge recalled that "Some of the girls were treated differently …

More blame would be put on them if something went wrong ... Like if they weren't filling their quotas."

In contrast to Jorge's account, both male and female workers reported that some supervisors exercised favoritism towards women, especially attractive women. As Samuel put it, "Some supervisors would favor the prettier girls like you know, people that they're cool with." Similarly, Paola claimed that "It was mainly the most attractive girls were getting the easy way." Likewise, Xavier reported that "Some women moved up and were promoted faster because of favors or relationships with some of the managers." Another former worker, a woman initially employed as a warehouse associate who later became an assistant manager, agreed with that assessment. Various workers also claimed that supervisors were more likely to select women, particularly attractive women, to become either "problem solvers" or "ambassadors." When describing supervisors' favoritism towards women, Samuel reported that "There was some favoritism with ... supervisors picking problem solvers. At first they were generally mostly women. So there was kind of a thing [rumor] going around like, 'you only pick the pretty girls to learn how to problem solve.'" Jimmy similarly noted that "Sometimes women would be promoted faster to ambassadors but it's hard to say if that was the reason. It was kind of favoritism with a cost." Although problem solvers and ambassadors did not earn more per hour, these positions were coveted as they were considered less onerous and tightly monitored compared to other jobs, such as picking or packing, and key positions for becoming promoted to assistant manager positions.

Blue-collar warehouse labor has long been male dominated. Workers, both male and female, observed the challenges for Amazon's blue-collar female workers in terms of the male-dominated or masculine workplace culture. For example, Destiny observed:

> Working at a warehouse is probably like the most, the most like sexist jokes of any other place ... It's a macho-like environment ... with all this heavy machinery and stuff. Like the women were kind of encouraged to be like more manly ... They had to like to put on this persona like you can't fuck with me.

Destiny also reported that "Some men not all, were like 'ok since I'm working at a warehouse, I can hit up any one of these females.' And the women who work there usually wear like workout clothes. So, women were usually seen as sex objects."

Like Destiny, other workers interviewed recalled various instances of sexual harassment experienced by themselves or coworkers, not all of which were reported to management or Human Resources. As Samuel reported, "There's a lot of ... things that go there as far as sexual talk and you know, verbal things that happened in between employees and sometimes supervisors." Similarly, Jimmy reported that "I think there were generally a lot of flirting, between younger people or older men with younger women. It was sometimes consensual or non-consensual." Fernando reported that

> Within the workers and the management, there is a lot of like not overt harassment, but there's a lot like there's a sense of like uncomfortability that is placed among the women ... There be [*sic*] like a lot of attention [towards] specific women ... If there were like really ... attractive ... you see like a lot of men gathered towards them, which I think would make it very difficult for them to do their job.

Anong claimed that "a lot" of women warehouse workers experience sexual harassment. He, along with several other workers, reported that Human Resources did not adequately address complaints about sexual harassment, and required witnesses, which was often difficult given the isolated nature of many warehouse tasks:

> Sexual harassment is not taken seriously, from my experience with my co-workers ... They've been to HR and HR doesn't do much about it, or from what I've been told. HR doesn't do much and tells them to switch departments if they can't work with that person. It seems like supervisors and managers tend to cater more toward what the company needs than what the employee needs. As a tier 1, it feels like you're left off on your own and there is not a lot of security there. I think it sucks that a lot of the female co-workers have to experience that. It's a really common thing. When they try to report to HR, they say they need concrete evidence, like telling us that if someone said something inappropriate, it isn't enough. You need to have witnesses, but it's hard when you do work since you're out there by yourself.

Paola similarly complained about HR's failure to fire a female worker that repeatedly sexually harassed her girlfriend, trying to kiss her and making unwanted sexual comments to her, despite multiple complaints being made against the worker. This worker also claimed that HR required a witness to these incidences, which was difficult because many of these incidences occurred when other workers were out of sight or earshot. After considerable delays and lost paperwork, HR simply moved the worker into another department. Unfortunately, the woman continued to harass the other woman during work breaks. The harassed worker finally "got fired because she stopped going to work because of the situation."

Similarly, Josh recalled that, after a worker filed a sexual harassment complaint against a man who showed naked pictures of her to other coworkers, "The whole thing got really messy and they didn't do anything to him. He ended up switching to a different department to avoid it ... I understand they had nothing to prove what he did, but she obviously was feeling intimidated and harassed by him and they weren't doing much about that." After reporting the incident to HR, this worker "felt really uncomfortable and she kinda felt like [co-workers who knew of the incident] ... were making her job harder, like making her feel uncomfortable 'cus they would be mentioning things about him to her and she would just kinda feel really uncomfortable about it."

Workers interviews also described various incidences of racism or racialized xenophobia carried out by fellow workers, supervisors, or managers. For example, Alejandro reported that

> There's been a couple of situations for example, about people from India ... People kinda stay away from [them] ... but there's been a couple of cases of Whites and Latinos or White and Black. Sometimes there was a couple [of] people, White people, that would just be rude to these other people so, that's something that was kind of racial.

Fernando, describing a coworker, reported that "He was African American ... He would get in trouble a lot by the upper management who were White ... It kind of seemed like they were purposely giving him hassle because he was African American and they were blaming the productivity for ... that certain area because of him."

Workers also reported various situations in which workers or managers were fired for racist and/or sexist behavior that was reported to Human Resources. For example, Alejandro reported that "This time ... it was a White male ... They ended up letting him go 'cause he was just being, just throwing sexual jokes or like racist jokes so, the manager said those things ... He ended up being fired because he was using too many racist jokes or sexual jokes ... Girls would put in complaints... He was let go."

Josh remembered another incident involving racialized and anti-Islamic discrimination that led to worker firings:

After the shooting, the San Bernardino shooting[17] ... I heard that there was people saying like really mean things about ... Muslims and the people that they thought were Middle Eastern or ... involved with ISIS ... I heard that people were making remarks to them, but literally like the next week the managers addressed that and said there wasn't going to be any tolerance to the person that was making those remarks and they got fired.

Yet, Amazon's upper management sometimes responded less forcefully to complaints about racial inequalities in the treatment of workers; they simply transferred the workers rather than firing them. For example, Alejandro recalled "That manager got moved to a different position ... It was because he was being really mean to [my friend] and I think it's 'cus he was White, and she was Hispanic. I think that had a lot to do with it. A lot of people put in a lot of complaints about him too that he was treating people [badly]." Various worker interviews also mentioned that racial and/or ethnic homophily among workers was common, another indicator of the racialized nature of warehouse labor.

WAREHOUSE LABOR AND WORK–FAMILY CONFLICTS

Most working parents, about one-third of the interview sample, reported difficulties juggling their dual responsibilities as a parent and an Amazon employee. This was especially the case for single mothers, those working full-time, and those employed in graveyard shifts, as well as those working extra long hours during holidays. Clara, a single mother, who typically worked more than 40 hours per week and as many as 70 hours per week during peak season as a process assistant, would pick her young son up when he was already asleep from her sister's house. As she described, "So I would just watch him sleep. That was the only time I would get to see him." Because of her long work hours, she was unable to get him involved in sports despite his desire to do so. Another single mother, Vanessa, reported that " I feel as if I miss out on a lot of my son's young age." Adriana reported that it was difficult to balance being a parent and an Amazon employee given the physical exhaustion she experienced at the end of her shift: "It could be hard sometimes when I'm tired and I don't want to do anything ... I just want to go upstairs and lay down." Destiny, a single mom who worked graveyard shift from 6:30 p.m. until 5 a.m. in San Bernardino four days per week, had a care provider to watch her children at night in Riverside, where she lived (about 30 minutes away from her workplace). Getting enough sleep was a challenge for her family. As she describes, "I would pick them up around 5:30 a.m. I would sleep in the parking lot at my kids' school, have them dressed and ready to go, and I would then drop them off at school by 8 in the morning." Kelly, another mother employed in a graveyard shift, struggled to take her infant daughter to daytime medical appointments and feared something might happen to her daughter if she fell asleep while watching her. After Amazon's management denied all four of her requests for a daytime shift, she finally accepted Amazon's "offer" of compensation for agreeing to quit and never work for the company again.

Given their low wages, all of the working parents in the interview sample regularly relied on family members or others to provide child care for free or below market prices. Most of these workers also lived with their parents, family members, or roommates, which helped them to pay for housing and other household expenses. Only a few of these parents, who benefited from family support for child care and household bills, viewed Amazon's healthcare plan as affordable. More than one-third of these families relied on Medicaid, a publicly subsidized health insurance program for low-income families.

CONCLUSION

Warehouse labor is deeply gendered and racialized in the United States in terms of who is employed to do what, and how workers are treated on the job. Jeff Bezos and other warehouse executives are predominantly white men, while the hard labor of handling goods within warehouses is largely carried out by underpaid black and Latinx male workers. Women, mostly of color, make up a growing proportion of warehouse workers, especially in the e-commerce sector. Former and current Amazon warehouse workers interviewed in Inland Southern California for this study, most of whom were Latinx, recalled various instances of gender and race discrimination, as well as sexual harassment and racialized xenophobia, sometimes carried out by fellow workers. Such practices are oppressive to the workers experiencing them and help to keep workers internally divided. Problems of racism and sexism within Amazon's warehouses are not isolated to Southern California. Warehouse workers and organizations across the United States are publicizing and resisting racist and sexist practices within Amazon.

For example, at least seven pregnant women, formerly employed in Amazon warehouses in the U.S., sued the corporation for pregnancy discrimination. The women were fired after reporting their pregnancies to management, who also refused their requests for pregnancy-related accommodations, such as longer bathroom breaks and fewer hours spent on their feet.[18] Other women have also reported employment discrimination against pregnant women in the warehouse industry.[19]

Meanwhile, black Muslim immigrants from Somalia and other East African nations in the Minneapolis region, organized through Awood Center, a workers' center, have engaged in collective action targeting Amazon to demand the right to have prayer breaks during work in order to exercise their religious freedom as well as other improvements in their working conditions. Three of these workers, all women, also filed federal complaints to the Equal Employment Opportunities Commission against Amazon for employment discrimination based on race. They claim that, compared to white workers, black warehouse workers have been given more physically taxing jobs, such as packing heavy items, and denied promotions and training opportunities.[20] Thus, while Amazon's warehouses exploit gendered and racialized labor, workers are fighting back to demand greater workplace equity and rights. In doing so, they help to raise consciousness about, and resist, the ways in which Amazon and other warehouse executives reinforce and take advantage of gender and racial inequalities among workers and pave the way for greater worker mobilization and solidarity.

ACKNOWLEDGMENTS

The author thanks the warehouse workers that provided interviews for this study and the UCR student research team that collected and transcribed these interviews.

NOTES

1. Sumi Cho, Kimberly Williams Crenshaw, and Leslie McCall, "Toward a Field of Intersectionality Studies: Theory, Application and Praxis," *Signs* 38(4) (2013): 785-810.
2. Jack Katzanek, "Here's How to Apply for 2,000 New Amazon Jobs," *Daily Bulletin*, June 4, 2019, www.dailybulletin.com/2019/06/04/heres-how-to-apply-for-2000-new-amazon-jobs/ Accessed September 1, 2019.
3. Daniel Flaming and Patrick Burns, "Too Big to Govern: Public Balance Sheet for the World's Largest Store", *Economic Roundtable*, November 26, 2019, pp. 1–82, https://economicrt.org/publication/too-big-to-govern/. Accessed December 1, 2019.
4. Transnational Social Strike Platform, *Strike the Giant! Transnational Organization Against Amazon*. Fall 2019 Journal, www.transnational-strike.info/2019/11/29/pdf-strike-the-giant-transnational-organization-against-amazon-tss-journal/. Accessed December 1, 2019.
5. Beth Gutelis and Nik Theodore. "The Future of Warehouse Work: Technological Change in the U.S. Logistics Industry," *UC Berkeley Labor Center and Working Partnerships USA*, October 2019, http://laborcenter.berkeley.edu/pdf/2019/Future-of-Warehouse-Work.pdf. Accessed April 1, 2020.
6. Juliann Allison, Joel Herrera, Jason Struna, and Ellen Reese, "The Matrix of Exploitation and Temporary Employment: Earnings Inequality Among Inland Southern California's Warehouse Workers," *Journal of Labor and Society* 1 (2018): 1–28; George Gonos, and Carmen Martino, "Temp Agency Workers in New Jersey's Logistics Hub: The Case for a Union Hiring Hall," *Working-USA: The Journal of Labor and Society* 14 (2011): 499–525; Kim Moody, *On New Terrain: How Capital is Reshaping the Battleground of Class War* (Chicago, IL: Haymarket Books. 2017); Warehouse Workers for Justice, "Boxed In: Gender Discrimination in Illinois Warehouses," March 2017, www.ww4j.org/uploads/7/0/0/6/70064813/boxed_in_small.pdf. Accessed September 1, 2019.
7. Among the three most recently employed in managerial occupations, only one had no experience as a blue-collar warehouse worker.
8. Allison et al., "The Matrix of Exploitation and Temporary Employment."
9. For a more detailed description of the sample and methods, see Chapter 5.

10. About Amazon Staff, "Working at Amazon. Diversity and Inclusion. Our Workforce Data," 2019, www.aboutamazon.com/working-at-amazon/diversity-and-inclusion/our-workforce-data. Accessed April 19, 2020.
11. Charles Duhigg, "Is Amazon Unstoppable?" *The New Yorker*, October 10, 2019, www.newyorker.com/magazine/2019/10/21/is-amazon-unstoppable. Accessed April 19, 2020.
12. Flaming and Burns, "Too Big to Govern."
13. Allison et al., "The Matrix of Exploitation and Temporary Employment"; Will Evans, "Growing Temp Industry Shuts Out Black Workers, Exploits Latinos," *Chicago Reporter*, June 8, 2016, http://chicagoreporter.com/growing-temp-industry-shuts-out-black-workers-exploits-latinos/. Accessed September 1, 2019; Jamie Peck and Nik Theodore, "Contingent Chicago: Restructuring the Spaces of Temporary Labour," *International Journal of Urban and Regional Research* 25(3) (2001): 471–496; Warehouse Workers for Justice, "Boxed In."
14. Allison et al., "The Matrix of Exploitation and Temporary Employment."
15. For example, see Jake Alimahomed-Wilson, *Solidarity Forever? Race, Gender and Unionism in the Ports of Southern California* (Lanham, MD: Lexington Books, 2016).
16. Warehouse Workers for Justice, "Boxed In."
17. The "San Bernardino shooting" refers to a mass shooting and attempted bombing that occurred during a training event and holiday party for about 80 employees of the San Bernardino County Public Health Department. A Pakistani couple, reported as being inspired by Islamic terrorist organizations, carried out the shooting, which killed 14 people and seriously injured 22 people.
18. "Muslim Workers Accuse Amazon of Discrimination at Shakopee Warehouse," *Washington Post*, May 14, 2019, www.twincities.com/2019/05/14/3-muslim-workers-accuse-amazon-of-discrimination-at-shakopee-warehouse/. Accessed September 1, 2019.
19. For example, see Warehouse Workers for Justice, "Boxed In."
20. *Washington Post*, "Muslim Workers Accuse Amazon."

7
A New Industrial Working Class? Challenges in Disrupting Amazon's Fulfillment Process in Germany

Nantina Vgontzas

The specter of deindustrialization continues to haunt organized labor. For nearly a century, the concentration of capital and labor in Europe and North America gave industrial workers two forms of leverage. The first was their position in the economy, or *positional leverage*, enabling workers to disrupt the production of goods central to the world market.[1] The second form of leverage was their proximity to each other, or *associational leverage*, fostering the ties through which they activated their positional leverage.[2]

By the 1970s, the limits of this regionally delimited power became evident as employers relocated factories to developing economies.[3] To rebuild their movement, workers in the deindustrializing North needed to coordinate with workers in the industrializing South, given a system of production that increasingly was spread across space.[4] But this coordination proved difficult amid a concomitant decline of the Global Left, contributing to a number of social and political setbacks over the course of several decades.[5] From a steady rise in wage inequality[6] to the election of far right populists in once social democratic heartlands,[7] the various consequences of labor's retreat have made identifying sources of its renewal an urgent task.

To be certain, it is not that workers in deindustrializing economies have *no* leverage.[8] In theory, autoworkers in Mississippi or Chattanooga could cause considerable dents to the profits of Nissan or Volkswagen. But so far organizing drives have floundered amid the paternalistic labor relations of the American South and an uninspiring track record of unions in the Midwest.[9] Meanwhile, though in recent years teachers from West Virginia to Los Angeles have brought city and state governments to their knees, on their own, such strikes leave much of the wider economy unaffected. In short, while workers in deindustrializing economies still have access to positional or associational leverage, relative to earlier periods of development, the potent combination of these two forms of power has waned.

It is within this context that Amazon has become an unlikely source of hope. As Kim Moody notes in this volume, the retail, tech, and logistics giant brings together massive investments of capital and labor similar to industries of the past.[10] In particular, Moody highlights the centrality of warehouses to Amazon's imperative of fulfilling customers' orders at increasingly faster speeds, leading the company to situate warehouses closer to urban markets and thus to communities with generally higher associational power relative to rural ones. Amid the rise of social and political movements since the Great Recession, this assessment has motivated organizing efforts by a number of leftist currents, from anarchists in Poland to the growing numbers of socialists in the United States.[11] Their wager is as follows. If Amazon warehouse workers can activate these "choke points," and if they can coordinate with workers in trucks, ports, and other distribution hubs, they can disrupt the circulation of goods in the wider economy.[12] They can form a "new industrial working class," one capable of leveraging both positional and associational capacities in the Global North as a basis for meaningfully forging solidarity with workers in the Global South.[13]

But just as old words take on new meanings, old forms of power come with new constraints. In this chapter, I examine the constraints on Amazon workers' positional and associational power. Drawing on research from Germany, where Amazon warehouse workers have been striking for seven years in what has been the longest attempt at disrupting the company's fulfillment network, I make three claims. First, the *constraint on positional leverage in Amazon fulfillment centers* is the company's trend toward network redundancy, or a capacity to redirect the fulfillment of orders in the event of blockages. Second, the *constraint on associational leverage of Amazon fulfillment workers* is a legal parameter that divorces wage bargaining from shop-floor conflict. This is especially stark in the German case, but applies to others throughout Amazon's fulfillment network. The third claim connects these positional and associational constraints by tracing the *process of organizing in German Amazon warehouses*. I find that, in confining itself to this legal parameter, the union has been unable to regenerate power on the shop-floor in a way that can overcome the constraint of network redundancy. I conclude that more successful efforts at disruption will depend on amassing and maintaining power on the shop-floor and scaling that up across the fulfillment network.

DATA, METHODS AND SCOPE CONDITIONS

This chapter is based on two years of fieldwork on Amazon in Germany that was collected as part of a larger project comparing Amazon's fulfillment networks in Germany and the United States.[14] Although the U.S. remains Amazon's largest market by a long shot, bringing US$160 billion in revenue, Germany is its second largest, with US$20 billion. My research on Amazon in Germany was partly based on a review of trade journals, investor reports, and the business press. I also read secondary literature on industries where workers historically seized the choke points, drawing a shadow comparison to the auto industry in the twentieth century.[15] In addition, I interviewed Amazon unionists in Germany and participated in a transnational grassroots network that exchanges knowledge and coordinates actions among Amazon workers in Germany, Poland, France, Spain, and the United States. Finally, I collected covert observations while working in a warehouse in Germany.

For this last item, I worked as a packer in an older, less-automated Amazon warehouse located on the outskirts of a medium East German city. I chose this warehouse because it featured one of the more established shop steward committees, organized by the United Trade Services Union, or Ver.di. For two months during Amazon's peak season, I worked 8-hour shifts five days a week, alternating biweekly between the morning and evening shifts. I was part of a seasonal workforce directly hired by the company, that doubled the warehouse's overall workforce. Most of my seasonal co-workers were immigrants, and specifically many were South Asian master's degree engineering students, while out of the permanent workforce, roughly 80 percent were white German and 20 percent people of color, mostly first-generation immigrants from the Middle East, Asia, and Africa.

This chapter seeks to identify the core organizing constraints of Amazon's fulfillment network using data from my German case study. It is thus important to delineate scope conditions from the outset. The key condition is that this analysis is focused on Amazon fulfillment centers, which are warehouses that store, pick and pack customers' orders. These are distinct from warehouses that sort or deliver already packed orders, referred to as "sortation and delivery" centers. For roughly the first two decades of its existence, Amazon specialized in fulfilling orders and left the sorting and delivery to third parties. In recent years, and especially in the United States, the company has begun building its last mile infrastructure, which is responsible for delivering packaged orders to customers' doors (see Chapter 4 of this volume).

With this expansion comes both vulnerabilities and redundancies. For now, delivery centers feature the highest level of associational leverage; management has yet to erode worker autonomy there to the degree it has in fulfillment centers. Delivery centers are also, for now, more resilient choke points, given that orders are already packaged and thus at immediate risk of not being delivered. At the same time, Amazon's continued expansion of its suite of delivery centers is already reducing the volume that goes through any one center. In this sense, the expansion of Amazon's network into sortation and delivery is replicating the trend of redundancy in its fulfillment network. As the company continues investing in the last mile, and hence creating the processes and technologies to increasingly restrict worker mobility in delivery centers, the analysis below of my fieldwork in Germany will become more relevant to the wider network.

POSITIONAL CONSTRAINT

Network redundancy is not a new phenomenon. In the post-war period, executives shifted production to facilities away from Detroit, Turin and other key industrial centers specifically to weaken union influence.[16] What is new is the additional element that information technologies introduced and artificial intelligence has deepened: companies can increasingly optimize the overall systems managing the flow of one process to another within their production and fulfillment networks. At Amazon, this is referred to as the Fulfillment Operating System, and it is cementing two features of the labor process.

The first feature is a *decoupling of the labor process within warehouses*, or a loosening of linkages along the assembly line that minimizes blockages in the event that any individual worker stops fulfilling orders. This is in contrast to tightly coupled production, in which every step along the assembly line affects subsequent steps.

Decoupling plays out on the Amazon shop-floor as follows. In online retail fulfillment, the key imperative is to receive goods; store, or stow them as individual units; pick the units once they are ordered; group them into orders to pack, and finally, ship those orders at ever-increasing speeds. This is a more complicated process than in discount retail fulfillment, which entails unloading and reloading large quantities that then get sent to stores. In online retail, more labor is needed to handle the same volume, and a balance between speed and precision is needed to ensure that that volume is efficiently picked, packed, and sorted for delivery. These needs have led to the partial automation of tasks like picking, where workers are stationed along fields while Kiva robots bring the shelves to them. If a worker does not pick an order in time, a "problem solver" sees on their touchscreen monitor that an order has been unfulfilled, locates it, manually picks it, and then coordinates with their counterpart in subsequent departments. The point of the Fulfillment Operating System is to remove the need for that coordination between problem solvers, or the need for problem solvers in the first place. The entire system will be able to automatically redirect orders that have not been fulfilled and, moreover, move them along the process without human assistance.

The second feature is a *dispersal of the labor process across warehouses*, or an expansion of nodes in the network that minimizes blockages in the event that any individual warehouse stops fulfilling orders. In most cases, management can simply block off that warehouse by pressing a "little red button," which tells the system to not send any new orders to that warehouse. In extreme cases, managers can select the "big red button," which re-plans orders within the warehouse and has them fulfilled elsewhere. The end goal of the Fulfillment Operating System is to remove from humans even that step of pressing the button.

Through these two mechanisms, Amazon is building ever-more redundancy within its fulfillment network, making its warehouses increasingly scattered and individual choke points thus weakened. This point can be crystallized through a comparison to the early automobile industry of Southeastern Michigan.[17]

In the twentieth century, Ford and General Motors' expansion relied on a tightly coupled and geographically clustered production process. Clusters of supplier plants fed assembly plants, where parts were added to the bodies of cars. In both supply and assembly plants, semi-skilled workers produced and processed cars that were sent down the line for final assembly by unskilled workers. This helped eliminate the need for stockpiles of supplies in every plant and promoted continuous innovation. But it also made the production process vulnerable in two key respects. Semi-skilled workers could create blockages by not feeding the assembly lines, and supplier plants could create blockages by not feeding assembly plants. This is precisely how workers won the sit-down strikes of the 1930s, by seizing those two choke points.

Amazon is safeguarding its network against such blockages through its loosely coupled and geographically dispersed fulfillment process. This demands that, for workers to be able to exercise their positional and associational power, they must build enough majorities within warehouses to trigger shop-wide shutdowns, and in enough warehouses so that orders cannot be as easily rerouted; doing so requires that they coordinate with workers in other nodes who can ensure that management does not otherwise bypass these blockages. The question, then, is why German Amazon workers, already organized through unions and active in works councils, have not yet met these requirements.

ASSOCIATIONAL CONSTRAINT

The key constraint on Amazon fulfillment workers' associational power stems from a labor relations framework that has been inherited from the twentieth century. Throughout the world, unions settled for a legally protected right to bargain over wages in exchange for retreating from daily conflict on the shop-floor. In Germany, the compromise was even starker. In the turbulent years following World War I, revolutionary workers' councils demanded control over their work. After the revolution was defeated, the Weimar administration narrowed the parameters of these councils.[18] The *works councils* it instituted were comprised of both managers and workers who met to regulate the work process, taking the daily conflict and negotiation away from the shop-floor. Suspended during Nazi rule, this system of "social partnership" was formalized amid the prosperous conditions that followed World War II.[19] It was a dual model whose core tenets were centralized collective bargaining and co-determination: unions negotiated agreements that raised wages, while works councils and supervisory boards met to approve changes to the workplace, from working time to the production process itself. Under this system, unions rarely went on strike; the credible threat of industrial action was usually sufficient for maintaining wage and productivity growth.

Once the profitability crisis hit in the 1970s, employers began pulling back from the social partnership. Trade union density has since been on a continuous decline from 40 percent at its peak in 1980 down to 16 percent today. This has led to an erosion of the dual model.[20] Without a daily shop-floor presence, unions were unable to counteract the offensive, and as they lost membership, works councils also became a shell of their former selves, given that there were fewer union-aligned workers elected onto the works councils who could regulate workplace changes.

As unions bled members, they have been amalgamating into mega-unions, as is the case with Ver.di. Ver.di has the contradictory tendency of decision making being centralized at the highest levels of leadership while its 13 sectoral divisions remain fragmented. As one staffer put it, Ver.di is comprised of 13 "fiefdoms," all of which are vying for money from the top. This produces competition among the sectors and a lack of strategic coordination, which became especially complicated in the Amazon campaign. The central Ver.di leadership put the campaign under the jurisdiction of its retail division so that the union could strike to raise hourly wages to the €13 set by the sectoral collective agreement, roughly €1.5 more than the starting wage at Amazon. The company countered that it is a logistics firm and does not need to agree to the higher standard in retail, and thus the retail division had even less of an incentive to collaborate with the logistics sector. The next section illustrates how this contest fed into the union's eschewal of organizing workers in other nodes beyond warehouses, to the detriment of the campaign.

TRACING THE ORGANIZING PROCESS IN GERMANY

Putting together these positional and associational constraints, I argue that Ver.di's confinement to the legal parameter of wage bargaining has constrained it from regenerating power on the shop-floor and thus from generating the capacity needed to disrupt Amazon's fulfillment network. This claim is based on tracing the process of Ver.di's campaign at Amazon, which can be distinguished into three key subprocesses. The first focuses on the early stages of the campaign, which saw some associational capacity built on the shop-floor. Due to resource competition within Ver.di, the union relied on workers to organize the campaign in its early stages, first through the formation of shop-steward committees that later helped to form strike committees. These committees were integral to launching strikes in four of the seven warehouses in Amazon's network in the spring of 2013. The second and third subprocesses focus on the constraints workers faced as the strikes carried on. The second subprocess focuses on the erosion of strike coverage in these warehouses over time, and the third focuses on the stasis of strike coverage across the network, as Amazon's expansion of warehouses outpaced Ver.di's ability to organize them. Currently, the union has coverage in seven of the twelve fulfillment centers in the German network, or 16 if we count those in Poland, which nearly exclusively serve the German market. Together, these three subprocesses have resulted in an erosion of workers' bargaining power and Amazon's continued refusal to collectively bargain with them.

In the first subprocess, the union initially built power in its three oldest warehouses, two in Bad Hersfeld and one in Leipzig, through shop-steward committees that eventually built strike committees. Shop stewards came largely from departments where workers enjoyed more mobility like picking and thus where they could speak on the job more. This budding power on the shop-floor was strengthened by union members becoming elected to the works' council and, in 2011, enforcing the *Bundesdatenschutzgesetz*, a federal data protection law dating to the 1960s. In this case, the activist works council used the law to prevent managers from formally disciplining workers according to their electronically monitored work rates; managers now had to ask workers if they even wanted their rates disclosed, and workers could simply refuse. Union activists made use of this law to continue recruiting their co-workers to the campaign. Between 2011 and 2013, works councils, now dominated by union activists, turned all-hands meetings in the fulfillment centers into assemblies to answer workers' questions, while strike committees trained workers offsite.

By the spring of 2013, after months of assemblies, members were ready to strike. Union officials have told me that they did not feel ready to take this action but that members decided to proceed regardless. The difference is that union officials worried that they would not be able to turn out a majority of workers in order to quickly bring Amazon to the table for a collective agreement. Members, on the other hand, felt the action could be the first in an escalation strategy that wasn't necessarily focused on bargaining over wages. And indeed, quantitative analysis by Sabrina Appicella and Helmut Hildebrant, who surveyed strikers in this initial phase, shows that wages were not relevant to workers striking.[21] Rather, it was union participation and issues of shop-floor control that animated strikers, such as stress and the lack of true co-determination, which would entail participation in supervisory boards at the company level and not merely works councils at the shop level. What stalled this momentum?

The second subprocess can be broken into two components. First, the decoupling of the labor process resulted in a curtailing of worker autonomy on the shop-floor. Whereas originally all workers had access to problem-solving tools, over time, that access was limited to problem solvers. This weakened the capacity that a minority of workers could have in impacting overall productivity. Second, management introduced "zone picking" as an innovation that confines workers to picking orders from one section of the warehouse. This allowed for quicker training of seasonal workers and limited the mobility of permanent pickers, who as a department initially had been able to amass the most strike participation.

Second, as older workers found their autonomy curtailed, newer workers were subject to conditional job security. All workers are hired on fixed-term contracts, which after two years must be made permanent. Probationary workers who struck or even decreased their work effort are denied permanent employment. This is where the data privacy law did not hold, for there was no restriction on not hiring someone on the basis of their performance. Here migration status and race have played a moderating role, as discussed in other analyses of shop-floor politics.[22] At a recent picket line in Bad Hersfeld, for instance, I saw a group of about ten immigrant workers who stood apart from the other strikers. For several hours, no one approached them. It turns out that, even though they had passed the probationary threshold, managers were still exerting pressure, because of their assumption that the visibly immigrant workers they encountered were all on fixed contracts. And though these permanent workers responded by joining the others on the picket line, the union failed to see this as an opportunity to recruit more of their co-workers, given its own assumption that immigrant workers were on probation and that this would not grow the union the stable numbers it felt would win them a collective agreement.

The third subprocess is the stasis of strike coverage across the network. Two factors stem from the dispersal of the labor process. First, in 2014, a year after the first outbreak of strikes, Amazon opened warehouses not only in other parts of Germany but also in Poland, where unemployment was higher and strike laws were more prohibitive. The second factor, over which Ver.di had greater control, was its lack of coverage of other nodes. As previously discussed, challenges related to its organizational structure led to the exclusion of other logistics workers. Indeed, early in the campaign, higher-level officials in the retail division had instructed field organizers to see if they could organize drivers, but the organizers knew that this was a symbolic exercise and reported that it was too difficult to organize them. Even more noteworthy is that a key Ver.di official who helped lead the Amazon campaign considers their lack of reaching out to tech workers, who were expected down the road to become members of another union, IG Metall, to have been a "fatal error of the campaign."

It is difficult to disagree with his assessment. By the time I arrived in Leipzig, strikes proceeded routinely. A minority of workers went out on strike, collected their strike payments and went home after a few hours on the picket line. Meanwhile, within the warehouse, seasonal workers were deployed to departments affected by the strike and in fact did not even know that we were breaking the strike; they did not even know that there was a union. Amazon carried on with lower productivity in the warehouse, while motivation for strategizing more effective disruption generally dissipated among the permanent strikers. In an organizing context where the wage-bargaining framework remained dominant, it was unclear to them how to proceed against employer intransigence.

CONCLUSION

This case study of German workers' attempts at disrupting the fulfillment of Amazon orders illustrates the organizing challenges in an ever-increasingly decoupled and dispersed network. Success remains limited so long as workers' power is not amassed on the shop-floor and scaled up across the network. But it is not impossible. Had Ver.di taken organizing probationary workers more seriously, with a focus on how management instrumentalizes racial divisions on the shop-floor, it may have regenerated the shop-floor power that gave it its initial momentum. Or had it not ignored tech workers or drivers, it could have better dealt with weakening strike coverage within and across nodes. That, too, would have required centering concerns around shop-floor control.

These challenges compel revising strategies inherited from the old industrial working class. While the form of power present in today's warehouses can be likened to that in yesterday's factories—that is, a combination of positional and associational power—the *scope* of its activation will need to be far more diffused. Amazon's fulfillment network will not be shut down by workers strategically placed along the assembly line in several key facilities, as in the interwar strikes that led to the initial unionization of mass industry. It will require a much wider level of coordination within fulfillment centers, across regions, and between nodes in Amazon's network, from fulfillment centers to the tech offices that optimize fulfillment work.

NOTES

1. Luca Perrrone, "Positional Power and Propensity to Strike," *Politics and Society* 12(2) (1983): 231–261; Luca Perrone, Erik Olin Wright, and Larry J. Griffin, "Positional Power, Strikes and Wages," *American Sociological Review* 49(3) (1984): 412–426; Howard Kimeldorf, "Worker Replacement Costs and Unionization: Origins of the U.S. Labor Movement," *American Sociological Review* 78(6) (2013): 1033–1062; Adaner Usmani, "Democracy and the Class Struggle," *American Journal of Sociology* 124(3) (2018): 664–704.
2. Beverly J. Silver, *Forces of Labour: Workers' Movements and Globalization Since 1870* (Cambridge: Cambridge Univeristy Press, 2003); Erik Olin Wright, "Working-Class Power, Capitalist-Class Interests, and Class Compromise," *American Journal of Sociology* 105 (4) (2000): 957–1002.
3. Robert Brenner, *The Economics of Global Turbulence* (London: Verso, 2006); Joshua Murray and Michael Schwartz, *Wrecked: How the American Automobile Industry Destroyed Its Capacity to Compete* (New York: Russell Sage Foundation, 2019).
4. Kim Moody, *Workers in a Lean World: Unions in the International Economy* (London: Verso, 1997).
5. Kate Bronfenbrenner, *Global Unions: Challenging Transnational Capital Through Cross-Border Campaigns* (Ithaca, NY: ILR Press, 2007).
6. Nathan Wilmers, "Wage Stagnation and Buyer Power: How Buyer-Supplier Relations Affect U.S. Workers' Wages, 1978 to 2014," *American Sociological Review* 83(2) (2018): 213–242; Tali Kristal, "Good Times, Bad Times: Postwar Labor's Share of National Income in Capitalist Democracies," *American Sociological Review* 35(5) (2010): 729–763; Tali Kristal, "The Capitalist Machine: Computerization, Workers' Power, and the Decline in Labor's Share within U.S. Industries," *American Sociological Review* 78(3) (2013): 361–389; Tali Kristal

and Yinon Cohen, "The Causes of Rising Wage Inequality: The Race Between Institutions and Technology," *Socio-Economic Review* 15(1) (2017): 187–212.
7. Michael McQuarrie, "The Revolt of the Rust Belt," *British Journal of Sociology* 68(S1) (2017): 120–152.
8. A number of studies have pointed particularly to associational capacities as a source of labor renewal, including Jane McAlevey, "The Crisis of New Labour: Revisiting the Role of the Organic Grassroots Leaders in Building Powerful Organizations and Movements," *Politics and Society* (2015): 1–27; Rick Fantasia and Kim Voss, *Hard Work: Remaking the American Labor Movement* (Berkeley: University of California Press, 2004); Ruth Milkman, *L.A. Story: Immigrant Workers and the Future of the U.S. Labor Movement* (New York: Russell Sage Foundation, 2006).
9. Nicole Aschoff, "Tennessee Car Sick Blues," *Jacobin* (2014); Chris Brooks, "Why the UAW Lost Again in Chattanooga," *Labor Notes* (2019).
10. Kim Moody, *On New Terrain: How Capital is Reshaping the Battleground of Class War* (London: Haymarket, 2017); Kim Moody, "High Tech, Low Growth: Robots and the Future of Work," *Historical Materialism* (2019).
11. Amazon Workers and Supporters, "Stop Treating Us Like Dogs! Workers Organizing Resistance at Amazon in Poland," in Jake Alimahomed-Wilson and Immanuel Ness (eds.), *Choke Points: Logistics Workers Disrupting the Global Supply Chain* (London: Pluto Press, 2018); Jane Slaughter, "Put Socialists to Work," *Democratic Left* (2018); Rand Wilson and Peter Olney, "Socialists Can Seize the Moment at Amazon," *Jacobin* (2018).
12. Alimahomed-Wilson and Ness, *Choke Points*; Edna Bonacich and Jake B. Wilson, *Getting the Goods: Ports, Labor, and the Logistics Revolution* (Ithaca, NY: Cornell University Press, 2008).
13. Joe Allen, "Studying Logistics," *Jacobin* (2015).
14. This work is in progress as part of my dissertation, tentatively titled, "The Micropolitics of Inequality in Amazon's Warehouses."
15. This is in the vein of research like Gary Fields's comparison of Swift Meatpacking and Dell as leaders in key industries of the nineteenth and twentieth centuries. Amazon and automakers of the past share parallels not just in terms of their vertical integration, as is usually noted, but also in terms of the vulnerabilities of their labor processes. For the meatpacking and software comparison, see Gary Fields, *Territories of Profit* (Stanford, CA: Stanford University Press, 2004).
16. Patrick V. Peppe, "The Struggle for Workers' Control in Italian Industry, 1968–1977," *Socialism and Democracy* 11(1) (1997): 55–86.
17. The following analysis draws heavily on insights from Murray and Schwartz, *Wrecked*.
18. Andrei Markovitz, *The Politics of the West German Trade Unions: Strategies of Class and Interest Representation in Growth and Crisis* (Cambridge: Cambridge University Press, 1986).

19. See Kathleen Thelen, *Union of Parts: Labor Politics in Postwar Germany* (Ithaca, NY: Cornell University Press, 1992).
20. Anke Hassel, "The Erosion of the German System of Industrial Relations," *British Journal of Industrial Relations* 37(3) (2002): 483-505.
21. Sabrina Appicella and Helmut Hildebrant, "Divided We Stand: Reasons for and against Strike Participation in Amazon's German Distribution Centres," *Work Organisation, Labour & Globalisation* 13(1) (2019): 172–189.
22. See, for example, Carolina Bank Muñoz, *Transnational Tortillas: Race, Gender and Shop Floor Politics in Mexico and the United States* (Ithaca, NY: Cornell University Press, 2008).

8
A Struggle for Bodies and Souls: Amazon Management and Union Strategies in France and Italy

Francesco Massimo

At the end of 2017, the press, the public, and the labor movement raised concerns about the frantic work pace, insane corporate culture, and deplorable working conditions at Amazon. What, then, has prevented labor unrest among Amazon's workers? To address this question, I interviewed and talked with Amazon workers. I also worked in a French Amazon Fulfillment Center (FC) as a temporary worker for two months, in July 2018 and October 2019, and in an Italian FC for four months, from May to August 2019. Drawing on this ethnographic and comparative research, this chapter provides insights on Amazon management and assesses union strategies within the French and Italian contexts.

Amazon has an expansive logistical infrastructure and a large concentration of workers (an FC employs hundreds or thousands of workers). The problem faced by management is how to govern these large hubs; they seek to ensure workers' commitment and acquiescence, hinder workforce unionizing and escape, and take advantage of loopholes in institutional constraints, such as labor regulations, on wage work in order to reduce labor costs and maximize profits. These tasks are particularly challenging in European countries where prior class conflict has institutionalized the relations between unions and corporations.[1] I argue that the company relies on a "corporate hegemony" regime, in order to "obscure and secur[e] the surplus value"[2] and gain workers' cooperation. In particular, Amazon combines bureaucratic techniques (real time control and performance evaluation) with a particular type of corporate culture[3] that depends upon gamification, meritocratic and diversity discourse, corporate welfare, and soft authoritarianism. As the Marxist sociologist Michael Burawoy describes it, the traditional Fordist hegemonic regime is built on a "compromise," i.e., the coordination of mutually antagonist interests for instance through collective bargaining.[4] In contrast, in Amazon's new "service factories," the company clearly negates class conflict and union legitimacy. Instead, Amazon's hegemony is built on the organized fragmentation of any potential antagonistic subjectivity by integrating a distinct combination of coercion, surveillance, and consent in the workplace.

COERCION AND SURVEILLANCE THROUGH THE LABOR PROCESS

Work in Amazon FCs is implicitly based on the three pillars of Taylorism, or scientific management, as defined by Harry Braverman in his classic 1974 work *Labor and Monopoly Capital*.[5]

(1) *The dissociation of the labor process from the skills of the workers*: The labor process is to be rendered independent of craft, traditions, and the workers' knowledge. Amazon often recruits people without any professional background, or even without work experience in the case of young workers: anyone can have their "chance." Tasks such as *picking*, *packing*, or *stowing* are so simple that no special skill is required. The technical division of labor is so intense that a few hours are usually enough to train workers to perform these tasks. This allows management to allocate the workforce in terms of organizational needs and in an arbitrary way, favoring some workers instead of others, thus dividing the workforce.[6]

(2) *Separation of conception from execution*: The fragmentation of the labor process into basic tasks implies that workers are merely expected to execute their jobs. Amazon's introduction of algorithmic management allows managers to plan and distribute work among FCs and, within them, among different departments and tasks. Both workers and managers lose significant autonomy, although that allows managers to naturalize their decisions in front of the workers. Workers do not master the organization of work, nor are they expected to do so. Thus, the organization presents itself as an *algorithmic bureaucracy*.

(3) *Monopoly over knowledge to control each step of the labor process and its mode of execution*: The divorce between conception and execution, however, does not correspond to the separation of mental from manual labor. Quite the opposite. Management is aware of the mental content of work—even

the most basic tasks imply workers' mental activity—and digital devices allow real-time control of work and also permanent flows of information from workers' devices to a centralized system. These devices capture real-time information about each worker on the job. Knowledge about the labor process thus becomes a crucial part of the extraction of value, which is placed strictly in the hands of management.[7] Such organization of the labor process has two key effects: it decreases the interdependence of workers and reduces workers' autonomous skills and knowledge, thereby allowing management to easily measure each worker's output and labor effort.[8]

COERCION THROUGH THE LABOR MARKET

Low interdependence and deskilling also weakens workers' structural power in the workplace and the labor market. The labor market can be divided in two parts: an external and an internal. In contrast to the Fordist era, today's conditions of the external labor market are completely different. Full employment gave way to mass unemployment. The two FCs I studied were both established in areas that had been enduring a wave of deindustrialization since the 1980s and was greatly affected by the 2008 economic crisis. In the department around the French site, the official unemployment rate was 9.2% in 2006, one year before the FC opened (2007), but jumped to 11.5% in 2011 and to 13.2% in 2016.[9] When the Italian FC opened in 2011, the unemployment rate was skyrocketing from 2% (2008) to 9.4% (2014) and then stabilized around 6% (2017).[10] In both cases, the unemployment rate was high enough to weaken workers' collective power. Particularly in the years in which the economic crisis was more acute, Amazon appeared to workers and their local communities as an opportunity to escape unemployment. Moreover, Amazon offered a compensation slightly higher than the minimum wage and the promise of a stable job in a big, successful company. However, the realization of such a perspective was not so close at hand, given the split structure of the internal labor market which included both permanent and temporary workers.

Observing the workplace, especially during the peak season, the firm treated these two groups of workers very differently. Amazon logistics performance relies on the presence of this "industrial reserve army" of precarious workers inside the labor process. Temps are recruited through agencies during the peak season and the large majority of them outperform permanent workers, pushed by the threat of immediate lay-off. Asymmetrical power relations between workers and management are exacerbated for temps. Permanent workers can rely on a relatively strong relation with their co-workers and on a relative high employment protection. In the case of temps, employment relations are much more individualized. The pace of work becomes more intense and surveillance more effective, creating a terrain favorable to opportunism and isolation. Turnover is high and only a small proportion of temps will ever obtain a permanent position, usually after at least six months of temporary contracts. The majority of temps are eventually laid off at the end of the peak season.

Amazon's production regime depends upon this split structure of its internal labor market and labor market conditions. Deskilling and mass unemployment increase the risk of job loss to workers and thus make it easier for managers to exploit them. Even so, management must also legitimize its industrial order and gain workers' consent and active participation. To do this, it must persuade workers that its industrial order is the only possible and desirable option, with no real competing alternative, so that workers come to view their interests as aligned with those of the corporation.

THE MANAGEMENT OF LEGITIMACY: THE DISCOURSES OF COMPANY LEADERSHIP AND CUSTOMER OBSESSION

Amazon's official doctrine is how the firm thinks about itself, its self-representation. The two pillars of Amazon's official doctrine are company leadership and customer obsession, both of which are used to manage its legitimacy among workers. First, Amazon is portrayed to workers as the most efficient e-commerce and logistics company in the world. During recruitment and training, daily meetings (the "brief") or periodic meetings (the "All hands"), workers are informed about the ruthless success of the company and its leadership on sales, employment, productivity, and technology. The company's corporate culture is founded on 14 "leadership principles" which are supposed to govern every choice, from the top to the bottom of the hierarchy; from engineers to warehouse workers, everyone is equal in front of these rules. Other norms which are important for the firm's legitimacy is the triad—safety-quality-productivity. These are the three basic norms that are supposed to govern the labor process. Amazon is presented to the workers as a leader in workplace safety—if the rules are respected, no workplace accident will occur—and in the quality of the service—deliver on time and with the good article in perfect condition—and productivity. The order of priority is clear: the official discourse establishes that safety "comes first," followed by quality, and last, productivity. Through these rules, especially the priority given to workplace safety, Amazon presents itself as socially responsible, helping to increase its legitimacy among workers and the broader public. However, the reality at work is quite different, as many workers stress, particularly during the peak season, productivity outranks workplace safety. As I observed, these rules are often used not to protect workers but to increase surveillance of them. Workers must continuously arbitrate between these different imperatives and opposite injunctions, especially safety and productivity. Frequently, workers receive negative feedback because, under the pressure of work, they did not respect a particular safety procedure.

In the building of consent, the algorithm also plays a role: it is an invisible authority that determines the organization of work. Managers rely on algorithms to predict the volume of goods to be handled, in addition to assigning tasks and in the evaluation of workers' performance. The algorithm does not accomplish these functions automatically but in concert with managers. This lends a technical character to managers' personal authority, thus fostering the whole legitimacy of the organization of work. Hence, we could define this kind of administration as *algorithmic bureaucracy* or *algorithm-assisted management*.[11]

If algorithm is presented as the ultimate authority, customer satisfaction is presented as the ultimate goal, in the face of which managers and workers appear to be equal. Management on behalf of customers helps to naturalize managers' power as an objective constraint and to foster workers' involvement. Training becomes a key site during which this belief is fostered: a video is shown to new workers which tells the story of a mother who orders a doll for her daughter but, because of a mistake committed by a worker during the labor process, the child receives the wrong doll and cries. Such a video illustrates through an example the importance of quality of work for fulfilling the service promised to customers, as well as the "harmful" consequences of workers' errors on customers' psychological well-being. In contrast to other comparable service companies, such as Walmart or Uber, for Amazon the customer is never physically present in the workplace. For this reason, customer satisfaction must be permanently evoked by managers during briefings. For example, they might declare: "Congratulations! Today we managed to satisfy our customers' demands." References to customers are also contained in instructions given to the workers, such as "If you are not sure if a product is damaged, make your decision as if you were the customer who ordered it." Or they are represented on walls and boards. For instance, the organizational chart of an FC is epitomized by a Maslow-like upside-down pyramid, in which customers are on the top, associates immediately below, followed by a team leader, area managers, operational mangers and finally, at the capsized summit, the general manager. Customers are therefore surreptitiously integrated into the labor process by management, although this goal is never fully achieved because of the technical impossibility of this.

Customer obsession in warehouse work is also frequently perceived and dismissed by workers as a clumsily disguised form of management control. However uncertain its assimilation by workers, it is important to stress that unions can also be sensitive to customer obsession: even a traditionally combative union such as the French CGT (*Confédération Generalé du Travail*) released flyers during a strike in 2014 in which they affirmed that their action was by no means an action against customers and for this reason trucks would not be blocked by strikers. The last element of legitimation is employment and investments. The company exerts a powerful influence on local communities by stressing its role as a job creator and as an investor. Legitimation provides the company with an official discourse through which it can justify its activity. However, self-representation does not automatically lead to consent. Legitimation means that the industrial order is perceived as the only possible and desirable one. However, management faces the problem of actively eliciting workers' cooperation in the workplace, and for that consent to be obtained, workers' interest must appear linked to the interest of the firm.

THE MANAGEMENT OF CONSENT

What distinguishes Amazon's corporate hegemonic regime from the Fordist hegemonic regime is the central role of management in Amazon and the exclusion of unions from the construction of consent. According to Burawoy, consent spreads from workers' activity, such as "*making out*,"[12] and from collective bargaining. In contrast, consent is built from the top in

Amazon, through corporate culture, and relies upon the managerialization of labor relations and the exclusion of unions from the workplace.

The management of consent links the interest of the worker to the interest of the company. In order to achieve these goals, the role of management—team leaders, area managers, and operational managers—becomes crucial. The first goal is to render the work meaningful in order to avoid dissatisfaction without renouncing the Taylorization of work, and it is sought through the labor process. The second goal is, borrowing Albert O. Hirschman's terms, to build loyalty, channel voice, and control exit,[13] and it is pursued through the internal labor market.

HARD WORK, MANDATORY FUN: CONSENT THROUGH THE LABOR PROCESS

Beyond technocracy and customer obsession, Amazon governs the workplace through a set of norms and activities, which in fact are nothing but rituals to foster workplace identity and workers' investment to their job. The result of these policies, such as gamification and workers' involvement, are the individualization of the employment relation and the breaking of workers' associational power. Workers are asked to actively participate in the organization of work and in the social life of the factory. For instance, they are encouraged to signal any problem and propose changes immediately to managers without a union or any other hierarchical or collective intermediation. Propositions, written on a suggestion board (called by the Japanese-Toyota-ist terms "*Kaizen Board*" or "*Gemba Walk*"), are then selected and evaluated by managers: all receive answers, whether positive or negative. Some propositions are rejected because they are not viable, while others are accepted, and the authors are publicly thanked on another board. In this way, management imposes the organization of work, keeps control of its ordinary functioning and can, sometimes, choose some ideas from workers' propositions. Most of all, they involve workers and make them cooperate in their own exploitation.

The slogan "Work hard, have fun, make history" is an exhortation not only to accomplish tasks successfully and with high performances (professional commitment), but also to mobilize the emotional sphere of workers' experience. This goal is approached through a broad set of practices that aim to improve workers' positive feelings about their work and to boost workers' cooperation with managerial goals. These practices include the gamification of work, understood not necessarily as the design of tasks in a game-like way but as the staging of a widespread spirit of play. As long as tasks are fragmented in elementary operations, scanners and other computer devices used by workers provide them with immediate feedback on their performance. Instructors train workers partly through the organization of contests and games which encourage more competitive workers to take the lead while leaving at the margins workers which, for any reason, do not "play the game." Team briefings are conceived of and organized as a school class: team leaders and area managers ask questions, cyclically the same, to workers on standard work, quality, and safety rules. After that, ranks are broken and workers chosen for the "fast start," i.e., realizing the first task (picking an article or packing a box) in the shortest time. During work, operators can receive on their device a message of congratulations by their manager or, alternatively negative feedback (several negative feedbacks can lead to the worker being laid off). Workers' behavior is measured along different dimensions (performance, quality, presence at work) and periodically rewarded with "swag," i.e., virtual coins they can spend to purchase Amazon gadgets and products. This system of symbolic rewards lubricates the execution of repetitive, fragmented, elementary tasks.

Another instrument to build consent is the diffusion of a spirit of competition among the workforce: temporary workers compete in order to have more chances to have their contract renewed; team and area managers compete in order to boost their careers. Every actor, whether worker or manager, has an interest in outperforming his or her peers even if, in some cases, such a competitive atmosphere threatens cooperation and fosters opportunism. Workers and managers thus both face competitive constraints. A flagrant example is the "Amazon connection," a daily survey given to the workers in which they answer questions about their satisfaction at work (if they feel respected at work, if their work respects safety rules, etc.). As the workers put it, "it is a way to control managers": managers are responsible for bad results, i.e., low levels of satisfaction. So managers compete to have the best feedback by their workers and workers are given an instrument that is supposed to give them a voice on particular problems. However this form of "domesticated" voice is completely individualized—workers answer questions through their individual account, even if the survey is supposed to be anonymous—and treatment of these data and the solution to possible problems is not in their hands.

CONSENT THROUGH THE LABOR MARKET

Another way in which workers and managers are under the same pressure involves careers. Workers cannot expect to radically improve their career in Amazon in terms of wage and position. A few of the "associates" become team leaders; becoming a manager is a rare exception. Yet, workers depend on management regarding "horizontal" career moves within the workplace. Workers know that if they behave properly—"work hard, have fun, make history"—and establish good personal relations with their supervisors, they can move from one position to another. Workers seek jobs with less arduous and monotonous tasks such as "problem solver" or "process guide" (though with no wage increase), or they strive to become "temporary" team leader and other forms of individual improvement of their working condition.

What happens to dissatisfied workers? Amazon has an answer for them too. In 2014, the company introduced a "Pay-to-Quit" program, called "*the Offer*," which is widely used in the United States: at least once a year, but sometimes even more frequently, associates are offered the opportunity to leave the company forever in exchange of €1000–2000 per year worked at Amazon. Referring again to Hirschman's triad of *Exit, Voice and Loyalty*,[14] we could say that the company encourages dissatisfied workers to *exit* in order to prevent *voice*. Also, unions and collective bargaining do not have any recognized and effective power on this key point of the workplace's social life.

THE RELATIVE AUTONOMY OF THE WORKPLACE

In contrast to the classic Fordist hegemonic regime, unions are usually excluded from the management of Amazon's internal labor market. Amazon is fiercely hostile to unions, which the company considers to be intruders. However, such a position toward unions is difficult to maintain in the Western European context, where union presence is stronger than in the U.S., and labor law as well as collective bargaining are still central in employment relations. Progressively, the degradation of working conditions and pressures from the labor movement set the terrain for union action. In some European countries, where unions are less weak and employment relations are part of the constitutional order, Amazon facilities have been touched by union action, strikes, and industrial conflicts. This was the case in Germany (2013), France (2014), Poland (2015), Italy (2017), and Spain (2018). In France and Italy, Amazon was forced by law and collective action to recognize the presence of unions inside its FCs. Even in those countries, the company goal is to reduce at any cost the influence of collective bargaining on the organization of work.[15] On the other hand, unions are still struggling to coordinate their actions and goals across workplace sections, sector federations, and different national settings.

UNIONS IN FRANCE AND ITALY: BETWEEN COLLECTIVE BARGAINING AND CONTESTING MANAGERIAL DISCOURSE AND PRACTICES

In France, where collective bargaining is compulsory at the company level and where every five years, workers' elections are celebrated, union presence is institutionally rooted and almost routinized. All French Amazon FCs are unionized, with different electoral rates among unions at every site. All Amazon employees have their representative bodies regularly elected (in 2011, 2015, and 2019). According to 2019 election results, the main unions are CFDT (*Confédération française démocratique du travail*, a former Catholic moderate union, 28%), *Solidaires* (a radical anarchist union, 25%), CGT (*Confédération générale du travail*, a radical former communist union, 25%), CAT (*Confédération autonome du travail*, known as a "yellow", i.e. non-independent, union, 13%). However, voter turnout remains low and union membership has always been weak (between 5 and 10 percent of warehouse workers), in line with the national average in the private sector in France. Inter-union competition can be very harsh, not only between unions (particularly the former communist CGT and the more business-friendly CFDT), but also inside the organizations themselves. One of the reasons for this harsh competition is the crucial importance of elections: competition in company elections determines the amount of resources and power unions obtain within the company. Union resources are used to maintain the organization and implement cultural and recreational activities with company funds and contribute to the relative influence of trade unions at the national level.

Surprisingly, Amazon management quickly adapted to this context and have used union divisions to contain their influence. Amazon management either favors one union to the detriment of others, or creates a company union. Amazon explored the first option of pitting unions against each other. It also pursued the latter path when, before professional elections in 2015, management informally encouraged the formation of a yellow union, the CAT, in order to break the union front and have a possible union ally. Finally, the company condoned threats of layoffs among union members and representatives, most recently during the Yellow Vest movement.

Despite management hostility, unions organized actions during the past years. Union strategy focused on health and safety issues, working time, and job classification. Modes of action alternate between episodic walkouts with legal action in labor courts. Strikes have been taking place frequently since 2014, with at least two per year but have never been promoted by all the unions at once and in every FC at the same time, which weakened these actions given the capacity of the company to reroute orders through its vast network. Moreover, strike participation is low: in general no more than a hundred workers walk out. Legal actions intensified and climaxed in the summer of 2019 as ongoing controversies about job classification arose. Unions challenged Amazon's internal system of classification, which is structured on only two levels (simple associates, level T1, and team leader, T3), because it does not respect job classifications established by sector-level collective bargaining.[16] Unions also commissioned studies on working conditions, which reportedly carry high psycho-social risks for workers. On the other hand, unions have been unable to enlarge their scope of action beyond standard FC employees to address the conditions of temporary agency workers which are employed heavily during seasonal peaks of activity. Nor have they been able to deploy a campaign of unionization of workers along Amazon's supply chain, i.e., smaller delivery stations and last mile drivers. This concentration of unions in the core may bring some residual benefit to many FC workers but not solidarity for all.

In Italy, Amazon is slightly younger (2011) than in France (2007), and had its first cycle of industrial conflict in 2017 when a strike took place during Black Friday, which had a strong impact across the media. In contrast to France, collective bargaining at the company level is not compulsory and

Amazon refused to recognize unions as interlocutors for several months after they declared their formation. Regardless, the main three Italian historic unions (CGIL, CISL, UIL plus the right-wing UGL[17]) put the corporation under strong public and political pressure with a strike during 2017s Black Friday. Thus management had to capitulate, at least formally, and allow union presence in Italian FCs. Workers' demands focused on health and safety, schedules, and respect from managers, and coalesced in a strike, which was organized and encouraged by unions. At that time, unions had no access to the workplace and workers had no means of expressing their concerns other than by making requests of management or through passive resistance.

After a three months' refusal to negotiate with the unions, two strikes, and government pressure (Ministry of Labor and the local Prefect), the company finally agreed to bargain with the unions. Parts of workers' demands were combined into a collective agreement and approved by a referendum. The main issue was an equal distribution of shifts and working time among workers. Significantly, the company accepted the deal but claimed that the agreement was signed only by workers' representatives and not by union officers. The agreement was presented as a historic win by unions and their national leaders. In a surprising turnaround, it was also publicly endorsed by Amazon Italy's top managers, who claimed to have good relations with the workers and a fruitful dialogue with "workers' representatives" (the word "unions" is carefully avoided).

However, many problems, such as yearly bonuses, job classifications, and health and safety issues remain unresolved. After the first collective agreement, no significant improvement resulted from the negotiations. In the summer of 2019, some Amazon workers, working outside of unions, collected approximately five hundred signatures for a petition. The petition called for better working conditions, particularly in terms of shift scheduling, but it was dismissed by the company and also by the unions, which is quite telling about the difficulties unions are facing in winning the trust of the workers. As in France, temporary workers are completely excluded from union representation and collective bargaining, although they are crucial for the functioning of the whole organization of work.

In contrast to France, as union presence and collective bargaining is protected but not imposed by legally binding norms, unions had to enlarge their legitimacy and during the strike opted for inter-union cooperation. Moreover, CGIL has been able to organize Amazon's drivers in the last two years and they organized a strike in 2018. In response, Amazon agreed to negotiate some aspects of the organization of work with unions, even though drivers are not Amazon employees but hired by outsourced small delivery firms.

Amazon's crucial battlefield is not in the arena of collective bargaining. Management is instead primarily concerned with gaining control over workers' minds and bodies, and secondarily, focused on behaving strategically once collective bargaining is settled. The company appears to be able to adapt to the institutional context and to take advantage of some parts of it, finding loopholes in labor legislation, unilaterally interpreting (or breaking) collective agreements, exploiting division among unions, and ultimately shielding its corporate regime. In these ways, it continues to exclude unions and workers from decisions on the organization of work. This could happen also at the transnational level, where the creation of a European Workers' Council with advisory prerogatives, is likely to be more a tool in the hands of the company for promoting its reputation than a weapon to improve working conditions and workers' political participation.

NOT THE END OF HISTORY

Far from behaving as a ruthless enemy of unions as it does in the U.S., Amazon in Europe accepts, at least formally, the institutional constraints imposed by unions and labor laws, and takes advantage of legal loopholes in terms of compensation. In the face of this counter-strategy, unions risk being co-opted and becoming part of workplace administration. Nevertheless, Amazon's hegemony is not uncontested. The corporation strives to maintain satisfying levels of productivity in its FCs, but this cannot be taken for granted. Workers' commitment is hard to secure and the workforce does not allow itself to be shaped by management without resistance. Amazon's hegemonic corporate regime cannot eradicate the latent antagonism in production relations, which emerges concretely in workers' account of their life in the workplace, especially when the issues of health, dignity, and respect are commonly evoked. French and Italian unions have been able to break the wall of anti-unionism built by the company. However, their activities have not yet successfully challenged managerial discourse, namely customer obsession, and all the sets of practices that safeguard corporate hegemony within the workplace. The mechanisms of unconscious consent described above take place in the everyday life of the workplace and are rarely questioned by unions. Unions must contest managerial discourses and workplace practices, and help workers to forge an alternative identity in order to empower workers *vis-à-vis* of management. The only ones who have been adopting a critical stand toward corporate hegemony management is a minority of workers, whether union members or not. Some of them occasionally comment with pessimistic irony on the official discourse of management: "Tomorrow I am not going to work: I am going to Amazon and make history …".

Table 8.1 General data on Amazon Fulfillment Centers in France and Italy

	France	*Italy*
Number of FCs	6	4
Number of FC employees	4700 (+ 3000 temp workers)	2800 (+ 2300 temp workers)
Main unions	CFDT, *Solidaires*, CGT	CGIL, CISL, UGL
Union membership	5–10%	20%[18]
Absenteeism	>10%	–
Days of strike	>10 (since 2014)	2 (since 2017)

Source: Author's fieldnotes

NOTES

1. Colin Crouch and Wolfgang Streeck (eds.), *Political Economy of Modern Capitalism: Mapping Convergence and Diversity* (London: Sage, 1997); Lucio Baccaro and Chris Howell, *Trajectories of Neoliberal Transformation: European Industrial Relations Since the 1970s* (Cambridge: Cambridge University Press, 2017).
2. Michael Burawoy, *Manufacturing Consent: Changes in the Labor Process under Monopoly Capitalism* (Chicago, IL: University of Chicago Press, 1979), p. 30.
3. Gideon Kunda, *Engineering Culture: Control and Commitment in a HighTech Corporation* (Philadelphia, PA: Temple University Press, 2006); Danièle Linhart, *La comédie humaine du travail: de la déshumanisation taylorienne à la sur-humanisation managériale* (Toulouse: Érès, 2015).
4. Burawoy, *Manufacturing Consent*, p. 120.

5. Harry Braverman, *Labor and Monopoly Capital: The Degradation of Work in the Twentieth Century,* (New York: Monthly Review Press, 1974).
6. Francesco S. Massimo, "Spettri del Taylorismo. Lavoro e organizzazione nei centri logistici di Amazon," *Quaderni di Rassegna Sindacale* 3 (2019): 85–102.
7. Massimo, 'Spettri del Taylorismo'; Alessandro Delfanti, "Machinic Dispossession and Augmented Despotism: Digital Work in an Amazon Warehouse," *New Media & Society*, December 2, 2019.
8. Regarding employers' ability to deconstruct tasks in order to "easily measure the output of each worker and thus monitor their level of labor effort", see Michael Burawoy and Erik Olin Wright, "Coercion and Consent in Contested Exchange", *Politics & Society* 18(2) (1990): 251–66. Massimo, "Spettri del Taylorismo"; Delfanti, "Machinic Dispossession and Augmented Despotism."
9. The French National Institute of Statistics.
10. The Italian National Institute of Statistics.
11. Francesco S. Massimo, "Burocrazie algoritmiche. Limiti e astuzie della razionalizzazione digitale in due stabilimenti Amazon," in *Etnografia E Ricerca Qualitativa* 1 (2020): 53–78.
12. In the factory studied by Burawoy "making out" was a game played by piece-rate workers on the shop-floor and one of the pillars of workers' consent to their exploitation. Burawoy, *Manufacturing Consent*, pp. 48–94.
13. Albert O. Hirschman, *Exit, Voice, and Loyalty: Responses to Decline in Firms, Organizations, and States* (Cambridge, MA: Harvard University Press, 1970).
14. Ibid.
15. Amazon workers and supporters, "Stop Treating Us Like Dogs! Workers Organizing Resistance at Amazon in Poland," in Jake Alimahomed-Wilson and Immanuel Ness (eds.), *Choke Points: Logistics Workers Disrupting the Global Supply Chain* (London: Pluto Press, 2018), pp. 96–109; Bruno Cattero and Marta D'Onofrio, "Orfani delle istituzioni. Lavoratori, sindacati e le 'fabbriche terziarie digitalizzate' di Amazon," *Quaderni di rassegna sindacale* 1 (2018): 7–28; Jörn Boewe and Johannes Schulten, "The Long Struggle of Amazon Employees," *Laboratory of Resistance: Union Organising in E-Commerce Worldwide*, 2nd ed. (Brussels: Rosa Luxemburg Stiftung, 2019).
16. The system of classification included in the sectoral collective agreement recognises workers' skills (for instance, forklift drivers) and better wages. Unions sued the company in front of the commerce-sector labor board in order to align the company's internal classification to the sectoral agreement. Amazon's reaction was to opt out from the commerce sector and apply another sector's collective agreement (transports).
17. *Confederazione Generale Italiana del Lavoro* is the former Communist and largest trade union in Italy. *Confederazione Italiana Sindacati dei Lavoratori* is the former Catholic and second largest union in Italy. *Unione Italiana del Lavoro* is the former Liberal-Socialist union and third largest union in Italy. *Unione Generale del Lavoro* is the former neo-Fascist union in Italy. Unions did not

precisely declare their membership. We know that in the Italian FC I studied, CISL had around one hundred members, CGIL also one hundred but slightly less than CISL, UGL around fifty members, and UIL around thirty. Considering that the FC's permanent workforce is around 1,600 workers, we can therefore estimate a membership rate of 20 percent, temp workers excluded.
18. Data refer to the only Italian FC with established union presence.

PART III

Communities Confronting the E-Commerce Giant

9
Company Town: What Happens to a City and its Democracy when Amazon Dominates?

Katie Wilson

When Amazon was founded in 1994, in the early days of the Internet, Seattle was a mellow, rainy city of half a million souls, known for grunge music and Starbucks coffee. Twenty-five years later, Seattle is a booming metropolis where dilapidated tents huddle in the shadows of glittering towers. The city's population has grown by nearly 50 percent. Amazon's rise from online bookseller to a many-tentacled global empire has driven this transformation, in the process creating something like a twenty-first-century company town. With over 50,000 employees and a fifth of the city's prime office space, Amazon dominates Seattle's economy.[1] Meanwhile, Amazon's founder and CEO Jeff Bezos has built up a vast personal fortune, vying with another Seattle-area tech magnate, Microsoft's Bill Gates, for the title of world's richest human.

Seattle offers plentiful advantages to tech firms, from a highly educated population to gorgeous natural surroundings, but perhaps none is more valuable than its favorable tax law. In Seattle, the rich are winning the tax war decisively. Every U.S. state's tax system is regressive, but Washington State's is the worst: the poorest quintile pay nearly 18 percent of their income in state and local taxes, while the wealthiest 1 percent pay less than 3 percent.[2] That's largely because Washington is one of a handful of states with no income-based taxes. Instead, it relies heavily on sales and excise taxes, property taxes, and a byzantine business and occupation tax that privileges high-margin and vertically integrated industries and is riddled with special-interest loopholes.

Tech industry titans have been instrumental in maintaining this status quo. In 2010, a community-labor coalition gathered signatures to place a measure on the state ballot to fund education and health services through a tax on high-income households. Microsoft CEO Steve Ballmer was the top contributor to the opposition campaign with $425,000, and Jeff Bezos made the top five with $100,000. The Washington Technology Industry Association explained: "The absence of a state income tax gives Washington companies a competitive advantage in their efforts to recruit and retain the best and brightest from across the country."[3] For Amazon, which has built an empire on tax avoidance,[4] it's like a generous publicly subsidized annual bonus for every high-paid employee. In eight months, Initiative 1098 went from polling two-thirds in favor to going down hard with two-thirds voting against. Seattle would remain a tax haven for the rich.

But Seattle has another face, too. From the 1919 Seattle General Strike to the WTO protests of 1999, the city has earned its place on America's Left Coast. Seattle Democrats lifted Bernie Sanders to a landslide 73 percent victory in the 2016 Washington caucus and Hillary creamed Trump by 87 to 8 percent. Seattle voters have thrice elected a Trostkyist council member and the city is home to a seven-ton statue of Lenin that some view with more reverence than irony. Seattle's labor movement is still relatively strong; Washington's union membership rate is 20 percent, nearly double the national average, making it the third most unionized state. In recent years Seattle has joined a handful of U.S. cities leading the charge on progressive policy, passing path-breaking labor standards laws including paid sick leave and a $15 minimum wage.

Amazon's rise in Seattle, and the resulting social and economic strains, set these dual identities—stronghold of global capital and bastion of left-leaning politics—on a collision course. At some point, people in Seattle would try to tax Amazon. That point came in the autumn of 2017. I was an active participant in the effort through my role as General Secretary of the Transit Riders Union (TRU), a grassroots membership organization that advocates on issues ranging from transportation to housing, homelessness, and tax policy. This chapter examines Round 1 of this collision, and what we can learn from it as we contemplate Round 2.

PRELUDE

Even as its economic footprint grew, Amazon was for a long time remarkably absent from Seattle's civic life—a reflection, perhaps, of the libertarian leanings of its founder and CEO. In 2012, Amazon came under heavy criticism for this lackluster performance,[5] and soon after began making tentative forays into local politics and philanthropy.

A look at Amazon's electoral spending in Washington State reveals that its first significant contribution—$5,000 to CASE (Civic Alliance for a Sound Economy), the Political Action Committee of the Seattle Metropolitan Chamber of Commerce—took place in 2013.[6] Over the next few years, Amazon made contributions of $25,000 or more to a handful of ballot measure campaigns, including several to fund transit service and transportation improvements—through regressive taxes, naturally. In 2016, Amazon began a partnership with the non-profit Mary's Place, donating space to shelter homeless families. At the same time Amazon came under fire for contracting with an anti-union security firm, not doing enough to improve the diversity of its tech workforce, and straining Seattle's housing market and urban infrastructure.[7]

The real turning point came in 2017. In the wake of Donald Trump's victory in the 2016 presidential election, a coalition calling itself "Trump-Proof Seattle" came together to channel the general outrage into local action on tax reform. Emboldened by an energetic campaign, in July 2017, the Seattle City Council unanimously passed a tax on high-income households, aware that the measure would face legal challenges. The Transit Riders Union co-convened this coalition, due to our interest in finding more equitable means to pay for public services like transit. Although the Washington State Supreme Court refused to review several legal rulings against Seattle's income tax in 2020, those rulings were hotly contested both in and out of court. A mayoral election was also underway, and skyrocketing rents and the deepening homelessness crisis were topics of intense debate. Sensing the activist mood, Amazon must have felt nervous—enough to contribute to CASE an unprecedented $365,000 to secure the election of now-Mayor Jenny Durkan over several rivals, all of whom were more critical than she of the company's role in Seattle.

Amazon was right to worry. By autumn 2017, the grassroots wing of Trump-Proof Seattle had reinvented itself as Housing For All, and propelled onto the political stage a plan to address homelessness through a tax on large businesses. The original proposal, which would have netted a modest $25 million annually, quickly won support from homeless service providers and one major labor union, SEIU Healthcare 1199NW, whose members include workers at one of Seattle's largest shelters. The Seattle Metropolitan Chamber of Commerce, the Downtown Seattle Association, and other business groups lobbied against the measure. In November 2017, after heated city budget deliberations punctuated by overflowing public hearings, occupations, and die-ins,[8] the city council narrowly rejected the tax, but voted unanimously to form a task force charged with crafting a more considered proposal in the new year.

TAXING BIG BUSINESS

In January 2018, the task force set to work. Appointees included service providers and affordable housing developers, business owners and labor representatives, experts and advocates; several, including me, were members of Housing For All. The business groups, belying their earlier complaints about lack of consultation and process, declined to participate. And it wasn't only the corporate establishment that seemed intent on delegitimizing the task force by ignoring it. Mayor Durkan made no acknowledgment of its existence, instead joining with the King County Executive to announce a new regional workgroup on homelessness called "One Table," which would include representatives of the Chamber, the Downtown Seattle Association, Amazon, Microsoft, and local real estate giant Vulcan Inc. The timing and publicity seemed calculated to undermine the task force by suggesting that solutions were forthcoming and that Seattle was needlessly and irresponsibly acting alone; "we need a regional approach" quickly became a rallying cry of business-tax opponents.

The task force became impossible to ignore when, in early March, it released a unanimous report calling for $150 million per year in new progressive revenue, including at least $75 million from a tax on large businesses.[9] Business opposition was swift and strong. Especially fierce controversy erupted over a recommendation the task force had considered minor, suggested by a small business owner reluctant to promote a tax he wouldn't himself pay: that a modest fee of a few hundred dollars be applied to firms below the exemption threshold, so that all but the very smallest would contribute something. Sensational news reports proclaimed that all businesses would be taxed, and confusion and misinformation multiplied. In fact, councilmembers were glad to nix the fee idea and exempt all but the very largest businesses; but this misstep gave opponents an early boost by making it easy to whip up fear and mistrust of the council's intentions. It wasn't an auspicious start.

As debate intensified, the campaign's weaknesses came into sharp relief. Housing for All had neither capacity nor resources to broadcast its message to the broad public; other supporters and the councilmembers now at the helm had no plan either. If anyone was prepared to grab the media spotlight, it was socialist Councilmember Kshama Sawant, who had positioned herself further to the left, calling for a business tax to raise the full $150 million named in the report. She and her party, Socialist Alternative, made Amazon their focal point, holding a "Tax Amazon Town Hall" in late March and rallying at Amazon's corporate headquarters soon after. Media coverage of these events gave much of the public their first impression of the tax's proponents. The effort appeared less about housing and homelessness, and more a crusade against Seattle's most notorious corporation led by Seattle's most notorious socialist. This might be a winning strategy to rally the left, but it also made easy fodder for opponents and reporters eager to paint a picture of a tax-happy, "activist" city council more interested in symbolic actions than real solutions.

Still, five of the nine councilmembers were solidly on board, and an early April poll suggested majority public support. At least two more councilmembers were engaging in productive discussions, and even the mayor seemed to be coming round; in mid-April, she transmitted a letter to the council, naming her desiderata without objecting to the overall project. "One Table" wasn't going anywhere fast,[10] so the big business tax was the only game in town.

In late April, four councilmembers unveiled legislation.[11] It would raise $75 million per year, exempting businesses with gross revenue under $20 million. The tax would begin at a flat $500 per employee, switching to a 0.7% employer-side payroll tax as soon as the city could set up the administration. Spending would be split between housing, shelter, and services. After a tense public hearing a few days later, the measure appeared to be trudging towards victory. Then Amazon entered the fray.

THE AMAZON FACTOR

On the morning of May 2, 2018, Amazon announced what amounted to a threat of a capital strike, pausing construction on a new downtown office tower pending the outcome of the council's vote. It would consider subleasing another skyscraper instead of occupying it, and was reconsidering its growth in Seattle to the tune of 7,000–8,000 jobs.[12] This was, ironically, just days after Bezos was dragged through the mud on social media for saying he couldn't think of a better way to spend his billions than launching rockets into space.[13]

National news commentators portrayed this move as a bullying tactic and likely a bluff, but a different attitude took hold in Seattle. A surprising amount of fear and even sympathy for Amazon emerged—or perhaps not surprising, given how much of Seattle's population works for Amazon or in a dependent industry, or has friends or family who do. The sense that Amazon really could abandon its hometown was heightened by the company's highly publicized search for a second headquarters. The HQ2 announcement the previous September had sent a ripple of consternation through Seattle, and business groups didn't hesitate to blame Seattle's politics.[14] While cities across North America prepared to grovel at Amazon's feet, offering everything from tax breaks to the keys to the city,[15] Seattle-area elected officials were writing an embarrassing letter asking to "hit the refresh button" on their relationship.[16] Amazon didn't reply.

Six months later, this was their reply. The tower in question was only in the planning stages, so "pausing construction" was a dramatic way of saying that some architects put down their pens. But it was enough to rouse the building trades unions to vehement opposition, driving a wedge into the labor support that had just begun to solidify. Sawant called another rally at Amazon's headquarters, where tax supporters met a crowd of angry iron workers.[17] It was a colorful scene for the news cameras, but not one that helped the cause. Seattle might have had more cranes in the sky than any other U.S. city for three years running,[18] but the image of construction workers supposedly fearful for their livelihoods had a powerful effect on the public consciousness.

Amazon's move overshadowed the release the following week of the McKinsey Report, an independent analysis of the homelessness crisis undertaken pro bono for the Seattle Metropolitan Chamber of Commerce. The Chamber had been trying to sweep this report under the rug for months,[19] with good reason: it flatly contradicted their talking points. "Even the most efficient response system will fail without more money"—double what was currently being spent. While hiding this analysis, the Chamber funded an anonymous social media campaign directing blame for the crisis squarely at a city council "spending millions without results".[20] Now the report was too late to make a dent in public opinion—the anti-council, anti-tax drumbeat was too strong. An early May poll suggested that a majority now opposed the measure.

Amazon's threat, the labor split, and the palpable shift in public opinion created an opening for a new wave of political opposition. Mayor Durkan announced she couldn't support the legislation in its present form, the County Executive opined that the "head tax" should be shelved,[21] even former mayors came out of the woodwork to oppose the plan.[22] The five council champions were increasingly isolated, and it became clear that their colleagues would follow the mayor's lead. But they pressed ahead and passed the original bill out of committee 5-4, setting up a potential veto showdown.

Over the weekend, intense negotiations took place among councilmembers, the mayor, and Amazon.[23] Amazon indicated that $250 per head would be acceptable enough to hit the "unpause" button; Amazon didn't like the more progressive payroll-based tax, which was duly nixed. Finally, on May 14, the council unanimously passed a tax of $275 per head, projected to raise $47 million per year, with a hard stop after five years. The compromise thrilled no one, but it was done: Seattle had approved a major revenue package for housing and homelessness, funded not on the backs of working and poor people but by Seattle's largest corporations.

THE REPEAL

But it wasn't over. The bill had passed on a Monday. *Kill harmful head tax by citizen initiative*, urged the *Seattle Times* editorial board on Tuesday, in the fourth of what would become a string of eight anti-head-tax editorials by the paper in less than two months. On Wednesday, the mayor signed the ordinance, and on Thursday morning, business groups met and decided to launch a referendum; in thirty days, the bill would become law, but if they submitted 17,632 valid signatures of Seattle voters before June 15, it would go to the November ballot instead. By Friday, they had commitments for over $300,000, including large sums from Amazon, Starbucks, Vulcan, and other heavy hitters.[24] Signature-gatherers hit the streets and "No Tax On Jobs" was on its way.

Over four weeks, the referendum campaign would spend nearly half a million dollars; $10,000 bought targeted Facebook and Twitter ads, other communications cost tens of thousands more. But the biggest chunk was the $350,000 signature-gathering operation, run by the conservative firm Morning In America. Signature-gatherers flew in from around the country to earn up to $6 per signature, and according to numerous reports and recordings,[25] some would say whatever it took—that the tax would be deducted straight out of employees' paychecks, or that it was already in effect and had caused grocery stores to shut down.

But it wasn't only paid signature-gatherers on the streets. Business groups had formed an alliance with several neighborhood groups that over the past year had become increasingly vocal: the Neighborhood Safety Alliance, Safe Seattle, Speak Out Seattle. The leadership of these groups skews to the right of Seattle's electorate, and their core audience—older, white home-owners in wealthier neighborhoods—were sick and tired: of needles in their kids' soccer fields, tents and garbage lining their sidewalks, RVs parked on their streets, and a City Hall they felt was unresponsive to their complaints and profligate with their tax money. These groups jumped at the chance to kill the "head tax," and Facebook and Nextdoor.com buzzed with discussion of the referendum and opportunities to sign or volunteer.

Many tax proponents wanted to write off these volunteers as reactionary Trump supporters, but it simply wasn't the case, though there were some in the mix. People who normally support every progressive cause and vote for every tax levy were saying they just couldn't get behind this one. They didn't trust the city council. They thought it was all about Sawant picking a fight with Amazon. Wasn't Amazon already helping the homeless? A jobs tax would be bad for the economy, they thought. Moody's and Fitch begged to differ,[26] but that was just another news blip that barely made an impact. For tax opponents, this referendum was about voters who'd had enough. They were tired of taxes, tired of ineffective spending on homelessness, finally taking action to keep an out-of-control city council in check.

The Transit Riders Union teamed up with progressive labor groups to mount a last-ditch counter-campaign, urging voters to "decline to sign" the referendum petition, but it was too little too late. As the deadline neared, it was clear they had their signatures. Meanwhile, a labor-commissioned poll seemed to confirm that the narrative battle was lost. Labor leaders consulted with councilmembers, and the odds looked to them insurmountable. The unions didn't want to throw money at a losing battle; they had other priorities, including the impending *Janus* v. *AFSCME* decision. Councilmembers worried that a frenzy of anti-tax sentiment could endanger other upcoming ballot measures and state elections—not to mention that five more months of ugly propaganda war would build momentum to unseat tax champions from the council in 2019. They concluded that cutting their losses and repealing the tax was the less bad of two bad endings.

The Seattle City Council convened on June 12 to an overflowing chambers. Councilmembers tried to convey the reasoning behind their abrupt about-face. Only Councilmembers Kshama Sawant and Teresa Mosqueda opposed the repeal, the latter explaining that she couldn't support it without another plan to address homelessness, the former decrying her colleagues' cowardice and capitulation to big business. As the repeal motion passed 7-2, Seattle's left (angry at the repeal) and the closest thing Seattle has to a right (still angry that the tax was passed in the first place) chanted in unison: "Vote Them Out!" It was, the *Seattle Times* reported, "a stunning reversal without parallel in Seattle's recent political history."[27]

LOOKING TO THE FUTURE

As of 2020, it's clear that Amazon's outsized role in Seattle politics is here to stay. Precisely one year after the repeal, a group of large donors including Amazon announced a $48.8 million gift to a local housing non-profit—a number suspiciously close to what the "head tax" would have raised annually, as if to underscore that philanthropy is their preferred mode of contributing to the common good.[28] In the summer and autumn of 2019, Amazon contributed an astounding $1.45 million to CASE, in a bold public bid to influence Seattle's local elections and secure a new city council more accommodating to the company's interests—a move that backfired spectacularly, as voters chose the more left-leaning candidate in six out of seven district council races.[29]

At the same time, the rent is still too damn high, the homelessness crisis continues unabated, and Seattle is still the city with the most regressive tax system in the state with the most regressive tax system in the country. Despite some posturing, Amazon shows no sign of reducing its footprint in the Seattle area. In short, not much has changed, and it's hard to imagine that the tensions produced by Amazon's omnipresence won't rupture again.

By the time this book goes to press, it's very possible that the next round of Amazon v. Seattle will already be underway. What can we learn from the "head tax" experience to guide us into the future?

If our only desire is a modest tax on big business, this episode offers some common-sense lessons. Foremost, we must be able to hold public opinion. As much as many people (myself included) wanted to fight it to the ballot, it's hard to imagine prevailing against Amazon's functionally unlimited resources given how far the tide had already turned. I believe we could have held public opinion had we done three things differently. First, prevent or minimize the building trades' defection, by securing stronger labor support at the outset and inoculating against Amazon's power moves. Second, more effectively shape the public narrative by running a strong public-facing campaign. Finally, narrow and isolate the opposition, for example, by designing a tax measure to affect even fewer and larger corporations and cultivating more vocal business support. In short, we needed to unite our allies, divide our opponents, and reach the "persuadables" first. A better-planned and resourced campaign should be able to win a measure like this in Seattle, as evidenced by the big business tax for homelessness that prevailed in San Francisco in the autumn of 2018, backed by a strong coalition and bolstered by the loud and generous support of one iconoclastic local tech titan.[30]

But of course, the challenge before us goes beyond this, and beyond Amazon. Over the past fifty years, corporate and financial elites, enabled by the globalization of productive capital,[31] have made a concerted grab for political control in the United States and around the world. They have successfully promoted neoliberal policies that lower taxes on corporations and the wealthy, deregulate markets, weaken organized labor, dismantle welfare-state programs, and privatize public services. With federal and state governments in their grip, shifting urban demographics and rising inequality are turning cities into a dynamic frontier where local movements can lock horns with global capital. In this struggle, capital has advantages: the ability to undermine local democracy with large infusions of cash, the leverage that comes with the ability to withdraw investment and jobs—or even, as we experienced in Seattle, merely the promise of future investment and jobs. The challenge before us is to build, against such odds, the people-power to begin winning this struggle.

In this endeavor there really are no shortcuts.[32] You can collect every progressive, left, and labor organization in a major U.S. city into a coalition and still its reach into the population will be narrow and shallow. We must figure out how to organize a larger section of urban populations into high-participation mass membership organizations, shrinking the part of the population that absorbs opinions from corporate-dominated media by growing the part that forms opinions through active participation in class-based civic organizations. While we must fight to maintain and increase labor union density, the challenges of organizing on this model in our new twenty-first-entury landscape of precarious work, anemic democratic infrastructure, and disintegrated community should prompt experimentation with a range of new models. Leftists should approach the organizing of workers, tenants, and residents on a geographic basis as energetically and seriously as radicals once approached the organization of industrial unions.

As we become more effective at building place-based movements, we must link these movements together, nationally and internationally. Coordination and solidarity are our only means to neutralize global capital's ability to pit cities and states against one another. We should also consider local and regional economic development and stabilization strategies to protect against capital flight and other punishments global capital under pressure may mete out. To give the obvious example, it's risky for a city to be so dominated by a single corporation as Seattle is by Amazon. A more diversified economy would give Amazon less leverage and our movements more opportunities to divide and conquer—even better would be an economy with significant sectors under public or cooperative control. Of course, putting such strategies into practice will depend on local movements' ability to achieve some degree of political ascendance.

The coming decades will be full of great possibility as well as great peril. It's up to us and to the generations that follow to learn from history, to experiment, and to draw lessons from our own failures and our own successes. We have a world to win.

NOTES

1. Mike Rosenberg and Ángel González, "Thanks to Amazon, Seattle is now America's biggest company town," *Seattle Times*, August 23, 2017, www.seattletimes.com/business/amazon/thanks-to-amazon-seattle-is-now-americas-biggest-company-town. Accessed December 1, 2019.
2. M. Wiehe et al., "Who Pays? A Distributional Analysis of the Tax Systems in All 50 States," 6th Edition, *The Institute on Taxation and Economic Policy*, October

2018, https://itep.org/wp-content/uploads/whopays-ITEP-2018.pdf. Accessed December 1, 2019.
3. Andrew Garber, "Ballmer and Bezos Opposing Income Tax Initiative I-1098," *Seattle Times*, September 20, 2010, http://old.seattletimes.com/html/politicsnorthwest/2012948586_ballmer_and_bezos_opposing_inc.html. Accessed December 1, 2019.
4. Alex Shephard, "Is Amazon Too Big to Tax?," *The New Republic*, March 1, 2018, https://newrepublic.com/article/147249/amazon-big-tax. Accessed December 1, 2019.
5. Amy Martinez and Kristi Heim, "Amazon a Virtual No-show in Hometown Philanthropy," *Seattle Times*, March 31, 2012, www.seattletimes.com/business/amazon-a-virtual-no-show-in-hometown-philanthropy. Accessed December 1, 2019.
6. The Public Disclosure Commission, www.pdc.wa.gov (accessed December 2019).
7. SEIU Local 6, "At Stakeholders Meeting, Amazon Urged to Drop Security Firm," *The Stand*, June 11, 2015. www.thestand.org/2015/06/at-stakeholders-meeting-amazon-urged-to-drop-security-firm/. Accessed December 1, 2019.
8. Joel Moreno, "Homeless Activists Stage Camp-out, 'Die-in' at Seattle City Hall," *KOMO News*, November 1, 2017, https://komonews.com/news/local/homeless-activists-stage-camp-out-in-seattle-city-hall. Accessed December 1, 2019.
9. City of Seattle, "Report of the Progressive Revenue Taskforce on Housing and Homelessness," March 9, 2018, www.seattle.gov/Documents/Departments/Council/Issues/ProgressiveRevenueTaskforce/Report-of-the-Progressive-Revenue-Taskforce-03-09-2018.pdf. Accessed December 1, 2019.
10. Josh Kelety, "Critics Say Draft Plan from Homelessness Task Force Underwhelms," *Seattle Weekly*, April 10, 2018, www.seattleweekly.com/news/critics-say-draft-plan-from-homelessness-task-force-underwhelms. Accessed December 1, 2019.
11. Daniel Beekman, "Seattle City Council Releases Plan to Tax Businesses, Fund Homelessness Help," *Seattle Times*, April 20, 2018, www.seattletimes.com/seattle-news/politics/seattle-city-council-releases-plan-to-tax-businesses-fund-homelessness-help. Accessed December 1, 2019.
12. Nick Wingfield, "Amazon Pauses Huge Development Plans in Seattle Over Tax Plan," *New York Times*, May 2, 2018, www.nytimes.com/2018/05/02/technology/amazon-development-tax.html. Accessed December 1, 2019.
13. Mike Wehner, "Jeff Bezos Confirms Plans to Spend His Billions like a Bond Villain," *New York Post*, May 3, 2018, https://nypost.com/2018/05/03/jeff-bezos-confirms-plans-to-spend-his-billions-like-a-bond-villain. Accessed December 1, 2019.
14. Heidi Groover, "Business Groups Blame City Politics for Amazon's Expansion Out of Seattle Because Of Course They Do," *The Stranger*, September 7, 2017, www.thestranger.com/slog/2017/09/07/25400984/business-groups-blame-

income-tax-for-amazons-expansion-out-of-seattle-because-of-course-they-do. Accessed December 1, 2019.
15. Danny Westneat, "This City Hall, Brought to You by Amazon," *Seattle Times*, November 24, 2017, www.seattletimes.com/business/amazon/this-city-hall-brought-to-you-by-amazon. Accessed December 1, 2019.
16. Monica Nickelsburg, "Seattle Politicians Seek to Renew Relationship with Amazon in Mea Culpa Letter to Jeff Bezos," *Geekwire*, October 16, 2017, www.geekwire.com/2017/seattle-politicians-seek-renew-relationship-amazon-mea-culpa-letter-jeff-bezos. Accessed December 1, 2019.
17. Vianna Davila, "Outside Amazon Spheres, Iron Workers Shout Down Kshama Sawant Over Proposed Head Tax," *Seattle Times*, May 3, 2018, www.seattletimes.com/seattle-news/politics/seattle-councilmember-iron-workers-face-off-over-proposed-amazon-tax. Accessed December 1, 2019.
18. Sarah Anne Lloyd, "Seattle Remains the Crane Capitol of the US," *Curbed Seattle*, July 24, 2018, https://seattle.curbed.com/2018/7/24/17608278/seattle-construction-crane-count-report. Accessed December 1, 2019.
19. Paul Constant, "The Case of the Missing Housing Report," *Civic Skunk Works*, May 11, 2018, https://civicskunk.works/the-case-of-the-missing-housing-report-edad7c7df1c4. Accessed December 1, 2019.
20. Eli Sanders, "Mystery Solved! Here's Who's Behind the Anonymous 'City Council: Make It Better' Ad Campaign," *The Stranger*, May 18, 2018, www.thestranger.com/slog/2018/05/18/26241533/mystery-solved-heres-whos-behind-the-anonymous-city-council-make-it-better-ad-campaign. Accessed December 1, 2019.
21. Jim Brunner, "Head-tax Plan Should Be Shelved, King County Executive Advises Seattle," *Seattle Times*, May 11, 2018, www.seattletimes.com/seattle-news/politics/head-tax-plan-should-be-shelved-king-county-executive-advises-seattle. Accessed December 1, 2019.
22. Tim Burgess and Charles Royer, "Tax on Jobs a Terrible Idea, Say Two Former Seattle Mayors," *Seattle Times*, May 8, 2018, www.seattletimes.com/opinion/tax-on-jobs-a-terrible-idea-say-two-former-seattle-mayors. Accessed December 1, 2019.
23. Daniel Beekman, "Amazon's Number: Inside the Battle Over Seattle's Head Tax," *Seattle Times*, May 17, 2018, www.seattletimes.com/seattle-news/politics/inside-seattle-head-tax-debate-a-battle-over-amazons-number. Accessed December 1, 2019.
24. David Kroman, "Here's Who is Funding the Campaign to Repeal the Business Tax," *Crosscut*, May 23, 2018, https://crosscut.com/2018/05/heres-who-funding-campaign-repeal-business-tax. Accessed December 1, 2019.
25. Steven Hsieh, "Audio and Video Show Canvassers Spreading False Information About the Head Tax," *The Stranger*, June 6, 2018, www.thestranger.com/slog/2018/06/06/27190451/audio-and-video-show-canvassers-spreading-false-information-about-the-head-tax. Accessed December 1, 2019.

26. Casey Coombs, "Ratings Agencies Say Head Tax Won't Slow Seattle's Economy; Moody's Warns of Amazon's Influence," *Puget Sound Business Journal,* May 31, 2018,www.bizjournals.com/seattle/news/2018/05/31/head-tax-economic-growth-amazon-moodys-fitch.html. Accessed December 1, 2019.
27. Daniel Beekman, "About-face: Seattle City Council Repeals Head Tax Amid Pressure From Businesses, Referendum Threat," *Seattle Times,* June 12, 2018, www.seattletimes.com/seattle-news/politics/about-face-seattle-city-council-repeals-head-tax-amid-pressure-from-big-businesses. Accessed December 1, 2019.
28. Katie Wilson, "Corporate Philanthropy Won't Solve Seattle's Housing Crisis," *Crosscut,* June 18, 2019, https://crosscut.com/2019/06/corporate-philanthropy-wont-solve-seattles-housing-crisis. Accessed December 1, 2019.
29. David Kroman, "Kshama Sawant Surges Ahead, Paving the Way for Seattle's 'Most Progressive Council' in Years," *Crosscut,* November 8, 2019, https://crosscut.com/2019/11/kshama-sawant-surges-ahead-paving-way-seattles-most-progressive-council-years (accessed December 2019).
30. Kevin Fagan, "SF Prop. C Homeless Tax—Measure to Raise $300 Million a Year Wins with 60%," *San Francisco Chronicle,* November 7, 2018, www.sfchronicle.com/politics/article/SF-Prop-C-homeless-tax-measure-to-raise-300-13369555.php. Accessed December 1, 2019.
31. William I. Robinson, *A Theory of Global Capitalism: Production, Class, and State in a Transnational World* (Baltimore, MD: Johns Hopkins University Press, 2004).
32. Jane F. McAlevey, *No Shortcuts: Organizing for Power in a New Gilded Age* (Oxford: Oxford University Press, 2016).

10
Lessons from New York City's Struggle Against Amazon HQ2 in Long Island City

Steve Lang and Filip Stabrowski

For three months between November 2018 and February 2019, the entire world, it seemed, was watching Long Island City, Queens. On November 12, 2018, nearly two years after Amazon CEO Jeff Bezos announced that the company would be holding a contest for its second corporate headquarters (Amazon HQ2), New York City Mayor Bill de Blasio and New York State Governor Andrew Cuomo jointly announced that Amazon had selected Long Island City as one of its two HQ2 locations. The project, outlined in a Memorandum of Understanding (MOU) between Amazon and New York City and State, would provide up to $3 billion in public (state and city) subsidies to Amazon in exchange for building 4–8 million square feet of office space on the East River waterfront and creating 25,000 jobs averaging $150,000 per year (over ten years).

No sooner had the ink dried on the MOU, however, than fierce opposition to the plan quickly emerged. A press conference at the proposed HQ2 site was convened the following day, and local elected officials joined a coalition of local labor and immigrant rights groups vowed to fight the deal. As the buzz (and controversy) concerning Amazon HQ2 continued to grow, Governor Cuomo and Mayor de Blasio announced the formation of a 45-member Community Advisory Committee to "help shape" the plan through "robust community engagement."[1] The next two months witnessed a series of public events dedicated to the Amazon plan—including meetings, discussions, teach-ins, city council hearings, canvassing operations, Internet discussion forums, and protests. Then suddenly, on Valentine's Day, in a tersely worded statement that cited the "number of state and local politicians

[that] have made it clear that they oppose [Amazon's] presence," Amazon announced that it was no longer planning to build its second headquarters in Long Island City.[2]

The shock waves from this second surprise decision emerged immediately and continue to reverberate today. Amazon's official announcement notwithstanding, there has been no shortage of blame (or credit) assigned for Amazon's sudden withdrawal from Long Island City. But while we may never know the true reason(s) for this decision, the struggle over the project and Amazon's attempt to control and manage community engagement in the planning process are instructive in their own right. From the arguments that emerged both for and against the Amazon plan we can discern the contours of the emerging struggles over urban space between big tech, the state, and immigrant and working-class communities in global cities such as New York City. The Amazon experience in Long Island City also sheds light on the power of organizing across multiple issue areas in struggles against big tech's designs on the contemporary city.

HQ2 IN LIC

Amazon's announcement that it would split its second corporate headquarters between Arlington, VA and Long Island City, NY, was the culmination of a nearly two-year-long "selection" process—likened to the "Hunger Games"—involving over 200 American cities, New York included. As part of this competition, cities pitched themselves to Amazon by offering up not just financial incentives (including subsidies and tax breaks) for HQ2, but also—and perhaps more consequentially—vast amounts of city data that Amazon would otherwise be challenged to obtain.[3] New York City's initial application included five potential urban sites (Midtown West, Lower Manhattan, Downtown Brooklyn, Long Island City, Governor's Island), with Long Island City ultimately winning out.

Significantly, the MOU also stipulated that the project would be designed as a General Project Plan, thereby enabling the state to impose eminent domain and bypassing the local, city council-mandated approval process known as the Uniform Land Use Review Process (ULURP). Bypassing ULURP, according to city and state planning officials, would allow for an expedited planning process that would better suit Amazon's time frame. It would also, critics emphasized, remove the opportunities for negotiation and compromise between the developers, the city, and local stakeholder groups afforded by ULURP. Instead, like the Atlantic Yards development project before it, the Amazon plan would be subjected to a less onerous approval process under the auspices of a New York State panel known as the Public Authorities Control Board (PACB).

THE CASE FOR HQ2

Though proponents of the Amazon plan emphasiszed the different aspects of the project that they felt would ultimately benefit the city and community, the core argument for HQ2 in Long Island City centered on quality job growth. Amazon's spectacular growth on a global scale promised further expansion and job creation with its second headquarters. Addressing the New York City Council in December 2019, James Patchett, head of New York State Economic Development Corporation (EDC), captured the logic behind this growth-oriented approach to economic and urban development. The anticipated job growth ("tens of thousands of jobs") was expected to yield $30 billion in tax revenue to the city and state—an "exponential return on investment" that could be used to deliver public benefits such as improved local schools, libraries, transit, and infrastructure. From this perspective, the multiplier effects of Amazon HQ2 represented a win-win opportunity for *all* New Yorkers. According to Patchett:

> From a jobs perspective, the Amazon opportunity will help real people in concrete ways. From the small business owner who will see an increase in foot traffic at her bodega, to the construction worker who will help build the headquarters, to the CUNY computer science student who will land a life-changing internship at the company, it is clear this deal is about New Yorkers, front and center.[4]

More importantly, the anticipated new jobs at Amazon were not just any jobs; rather, they were "tech" jobs whose growth would provide a kind of insurance against any future downturn or recession that might negatively affect the finance industry—a sector whose disproportionate power/influence in New York City has been made abundantly clear following the downturns of the early 1990s, the early 2000s (following the terrorist attacks on 9/11), and the Great Recession of 2008. Building HQ2 in Long Island City, Patchett claimed, would create a "reliable financial anchor," thereby "cushioning the city against slumps we know will come."[5]

With Amazon HQ2 firmly ensconced in the city, moreover, local educational institutions such as the City University of New York (CUNY) and the State University of New York (SUNY) would be well-positioned to create "talent pipelines" to employers such as Amazon. Along with the city and state, Amazon would invest into job-training programs focusing on under-represented New Yorkers. Students from nearby LaGuardia Community College, one of the most diverse institutions of higher learning in the world, and residents from the Queensbridge Houses, the largest public housing development in North America, were the intended targets of these new initiatives.

Patchett also lauded the Amazon HQ2 plan for the "unprecedented infrastructure investments in Long Island City" that would follow. In a neighborhood that had witnessed a massive boom in residential construction over the past decade, the Amazon plan for jobs and office space would complement the newly built housing, while reversing the existing commuting patterns that have characterized Long Island City as a bedroom community for workers in Manhattan. Far from taxing further the local infrastructure (such as sewers and subways), the plan would actually improve it by balancing out the live/work ratio in Long Island City and generating tax revenue for infrastructural investment. Amazon HQ2 was thus promoted as an example of smart and "comprehensive" urban planning, an innovative and forward-looking post-industrial waterfront project in the hyper-diverse borough of Queens. Unlike more traditional corporate office parks and technology campuses, moreover, HQ2 would not turn its back on the surrounding city by providing services (especially food and drink) in-house. Instead, limited on-site offerings would encourage Amazon workers to venture out into Long Island City and patronize its shops and restaurants.[6]

Finally—and perhaps most importantly—Amazon HQ2 would sit prominently, and visibly, on the East River waterfront across from the United Nations. A stone's throw from the sparkling new Cornell Tech campus on Roosevelt Island, and perched on the western end of the world's most diverse urban area (Queens), HQ2 would serve as a powerful symbol of the tech industry in New York City. By locating outside of Manhattan, moreover, the world's most powerful corporation would have space in which to settle and expand, nurturing an ecosystem of start-ups and solidifying New York City's place as a rival to Silicon Valley in the process.[7]

THE CASE AGAINST HQ2

Opposition to the Amazon HQ2 plan emerged forcefully and immediately. In fact, the seeds of the anti-Amazon coalition that emerged had been planted well before the company's announcement in November 2018. More than a year prior, in October 2017, a coalition of grassroots community and labor groups, including New York City Communities for Change, Make the Road New York, the Retail, Wholesale and Department Store Union (RWDSU), and the Alliance for a Greater New York (ALIGN) drafted a letter to Mayor Bill de Blasio and Governor Andrew Cuomo stating their opposition to any state or local financial incentives for Amazon, including sales tax exemptions, property tax abatements, or corporate income tax credits. The following July, just months before the HQ2 announcement, the same coalition of local labor and community groups organized a protest against Amazon for reportedly selling white-supremacist products on its website. Rallying outside an Amazon-sponsored summit in Manhattan, one protest organizer stated that "Amazon CEO Jeff Bezos wants taxpayer dollars and community resources to bring HQ [headquarters] to here. But we are here to say no … ."[8]

It was in such a context that Amazon HQ2 in Long Island City was announced. Critics, including city council member Jimmy Van Bramer and state senator Michael Gianaris—both of whom represented districts in which the proposed HQ2 site was located—assailed the plan on several fronts. They expressed outrage that $3 billion in public subsidies would be going to the world's richest man, at a time when New York City's own subways were falling apart and its public housing deteriorating. More substantively, critics pointed out that tax breaks rarely if ever make a difference in corporate headquarter location decisions, and were thus perfectly unnecessary.

The much-trumpeted jobs that HQ2 would create also came under fire. For low-income and working-class residents, the $150,000 per year jobs were clearly not intended for them. In place of job guarantees for local residents of public housing, Amazon offered job fairs and resume-building workshops. When pushed by council members and protesters at city council hearings, it offered just 30 customer service center jobs for Queensbridge residents. Moreover, critics viewed the $5 million that Amazon had pledged for tech training programs as a pittance at best, and entirely self-serving at worst—particularly considering how the city and state were also expected to contribute $5 million each to these programs.

Another issue of deep concern for the opposition to HQ2 was the anticipated residential displacement effects of the project. In the midst of an affordable housing crisis, with a spate of luxury residential developments already pushing rents steadily higher, tenant organizers in Western Queens were highly critical of the further gentrification that HQ2 would unleash. The thousands of new high-income individuals working for Amazon would not just be living in the newly built housing of Long Island City, but would be colonizing the working-class and immigrant "frontline" communities of Astoria, Sunnyside, Woodside, Jackson Heights, Elmhurst, and Corona as well. Local anti-gentrification activist groups such as the Justice For All Coalition and Queens Neighborhoods United saw Amazon as, in the words of one activist, a "great neutron bomb of gentrification" in Western Queens.

For the local elected leaders who opposed Amazon HQ2, however, perhaps the most egregious flaw in the plan was the way it sought to subvert the urban policy-making process itself. Specifically, by bypassing ULURP in favor of the General Project Plan, critics argued, vital public input and consultation would be excluded from the HQ2 planning process. This, according to Van Bramer, was nothing less than a state-backed, corporate subversion of democracy:

> Bypassing ULURP is a direct assault on community engagement and consultation on a project that would change the face of Queens ... It's outrageous, secretive and the height of corporate Democrats tripping over themselves to provide corporate welfare to the richest man in the world without any community review or votes.[9]

Reinforcing this argument was Amazon's track record in Seattle, Amazon's first and only headquarter city. In a meeting co-organized by RWDSU and Make the Road New York, in the time period between the two city council hearings on Amazon, local elected officials, union members, and community activists heard directly from a delegation from the Seattle City Council. At the meeting, the Seattle delegation discussed Amazon's impact on local rents and income inequality, as well as the methods and tactics (including threatening to freeze all construction in the city) it employed in battling against efforts by local elected officials to enact a worker tax on corporations to fund affordable housing and homeless services.

Thus, as the debate over HQ2 intensified in late 2018 and early 2019, the opposition mobilized around an expanding set of concerns that moved quickly beyond the local effects of the plan, linking groups across space and issue area in the process. For example, though the plan itself included no warehouse worker jobs, Amazon's track record of poor and dangerous labor conditions and aggressive union-busting efforts in its fulfillment centers across the country came under scrutiny. Organizers shared Amazon "horror stories" at public meetings and Internet chat groups and drew attention to existing conditions at one of its fulfillment centers on Staten Island, where more than 2,500 workers were employed. This issue emerged most visibly in the two New York City Council hearings devoted to Amazon HQ2 in December 2018 and January 2019. In the December hearings, as a group of Staten Island workers announced their plans to unionize on the steps of City Hall, inside the council chambers Amazon's Vice President for Public Policy was grilled by council members about Amazon's warehouse working conditions. During the hearings, the executive stated that he could not guarantee that Amazon's Staten Island workers would not be required to work more than eight hours per day.[10] At the follow-up hearings in January, the same Amazon executive admitted that Amazon would not commit to remaining neutral in any attempts by its workers to unionize. This took several city council members aback, as it presented a clear challenge to the image of New York City as a "union town." It also brought members of the RWDSU and the Teamsters to join local activist groups on the steps of City Hall to protest the HQ2 plan during the January hearings.[11]

An even more significant issue serving to mobilize the diverse coalition of grassroots groups in opposition to the HQ2 plan was Amazon's history of providing products and services, including cloud computing and facial recognition technology, to the Immigration and Customs Enforcement (ICE) agency. The issue was first highlighted as politically significant at a meeting of some 150 activists, Queens residents, local businesses, and citywide community-based organizations, initiated by ALIGN just days after the HQ2 announcement. It emerged much more spectacularly in the first Amazon city council hearing (December 12), when Amazon's Vice President of Public Policy implicitly admitted that Amazon had provided ICE with services and products, by simply stating that "We believe the government should have the best available technology."[12]

The comment was immediately captured, edited, and re-exported via social media by MPower Change, an online "Muslim grassroots movement" co-founded by Linda Sarsour, and ALIGN. In another video that had gone viral, Mayor Bill de Blasio was asked directly on camera whether he had known previously about Amazon's relationship with ICE—to which he gave an awkward non-response. In Queens, where an estimated 1.1 million immigrants live, an estimated 138 languages are spoken, and raids by ICE agents have become a regularity under the current presidential administration, these revelations were more ammunition for the fight against HQ2. Local immigrant-serving groups such as Desis Rising Up and Moving (DRUM) and Make the Road New York mobilized grassroots opposition to HQ2 on the basis of Amazon's relationship with ICE, among other issues.[13]

NO NEGOTIATIONS

For a core group of activist organizations fighting against HQ2, Amazon's well-established track record made any cooperation or negotiation with the company a non-starter. This position was expressed most clearly by the grassroots activist group Queens Neighborhoods United in a statement issued in December 2019. The statement included four "Principles of Engagement":[14]

1) We will not meet or communicate with Amazon or any of its representatives.
2) We will not meet or communicate with any politicians who have previously endorsed AmazonHQ2 or have connections to the Real Estate Industry. This includes every politician who signed the statement, dated October 16, 2017, endorsing AmazonHQ2.
3) We will oppose AmazonHQ2 in its entirety—with or without public subsidies—and reject any discussion about concessions or negotiation.
4) We respect the diversity of tactics used in the fight against Amazon HQ2.

Facing intense political pressure (and potential primary challengers) from the left, both Van Bramer and Gianaris also adopted a position of no negotiation with Amazon. Both incumbents had witnessed the shocking unseating of long-time congressperson and Democratic Party boss Joseph Crowley by Alexandria Ocasio-Cortez (AOC) just months earlier, and were loathe to test their political fortunes against these same groups (including members of the Queens Democratic Socialists of America, the group most responsible for AOC's stunning victory) in future electoral contests. Initially staked out just after the announcement, their position of no negotiation with Amazon was put to the test less than a month later, when Governor Cuomo announced the formation of the 45-member Community Advisory Committee (CAC). This group of local and citywide "community stakeholders" was charged with "helping ensure that community priorities and needs are considered throughout the process."[15]

Amid the discussions over the value, purpose and legitimacy of the CAC, questions of who actually represented the "community" and what "community priorities and needs" really meant quickly arose. Two local stakeholder institutions that have long represented the poor and underserved in the area—LaGuardia Community College and NYCHA's Queensbridge Houses—emerged as key players in this debate. Both institutions had representation on the CAC. President Mellow of LaGuardia Community College was appointed co-chair of the Workforce Development Committee, a position she shared with Bishop Michael Taylor, CEO and President of Urban Upbound. April Simpson, President of the Queensbridge Houses Tenant Association, was also a key member of the CAC. President Mellow welcomed the CAC as a way of building "a robust workforce development process that creates the human infrastructure necessary to maintain a vital and equitable workforce for our community," while Bishop Taylor gushed about how "the arrival of Amazon will revitalize neighborhood businesses and jumpstart young entrepreneurial minds in our communities."[16]

As representatives of underserved and disadvantaged members of the Long Island City "community", Mellow, Taylor, and Simpson constituted the organizational infrastructure that would be required to form an effective "pipeline" connecting the minority and low-income residents of Queensbridge and students at LaGuardia with local tech employers, chief among them Amazon. Under President Mellow, LaGuardia Community College had embraced the notion that a major function of the institution is workforce development and that the future of employment for first-generation community college students is in the tech sector. LaGuardia was also no stranger to corporate partnerships and workforce training initiatives. Long before Amazon, it partnered with Goldman Sachs on a small business center, the Weill Cornell Medicine for a program in medical billing, and Google for a certificate program to train IT support workers. Within a day of the surprise HQ2 announcement, the LaGuardia home page displayed a banner welcoming Amazon to Long Island City.

Similarly, Urban Upbound, which provides employment services for public housing and low-income residents, figured prominently in the public debate over whether the Amazon plan would bring concrete benefits to residents of Queensbridge Houses. Beyond serving as co-chair of the Workforce Development Subcommittee of the CAC, Taylor issued press statements and organized a pro-Amazon rally at Queensbridge Houses, where he denounced the "people from Connecticut, from other boroughs, from other places ... knocking on doors telling people because of Amazon, because of this, you're going to lose your apartment."[17]

The third key member of the CAC was April Simpson, President of the Queensbridge Houses Residents Association. She too chided the hard opposition to Amazon HQ2, likening them to "sneaky thieves in the night" infiltrating Queensbridge Houses and other NYCHA developments in an effort to spread misinformation about the Amazon plan and the role of the CAC. Days after the Amazon withdrawal, Simpson excoriated Van Bramer and Gianaris, calling them "grandstanding politicians" and holding them responsible for New York missing "a generational opportunity to cement its place as the tech hub of the future."[18] Several months later, she continued to lament Amazon's departure on the editorial pages of the *Daily News*, claiming that she and other community leaders "had a seat at the table" with Amazon and had been making progress towards concrete benefits when the company, in the face of opposition from political opportunists, pulled the plug on the plan.[19]

With such high-profile leaders of community institutions such as LaGuardia Community College, Urban Upbound, and the Queensbridge Houses Residents Association serving on the CAC, the refusal of Van Bramer and Gianaris to join the committee was all the more consequential. Facing constant pressure from grassroots organizers to remain committed to their initial position of no compromise, Van Bramer and Gianaris issued a joint statement in which they described the CAC as "a thinly veiled attempt to present the Amazon development as a fait accompli." Without the participation of local elected officials at both the city and state levels, the CAC's community bona fides were directly called into question.

Of the two local elected officials to refuse to participate in the CAC, it was Gianaris whose decision was most impactful. As the deputy majority leader of the New York State Senate representing the site of the future Amazon HQ2, Gianaris was a logical choice to serve on the PACB, the obscure state board whose approval was necessary for the plan to move forward. As one of the three voting members of the PACB, Gianaris would wield veto power over the plan. Ultimately, however, the threat of a Gianaris veto sinking HQ2 never materialized; on February 14, 2019, Amazon abruptly announced that it would be canceling its plans to establish its second headquarters in Long Island City.

AFTER AMAZON: LESSONS FROM THE STRUGGLE

With Amazon's thinly worded withdrawal from the HQ2 plan, proponents and opponents alike were left wondering what killed the deal. How and why did the world's most powerful corporation fall flat in its New York City debut, and what might this portend for corporate urban futures more generally? While the answer to the former question will have to await future historians, the latter question is worth considering and there are certainly important lessons to be learned from the Amazon HQ2 experience in Long Island City.

First, it is clear that Amazon will seek to bend state and municipal governments to its will. The nearly two-year-long HQ2 "competition" enabled Amazon to play cities against each other, reinforcing the notion that cities need the company—and not the other way around. When Amazon did "select" Long Island City, it did so on the condition—and presumably under the expectation—that it would enjoy an expedited planning and approval process that would bypass local layers of scrutiny and negotiation. When challenged on this (and several other points of its plan), rather than yield to local representatives, Amazon chose instead to replace them with an unelected "Community Advisory Committee."

Second, the scale and scope of Amazon's operations—which make it an economic behemoth the likes of which have not been seen since the age of the great trusts—are also, paradoxically, the source of its political vulnerability at the local level. Having inserted itself into our daily lives through its cloud computing, online shopping platform, vast logistics network, and much, much more (including Whole Foods and *The Washington Post*), Amazon has become the invisible backbone to our everyday economic lives. Yet this very ubiquity has made it an expansive target for the opposition. The inescapability of Amazon has made it an almost impossible-to-miss target, allowing for links to be forged across different groups, campaigns, and areas of concern. In New York City, the Amazon announcement immediately set off a chain reaction among scores of labor and community groups, immigrant rights organizations, and academics at the local and extra-local levels. This concatenation of opposition forces targeted Amazon at various sites through New York City, from its fulfillment center on Staten Island, to its first "brick-and-mortar" store in Manhattan, to its Whole Foods stores, to the very site of the proposed HQ2 in Long Island City. Over a three-month period, from the announcement to the withdrawal, the opposition to Amazon HQ2 presented itself vocally and visibly at every turn.

Finally, and perhaps most importantly, in dealing with an adversary of such size, power, and inflexibility as Amazon, it is vital that the opposition contain a kernel that is committed to no compromise and no negotiation. This is particularly important given Amazon's efforts to manufacture community and consent through bodies such as the CAC, where the price of participation is the legitimization of the process and the acceptance of the (likely preordained) outcome. Significantly, however, in order for this position to stand a chance of success, it must be supported by a credible political threat that would bring with it serious political consequences. In the case of New York City, the volatile political landscape of Western Queens and the rise of an insurgent left following the shock victory of AOC presented just such a possibility. While we will never know if Gianaris would have vetoed the plan or not—and there is no guarantee that a position of no compromise will always succeed—in the absence of such a position, failure is a near certainty.

POSTSCRIPT

In December 2019, less than a year after its surprise withdrawal from HQ2 in Long Island City, Amazon quietly announced that it had signed a lease for 335,000 square feet of office space in the new Hudson Yards development on Manhattan's Far Westside. While far smaller than HQ2, the space is intended for at least 1,500 employees from its consumer and advertising groups and represents a sizeable increase in Amazon's corporate presence in New York City. It also comes with no city or state tax breaks—a point that was lost on neither Gianaris nor AOC, both of whom were quick to embrace the announcement as a vindication of their staunch opposition to HQ2. Upon learning of the lease, Gianaris stated, "Amazon is coming to New York, just as they always planned. Fortunately, we dodged a $3 billion bullet by not agreeing to their subsidy shakedown earlier this year." In a similar vein, AOC quickly took to Twitter: "Won't you look at that: Amazon is coming to NYC anyway—*without* requiring the public to finance shady deals, helipad handouts for Jeff Bezos, & corporate giveaways."[20]

Beyond vindication for two of HQ2's most reviled political critics, Amazon's expansion into the Hudson Yards may signal an important shift in the perceived balance of power between cities and tech giants such as Amazon. Whereas the Hunger Games-like competition for HQ2 and the winner-take-all urbanism it represents posit a world in which cities must hand over their keys to court big tech "saviors" such as Amazon, the HQ2 experience (and its aftermath) in New York City suggests the opposite: that it is the big tech corporations that are dependent on cities with their deep talent pools, world-class amenities, and industry ecosystems. None of this is of course a foregone conclusion; what is ultimately necessary is the political will to call the bluff of corporations such as Amazon—and their enablers at the state and local levels.

NOTES

1. Kenneth Lovett, "Cuomo, de Blasio Announce After-the-Fact Community advisory committee for Amazon project," *Daily News*, December 11, 2018, www.nydailynews.com/news/politics/nypol-cuomo-deblasio-amazon-advisory-committee-20181211-story.html. Accessed December 1, 2019.
2. J. David Goodman, "Amazon Pulls Out of Planned New York City Headquarters," *New York Times*, February 14, 2019, www.nytimes.com/2019/02/14/nyregion/amazon-hq2-queens.html. Accessed December 1, 2019.
3. Karen Weisse, "High-Tech Degrees and the Price of an Avocado: The Data New York Gave to Amazon," *New York Times*, December 12, 2018, www.nytimes.com/2018/12/12/technology/amazon-new-york-hq2-data.html. Accessed December 1, 2019.
4. James Patchett, "NYCEDC President James Patchett Testimony—NYC Council Finance Committee Hearing," *NYCEDC*, January 30, 2019, https://edc.nyc/

press-release/nycedc-president-james-patchett-testimony-nyc-council-finance-committee-hearing Accessed December 1, 2019.
5. Ibid.
6. J. David Goodman, "Amazon has a New Strategy to Sway Skeptics in New York," *New York Times*, January 29, 2019, www.nytimes.com/2019/01/29/nyregion/amazon-new-york-long-island-city.html. Accessed December 1, 2019.
7. Josh Barro, "Here's Why New York is Resorting to Paying Amazon $3 Billion for what Google will do for Free," *New York Magazine*, November 13, 2018, http://n.ymag.com/intelligencer/2018/11/why-new-york-is-paying-amazon-usd3-billion.html. Accessed December 1, 2019.
8. Jimmy Tobias, "The Amazon Deal was not Brought Down by a Handful of Politicians: It was Felled by a Robust Grassroots Coalition," *The Nation*, February 25, 2019, www.thenation.com/article/the-amazon-deal-was-not-brought-down-by-a-handful-of-politicians/ Accessed December 1, 2019.
9. Jimmy Van Bramer, twitter account, 2018, thttps://twitter.com/JimmyVanBramer/status/1061031513029050374. Accessed December 1, 2019.
10. Gabby Del Valle, "New York Already has Thousands of Amazon Workers—and Some are Unionizing to Demand Better Conditions," *Vox*, December 12, 2018, www.vox.com/the-goods/2018/12/12/18138246/amazon-hq2-new-york-city-hearing. Accessed December 1, 2019.
11. Samantha Maldonado, "Amazon's Anti-union Stance Exacerbates Opposition," *Politico*, January 30, 2019, www.politico.com/states/new-york/city-hall/story/2019/01/30/amazons-anti-union-stance-exacerbates-opposition-825839. Accessed December 1, 2019.
12. Paige Leskin, "Amazon's Public Policy Exec Got Booed at a Meeting with New York Council Members," *Business Insider*, December 12, 2018, www.businessinsider.com/amazon-ice-government-provides-facial-recognition-tech-2018-12. Accessed December 1, 2019.
13. Daniel Medina, "The Grassroots Coalition that took on Amazon ... and Won," *The Guardian*, March 24, 2019, www.theguardian.com/technology/2019/mar/23/the-grassroots-coalition-that-took-on-amazon-and-won. Accessed December 1, 2019.
14. Queens Neighborhoods United, "No AmazonHQ2 Principles and Statement," *Queens Anti-Gentrification Project*, December 12, 2018, https://queensantigentrification.org/2018/12/24/fuck-off-amazon-no-amazonhq2-principles-of-engagement-statement/. Accessed December 1, 2019.
15. New York State, "Governor Cuomo and Mayor De Blasio Announce Community Advisory Committee to Guide Amazon Project," December 11, 2018, www.governor.ny.gov/news/governor-cuomo-and-mayor-de-blasio-announce-community-advisory-committee-guide-amazon. Accessed December 1, 2019.
16. Ibid.
17. Mark Hallum, "'You can't speak for us': Astoria & Long Island City Residents Blast Opponents of Amazon HQ Proposal," *QNS*, February 19, 2019, https://

qns.com/story/2019/02/11/you-cant-speak-for-us-astoria-long-island-city-residents-blast-opponents-of-amazon-hq-proposal/. Accessed December 1, 2019.
18. Bill Parry, "'They let us down': Queens NYCHA Reps Blast Gianaris & Van Bramer for Amazon Deal Failure" *QNS*, February 15, 2019, https://qns.com/story/2019/02/15/they-let-us-down-queens-nycha-reps-blast-gianaris-van-bramer-for-amazon-deal-failure/. Accessed December 1, 2019.
19. April Simpson, "After Amazon Left, Silence: A Public Housing Resident Says Politicians and Others who Claimed to Care About Jobs have Done Nothing Since," *New York Daily News*, July 29, 2019, www.nydailynews.com/opinion/ny-oped-after-amazon-left-silence-20190729-msx7fbuqrfhhrfzo6er2s4vmim-story.html. Accessed December 1, 2019.
20. Ed Shanahan, "Amazon Grows in New York, Reviving Debate Over Abandoned Queens Project," *New York Times*, December 9, 2019, www.nytimes.com/2019/12/06/nyregion/amazon-hudson-yards.html. Accessed December 1, 2019.

11
What Happens when Amazon Comes to Town? Environmental Impacts, Local Economies, and Resistance in Inland Southern California

Juliann Emmons Allison

Inland Southern California, which includes Riverside and San Bernardino counties, is one of the nation's, if not one of the world's, largest logistics clusters[1] or geographic concentrations of logistics-related companies and activities, including: transportation and fleet management, warehousing, materials handling, order processing and fulfillment, logistics network design, inventory management, supply and demand planning, third- and fourth-party logistics (3PL and 4PL) management, and other services.[2] By 2015, more than 598.3 million tons of freight valued at $1.7 trillion moved from the Los Angeles and Long Beach megaports through the region's 1 billion-plus square feet of warehouse and distribution center (DC) space annually.[3] The region's rise to prominence is attributable to its spatiality: proximity to the ports of Los Angeles and Long Beach, rail freight corridors, interstate highways, and airports; access to Southern California's large consumer and labor markets; relatively "cheap" land, and weak political resistance relative to increasing collaborations among local political and business leaders to promote warehousing.[4]

The expansion of warehousing in the region, under way since 1980, has both accelerated and changed due to the growth of e-commerce and the integration of online and brick-and-mortar transactions—i.e., omni-channel fulfillment, which might pair online purchase with in-store pick-up.[5] Contemporary logistics operations eschew warehouses designed for long-term storage in favor of spacious DCs, which process frequent, relatively small shipments, often under tight time constraints. The average "warehouse" size more than doubled during the 2007–17 decade to 184,000 square feet[6] to provide space for multiple and varied fulfillment activities as well as product storage. In comparison, Amazon fulfillment centers (FCs) are monstrous, ranging from 600,000 to 1.5 million square feet in Inland Southern California. These large facilities foster economies of scale by processing more goods at lower costs due, in part, to extended hours of operations and automation.[7]

Amazon has opened 15 "warehouses" in the region since establishing its first California FC in San Bernardino in 2012. Amazon facilities include, as noted in Table 11.1: automated "sortable" FCs that process smaller items; "nonsortable" FCs that handle large or bulky items; sortation centers tasked with consolidating orders onto trucks to accelerate delivery; receiving or inbound cross-dock (IXD) centers for redistributing large inventories; delivery stations where orders are prepared for "last mile" delivery, and, at least, one "media on demand" (MOD) center, which publishes and distributes vendors' video and audio products only when Amazon customers place an order.

Some of these facilities are the sortable FCs featured in typical first-person accounts and Amazon exposés, where robot-assisted "picking," packing, and shipping occur.[8] Among the other facilities are two Amazon "last mile" delivery stations that coordinate independent contractors who hire drivers and lease vans to supplement delivery services provided by FedEx, UPS, and other delivery partners.[9] Amazon's Inland Southern California "push" proved to be a "game changer" for logistics in the region. Half of the nearly 600 million tons of freight that crossed the region in 2015 was processed in Amazon FCs![10]

Table 11. 1   Amazon facilities in Inland Southern California

Facility Code	Location	Opened	Type	Purpose	Size	FT Employees[11]
ONT2	San Bernardino	Oct. 2012	FC	Small sortables/ Public Tours	1.5 million ft^2	1500+
ONT3	San Bernardino		MOD	Content Publishing and Distribution		

Facility Code	Location	Opened	Type	Purpose	Size	FT Employees[11]
ONT5	San Bernardino	Oct. 2013	Sortation Center	Delivery Consolidation		Varies
ONT8	Moreno Valley	Aug. 2014	FC	Small sortables	1.2 million ft^2	1500+
ONT6	Moreno Valley	Oct. 2014	IXD	Large, high-demand inventory	800,000 ft^2	Varies
ONT9	Redlands	Oct. 2014	FC	Large items	800,000 ft^2	1000+
SNA4	Rialto	Nov. 2015	FC	Large items	900,000 ft^2	1000+
SNA7	San Bernardino	Mar. 2016	FC	Small sortables	1 million ft^2	1500+
	Riverside	Apr. 2016	Delivery Station	"Last mile" Small items	36,000 ft^2	500
SNA6	Eastvale	Oct. 2016	FC	Small sortables	1 million ft^2	1500+
	Chino	Mar. 2017	Delivery Station	"Last mile"		500
LGB4	Redlands	June 2017	FC	Large items	800,000 ft^2	1000+
LGB8	Rialto	Oct 2017	IXD	Large, high-demand inventory	600,000 ft^2	Varies
LGB6	Riverside County	Mar. 2018	FC	Large items	1 million ft^2	600–900[12]
LGB3	Eastvale	Mar. 2018	FC	Small sortables	1 million ft^2	3,000[13]
LAX9	Fontana	June 2019	FC	Small Sortables	6,000 ft^2	1,000+[14]
LGB7	Rialto	June 2019	FC	Small sortables	850,000 ft^2	1,000+[15]
	Beaumont	TBA	FC	Small sortables	640,000 ft^2	1,000+[16]
PCA3	Fontana					

AMAZON: LINCHPIN IN SOUTHERN CALIFORNIA'S SPATIAL INEQUALITY

Amazon's dominance among Inland Southern California's e-commerce companies and logistics operations makes the company complicit in sustaining the spatial injustice that has long plagued the region.[17] Attention to spatiality extends social justice perspectives by recognizing that social, economic, and environmental conditions and inequalities have spatial dimensions that both reflect and enable the prioritization of some individual, group, and corporate demands over the needs of particular types of communities and societies.[18] Journalist Noah Smith's[19] characterization of Inland Southern

What Happens when Amazon Comes to Town?

California as the Southland's "back lot," a vast logistics staging ground and distribution hub that serves the more prosperous counties on its borders is apt. The summary provided in Table 11.2 indicates that, in contrast to these coastal counties, Inland Southern California is younger, browner, poorer, far more dependent on warehousing, distribution, and transportation services, and subject to higher levels of air pollution. Warehousing in Inland Southern California represents over twice as much of the industrial capacity as is the case in Orange County and the San Diego-Carlsbad Metropolitan Statistical Area (MSA), 1½ times as much as in the Los Angeles-Long Beach-Anaheim MSA. San Bernardino County experienced nine times as many high ozone days as neighboring Orange County did.

Table 11. 2   Spatial Inequality in Southern California

Metropolitan Statistical Area (MSA)	Racial/Ethnic Diversity	Ave. Age	Median Income	Poverty	Poorest Social Group	Primary Employment Sectors[20]	High Ozone Days 2015–17[c21]
Riverside-San Bernardino-Ontario	Latinx/Hispanic: 51% White: 32%	35	$62K	17%	Hispanic Women 25-34	Retail Trade: 13% Health Care: 13% Warehouse: 8%	SB: 161 Riv: 130
Los Angeles-Long Beach-Anaheim	Latinx/Hispanic: 45% White: 29%	37	$70K	16%	Hispanic Women 25-34	Health Care: 12% Retail Trade: 10% Manufacture: 10% Warehouse: 5%	LA: 119
Orange County	Latinx/Hispanic: 34% White: 40%	38	$86K	12%	White Women 18-24	Manufacture: 13% Health Care: 12% Retail Trade: 10% Science-Tech: 10% Warehouse: 3%	OC: 18
San Diego-Carlsbad	Latinx/Hispanic: 34% White: 45%	36	$76K	13%	Hispanic Women 25-34	Heath Care: 13% Retail Trade: 11% Science-Tech: 10% Warehouse: 3%	SD: 37[d]

Amazon's siting of warehouses, FCs, and delivery stations in Inland Southern California to serve more prosperous regions is consistent with the disproportionate siting of warehouses in socioeconomically disadvantaged communities throughout Southern California.[22] This phenomenon reeks of spatial injustice; however, until recently, there was not much research on the processes that relate warehousing, distribution, and associated transportation activities to social, environmental, and health disparities in poor communities of color. Yuan's[23] longitudinal examination of warehouse siting in Southern California suggests that "unregulated logistics expansion" is responsible for environmental disparities across communities differentiated by social and economic factors.

Most of the bases for siting decisions that Yuan[24] identifies would be ideal for any logistics cluster—i.e., the affordable real estate; proximity to rail freight corridors, interstate highways, and airports; availability of low-wage labor, and access to a large customer market—previously noted.[25] In addition, Yuan[26] emphasizes "inexpensive housing," which may draw low- and lower-middle-income people, often also of color, to neighborhoods near warehouses and DCs, and the political institutions that condition interactions among logistics companies, real estate agents, and municipalities. Local governments develop and implement the zoning restrictions, tax and other economic incentives, and environmental regulations that encourage or discourage proposed developments; once a warehouse, DC, or logistics center gains approval and is under construction, commercial realtors mediate negotiations between the developers or owners of these facilities and prospective tenants.[27] Cooper Smith, a specialist in business analytics, argues that Amazon's interactions with municipalities and developers have been calculated to capitalize on wealthy millennials' reliance on e-commerce.[28] Moreover, a recent analysis by *The Economist*[29] indicates that Amazon's arrival drives warehouse workers' wages down by an average 3 percent, deepening the divide between regions like Inland Southern California and their more affluent neighbors.

The warehouses and DCs that are essential to Amazon and other e-commerce companies are distinguished from other "locally undesirable land uses" (LULUs) because their negative social and environmental impacts flow primarily from their appearance and role in traffic congestion, rather than their operations. Some warehouses do store flammable, explosive, and/or toxic goods; however, warehouses and DCs more often degrade (sub)urban landscapes and require hazardous transportation activities *outside*.[30] The movement, operation, and maintenance of freight trucks make neighborhoods near warehouses and DCs louder, more polluted, and dangerous to navigate. Warehousing, distribution, and transportation processes contributed to local warming, increased air pollution and related respiratory illnesses, and road damage.[31] The public health consequences associated with diesel truck traffic and congestion pose the greatest threat to Inland Southern California neighborhoods adjacent to, or along transportation corridors connecting, warehouses and DCs in the region. Penny Newman, founding Director of the Center for Community Action and Environmental Justice (CCAEJ), referenced the region's high levels of deadly ozone and particulate matter to explain why "children born in San Bernardino or Riverside county will be exposed to as many carcinogens in the first 12 days of their life as most people are in 70 years."[32]

The magnitude of Amazon FC and delivery operations makes the company complicit in the increasing truck (and delivery van) traffic congestion, air pollution, and incidences of respiratory illnesses in Inland Southern California. In addition to Amazon's contribution to these impacts from transportation services associated with its warehouse and FC operations, the company is more directly responsible for emissions and related health disparities associated with its deliveries—45 percent of which are handled by Amazon.[33] Amazon's initial investment in delivery centers included dual gasoline-diesel fuel Mercedes Benz Sprinter Vans, an investment which was criticized by more climate-forward competitors, including Walmart and UPS, and its own employees, as well as environmental activists. A year later after "thumbing its nose"[34] at climate action and in response to concerted pressure from environmentally conscious high-tech Amazon employees, the company's 2019 Climate Pledge to have, at least, half its shipping operations carbon neutral by 2030 includes transition from Sprinter Vans to electric Rivians beginning in 2021.[35]

AMAZON JOBS: LOW-WAGE AND SUBJECT TO AUTOMATION

The primary justification that city and county officials provide for continuing to permit new construction of warehouses and DCs in Inland Southern California is "jobs." When the region's (and the state's) first Amazon "megawarehouse" opened, it was lauded by then San Bernardino Mayor Pat Morris as a "rare and wonderful thing"[36] that would put "hundreds of people to work."[37] Jobs remained the story six years later, when Eastvale's "robotic" FC opened. Responding to fears that automation might cost the region jobs, economist John Husing said, "Well this is a very technologically oriented facility, and there are more than 3,000 employees working …."[38] In addition to employees' wages—$15/hour minimum, relatively high for warehouse workers regionally[39]—and applicable sales taxes, Amazon contributed to growth in businesses, such as "hair salons, restaurants, industrial supply firms, and grocery stores generating a secondary [boon] of $2.7 billion" by 2016.[40] Amazon's investment in the region has also included street and traffic control improvements, landscaping and other infrastructure upgrades required for its operations. Considering Amazon's role in perpetuating the Southland's spatial inequality, Anthony Victoria, CCAEJ Communications Director says, "that's not enough …."[41]

Job promises are at the heart of Amazon's impact on Inland Southern California.[42] Warehousing, distribution, and transportation were responsible for 20 percent of job growth in Inland Southern California between the 2007–09 recession and the end of 2018, with Amazon providing over 30 percent of the 53,400 "warehouse" jobs recorded by the California Employment and Development Department (EDD) in November 2018.[43] There's the rub. Amazon FC jobs do not necessarily increase overall employment growth. According to Jones and Zipperer,[44] each Amazon FC increases warehousing jobs by 30 percent; however, these gains are entirely offset by job losses in other industries. Additionally, the region's higher employment rate has not been accompanied by increased earnings. Even Amazon's lauded $15/hour minimum wage barely qualifies as a living wage in Inland Southern California, and then only for a single adult, a working couple, or a family of three in which two adults are employed full time and all year.[45] Part-time warehouse workers, temporary employees, or "temps," and seasonal employees are in a far more precarious position.[46] Amazon reports that most of its associates work full time and a 2018 federally mandated pay disclosure indicates that the company's median employee pay during the previous year was $28,446. In contrast, Amazon managers and executives earned an average $110,000 annually.[47]

Inland Southern California's warehouse boosters claim that the region's warehouses and DCs represent the bottom rungs of ladders to the middle class. Yet, there is little evidence to support this claim.[48] The lack of social diversity among managers at Amazon also does not bode well for the region's predominantly Latinx warehouse workers.[49] According to Amazon's global workforce data, whites make up 39 percent of the company's employees and 62 percent of its managers.[50] The narrative that warehouse work provides a path to the middle class is also undermined by increasing reliance on automation in warehouses and DCs, which reduces employment opportunities in warehousing.[51] In the 2014–16 period, Amazon, which leads the automation curve, added over half as many robots as associates to its California warehouses alone.[52] While Amazon claims that fully automated fulfillment processes remain, at least, a decade away,[53] it has been making rapid advancements in warehouse automation, such as its adoption of Italian CartonWrap machines capable of packing boxes four to five times faster than a manual laborer can.[54] Amazon will certainly require a number of highly skilled employees to install, service, and operate its growing robot workforce, but not enough to offset long-term job losses expected in warehousing[55] and among retail among Amazon's competitors.[56] Industry-wide, up to 79 percent of warehousing and storage operations and up to 59 percent of fulfillment activities were automated by mid-2019, according to a survey of warehouse operators by Peerless Research Group.[57]

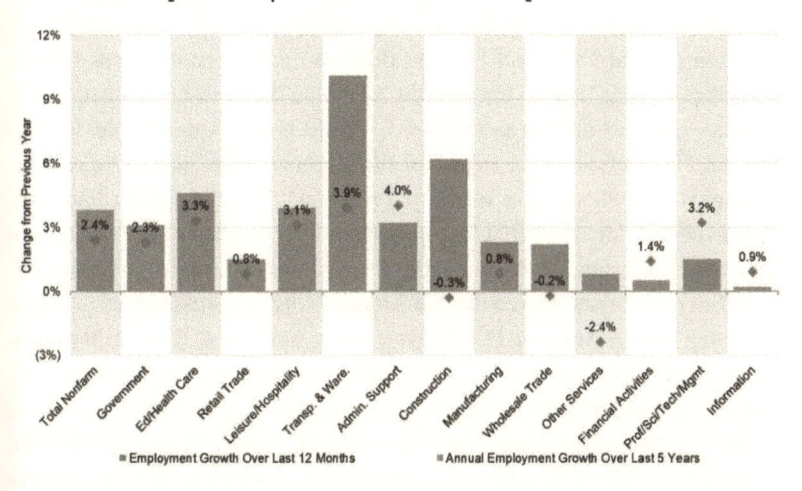

Figure 11.1 Slowing growth in warehousing, distribution, and transportation in Inland Southern California

Source: Reproduced from Rafael De Anda, "Year over Year Job Growth Across California's Inland Empire Hits 2.4%." *CoStar*, 21 August 2019. https://www.costar.com/article/173856585/year-over-year-job-growth-across-californias-inland-empire-hits-24 (accessed April 19, 2020).[58]

GRASSROOTS RESISTANCE TO AMAZON'S ADVANCE INTO INLAND SOUTHERN CALIFORNIA

The effects of Amazon's rapid rise in Inland Southern California, and growing popular resistance to Amazon in the region provides several important lessons for other communities. First, the rapid expansion of Amazon warehouses has exacerbated traffic congestion, air pollution and respiratory disease, and declining job prospects in Inland Southern California. This situation provides evidence that state and local governments do not receive a "commensurate return" for their investment in Amazon.[59] Cities where Amazon FCs are located have returned as much as 80 percent of the California sales tax earned to the company as an incentive for the company to invest there.[60] In California, roughly a tenth of the state's 7.25-percent sales tax is directed to the city or jurisdiction where a retailer operates; the remainder goes to the relevant counties and the state. Until 2012, when Amazon opened its first DC in San Bernardino, sales tax generated by Amazon sales to California residents was shared among all of the state's cities; immediately afterward, it was shared between San Bernardino and Patterson, where Amazon opened its second FC later that year.[61] Amazon designated these two cities as their legal "points of sale," meaning they earned 100 percent of the tax—about $8 million annually *each*—collected for Amazon sales in California. That's a hefty price to pay for the presence of an "aggressive retailer [that grows] at the expense of existing retailers."[62] Yet San Bernardino officials expected Amazon's first San Bernardino FC to catalyze recovery from the Great Recession, which had badly affected the city's working-class communities of color and driven the "All America City" to bankruptcy.[63] Despite "winning" three Amazon FCs between 2012 and 2016, San Bernardino's poverty rate increased from 23.4 percent in 2011, the year before Amazon's first FC opened there, to 30.6 percent in 2019.[64]

The rise of local resistance to "warehousing," generally, and Amazon in particular in Inland Southern California also provides important lessons for activists in other communities by demonstrating the critical role that labor-community alliances can play in building a broad-based popular resistance movement. Local resistance to "warehousing" is founded on long-standing collaborations among the region's environmental justice and labor rights organizations. CCAEJ is Inland Southern California's most prominent social and environmental justice organization. Long before Amazon arrived, CCAEJ recognized that the pollution associated with the warehousing, distribution, and transportation far outweighed the benefits from potential economic development.[65] A 2011 campaign aimed at a project that would have added 1.4 million square feet of storage space adjacent to Mira Loma, a village in Jurupa Valley that experienced 800 trucks passing *every hour* less than 20 feet from residents' homes; the campaign included a successful lawsuit against Riverside County and the developer.[66] The Warehouse Workers Resource Center (WWRC) is an education and advocacy organization devoted to improving working conditions via collective action and litigation for Southern Californians employed in the logistics sector. For example, with WWRC's support, 600 workers at the Walmart distribution center in Mira Loma won more than $4.7 million from Schneider Logistics, the contractor that had systematically stolen their wages.[67]

Amazon's advance into the region has provided opportunities for intentional, strategic collaboration among CCAEJ, the WWRC and other environmental justice, community and labor organizations. These organizations, together with community members and sometimes also municipalities, have joined in resisting new warehousing developments and logistics centers in Bloomington, a small predominantly Latino community in Riverside County,[68] Fontana,[69] Moreno Valley,[70] and San Bernardino.[71] The most recent of these joint initiatives concerns the proposed Eastgate Air Cargo Logistics Center, a 2-million-square foot warehouse and distribution facility adjacent the San Bernardino International Airport that entails a 35-year lease between the developer—Hillwood Enterprises—and its undisclosed tenant, rumored to be Amazon.[72] The Eastgate center will purportedly bring as many as 4,000 new jobs, in exchange for, at least 26 additional flights daily—and considerable airport traffic, air pollution, and noise.[73]

Opposition to the Eastgate Air Cargo Logistics Center reflects the dual strategy that Reese and Struna[74] argue was effective in earlier campaigns against warehousing in Inland Southern California. First, this opposition consists of a broad coalition directed at a visible, significant target. Community organizations opposed to the new development include: Inland Congregations United for Change (ICUC), San Bernardino Generation Now (SBGN), Teamsters 1932, Service Employees International Union (SEIU) 2015, the IE Central Labor Council, Sierra Club's My Gen Campaign, and the Inland Coalition for Immigrant Justice (IC4IJ), as well as CCAEJ and WWRC. Together with community members, they demand a community benefits agreement (CBA), or a contract with Hillwood Enterprises to limit pollution associated with the Eastgate center, require Hillwood to provide air quality monitors and air filters to those living nearest the center and airport, and ensure that its tenant provide living wages with benefits to the center's employees.[75]

Second, the coalition's appeals—for environmental quality, public health and labor justice—are based on moral and legal claims designed to motivate public support and policy change. Inland Southern California residents—individually, collectively, and under the auspices of CCAEJ, the Sierra Club, and other organizations—have added their concerns about the Eastgate center to long-standing demands for policy makers to do *something* to reduce the air pollution and related health impacts associated with warehousing, distribution, and transportation. Some demands have engendered lawsuits, such as CCAEJ and residents' challenging the Mira Loma warehouse complex, which yielded air filters for impacted homes among other measures to improve environmental quality and health.[76] More recently, the South Coast Air Quality Management District (SCAQMD) rolled out voluntary measures and regulations to reduce hazardous emissions from indirect sources, including the Amazon "mega-warehouses" located throughout Riverside and San Bernardino counties. While logistics industry leaders are worried, critics charge that the proposed rules are weak and unenforceable.[77]

The potential effectiveness of this strategy lies in its combination of coalitional and institutional power sources[78] to leverage the influence of workers, residents, and others marginalized by the financial and political processes spurring the growth of logistics operations in Inland Southern California. So far environmental, labor, ecumenical, immigrant and other organizations opposed to the Eastgate Air Cargo Logistics Center have united in action. Moral and legal claims pertaining to workers' and residents' rights to fair compensation and environmental health hold the capacity to elicit broad-based public support for stronger regulation of logistics industries to improve environmental protection, public health, and workers' safety and compensation. Amazon's Climate Pledge as well as its wage increase and training programs for warehouse workers threatened by automation represent responses to public criticism and demands for justice. These innovations are commendable; however, redressing Amazon's complicity in sustaining the spatial injustice faced by Inland Southern Californians will require persistent organized resistance, as well as greater legal and regulatory protections from exploitation.

What Happens when Amazon Comes to Town?

NOTES

1. "North America's Top Distribution Hubs," Supply Chain Link. 5 July 2016. https://www.nfiindustries.com/blog/north-americas-top-distribution-hubs/ (accessed November 2019).
2. Y. Yossi Sheffi, *Logistics clusters: delivering value and driving growth* (Cambridge: MIT press, 2012).
3. Los Angeles Economic Development Corporation, "Goods on the Move: Trade and Logistics in Southern California." *Institute for Applied Economics,* June 2017, https://laedc.org/wp-content/uploads/2017/06/TL_20170515_Final.pdf (accessed November 2019).
4. Tyler Finn, "Inland Empire Outlook: Logistics Flies High," *Rose Institute of State and Local Government. Claremont McKenna College,* 4 March 2016, http://roseinstitute.org/inland-empire-outlook-logistics-flies-high/ (accessed November 2019); Miguel Jaller and Leticia Pineda. "Warehousing and Distribution Center Facilities in Southern California: The Use of the Commodity Flow Survey Data to Identify Logistics Sprawl and Freight Generation Patterns," *National Center for Sustainable Transportation, University of California-Davis,* 2017. https://escholarship.org/uc/item/5dz0j1gg (accessed November 2019).
5. Finn (2016).
6. "Average Size of Newly Built Warehouses Swells due to E-Commerce," *CBRE,* 20 December 2017. https://www.cbre.us/about/media-center/average-size-of-newly-built-us-warehouses-swells-due-to-ecommerce (accessed November 2019).
7. Jaller and Pineda (2017).
8. Alex Press, "No Space to be Human," *The Nation,* 20 December 2018. https://www.thenation.com/article/heike-geissler-seasonal-associate-amazon/
9. Aldo Svaldi, "Amazon delivery centers look to bridge last mile," *Denver Post,* 19 November 2019. https://www.denverpost.com/2018/11/09/amazon-delivery-center-centennial/ (accessed November 2019).
10. Los Angeles Economic Development Corporation, "Goods on the Move: Trade and Logistics in Southern California," *Institute for Applied Economics,* 2017. https://laedc.org/wp-content/uploads/2017/06/TL_20170515_Final.pdf (accessed November 2019).
11. About Amazon Staff, "Fulfillment in our buildings," Amazon, 2019. *https://www.aboutamazon.com/amazon-fulfillment/our-fulfillment-centers/fulfillment-in-our-buildings/* (accessed November 2019).
12. Fielding Buck, "Why Amazon already has a Strong Presence in Southern California," The Sun, 18 January 2018, https://www.sbsun.com/2018/01/18/why-amazon-already-has-a-strong-presence-in-southern-cali*fornia*/ (accessed November 2019).

13. Press Release, "Amazon Shows off New Robotics Fulfillment Center in Eastvale," InlandEmpire.US, 22 May 2019. https://inlandempire.us/amazon-shows-off-new-robotics-fulfilment-center-in-eastvale/ (accessed November 2019).
14. Steve Ganey, "Amazon Hiring more than 2,000 Workers for Upcoming Fulfillment Centers in Fontana and Rialto. KTLA5," 4 June 2019, https://ktla.com/2019/06/04/amazon-hiring-more-than-2000-workers-for-upcoming-fulfillment-centers-in-fontana-and-rialto/ (accessed November 2019).
15. Ganey (2019).
16. Jack Katzanek, "Amazon grows its Inland Empire state with new center coming to Beaumont," The Press Enterprise, 2 November 2018. https://www.pe.com/2018/11/02/amazon-building-new-distribution-facility-in-beaumont-will-hire-1000/ (accessed November 2019).
17. David Pierson and Andrew Khouri. "Amazon plans fifth warehouse in the Inland Empire," *The Los Angeles Times*, 31 March 2016. https://www.latimes.com/business/la-fi-amazon-center-20160401-story.html (accessed November 2019).
18. Andrew Biro, "Spaces of environmental justice," *Contemporary Political Theory*, 14(4) (2015), pp. e45-e47; Jennifer Manuel, "Social and Spatial Justice: Grassroots Community Action," *Newcastle University*, May 2016. http://depts.washington.edu/tatlab/socialjustice/wp-content/uploads/2016/02/Manuel-Social-and-Spatial-Justice-Supporting-Grassroots-Community-Action.pdf (accessed November 2019).
19. Noah Smith, "In California's Inland Empire, Economic Recovery Brimming with Industrial Complexes," *The New York Times*, 4 April 2015. https://www.nytimes.com/2015/08/05/realestate/commercial/an-economic-recovery-brimming-with-industrial-complexes-in-southern-california.html (accessed November 2019).
20. "The most common employment sectors for those who live in Riverside-San Bernardino-Ontario in 2017," DataUSA, 2017. https://datausa.io/ (accessed November 2019).
21. Paul Krueger, "Lung Association Says San Diego's Air is Among the Nation's Dirtiest," *NBC San Diego* 7, 18 April 2018. https://www.nbcsandiego.com/news/local/lung-association-says-san-diegos-air-is-among-the-nations-dirtiest/45473/(accessed November 2019); Martin Wisckol, "5-county greater Los Angeles area ranks as nation's worst for smog, again," *Los Angeles Daily News*, 23 April 2019, https://www.dailynews.com/2019/04/23/5-county-greater-los-angeles-area-ranks-as-nations-worst-for-smog-again/ (accessed November 2019).
22. Kim Moody, *On new terrain: How capital is reshaping the battleground of class war* (Chicago: Haymarket Books, 2017); Quan Yuan, "Environmental justice in warehousing location: State of the art. *Journal of Planning Literature*, 33(3) (2018a), pp. 287-298.

23. Quan Yuan, "Location of warehouses and environmental justice," *Journal of Planning Education and Research* 33(3) (2018b), pp. 287-298.
24. Yuan (2018a, 2018b).
25. Edna Bonacich and Jake B. Wilson, *Getting the goods: Ports, labor, and the logistics revolution*. (Ithaca: Cornell University Press 2008); Juan DeLara, *Inland Shift: Race, Space, and Capital in Southern California* (Oakland: University of California, 2018; Finn (2016); Jaller and Pineda (2017); Sheffi (2012).
26. Yuan (2018b)
27. De Lara (2018); Yuan 2018b; and Zhaohua Zhang, Derrick Robinson, and Diane Hite, "Racial Residential Segregation: Measuring Location Choice Attributes of Environmental Quality and Self-Segregation," *Sustainability* 10(4) (2018), p. 1114.
28. Sisson, Patrick, "How Amazon's 'invisible' hand can shape your city," *Curbed.*, 2 May 2017. https://www.curbed.com/2017/5/2/15509316/amazon-prime-retail-urban-planning (accessed November 2019).
29. "Unfulfillment Centers: What Amazon does to Jobs," *The Economist,* 20 January 2018. https://www.economist.com/united-states/2018/01/20/what-amazon-does-to-wages (accessed November 2019).
30. Sisson (2017); Yuan (2018a).
31. Yuan (2018b).
32. Eric Kirkendall, "Environmental & community groups file suit to prevent more diesel exhaust pollution in Inland Empire," *Moving Forward Network*, 2016. http://www.movingforwardnetwork.com/2016/06/environmental-community-groups-file-suit-to-prevent-more-diesel-exhaust-pollution-in-inland-empire/ (accessed November 2019); Penny Newman, "Inland Ports of Southern California–Warehouses, Distribution Centers, Intermodal Facilities Impacts, Costs and Trends," *Center for Community Action and Environmental* Justice, 2012. http://ccaej.org/wp-content/uploads/2016/11/Inland-Ports-of-Southern-California.pdf (accessed November 2019).
33. John Paul Hempstead, "Amazon in-sourcing nearly half of its parcel transportation needs," *American Shipper*, 28 June 2019. https://www.freightwaves.com/news/amazon-in-sourcing-nearly-half-of-its-transportation-needs (accessed November 2019).
34. Steve Hanley, "Amazon Thumbs Its Nose At Sustainability, Orders 20,000 Conventional Mercedes Sprinter Vans," *Clean Technica*, 10 September 2018. https://cleantechnica.com/2018/09/10/amazon-thumbs-its-nose-at-sustainability-orders-20000-conventional-mercedes-sprinter-vans/ (accessed November 2019).
35. David McCabe and Karen Weiss, "Amazon Accelerates Efforts to Fight Climate Change," *The New York Times*, 19 September 2019. https://www.nytimes.com/2019/09/19/technology/amazon-carbon-neutral.html (accessed Novewmber 2019); Alan Peters and Peter Fisher, "The failures of economic

development incentives," *Journal of the American Planning Association* 70(1) (2004), pp. 27-37; see also Chapter 7 in this volume.
36. Alana Semuels, "What Amazon Does to Poor Cities," *The Atlantic*, 1 February 2018, https://www.theatlantic.com/business/archive/2018/02/amazon-warehouses-poor-cities/552020/ (accessed November 2019).
37. Steven Cuevas, "Amazon holds grand opening for San Bernardino mega warehouse," *89.3 KPCC*, 18 October 2012, https://www.scpr.org/news/2012/10/18/34677/amazon-holds-grand-opening-san-bernardino-mega-war/ (accessed November 2019).
38. InlandEmpire.US (2018).
39. Juan De Lara, J. "Warehouse work: Path to the middle class or road to economic insecurity?" *USC Program for Environmental and Regional Equity*, September 2013. https://dornsifecms.usc.edu/assets/sites/242/docs/WarehouseWorkerPay_web.pdf (accessed November 2019).
40. Day One Staff, "Amazon's impact in Southern California," *Amazon Day One*, 8 February 2018. https://blog.aboutamazon.com/job-creation-and-investment/amazons-impact-in-southern-california
41. Buck (2018).
42. Janelle Jones and Ben Zipperer, "Unfulfilled Promise: Amazon fulfilment centers do not generate broad-based employment growth," *Economic Policy Institute*, 1, 2018.
43. Buck (2018).
44. Jones and Zipperer (2018).
45. Amy Glasmeier, "Living Wage Calculator," *Massachusetts Institute of Technology*, 2019, https://livingwage.mit.edu/ (accessed November 2019); see also John Husing, "Opinion: Amazon has powerful impact on the Inland Empire Economy," *The Orange County Register*, 5 February 2018. https://www.ocregister.com/2018/02/05/opinion-amazon-has-powerful-impact-on-the-inland-empire-economy/(accessed December 2019).
46. De Lara (2013).
47. Matt Day, "Amazon workers' median pay in 2017: $28,446," *The Seattle Times*, 18 April 2018, https://www.seattletimes.com/business/amazon/amazon-workers-median-pay-in-2017-28446/ (accessed November 2019).
48. De Lara (2018), Husing (2019).
49. Juliann Allison, Joel Herrera, and Ellen Reese, "Why the City of Ontario Needs to Raise the Minimum Wage: Earnings among Warehouse Workers in Inland Southern California" (2015); Edna Bonacich and Juan David De Lara, "Economic crisis and the logistics industry: Financial insecurity for warehouse workers in the Inland Empire" (2009); De Lara (2013).
50. Amazon Staff, "Our workforce data," *Amazon Day One*, nd. https://www.aboutamazon.com/working-at-amazon/diversity-and-inclusion/our-workforce-data (accessed December 2019).

51. Marc Wells, "California's Inland Empire: a Model of Low Wage "Growth." *World Socialist*, 22 April 2015.
52. Natalie Kitroeff, "Warehouses Promised Lots of Jobs, but Robot Workforce Slows Hiring," *Los Angeles Times*, December 4, 2016, www.latimes.com/projects/la-fi-warehouse-robots/. Accessed November 2019.
53. Nick Statt, "Amazon says Fully Automated Shipping Warehouses are at least a Decade Away," *The Verge*, 1 May 2019. https://www.theverge.com/2019/5/1/18526092/amazon-warehouse-robotics-automation-ai-10-years-away (accessed November 2019).
54. Jeffrey Dastin, "Exclusive: Amazon rolls out machines that pack orders and replace jobs," *Reuters*, 13 May 2019. https://www.reuters.com/article/us-amazon-com-automation-exclusive/exclusive-amazon-rolls-out-machines-that-pack-orders-and-replace-jobs-idUSKCN1SJ0X1(accessed November 2019).
55. Gutelis, Beth and Nik Theodore. 2019. "The Future of Warehouse Work: Technological Change in the U.S. Logistics Industry." UC Berkeley Labor Center and Working Partnerships USA. http://laborcenter.berkeley.edu/pdf/2019/Future-of-Warehouse-Work.pdf (accessed April 19, 2020).
56. David Edwards and Helen Edwards, "There are 170,000 fewer retail jobs in 2017, and 75,000 more Amazon robots," *Quartz*, 4 December 2017. https://qz.com/1107112/there-are-170000-fewer-retail-jobs-in-2017-and-75000-more-amazon-robots/ (accessed November 2019).
57. Bridget McCrea, "Annual Warehouse and Distribution Center Automation Survey: More automation, please", *Modern Materials Handling*, 2019. https://www.mmh.com/article/annual_warehouse_and_distribution_center_automation_survey_more_automation (accessed November 2019).
58. De Anda (2019).
59. Jones and Zipperer (2018).
60. Marc Lifsher, "Amazon poised to get a cut of California sales tax," *The Los Angeles Times*, 19 May 2012, https://www.latimes.com/business/la-xpm-2012-may-19-la-fi-amazon-sales-taxes-20120520-story.html (accessed November 2019).
61. Lifsher (2012).
62. Thomas Cafcas and Greg LeRoy, "Will Amazon Fool Us Twice: Why State and Local Governments Should Stop Subsidizing the Online Giant's Growing Distribution Network," *Good Jobs First*, 2016, https://www.goodjobsfirst.org/sites/default/files/docs/pdf/amazon-subsidies.pdf (accessed November 2019).
63. Joe Mozingo, "San Bernardino: Broken City," *Los Angeles Times*, 14 June 2015. http://graphics.latimes.com/san-bernardino/ accessed November 2019; Amazon staff, "Our Workforce Data" (2019); Cuevas (2012).
64. DataUSA (2019) https://datausa.io/ (accessed November 2019).
65. Newman (2012); Buck (2018); Anthony Victoria "Amazon Delivers Low Paying Jobs and Dirty Air to California's Poorest," *Truthout*, 11 September 2018,

https://truthout.org/articles/amazon-delivers-low-paying-jobs-and-dirty-air-to-californias-poorest/ (accessed November 2019).
66. Newman (2012); Brinda Sarathy, "Legacies of Environmental Justice in Inland Southern California," *Race, Gender & Class* (2013), pp.254-268.
67. Dave Jamieson, "Walmart Warehouse Contractor to Pay $21 Million to Settle Wage Theft Allegations," *Huffington Post*, 14 May 2014. http://www.huffingtonpost.com/2014/05/14/walmart-warehouse-wage-theft_n_5324021.html (accessed December 2019); Ellen Reese and Jason Struna. "'Work Hard, Make History': Oppression and Resistance in Inland Southern California's Warehouse and Distribution Industry," in Jake Alimahomed-Wilson and Emmanuel Ness (eds.), *Choke Points: Logistics Workers and Solidarity Movements Disrupting the Global Capitalist Supply Chain* (London: Pluto Press, 2018), pp.88-95.
68. Alejandra Molina, "Enough with the Warehouses," *Next City*, 10 August 2018. https://nextcity.org/daily/entry/this-inland-empire-community-says-enough-with-the-warehouses (accessed November 2019).
69. Sandra Emerson and Jack Katzanek, "San Bernardino County, environmental groups sue Fontana over massive warehouse complex," *Daily Bulletin*, 16 April 2019. http://ccaej.org/san-bernardino-county-environmental-groups-sue-fontana-over-massive-warehouse-complex/ (accessed November 2019).
70. Kevin Stark, "Among e-commerce surge, California cities want relief from truck pollution," *Energy News Network*, 14 March 2019. http://ccaej.org/amid-e-commerce-surge-california-cities-want-relief-from-truck-pollution/ (accessed November 2019).
71. Manny Sandoval, "Hundreds of San Bernardino residents speak out at FAA hearing on Eastgate air-cargo logistics project," *Inland Empire Community News*, 13 August 2019. https://iecn.com/hundreds-of-san-bernardino-residents-speak-out-at-faa-hearing-on-air-cargo-logistics-project-eastgate/ (accessed November 2019).
72. Steve Brown, "Amazon's formal announcement of two big warehouse developments. *The Dallas Daily News*, 31 January 2013. https://www.dallasnews.com/business/2013/01/31/new-amazon-warehouses-are-big-projects-for-developer-hillwood/ (accessed November 2019); Warehouse Workers Resource Center, "Holding San Bernardino to a Higher Standard," 9 July 2019. http://www.warehouseworkers.org/holding-san-bernardino-to-a-higher-standard/ (accessed November 2019).
73. Sandoval (2019).
74. Reese and Struna (2018).
75. DaJonae Shaw, "A Community Benefits Agreement at Eastgate is the beginning of changing how we do business," *Inland Empire Community News*, 30 July 2019. https://iecn.com/a-community-benefits-agreement-at-eastgate-is-the-start-of-changing-the-way-we-do-business/ (accessed November 2019); see also Chapter 11, in this volume.

76. Emily Guerin, "Cracking down on warehouses to stem pollution—will it work?" *89.3 KPCC*, 4 May 2018. https://www.scpr.org/news/2018/05/04/82129/truck-pollution-is-harming-californians-is-crackin/ (accessed January 2020).
77. Guerin (2018); Steve Scauzillo, "AQMD to tackle pollution from warehouses, rail yards, ports, and airports, not everyone is happy," *Daily Bulletin*, 27 June 2019. https://www.dailybulletin.com/2019/06/27/aqmd-to-tackle-pollution-from-warehouses-rail-yards-ports-and-airports-not-everyone-is-happy/ (accessed January 2020).
78. Marissa Brookes, "Varieties of Power in Transnational Labor Alliances: An Analysis of Workers' Structural, Institutional, and Coalitional Power in the Global Economy," *Labor Studies Journal* 38(3) (2012), pp. 181-200; Reese and Struna (2018).

12
Worker and Community Organizing to Challenge Amazon's Algorithmic Threat

Sheheryar Kaoosji

Since Walmart established its ground-breaking logistics data systems in the mid-1980s, logistics and goods movement has been a key sector where corporations innovate and test technologically derived production standards and rates on vendors, consumers, workers, and regulators. In the past decade, Amazon has established itself as the key innovator in the retail, e-commerce, and logistics sectors, developing a set of interlaced technologies, machine learning, and production systems that can broadly be grouped under the term "algorithmic management."[1] As Shoshana Zuboff persuasively argues, the increasing use of these technologies by corporations and the state is unleashing a new level of surveillance, control and most concerning, data aggregation and artificial intelligence that is breaking down the walls between surveilled worker and data-rich customer, between citizen and surveilled criminal suspect; its influence stretches from workers to customers into the worlds of policing, intelligence, and American empire.[2]

These models of management have technologized and, to an extent, automated both traditional Taylorist work-flow models and even more traditional forms of workplace management, coercion, and pressure. Amazon is in the process of creating a perfect combination of intense surveillance, never-quite-attainable production rates and quotas, and employment insecurity to squeeze more out of every worker than any company in our economy. This results in a new level of intensity, fear, and pressure on workers, resulting in increased workplace injuries, wage theft, and a variety of other workplace hazards. Amazon's tools of algorithmic management and control are a key space of contestation for many aspects of our society, from workplaces to law and border enforcement to personal privacy. Without a direct challenge, these tools will spread across the economy and to consumers. Amazon's centering of algorithmic management, surveillance, and data aggregation make it a threat to communities and workers on a different scale than any other company, one that requires an organizing strategy that similarly centers on this logic. In order to address the broader application of these technologies in our society, challenging Amazon's rising power and influence through mass mobilization must be a key activity.

THE HUMAN IMPACTS

The human effects of these technologies are predictable but devastating. I speak all the time to seasoned warehouse workers who remark at the speed and constant pace of work in Amazon warehouses. The rates are generally seen as unattainable but for a few of the most productive workers, who either get a lucky assignment or position that day or are just working out of their minds all day. Workers who do not attain the rate for the day are in peril of losing their jobs, sometimes through direct discipline from their managers and sometimes even being terminated by the algorithm itself.

The most direct impact of the algorithm is the fact that the work rate is high and constantly going up. Depending on the job, speed causes different hazards, but in each case, mitigation training or expertise is not enough to prevent injury. If you have a certain number of picks to make from racks in a million-square-foot fulfillment center each hour, you know you must run. If you have to move six boxes off a conveyer each minute, you must pick up multiple boxes at a time, and jostle with co-workers to put them on pallets. If you must deliver 250 boxes to homes every shift, you have to roll through stop signs, park illegally and not bother with the seat belt. There is no way to safely make these rates.

When workers slow down, they face immediate discipline, reminding them of the level of surveillance they are under. Workers can also be disciplined for something observed on camera days later—a conversation, a quick breather, anything that looks like "time off task" (TOT). This constant control of the workplace is the apotheosis of the managerial dream of complete control, keeping workers constantly looking over their shoulders to see where they are being observed. Facing surveillance for half their waking hours has a serious impact on people. Workers report feelings of surveillance after they leave work and they have trouble sleeping. Workers self-medicate to recover from the intensity of the work but also from the feeling of being under intense surveillance. We also see high turnover in Amazon warehouses relative to other warehouses or jobs. Workers tell us that they do not want to stay at a job that has these kinds of conditions, but they must in order to survive.

The effects of these technologies are being tested out in real time on this workforce. After only a few years, hundreds of thousands of people have worked in these warehouses, but we are not tracking the physical and mental impacts of technological surveillance on workers, many of them in their first real jobs. As more and more people begin their careers in these kinds of workplaces, the minimal assumptions of privacy that exist in the workplace will likely dissolve. Workers are routinely called back from or asked about their reason to go to the bathroom, which the company has identified as the last uncontrollable place in the workplace. Workers are deprived of their own technology, namely phones, and cannot track or communicate about their working conditions outside of the workplace. These systems of control are the new normal for a generation of young warehouse workers.

WHERE IS AMAZON HEADED?

These efforts represent a logical but still shocking progression of Amazon and other corporations' expansion of their control of the workplace, using the tools afforded by technology to establish a new level of surveillance, data collection, and analysis of its workforce. The authoritarian control of workplaces is nothing new, but these tools allow Amazon to expand this control in several directions at once, quickly decimating what little workplace power warehouse workers had before Amazon's technological innovations.

Amazon is the only big tech company with a significant blue-collar workforce, something that positions it uniquely to have a role in disrupting both industrial relations and the general consumer public. Most recently, Amazon is adding a third leg to this stool, contracting with federal, state, and local government agencies to support police, and surveillance and data collection activities, and to aggregate datasets across these levels to establish massive sets of information on residents of the US and other countries. This includes contracts to provide technology and services to agencies including the Central Intelligence Agency (CIA), Immigration and Customs Enforcement

(ICE), Border Patrol, and the National Security Agency (NSA). As of 2020, Amazon is challenging its loss to Microsoft of the Department of Defense's proposed "Joint Enterprise Defense Infrastructure" (JEDI) contract, a $10 billion federal contract to establish a defense-focused dataset that integrates facial recognition, data fusion, and foreign surveillance to establish a global defense dataset. These tools position Amazon as the pivotal player in the transition of the key attributes of the long-established authoritarian workplace to augment and facilitate the growth of authoritarian modes of surveillance and control in the U.S.'s civil society and especially at the U.S.'s borders and ports of entry, and, in the future, its foreign policy and intervention.

Workers in Amazon's supply chain cross multiple contractors and subcontractors and have highly variant work experiences. Amazon's business model is to test out each of these models simultaneously and gauge the productivity and cost of each form of work. The data Amazon collects is what helps the company understand how they want to invest future resources in that line of business, and how to treat the workers and communities involved.

In the core logistics and goods movement area of Amazon's business, this consists of some business activities that have been established as insourced. More than other retailers like Walmart, Amazon operates its core fulfillment and sortation operations in-house, with limited use of third-party logistics firms and staffing agencies. As goods come closer to customers, however, Amazon operates with a variety of models. Much of its delivery is executed through a contract with the U.S. Postal Service. United Parcel Service (UPS) also has a significant amount of the delivery business that Amazon outsources. Further, Amazon operates its own network of delivery stations in urban markets through which they contract with delivery and courier companies that deliver goods in Amazon-branded vans. Finally, they are also testing out the models of independent drivers, operating Amazon Flex as a network of independent drivers and using Uber drivers for delivery.

Each piece of this system has its own level of tracking, surveillance, and profitability. An untrained Uber driver working piece rate is going to be much less efficient than an experienced, professional full-time UPS driver employed with a good salary and pension, but also costs a quarter of what a unionized worker costs. Amazon's data analysis is testing when each model is most efficient, and when to switch to a different mix of activities.

This variety of employment and contract models allows Amazon to customize its operation constantly. At the same time, the company is collecting a set of data that can be used in multiple ways. They track not only the movement of delivery vehicles but also the activities of delivery drivers, including breaks, delays, driving methods, and safety. This data benefits the corporation by allowing it to determine minute changes in labor and work flows and to constantly test new concepts. This always results in new forms of control of the workforce. While this data could easily be used to benefit worker safety and health conditions or other aspects of work, in reality the benefit only moves in one direction.

CONSUMER SURVEILLANCE IN SERVICE OF RETAIL DOMINANCE

Consumer surveillance is the most commonly discussed aspect of the data collection of the major tech companies like Facebook, Google, Amazon, Apple, and Microsoft. Consumers of these companies' products are via their consumption sharing vast amounts of data that the companies are using to develop deep and comprehensive customer profiles. Google perfected data harvesting as a business model, one that Amazon is expanding on with its entry into data services, media production, and speculation in dozens of other sectors. The establishment of Alexa and Ring create huge amounts of data flowing back to the company daily, with no regulation of how this data is used or marketed. This core of consumer data represents Amazon's primary asset, especially in the depth of its relationships to its 150 million Prime members in the United States. This represents a massive and growing liability for customers that could be an opportunity for organizing.

SURVEILLANCE IN SERVICE OF WORKPLACE AUTOMATION

Amazon has explicitly stated that its goal is to automate its warehouse and delivery driver workforces. This is a process to track and map the activities of workers through video footage collection, one that Amazon expects to be able to begin relatively soon, given its recent claim that it will invest $700 million in retraining redundant workers. These tools include camera surveillance in the warehouses, which allows the company's industrial engineers to understand the movements workers make and identify opportunities for technological assistance or replacement. This process occurs through the collection of thousands of hours of motion studies every day, tracking the movements of over 400,000 workers throughout 8–10-hour shifts around the world. This data can then be analyzed for improvements that seek to maximize workplace efficiency rather than to make the workstations more ergonomically suited to the human body, or to make the work safer or healthier.

Likely, these jobs will not all disappear, but will increasingly be tied to automatic assistance machines and technology. The twinning of human and machine creates a more integrated form of speed-up, where workers must keep up with their buddy robot or scanner, and feel rushed by a machine that can always move faster. Often the machines take the easier, more repeated tasks, leaving more complex and strenuous tasks for humans. The machines that increase productivity are potentially beneficial to the workers—if the work rate is increased and the worker is allowed to benefit from the increased productivity. But when all the benefits of productivity are retained by the company, and the worker must just work faster for the same pay, there is no end to the potential speed-up that technology places on the workers.

SURVEILLANCE AND DATA COLLECTION IN SERVICE OF JOB INSECURITY

The prevalent employment model in the major warehouses of the U.S. and globally is enforced employment insecurity. The sector grew up in the neoliberal era starting in the late 1980s with little threat of worker organizing or strict employment and labor law. The use of staffing agencies is the most obvious and discussed attribute of this insecurity. Many major warehouses commonly employ half of their workforce through staffing agencies at or close to minimum wage. Elsewhere in the supply chain, the misclassification of truck and delivery drivers is another tool of offloading liability onto workers, often forcing workers to finance trucks, but giving them no authority to decide where and how to use them. Shippers' (major retailers' and manufacturers') use of small logistics and trucking firms creates a middle layer of powerless players contingent on shippers' whims and demands for survival. Mostly this leads to worsened conditions in the workplace.

While explained by industry as a measure to establish flexibility or, at worst, keep wages low, the use of staffing agencies and, in the case of Amazon in California, direct seasonal employees, has created a much larger and economy-wide problem. The logistics sector and other insecure sectors have created a surplus workforce of thousands of partly employed men and women. Amazon and other warehouse operators use a variety of schemes to keep this surplus workforce loyal—working 20 hours a week creates a hungry, desperate, and competitive workforce committed to cutting out their co-worker to get the next open shift or overtime opportunity, the next permanent job, or the next promotion. Using algorithmic schedule management and data management of freight, Amazon is working to establish a perfect on-off switch for labor, calling people in an hour or two before to go in for a shift, or sending people home as soon as the freight is loaded. This day-to-day insecurity of operating a business is thus offloaded to people least prepared to handle it—young parents, workers with high school degrees, trying to hold onto the only jobs available to them in their communities. Technology does not create Amazon's decision to operate this way, but it facilitates this push of stress and insecurity down to the workers.

SURVEILLANCE IN SERVICE OF COMMUNITY INSECURITY

Amazon has operated at a loss for almost the entirety of its existence. Venture capital has flowed into the company based on speculation that its business model will eventually lead to the kind of market power that would create dominance of the online retail space, something that is coming true at this time but is still not clearly a profitable business model. While Amazon's e-commerce operations are its most prominent line of business, the company's technology services operations are in fact the space where Amazon is growing most rapidly and making a profit. Amazon Web Service (AWS) is the provider of web services to a third of the Internet. The company most recently has moved into contracts with public agencies as a profitable area for growth, marketing surveillance and data systems designed originally for the inside of warehouses, as well as the home, into governmental, and especially policing, activities. This is an especially resonant activity for the Inland Empire region, an area that has become dominated by Amazon in the past nine years. Amazon is the largest private employer in the region, an area with a large and diverse immigrant and Latinx population that depends heavily on Amazon and the rest of the goods movement sector for economic activity. The coordination of Amazon with ICE, which operates two major detention centers in San Bernardino County, as well as local police agencies and the Border Patrol operating 100 miles south is illustrative of exactly how Amazon sees this community—a space to be dominated, policed, and exploited through extraction of resources and labor.

MODES OF RESISTANCE

As always, the most effective form of resistance to consolidation of corporate power is workplace organizing. Amazon has used years of workplace data and designed its warehouses and workplaces specifically to be difficult to organize. They have high turnover and workforces who are insecure and have no job security. They have also staggered breaks and shift changes, which makes it difficult for large numbers of workers to talk to one another. Workers in some workplaces are split among various contractors and staffing agencies. Other workforces are split by race, gender, or national origin. These systems can be overcome but only with strategic and deep organizing that addresses them from the beginning.

Workers in some high-surveillance workplaces are beginning to organize around their work rate and surveillance as the source of the problems they face in the workplace. The work rate is an issue with a long history within both agricultural and industrial labor action, because it is so critical to the basic operation of the company but also because it, along with wage, is the basic unit of negotiation in the workplace. In the warehouse context, the rate, bolstered and turbocharged by surveillance, makes the rate both unattainable and ever present. Because this rate is high and tightly enforced, workers are likelier to rush, to twist, resulting in more injury, resulting in more workers quitting or being let go after an injury. This has implications on the workplace but also is a negative externality to their broader communities. The workers in these warehouses are often paid somewhat better than minimum wage and receive some benefits. Focusing on issues like surveillance and rates and demanding that they be reformed and reduced can be a site of critical resistance.

WORKER-DRIVEN POLICY

Much of the discourse on the issues of data and algorithmic management has landed in the area of technology policy and regulation. While this is a critical area for action, such efforts for regulation are a distraction if they are not generated from affected communities and workplaces. This is for two reasons: first, if the affected workers and communities don't have a say, the policies will likely not address the issues they feel are most important. Second, if the issues are not things people are willing to fight for in their workplace or the public, they will not be able to overcome corporate money and power in the policy and rule-making space and will likely not be implemented.

Worker- and community-driven policy will have to be a key part of the way we change the way the company operates. As always, Amazon is testing how much it can get away with. In California, the company was using independent contractors for delivery until it faced lawsuits, then changed to employing workers directly. They used staffing agencies to employ many of their workers, until it was clear they were still liable for wage and hour violations and insourced most of their workers, even the seasonal ones. California's AB 5, which passed in September 2019 and reinforced the Dynamex ruling that first determined a higher standard for independent contractors, will be a test of the Flex and Uber models in California and may push more business toward employee contractors. Policy and litigation are key parts of how to push back against Amazon's direct push downward on standards, if community members and workers lead.

Another key area of engagement is the question of data ownership. Workers who are being surveilled are a source of valuable information that is related to their activity levels, their productivity, the methods by which they solve problems, even their physical actions. All this information is being stored by Amazon and analyzed to develop solutions to the company's concerns. When there is a "power hour"—where workers are encouraged to work at a highly accelerated rate for an hour and incentivized with gift cards or recognition—workers are essentially participants in a logistics stress test, where the company can see the result of an operation at maximum effort. The information collected from this data is used to determine opportunities for technological fixes, automation, or movement of labor. If workers could collectively bargain the rates and actions of the company, they could have access to this data to benefit themselves, not just the productivity of the company. The data that is "neutral" is currently only used for one purpose: to maximize productivity with minimal errors and at minimal cost. If workers had access to corporate data as well, they could analyze the path the company is taking with regard to compensation, health and safety, work rates, and other factors and determine their best response. The data should be shared between all affected parties, for the benefit of all.

There is a space for regulation of this data as well. Without anonymization, workers are vulnerable to discipline through electronic surveillance techniques. In Germany, it is illegal to use data to pick on any one worker. The right to relax—the right to be human—is something we must return to the workplace. Amazon and other employers have pushed their mandate for productivity as far as they can get it. Workers and the state have every right to push back, to acknowledge that preservation of human health and life are more important than Amazon's right to maximize profit. Only with clear and bold demands can we retake the space of the workplace, which has been ceded completely to capital in the United States.

COMMUNITY ORGANIZING

As detailed above, Amazon has a massive impact on people in all sorts of ways, including people who don't work in warehouses. Organizing Inland residents on these issues gives us an opportunity to establish a mass movement around the various aspects of Amazon. In our region, which is majority Latinx and people of color, the racial justice implications of Amazon's plans and activities are a core part of our message.

Amazon has rapidly become a leading vendor of surveillance technologies in the public, mostly to police and military agencies like ICE. The use of these technologies is transforming public spaces into areas of surveillance and control. Amazon is adopting its workplace structures to these public spaces. A coordinated resistance, between people inside workplaces and those who are in public spaces, will be a necessary piece of this fight. Americans have mostly ceded workplaces to corporate power. People still believe they have the right to some privacy at home and in public, however. Data collection through phones, Alexa, Ring, and AWS tech in the home, and collection by state agencies through Amazon services are creating massive databases that agencies like ICE join together in "Fusion Centers." These datasets are opportunities for both state and corporate manipulation, and the increasingly close relationship between Amazon and the state creates an opportunity for seamless merging of the two. Only strong government regulation of how this data is collected and used, and a strong data destruction policy, will prevent the abuse of these unprecedented and massive tools of control that are being built without our consent or knowledge.

Customers must play a huge role in standing up for changes in Amazon's business model. Over half the households in the United States have Amazon Prime accounts, and half of all online sales originate with an Amazon search. Retail customers face impacts of data gathering and surveillance that impact their pricing, is sold to marketers and governments, and cannot be destroyed or controlled. The public also has a voice in the way public agencies like universities and local government agencies contract with Amazon for goods and services. Customers are ultimately who the company will listen to, and they can have massive impacts through tactics including but not limited to petitions, boycotts, and direct action.

The workers and communities of Southern California are organizing to resist this domination. Even though high turnover, employer surveillance, and permanently insecure work make it extremely difficult for the thousands of workers in the warehouses to organize using the methods laid out in the National Labor Relations Act, there are groups of workers joining together to act and challenge Amazon's business model. The community has begun organizing actions protesting Amazon's relationship to ICE, which operates two major detention centers in the area and has a huge impact on the large immigrant community in Inland Southern California.

In San Bernardino, community, labor and environmental leaders have joined together to challenge Amazon's proposed Eastgate Air Cargo Terminal, an airfreight project expected to establish an Amazon Prime Air hub in San Bernardino, a key part of the company's growth strategy. The groups, including Warehouse Worker Resource Center (WWRC), Inland Coalition for Immigrant Justice, the Sierra Club, local PICO affiliate Inland Congregations United for Change, Center for Community Action and Environmental Justice, the Inland Empire Central Labor Council, Building Trades Council, and Teamsters Local 1932, have joined together to establish San Bernardino Airport Communities, a coalition organizing with the demand of an enforceable community benefits agreement relating to the impacts of the project on the region. These forms of deep and intersectional resistance integrate concerns about wages and working conditions, job access for local residents, environmental impacts such as noise and air pollution, but also demand that Amazon sever its contracts with ICE and other policing agencies, and establish transparency in its operations in the region. As the largest employer in the region, Amazon has a responsibility to the community. This coalition intends to hold Amazon accountable not just to the local community; it also seeks to contribute to the national and international critique of Amazon, and its efforts to expand its authoritarian employment practices to the market for goods and services and civil society, both in the United States and beyond.

As this chapter was going to press, the COVID-19 pandemic was taking hold in the United States, making Amazon's dominant presence in our economy even more stark and considerable. Thousands of retail businesses have closed, customers are dependent on deliveries while sheltered in their homes, and Amazon is one of the only companies operating at full capacity—even growing at this time.[3] At the same time, worker revolt is beginning across Amazon's supply chain, as workers deemed essential find that their employer is taking insufficient measures to ensure workers or customers are protected from infection at a time when the company is growing and profiting greatly. If challenging Amazon was a good idea before this pandemic, it is a critical part of any plan to establish democracy and economic justice in the United States.

These efforts represent a community coming to terms with the domination that Amazon has established in the region and drawing a line in terms of how much a community is willing to take. Other communities around the U.S. and the world are organizing in ways that make sense locally but also reflect coordinated strategies around Amazon's national and global systems. When we educate workers and local communities with information of how Amazon is more than just a retailer, and the potential impacts of its data and surveillance systems, they understand that the effects of standing up to Amazon benefit more than just their workplace and community, but have an impact on the nature of our democracy and workplaces.

NOTES

1. A. Aneesh, "Global Labor: Algocratic Modes of Organization," *Sociological Theory* 27(4) (2009): 347–370.
2. Shoshanna Zuboff, *The Age of Surveillance Capitalism: The Fight for A Human Future at the New Frontier of Power* (New York: Public Affairs, Hachette Book Group, 2019).
3. In mid-April 2020, Amazon reported that it was creating an additional 75,000 jobs, even after hiring another 100,000 new workers, mostly warehouse and delivery workers, in the previous month. See Annie Palmer, "Amazon to Hire 75,000 More Workers as Demand Rises Due to Coronavirus," CNBC.com, April 13, 2020, www.cnbc.com/2020/04/13/amazon-hiring-75000-more-workers-as-demand-rises-due-to-coronavirus.html. Accessed June 22, 2020.

PART IV

Struggling to Win against Amazon

13
Amazon Strikes in Europe: Seven Years of Industrial Action, Challenges, and Strategies

Jörn Boewe and Johannes Schulten

A banner on the Amazon site at the former Westfalenhütte steel plant in Dortmund, Germany announces the elections for the works council. However, it was not the responsible trade union Ver.di that displayed it but the management of the fulfillment center (FC), which opened at the end of 2017 and employs over 1,600 people. "Direct communication and cooperation with the works councils," says a press spokeswoman, "is the best way to understand and respond to the concerns of the workforce."[1]

Many critical observers, who have known Amazon for years for their strict performance pressures on employees, intensive employee monitoring, and anti-union activities, are surprised by this direct support for workers' representation. For German unionists, it causes headaches. Works councils (*Betriebsräte*) are a special feature of German industrial relations and are independent of trade unions. While the latter are responsible for negotiating collective rules with employers' associations, works councils represent employees at the company level *vis-à-vis* management. To this end, they have so-called statutory co-determination rights, which include, among other things, a say in working-time issues. By recognizing this "symbolic national institution"[2]—whose establishment is even actively promoted by the printing of flyers for all candidates—the company can present itself in an employee-friendly manner and take the wind out of the sails of publicly omnipresent criticism directed at them by trade unions. Amazon is also taking various measures to ensure that trade unionists remain in the minority on the works council and that the committee does not cause any trouble. This is due, on the one hand, to the combination of a very high number of temporary employees at newly opened locations and an antitrade union atmosphere spread by the management. Hardly anyone dares to appear openly as a union member. At the same time, the bid for elections ensures that ten or more different lists often appear (which is very unusual in Germany). The chance is therefore high that the votes will be distributed among a large number of candidates, which in turn will lead to a strong political fragmentation of the works councils.

As demonstrated by "the long struggle of Amazon employees"[3] that began in the spring of 2013, Amazon has proved to be a company capable of learning. It has been relatively quick to respond to union activity and workers' desire for a representation of interests with different and flexible methods. But these do not always work in the corporation's favor. In the 2018 works council elections, trade union lists emerged as winners for the first time at many locations, including Dortmund.

This chapter is divided into two parts. First, we give an overview of the development of trade union resistance against Amazon in Germany, Poland, the United Kingdom, France, Italy and Spain. This resistance has intensified in many countries since the beginning of the strikes in Germany, not least because of the advancement of international trade union networking. Even though Amazon continues to refuse in principle to recognize trade unions as collective representatives of workers' interests, the balance of power between the corporation and its employees has shifted significantly in favor of the latter since 2013. Second, we use the example of the situation in Germany to formulate two trade union challenges for successful union representation that, in our opinion, extend beyond the specific situation in Germany.

TRADE UNION RESISTANCE IN EUROPE: FROM BAD HERSFELD TO BRUSSELS

Founded in 1994 in the U.S. state of Washington as an online bookstore, Amazon expanded to Europe just four years later. In 1998, the first fulfillment center (FC) opened in Slough, just outside London. In 1999, the first German FC started operations in Bad Hersfeld, Hessen. One year later, the company entered the French market. Further dispatch centers followed in 2011 in Italy (Piacenza) and Spain in 2012 (Madrid). Throughout Western Europe, especially Germany, France, Italy, and the U.K., a significant share of Amazon's warehouse workers are immigrants. The corporation's expansion into Eastern Europe is particularly important for the German situation. Amazon more or less openly threatened to relocate jobs from strike-happy Germany to Poland and the Czech Republic beginning in the autumn of 2013.[4] Above all, the expansion into Eastern Europe appears to be aimed at supplying the Western European market employing labor that is still much cheaper, while at the same time undermining the successes achieved by trade unions in Germany and France.

Although the operational organization of FCs across Europe is similar, wages, working hours, and work contracts sometimes differ considerably, especially between Western and Eastern Europe.[5] As a general rule, Amazon is consistently trying everywhere to exploit the leeway allowed by national laws. This applies to taxes and duties as well as to labor costs and conditions. Collective agreements are only applied where there is a legal obligation. National differences in the state of trade union struggles for humane wages and working conditions at Amazon partly reflect differences in union strategies, as well as national differences in labor laws and trade union strength and influence. Table 13.1 shows the variation in trade union density, the percentage of employed workers belonging to unions, across European countries in 2018.

Table 13.1 Trade union density in European countries, 2018 (percentage of employed workers belonging to a union)

Country	Germany	United Kingdom	France	Poland	Spain	Italy
Density	16.5	23.2	8.1	12	14.8	34

Source: "Trade Union Density," *Organisation for Economic Co-operation and Development*, 2019, https://stats.oecd.org/Index.aspx?DataSetCode=TUD. Accessed April 19, 2020.

GERMANY

For years, union resistance played no role at Amazon and unions had hardly taken an interest in the expanding online retailer. However, this has changed since the beginning of industrial action in Germany. When several hundred workers gathered outside the gates of the warehouse known as FRA 3 on April 9, 2013, it was not only the first strike at Amazon in Germany but also the first strike in the almost 20-year history of the online retailer. How did this happen? The strike in Bad Hersfeld was not a spontaneous uprising of Amazon workers. It was the result—albeit probably not intended—of a coordinated development of trade unions' *associational power* in the form of a two-year organizing project of the United Services Union (Ver.di).[6] By associational power, we refer to the capacity of workers to mobilize in order to act collectively.[7] Just two years before the strike, Ver.di, with just 79 members among the more than 3,000 employees of both Bad Hersfeld FCs, played practically no role. Although there was a works council, it, like large sections of the workforce, was "rather distanced" from the union, as one union organizer put it.

With the organizing project, Ver.di succeeded for the first time in maintaining a regular presence in the company over a longer period of time. The two organizers had the necessary time to identify various experiences of injustice among the workforce and to develop solutions. For this purpose, there were various actions in front of the gate as well as work council meetings, which gave the organizers the opportunity to present themselves and their plans to up to 700 workers. At these events, which are regulated by the German Works Constitution Act, the works council (*Betriebsrat*) has the opportunity to inform the workforce quarterly about matters related to the company and to invite a trade union representative to participate. Interestingly, there was no resistance from the local management to these actions by Ver.di. One of the union officials interviewed at the time described the attitude of the local management as "friendly, American, non-binding."

Built up over months, these intensive contacts with workers were essential to ensuring that a considerable proportion of the employees identified with the central themes of the campaign and were prepared to take action. Moreover, organizers did not present "trade unions" as "service providers," but as a tool for company organization, to which everyone has to contribute. Thus, in Bad Hersfeld, an understanding that "We are the trade union" was cultivated that is still decisive today.

Within two years, nearly a thousand workers joined the union, an enormous number given the high proportion of fixed-term contracts and high employee turnover, and it was possible to establish sustainable activist structures that still exist today. This small example from Bad Hersfeld is in a way exemplary of the trade union situation at Amazon in Europe. It shows the importance of direct contact between the trade union and the workers and the collective experience of being able to carry out joint actions.

Labor Revitalization Studies (LRS) regard trade unions as strategic actors who, even if they act in adverse conditions, always have the possibility of a "strategic choice."[8] After almost 15 years of presence in Germany, Ver.di's decision to regard Amazon as a strategically important actor that had to be countered not with a strategy based on social partnership but with a conflicting strategy aimed at building workers' organizational power, must be regarded as such a strategic choice. This includes above all the decision of the Federal Executive Board to support the chronically financially weak state districts in the development of further locations with additional personnel resources or organizers. Over the following years, this was a key factor that helped in significantly improving the trade union position at Amazon and creating structures at most locations. In FCs at older locations, the degree of organization was increased from practically zero to 30–50 percent.

Even though Amazon still refuses to negotiate a collective agreement with the union, organized workers have gained significant improvements in working conditions since the start of trade union activities, such as a significant increase in wages and the payment of a Christmas bonus. Workers have also gained other improvements, such as better workplace safety, or ergonomics like height-adjustable tables, decentralized common rooms, or, at least in some FCs, the abolition of unpopular feedback talks.[9] But it is also true that works councils and trade unions have failed to solve key problems for workers. Intensive employee monitoring and strict pressures to perform their jobs quickly and with minimal errors remain high. Moreover, the monotony of work is likely to have increased with increasing mechanization at many locations. In short, many employees still feel like robots.

POLAND

Poland is an early example of how international networking can help to counter Amazon's attempts to play different locations off against each other. When employees at the Polish Amazon FC in Poznań were told at the end of June 2015 that their shifts would be extended by an hour at short notice, spontaneous protests broke out, resulting in a "go-slow" strike. The protests, however, had their origin not in the Polish industrial city, but some 650 kilometers further west, in the town of Bad Hersfeld. The employees had again staged a walkout there. By ordering overtime in Poznań, the workers at that site feared that Amazon was trying to undermine the industrial action in Germany and turn them into strike-breakers. The fact that the staff in Poznań were so well informed about events in Bad Hersfeld was chiefly due to the anarcho-syndicalist rank-and-file union OZZ inicjatywa Pracownicza (IP),[10] which is active there and has close ties with the group of Ver.di activists in Bad Hersfeld and Leipzig.

Amazon started its operations in Poland in October 2014 and today operates a total of seven FCs, a software development center and an Amazon Web Services (AWS) site with a total of approximately 16,000 regular employees in Poland. There is much to suggest that Poland will fulfill the role of the extended packing table. Remuneration and working hours differ significantly from the situation in Germany. In 2019, the hourly wage in Poland ranged from €4.12 to €4.36 , compared to a range from €10.96 to €13.04 among the great majority of German workers. Meanwhile, as a sales market, Poland has so far not gained the interest of online retailers; as of August 2019, there was still no Polish-language customer website on the Internet.

In Poland, two trade unions, IP (combative and militant) and NSZZ Solidarność (based on social partnership), are seeking to represent Amazon employees.[11] This is problematic, since they not only embody two fundamentally different trade union models, but also have a tense relationship with each other. This became clear in the evaluation of the slowdown strike in Poznań in 2016. While the IP actively supported the action, Solidarność subsequently issued a statement indicating that it viewed many of the IP's demands as legitimate but its confrontational methods as counterproductive.[12] At the same time, the trade unions in Poland were able to mobilize relatively quickly. In Wrocław, Solidarność stated that it began recruiting its first members three months after the centers opened, and is still the organization's geographical focus. In Poznań, on the other hand, the IP achieved *organizational success.*

In 2016, the IP even felt strong enough to initiate a strike ballot in Wrocław and Poznań. According to the union, more than 2,000 workers voted for a strike.[13] However, only 2,150 of the 5,500 workers employed at both locations participated. Thus, participation remained below the 50 percent quorum required in Poland. Even though the strike ballot was not successful, the substantial number of people willing to go on strike indicates a certain mobilization potential of IP. All in all, however, trade union organizing at Amazon in Poland is still weak.

In the recent past, at least a relaxation of the relationship between the IP and Solidarność and a serious effort for cooperation are emerging. In May 2019, for example, both unions jointly called on Amazon to discuss wage increases. Amazon offered to negotiate exclusively with Solidarność—not with the IP. Solidarność rejected the offer. Since 2019, Solidarność and the IP have been running a joint campaign to eliminate feedback talks, which can be seen as a slow departure from the course of social partnership towards a stronger willingness to confront on the part of Solidarność.

THE UNITED KINGDOM

After Germany, the U.K. is the largest market for Amazon in Europe. About 27,500 workers are employed there, of which 22,500 are employed in 17 FCs. However, almost 20 years after entering the market, Amazon is still largely union-free. In addition to the lack of union-friendly British labor laws, this has a lot to do with the vehemence with which Amazon has countered previous attempts to establish trade union representation in its FCs. As early as 2002, Amazon succeeded in forcing the British Graphical, Paper and Media Union (GPMU) out of the company in an unprecedented union-busting campaign. In 2001, the GPMU—which today belongs to the umbrella trade union Unite the Union (know as Unite) founded in 2007— started an organizing project at its Milton Keynes site, about 75 kilometers from London. The aim was to persuade at least 10 percent of the employees to sign on as members, in order to apply for union recognition from the Central Arbitration Committee (CAC). The GMPU succeeded in organizing about 200 employees, but Amazon responded with a classic U.S.-style anti-union campaign. On the one hand, it granted the workforce several wage increases. Meanwhile, it dismissed leading union members and agitated against the union on the shop-floor. In a vote in the autumn of 2001, in which 90 percent of the workforce participated, 80 percent voted against the GPMU, 15 percent in favor, and 5 percent had invalid votes.[14] For the union, it was a heavy defeat that still burdens the trade unions, as one former GPMU trade union official told us.

The low wage and poor working conditions have changed little for a long time.[15] According to the union, Amazon paid £7.10 per hour for years, slightly more than the minimum wage of £6.70 per hour (€9.10). A substantial improvement did not come until the end of 2018, when the company announced that it would raise the starting wage in Greater London to £10.50 per hour and in the rest of the country to £9.50 per hour (€10.61 and €11.73 respectively).[16] In contrast to Germany, employees and trade unions in the U.K. must contend with a high proportion of part-time contracts (so-called "zero-hour contracts").

Under an agreement within the Trade Union Congress (TUC), the GPMU and Unite are no longer responsible for organizing Amazon workers, and the job falls to the GMB, the third largest trade union in the country. It considers the situation to be "very difficult." The lack of access to the Amazon FCs is a particular problem for the trade union: "We have enormous problems coming into contact with our colleagues at all because we are only allowed to address them outside the company boundaries."[17] In this context, the GMB's strategic focus is to influence public opinion by pointing out bad working conditions at Amazon. Meanwhile, the trade union is making efforts to organize truck drivers for inbound and outbound deliveries. According to a trade union official, "If we have control over the last mile, we have a lever to get into [the] FC."[18] At the same time, attempts are being made to sensitize institutional investors to Amazon's working conditions and rejection of basic trade union rights. For this purpose, a special lobby organization was founded: the Trade Union Share Owners (TUSO). The union's central political demand, however, remains the right of union representatives to talk with workers at the Amazon FCs. This presupposes a fundamental change in collective labor law, which can probably only be expected under a Labour government.

FRANCE[19]

After Germany, France was the second country in which there were noticeable strikes against Amazon. In June 2014, the three trade unions—*Confédération générale du travail* (CGT), *Force ouvrière* (FO), and *Union syndicale solidaires* (SUD)—called for a first industrial action, also inspired by the Ver.di strikes in Germany. The aim was to persuade Amazon to talk about wages, working conditions, and respect for trade union activities. Afterward, the employees managed to win a year-end bonus.

In December 2014, CGT members in Saran near Orléans again went on strike for more pay and better working conditions. The protests against a planned labor market reform by the government under François Hollande led to a major wave of industrial action in 2016. The workforces in Lille, Montélimar, and Dijon were involved, and there were repeated blockades in Orléans. That year, the trade unions were able to implement Saturdays off work, a 0.5 percent wage increase, and a doubling of individual bonuses. In the spring of 2018, news of a strike at Amazon at an FC near Madrid triggered a spontaneous strike in Lille. In the politically prescribed regular annual rounds of negotiations, the unions were able to agree on annual wage increases. In 2018, this increase was 2.2 percent.

The last major success of the CGT union was the enforcement of a €500 bonus payment for French Amazon workers at the turn of 2018/19, based on a proposal by President Emmanuel Macron, who, following protests by "Yellow Vest" women entrepreneurs, called for bonuses to be paid to their workers.[20] In general, Amazon was one of the targets of protests by the "Yellow Vest" movement in various locations. After Germany and the U.K., France is the most important market for Amazon in Europe. Today there are five FCs in France. The degree of unionization at Amazon France is very low, as is generally the case in France (see Table 13.1).

ITALY

Since Amazon's market entry in 2011 with the construction of an FC in Castel San Giovanni near Piacenza which has 1,600 employees today, the company has increased the number of its distribution centers to a total of six. In Italy, many collective agreements are generally binding, applying even without the consent of the employer. However, Amazon's rejection of any trade union cooperation for years prevented trade unions from verifying its correct application.[21]

Trade union presence at Amazon in Italy is generally weak. According to trade union estimates, there are a total of 250–400 members, mainly organized in the three main trade unions, the *Confederazione Generale Italiana del Lavoro* (CGIL), the *Confederazione Italiana Sindacati Lavoratori* (CISL), and the *Unione Italiana del Lavoro* (UIL). Cattero and D'Onofrio have come to the conclusion that Amazon in Italy does not even have to apply specific defence strategies against trade unions, as the high proportion of temporary workers "already works as an effective deterrent to enrollment in the unions."[22] Despite this, on "Black Friday" in November 2017, employees in

Piacenza participated for the first time in strike actions coordinated with Germany's Ver.di.

It caused an international sensation when the CGIL negotiated an in-house collective agreement in Piacenza in May 2018 to regulate weekly working hours. The agreement was considered "historic" by the UNI Global Union, as it was the first collective agreement par excellence negotiated at Amazon.[23] However, the agreement regulates content "which, although very important, does not significantly affect some of Amazon's most obvious problems in terms of work organization and human resources management."[24] Overall, there has been little evidence since then that the Piacenza Agreement marks the turnaround that unions hoped for in terms of Amazon's attitude towards collective agreements and trade unions. A traditional approach to proxy politics still seems to predominate. There are no pronounced shop-floor activist structures like those in Germany, and apparently there are hardly any serious attempts to build them up. An additional problem is that in addition to the three major trade unions, the *Unione Generale del Lavoro* (UGL), has close ties to the right-wing populist *Lega Nord*.

SPAIN

Besides Germany, Italy, Poland, and France, Spain is the country in which Amazon employees regularly take part in strikes. Also, they have succeeded in achieving certain successes in union representation. In September 2015, three union representatives were elected to the factory committee for the first time at the FC in San Fernando de Henares. The *Confederación Sindical de Comisiones Obreras* (CCOO), a trade union close to the *Izquierda Unida* party, won two seats, and the moderately anarcho-syndicalist *Confederación General de Trabajo* (CGT) won one seat. The remaining 10 of the 13 seats on the panel were held by an "independent" list, but according to the CCOO's assessment, the list was closer to the management.

In autumn 2018, a factory committee was also elected at the El Prat fulfillment center at Barcelona Airpor, which employs around 1,500 employees. The CCOO emerged as the strongest list and won eleven of the 23 seats. The third Amazon plant with an elected representation of interests in Spain is the much smaller site in Castellbisbal, also near Barcelona, with around a hundred employees. According to the CCOO, the rest of the now 27 Amazon facilities in Spain have no collective representation of interests.[25]

In March 2018, workers at the FC in San Fernando de Henares suspended their work for two days.

At that time, 1,100 permanent employees and 900 temporary workers were working there.[26] The strike was a response to attempts by Amazon to worsen existing conditions, such as wages. This was followed by another three-day strike around Amazon Prime Day in July 2018, coordinated with simultaneous work stoppages in France, Germany, and Italy. Further strikes followed at the end of November on Black Friday, on four days in December, and at the beginning of January 2019 before Epiphany.[27] The San Fernando de Henares site is the only Amazon strike operation in Spain to date. So far it is only in Spain that unions are capable of mobilizing an overwhelming majority of workers of a FC for the strikes; according to trade union figures, around 60–70 percent of workers took part, and shut down at least large parts of the work process.

INTERNATIONAL NETWORKING

We have seen that since the beginning of the strikes in Germany, a slight trade union offensive has gotten under way in various European countries with Amazon locations. The conflict at Amazon has now taken on a transnational dimension. This takes place on both activist and institutional levels. In 2015, UNI Commerce founded the Amazon Alliance, which initially brought together trade unions active in European Amazon logistics centers. Meetings usually take place every six months. Trade unions from overseas have been participating for about a year now. In spring 2019, in Berlin, 70 delegates (mainly union officials) from 15 countries participated, including from the U.S., Latin America and Australia. Increasingly involved in networking are also trade unions from countries in which Amazon is still little represented or not represented at all, but where expansion is expected, such as Austria, Sweden, Ireland, and the Netherlands.

Unions have successfully coordinated various joint protests and strike activities across nations. In September 2016, workers and trade union representatives from eight European countries demonstrated in front of the Amazon headquarters in Luxembourg for the improvement of working conditions in their countries.[28] Since 2017, with the help of the Amazon

Alliance, trade unions in Germany, Italy, Poland, and Spain went on strike together regularly on occasions such as Amazon Prime Day or Black Friday.

A problem is the lack of commitment in the formulation of common strategies. An example of this is the establishment of a European Works Council (EWC). In 2017, the Alliance decided not to pursue this goal any further but to expand the alliance beyond Europe—with a clear focus on building organizational power. Nevertheless, some of the unions involved continued to pursue the EWC project on their own initiative, including the Spanish CCOO, the Italian CGIL, and the French CGT. Amazon gratefully takes up this special path, as it offers the opportunity to present itself as an employee-friendly company and at the same time play off the national trade unions against each other.

AMAZON IN GERMANY: LESSONS FROM SEVEN YEARS OF STRIKE

With nearly seven years and over 300 days on strike,[29] Amazon employees not only hold the "dubious record for the longest dispute in the history of industrial action in the Federal Republic,"[30] but their strike is also one of the most innovative and certainly most exciting disputes of recent years. This has resulted in a wealth of experience that is also of interest to other countries. We believe two key challenges for successful trade union representation should be addressed here.

KEEPING PACE WITH AMAZON

Twenty-five years after its foundation, Amazon's growth remains rapid. In Germany alone, the company opened four new FCs since the beginning of 2017, and numerous other logistics centers, its own delivery services, etc. A trade union official summarizes the problem for Ver.di thus: "As soon as we have organized a site, Amazon opens the next one."[31] So far, trade union organizing at Amazon in Germany has shown that the potential number of Amazon workers who are willing to organize is huge.[32] However, building of workers' awareness of the necessity to assert their interests collectively through trade union action must always be developed through patient persuasion. In addition, there are new challenges, such as the fact that since around 2016 Amazon has been increasingly recruiting refugee workers at the new sites, who for various reasons are more difficult to organize and predominantly have fixed-term employment contracts. In short, a strategic master plan is needed. Without additional resources that go beyond "regular care," no breakthrough will be possible in the conflict in the long run.

EMPOWERING SHOP-FLOOR ACTIVISM

The second challenge concerns the well-organized Amazon sites, where union members make up between 30 and 50 percent of the core workforce. Such degrees of organization are unique to Amazon worldwide. But it is still a minority strike. On average, in a typical single FC affected by strikes, between 300 and 800 workers take part in the work stoppages. To measure the effectiveness of the strikes, we compared the units settled in one day (Amazon calls it "throughput") during a five-day strike at a well-organized German FC in 2017 with those of the weeks before and after. We found that in the weeks before and after the strike week, the throughput fluctuated at 620,000 and 650,000 processed units. In the strike week, the throughput dropped to 540,000 units (a 14–17 percent decrease). However, these effects and related financial losses are likely to be acceptable for Amazon, taking into account that during 2017 workers went on strike for 43 days, so worked more than 260 working days.

To really harm Amazon economically, even at well-organized locations, associational power must therefore be increased.[33] The fact that Ver.di was able to become so strong at all is primarily due to the strong shop-floor activist structures. It is shop-floor activists who credibly represent their union in the workplace, who are available as competent contacts for employees and who take over a large part of the strike organization. However, volunteer structures at many locations tend to be overburdened. Here, too, the trade union is called upon to provide more assistance to adequately support the few activists under pressure—especially in training activists and imparting organizing skills. Cross-site workshops for the training of one-to-one interviews, the creation of company maps, and concrete campaign planning could be helpful tools in such a process. Shop-floor activists are the backbone of this enduring struggle with Amazon; they are the real aces in the hands of unions worldwide. Unions should play wisely and not gamble them away.

NOTES

1. Sandra Schaftner, "Betriebsrat bei Amazon Dortmund: PR-Masche oder guter Wille?," *ruhr24.de*, August 24, 2018, www.ruhr24.de/dortmund/betriebsrat-bei-amazon-dortmund-pr-masche-oder-guter-wille-152523/. Accessed September 1, 2019.
2. Bruno Cattero and Marta D'Onofrio, "Organizing and Collective Bargaining in the Digitized Tertiary Factories of Amazon: A Comparison Between Germany and Italy," in Eduardo Ales, Ylenia Curzi, Tommaso Fabbri, Olga Rymkevich, Iacopo Senatori, and Giovanni Solinas (eds.), *Working in Digital and Smart Organizations: Legal, Economic and Organizational Perspectives on the Digitalization of Labour Relations* (Cheltenham: Palgrave Macmillan, 2018), p. 154.
3. In 2017, the authors published a chronicle of worker resistance against Amazon in Europe. In 2019, the authors updated the study to include developments in the U.S., Australia and Latin America. Unless otherwise indicated, the present article is based on these results; Jörn Boewe and Johannes Schulten,*The Long Struggle of the Amazon Employees: Laboratories of Resistance*, 2nd edition (Brussels: Rosa-Luxemburg Foundation), December 10, 2019, www.rosalux.eu/en/article/1557.the-long-struggle-of-the-amazon-employees.html. Accessed December 1, 2019.
4. Agence France Presse, "Amazon plant Logistikzentren", *Handelsblatt*, 2013. www.handelsblatt.com/unternehmen/handel-konsumgueter/neue-werke-in-osteuropa-amazon-plant- logistikzentren/8866962.html. Accessed April 19, 2020.
5. Cattero and D'Onofrio, "Organizing and Collective Bargaining"; Dominik Owczarek and Agata Chełstowska, "Amazon in Polen. Arbeitsbedingungen und Arbeitsbeziehungen Fundacja Instytut Spraw Publicznych," *Friedrich-Ebert-Stiftung*, 2018, https://library.fes.de/pdf-files/bueros/warschau/14103.pdf. Accessed September 2019.
6. With nearly 2 million members in 2018, Ver.di is the second largest trade union in Germany (behind the IG Metall). It organizes large parts of the public and private service sector—from former state-owned services such as postal services to banks and insurance companies, retail, logistics and the health sector.
7. Stefan Schmalz and Klaus Dörre,"The Power Resources Approach," *Friedrich-Ebert-Stitung*, n.d., www.fes.de/index.php?eID=dumpFile&t=f&f=32816&token=ce072af9d0b7670be9047b640338abd717f87033. Accessed September 1, 2019; Stefan Schmalz, Carmen Ludwig, and Eddy Webster, "The Power Ressources Approach: Developments and Challenges," *Global Labour Journal*, 9(2) (2018), pp. 113-134.
8. Lowell Turner, "From Transformation to Revitalization: A New Research Agenda for a Contested Global Economy," *Work and Occupations* 32(4) (2005): 383–399.

9. A feature of Amazon's control regime are the so-called "feedback talks," in which managers and employees meet with a view to optimizing the workers' performance. The problem is that these talks are based on performance data collected by digital devices like hand-held scanners operated by both the *pickers* and the *stowers*.
10. The Workers' Initiative was founded in Poznań in 2002 and has its roots in the tradition of anarcho-syndicalism. According to them, the IP organizes between 1,000 and 5,000 workers and they gather workers from various industries—e.g. the health service, the shipyard industry, public administration, retail, art and culture workers. One difference to Solidarność is that Solidarność does not represent temporary workers, which the Workers' Initiative tries to integrate: see Owczarek and Chelstowska, "Amazon in Polen," p. 59.
11. NSZZ Solidarność emerged in 1980 from the strikes of Gdańsk shipyard workers against the Communist leadership and became the first independent trade union in Poland According to the International Trade Union Confederation, Solidarność has about 550,000 members and organizes branches in education, industry, and parts of the service sector.
12. Owczarek and Chelstowska, "Amazon in Polen."
13. According to IP's figures, 1,605 permanent employees and 496 temporary workers voted yes, 39 permanent employees and 10 temporary workers voted no, and 9 votes were invalid. Yes votes accounted for 97.3 percent of total votes; OZZ IP—Ogólnopolski Związek Zawodowy Inicjatywa Pracownicza, "Amazon Polen: Über 2.000 Beschäftigte wollen streiken," December 29, 2016, www.ozzip.pl/english-news/item/2138-amazon-polen-ueber-2000-beschaeftigte-wollen-streiken. Accessed September 1, 2019.
14. Gregor Gall, "Union Busting at Amazon.com in Britain," *IndyMedia*, January 21, 2004, www.indymedia.org.uk/en/2004/01/284179.html. Accessed September 1, 2019.
15. Kendra Briken and Phil Taylor "Fulfilling the 'British Way'. Beyond Constrained Choice—Amazon Workers' Lived Experiences of Workfare," *Industrial Relations Journal* 49(5) (2018): 438–458.
16. Richard Partington, "Amazon Raises Minimum Wage for US and UK Employees", *The Guardian*, October 2, 2018, www.theguardian.com/technology/2018/oct/02/amazon-raises-minimum-wage-us-uk-employees. Accessed September 1, 2019.
17. Telephone interview with GMB official, Martin Smith, conducted by Johannes Schulten on June 7, 2015.
18. Interview with a GMB official in charge of Amazon, conducted by Johannes Schulten on April 30, 2019 in Berlin during the Amazon Alliance union meeting.
19. We would like to thank Francesco Massimo, who provided us with important information about this part of France.
20. UNI Global Union, UNI Global Amazon Alliance, "Victory in France, Strikes in Spain and Germany, Pressure in the U.S., and More," January 25, 2019, www.

uniglobalunion.org/news/uni-global-amazon-alliance-victory-france-strikes-spain-and-germany-pressure-us-and-more. Accessed October 30, 2019.
21. Cattero and D'Onofrio, "Organizing and Collective Bargaining," pp. 157–158.
22. Ibid., p. 158.
23. UNI, "Historic Agreement Between Amazon and Sector Unions," *UNI Global Union*, May 25, 2018, www.uni-europa.org/2018/05/25/historic-agreement-between-amazon-and-sector-unions/. Accessed September 1, 2019.
24. Cattero and D'Onofrio, "Organizing and Collective Bargaining," p. 158.
25. Javier Salvatiera, "The Staff of the Largest Amazon Warehouse in Spain Strikes in the Middle of Black Friday," November 23, 2018, https://elpais.com/economia/2018/11/22/actualidad/1542902975_062509.html. Accessed September 1, 2019.
26. CCOO, "Convocada la primera huelga in Amazon España," *Confederación Sindical de Comisiones Obreras*, March 20, 2018, www.fsc.ccoo.es/noticia:271775-Convocada_la_primera_huelga_en_Amazon_Espana. Accessed September 1, 2019.
27. Jesús Martínez, " La solitaria lucha sindical en Amazon," *La Información*, January 5, 2019, www.lainformacion.com/empresas/solitaria-lucha-sindical-amazon-comite-empresa/6484445/. Accessed September 1, 2019.
28. Ver.di, "Proteste vor Amazon-Zentrale in Luxemburg," Press release, September 30, 2016. www.Ver.di/de/themen/nachrichten/++co++c709658c- 86ec-11e6-9f4f-525400b665de. Accessed October 30, 2019.
29. Some of these strikes were limited to individual FCs, but most took place simultaneously at different locations in Germany. Currently Ver.di is able to strike at seven out of twelve locations.
30. WSI—Wirtschafts- und Sozialwissenschaftliche Institut, WSI-Arbeitskampf bilanz 2015, 2016, www.boeckler.de/pdf/pm_ta_2016_03_03.pdf. Accessed September 1, 2019.
31. Interview with Lena Widmann, Ver.di's national coordinator for the retail sector until mid-2019, conducted by Johannes Schulten on January 10, 2019.
32. For the question regarding why Amazon employees take part in the strike or not, see also Sabrina Apicella and Helmut Hildebrandt, "Divided We Stand: Reasons For and Against Strike Participation in Amazon's German Distribution Centres," *Work Organisation, Labour & Globalisation* 13 (2019): 172–189.
33. Georg Barthel, "Against the Logistics of Amazon. Challenges to Build Effective Power," *Strike The Giant. Transnational Organization against Amazon*, Fall 2019, pp. 64–72, www.transnational-strike.info/2019/11/29/pdf-strike-the-giant-transnational-organization-against-amazon-tss-journal/. Accessed December 1, 2019.

14
Bursting the Bubble: The Emerging Tech Worker Movement at Amazon

Spencer Cox

In early March 2017, a large swath of the Internet hosted on Amazon Web Services (AWS) went offline for several hours, costing S&P 500 companies over $150 million in lost revenue and $160 million in losses for U.S. financial-service firms.[1] The cause? A mistaken keystroke by an Amazon engineer in Seattle.

Tech workers, in particular those at FAANG (Facebook, Amazon, Apple, Netflix, Google, and Microsoft) firms, are uniquely positioned in today's capitalist economy that depends on their labor to make industrial processes run. When they stop, so does everyone else. For the majority of the past 40 years, tech workers aligned themselves with the capitalist class, building a shared political project and ruling bloc that dominated U.S. politics. This political alliance is coming undone, and the opportunity to transform the world may depend on further shifts in tech workers' politics.

THE BUBBLE

In the late 1970s, capitalism was in crisis. Profit rates in the advanced industrial economies had been falling for decades, leading to declining rates of investment, slow growth, high inflation, and dwindling power among the capitalist class. Facing this crisis, the capitalist class unleashed a brutal era of economic, political, and social reforms that sought to restore profitability and capitalist-class power. The capitalist class introduced automating technologies into the production process, reorganized work around increasingly "flexible" employment relations, and spatially relocated production to low-wage areas in the global periphery.[2] These transformations—often understood through the bracket term of "neoliberalism"—radically transformed production relations in advanced capitalist economies, temporarily restoring falling rates of profits and driving a short but sustained period of economic growth in the late 1990s.

During this period, information and communication technologies became central to automating work and coordinating vast global supply chains of transnational corporations. Investment in information and communication technologies during the 1990s and the early 2000s reached up to one-third of all non-residential fixed capital investment in the United States, leading the prominent economist David Autor to claim "It's hard to think of a prior historical episode where a single category of capital investment came to rapidly dominate all others."[3] Tech hubs in Silicon Valley and Seattle grew at a rate far outpacing other urban regions, transforming the relatively small manufacturing regions into high-growth hubs of the new economy.[4]

The tidal wave of investment into information and communication technology led to a historic burst in demand for skilled workers who required substantial education to master the skills for the information technology (IT) economy.[5] The term "tech worker" became synonymous with the rapidly expanding information and computing technology sector, with a broad array of jobs—software engineers, data scientists/analysts, systems engineers, user-experience designers, product managers—increasingly crucial to a wide array of labor processes. Because these skills were essential to the competitive advantage of capitalist firms but rare in the labor market, tech corporations viewed the retention of particular skills to be essential to their core competencies. Tech corporations piloted stock-based compensation as a means of tying the financial interests of tech workers to the broader interests of the corporation, turning tech workers into owners.[6] The historic burst of market power afforded tech workers high salaries, luxurious workplaces, and relative control over their own labor relative to other layers of the working class.

This process solidified tech workers as a global *labor aristocracy*. Much like how Lenin used the term in the 1920s, during the recent IT boom, tech workers emerged as a privileged segment of the working class who benefited from monopoly capital's imperial expansion into hyper-exploitable geographic peripheries.[7] Super-profits generated from exploited FoxConn or retail workers in China and Amazon warehouse workers were captured by tech corporations, and selectively redistributed to particular workers, managers, and venture capitalists as a means of producing political alliances. Much like the spheres on Amazon's downtown Seattle campus, tech workers were brought under the "bubble" of tech wealth, while the majority of the working class were left on the outside looking in.

This alliance was not just economic. On the *political* terrain, tech workers in Silicon Valley and Seattle become enrolled in a political project called the "California Ideology."[8] The California Ideology articulated a vision where information technologies, combined with entrepreneurial smarts and free markets, could emancipate individuals from the hierarchies and stagnant intellectual terrain of the post-WWII order. This ideology was rooted in the venture capitalist offices of Sand Hill Road and the tech campuses of Apple, Bell Labs, and later, Google, Amazon, and Facebook. These ideas were broadcast to the world through magazines such as *Wired*, TED Talks, and spectacles of the California counterculture such as Burning Man. Tech workers could see their work as a truly transformative project, bringing new products to a global market that made business faster, sparked human connection at the click of a mouse, and made the world's information accessible in your living room. Technology became its own force of liberation; "make information free" became the dogma of a new world order. Google's ideology of "Do No Evil" and the promotion of "mission-based work" enshrined tech corporations as a place where a social project of emancipation and the logic of capitalist accumulation could be aligned. Here, you could "make a difference" and get rich in the process.

In a sense, the California Ideology was a pillar of what Nancy Fraser calls "progressive neoliberalism," a hegemonic ideology that dominated U.S. politics in the thirty years prior to Trump.[9] Progressive neoliberalism legitimated brutal neoliberal economic reforms with a veneer of progressive language. Forging itself around emerging environmentalist, feminist, racial justice and LGTBQ+ rights movements, progressive neoliberalism reinterpreted these movements through a language of individual meritocracy and social mobility:

> The progressive-neoliberal program for a just status order did not aim to abolish social hierarchy but to "diversify" it, "empowering" "talented" women, people of color, and sexual minorities to rise to the top. And that ideal was inherently *class specific*: geared to ensuring that "deserving"

individuals from "underrepresented groups" could attain positions and pay on par with the straight white men *of their own class*.[10]

This ideology includes not just an ethical evaluation of right and wrong (discrimination around individual opportunity), but more importantly a set of tactics (market-based, technocratic, and individualistic) to address oppression. This ideology emerged from the specific class experiences of the higher-skilled strata of the working class and the professional-managerial class, for whom a progressive political agenda was not incompatible with neoliberal capitalist reforms. In stark contrast to low-income workers, such as subcontracted Uber drivers or warehouse workers, who failed to benefit and often experienced oppression from liberal institutions, liberal social institutions worked in the favor of tech workers, producing a sense that if one followed the rules and the rules applied to all, opportunities for the good life abound.

The progressive neoliberal ideology found its concrete expression in Bill Clinton's "New Democrats" agenda, consolidating power upon a base of skilled workers, the professional and managerial class, and segments of the capitalist class. What Clinton pioneered, Obama mastered. Obama became a spokesperson for big tech, advocating an agenda of open borders, free markets, and innovation with a rhetoric of opening up middle-class aspirations to all who work hard, regardless of race or gender.[11] Many of Obama's staffers and campaigners filled the ranks of tech's political relations teams, infusing the progressive ideology of the Democratic Party into the DNA of the tech industry, while also using these connections to lobby for the interests of tech.[12] Tech workers are disproportionately Democrats. A *Wired* study documenting campaign contributions from tech workers at Facebook, Apple, Google, and Amazon indicates that tech workers overwhelmingly support Democratic candidates, with campaign contributions of $15 million for Hillary Clinton outweighing $2,400 contributions to Trump.[12]

THE BUBBLE WEAKENS

Tech workers are structurally part of the working class: tech corporations have an interest in maximizing the productivity of tech-worker labor, while in the long run weakening the market power they possess. This process operates across a broad array of terrains, including non-compete clauses that lower inter-firm mobility, the increased use of lower-waged subcontracted, temped, gigged-out, and immigrant workers, increasing the supply of labor through funnelling tech dollars exclusively into computer science programs, deskilling work that allows for less skilled (and often younger) workers to complete tasks, outright collusion, and spatial relocations of skilled work to lower-wage locations. As a consequence of tech's efforts to suppress wages, tech-worker wages increased at a *slower* rate than deskilled workers since the 2008 recession.[13] With the average salary in IT hovering at $81,000 but now matched with a soaring cost of living in a tech hub and burdensome loans from exploding costs of higher education, the financial benefits returning to tech workers are dwindling.[14]

If the economic prospects of tech workers as a broader group are dimming compared to the 1990s boom, tech workers at the heart of FAANG firms—an elite layer even among tech workers—are largely not driven by the bread-and-butter union issues of wages, job security, or benefits. Rather, it is their enrollment into unfulfilling, meaningless, and ethically dubious work, and ongoing sexism and racism in the industry that drives their political action.

Due to the vast amount of wealth captured by monopoly firms in the tech industry, the capitalist class commands the trajectory of science and technology with an iron fist. FAANG corporations dictate what technology gets produced, and the "entrepreneurial" wing of the technology industry largely reinforces and compliments the power of FAANG firms rather than driving growth through innovation and new firm formation.[15] Rather than redirecting investment and our social capacity for reason, science and technology to address the largest-scale crises facing humankind, capital largely aligns scientific knowledge for the pursuit of monopoly profits alone. What might appear as the rational use of science and technology from the perspective of the capitalist class is, from the perspective of those who labor to make these corporations run, a deeply irrational, immoral, and ultimately *inhumane* social project.

This irrationality is not lost on tech workers. In daily life, the contradictions between what corporations proclaim and the subtending reality workers observe produce a disjuncture, a sense of cognitive dissonance between what one ethically holds to be right, and the reality of one's own complicities of contributing labor to a banal and morally bankrupt project of private wealth accumulation and mass oppression. Caught between being complicit with furthering oppression and holding an ethical commitment for the greater good is not a matter of personal choice; it is the structure of capitalist society that compels one to sell one's labor, and skills, to the capitalist class in order to survive. The more tech workers engage in production on behalf of the capitalist class on capital's terms, the more the objects of their labor appear as a force that confronts the *humanity* of the person. The result is *alienation* from one's own sense of self, from others, from the product of one's work and from the broader environment. This drives not only social anomie and a lack of personal fulfillment, but a crisis around depression and anxiety that permeates all levels of the industry.[16]

Further, tech workers confront historic forms of oppression that operate within racialized and gendered capitalism. Capital benefits from a racial and gendered division of labor that devalues black and brown lives and so-called "women's work." The tech industry is notoriously a white male club, with white men over-represented at all levels of the industry, but even more so in managerial and executive positions.[17] As of late 2019, Amazon's overall workforce is 58 percent men and 42 percent women, managers are 73 percent men and 27 percent women, and Amazon's top executives are 86 percent men and 14 percent women.[18] Sexual harassment and gender-based discrimination are common, leading women to exit the industry at a faster rate than their male counterparts.[19] In conjunction, racialized forms of exploitation, oppression, and violence devalue black and brown lives and exclude them from institutions that act as gateways to working in tech, resulting in workplaces that are far from reflecting the racial composition of the U.S.[20]

For tech workers, the growing contradictions of their class position are becoming untenable, leading to new forms of political expression. Many joined tech in pursuit of meaningful mission-driven work, but find themselves disillusioned, working on optimizing food delivery apps, or new ways of surveilling and punishing workers. Many care about climate change and understand it as an issue of social justice, but are frustrated working for firms that further entrench consumerism, waste, and carbon emissions. Many recognize that automation has the capacity to free people from grueling work, but find themselves haunted by the inhumane conditions of warehouse work and the stark poverty and oppression bearing down on working-class lives. Many tech workers desire to live in culturally rich, diverse, ecologically resilient cities, but are repulsed at a housing crisis that force thousands onto the street and displaces all but the elite from the urban core. Many experience racism, sexism, and heterosexism but are furious at the inability of firms to develop real accountability to transform workplace culture.

Until recently, however, tech workers have largely stuck to the class playbook of the professional and managerial elite. Within companies, tech workers have often put faith in the corporation to address the concerns of tech workers, as if they and their bosses are on the same team. Open forums, town halls, and relatively free political speech on the tech campus produce space for political dialogue. Within Amazon, Employee Resource Groups (ERGs) or Affinity Groups provide a moderated but nonetheless real outlet for under-represented and historically oppressed groups in tech. Tech corporations maintain substantial departments, such as Amazon's Sustainability Team, directed towards addressing the concerns of their progressive workforce. These company-run unions channel righteous anger into digestible channels, often repackaging and co-opting tech worker concerns through a HR-friendly language and strategies that reinforce power structures while precluding collective organization. Real change remains elusive.

Tech workers also express their politics through the myriad non-governmental organizations (NGOs) in the tech-industry bubble. Often corporate backed and led by industry insiders, NGOs articulate the class interests of tech workers through individualistic, meritocratic, and technocratic frames. NGOs recommend professional women to "lean in," a means of contesting gender inequality by bargaining harder and climbing the corporate ladder, or to foster mentorship programs that help professional women and/or people of color advance their careers. Political problems are often reduced to a technical problem; designing the right technology or algorithm substitutes for democratic debate and an analysis of power.[21] Further, and more damning for those outside the bubble, they circumscribe solidarity to a small ring of professionals interested in advancing their own career interests rather than a more radical feminism or anti-racism that seeks to fight oppression in all its forms. The Black Employee Network at Amazon or the Anita Borg Institute may care about the issues facing black, brown, queer, and/or women tech workers, but are silent about the oppression of the predominantly black and brown workforce in the warehouse, queer and/or women warehouse workers, or those displaced from their homes in the San Francisco Bay Area or Seattle.

BURSTING THE BUBBLE

Trump's election was a catalyst for dismantling the hegemony of progressive neoliberalism. Trump's patriarchal, white, economic nationalism challenged narratives that economic neoliberalism and an elite's interpretation of social justice could persist as a ruling bloc. Once neglected from the progressive neoliberal agenda, the working class mattered again. While many U.S. tech workers and the NGO apparatus fled into the machinery of the Democratic Party to optimize elections, many tech workers protested at the Womxn's March or the March for Science and attended political meetings for the first time.[22]

Not long after the election, a pledge circulated through the tech community called "Never Again."[23] The pledge, citing IBM's collaboration with Nazi Germany to make genocide more efficient, argued tech workers have a responsibility to ensure technologies tech workers build are held to an ethical standard. The Never Again pledge articulated a new strategy. The argument was simple: tech users, although numbering in the billions, have no power to transform tech companies. Policy makers, especially in a conservative government, neither had the political will nor a shared analysis to push tech corporations along an ethical path. Consequently, it was only workers, in particular collectively organized workers, who could hold companies accountable. Organizations such as Tech Solidarity and the Tech Workers Coalition sought to carry this momentum into workplace organizing.[24] Tech campuses became spaces of heated debate, often with CEOs leading the charge.

As Trump's presidency carried on, the progressive rhetoric of tech leaders persisted but changes did not come. Contracts with the U.S. Immigration and Customs Enforcement (ICE) and the federal government were vigorously and unquestionably pursued, accountability for sexual harassment and gender/racial discrimination was nonexistent, and efforts to address the climate crisis negligent.[25] New tactics were necessary. At Amazon, new tech-worker organizations emerged around two specific campaigns. In the first campaign, Amazon Employees for Climate Justice, workers organized internally to push Amazon to lead in addressing the climate crisis. Starting with smaller petitions and a shareholder resolution, their actions escalated to a game-changing 3,000-worker walkout in September, 2019. A second campaign, part of a broader tech-worker movement called #WeWontBuildIt, is challenging Amazon's tight relationship with the military industrial complex, demanding Amazon cease selling facial recognition technologies to ICE and the police.

These two campaigns are just part of a growing tech-worker movement taking collective action to address political problems. In 2018, Google workers organized more than 20,000 of their co-workers to walk out in protests against gender-based discrimination and sexual harassment; as of 2019, a similar fight was brewing at Amazon. Today, this movement—often heralded as the emergent "Tech Left"—is conjoining with activists around climate change, spilling over into fights around the social use of technology, and buttressing struggles around temping, subcontracting, and the exploitative use of restrictive H1B visas. Each campaign focuses on the heart of the alienation and forms of oppression experienced by tech workers. Tech workers are demanding that their labor serve people and planet, rather than just the financial interests of the capitalist class. Through collective struggle, the Tech Left is also demystifying the fundamental class relation between tech workers and their employers, leading tech workers to rediscover that they are, indeed, working class. Scrapping the individualistic and meritocratic progressive neoliberal playbook, the Tech Left is putting into practice democratic structures, determining demands through deliberation and debate, and articulating a broader politics of emancipation that extends beyond the interests of tech workers alone.

Unlike the March for Science and Womxn's March two years prior, the climate walk-out demonstrated the specific power tech workers in FAANG corporations have to make broader demands for the common good. Tech-worker power stems not from their capacity to swing elections, but rather their decisive and growing position in the technical division of labor. The power to stop production and therefore create a crisis for the capitalist class (structural power) is historically concentrated in the tech industry. One could imagine strikes in key chokepoints that leverage the ability of engineers to shut down key aspects of the production process. Shutting down websites, access to the cloud, or monkeywrenching logistical systems can shut down not just the fulfillment logistics network, but the entire economy. Demands could link together the issues of warehouse, community organizations, and tech workers alike, using the structural power of tech workers to advance the interests of the working class as a whole. It is no surprise tech bosses are terrified, brazenly firing activists and hiring anti-union firms to quell the political self-expression of their workforce.

While tech workers in major corporations are organizing around their own self-interest, a broader question of how tech workers relate to the rest of the working class persists. A politics of alienation and the pursuit for self-fulfillment of tech workers does not *necessarily* align with the disempowered and exploited workers in Amazon's fulfillment centers. It is an open question whether the economic and political interests of the labor aristocracy and broader layers of the working class align. A politics of altruism or sympathy for the oppressed are weak bonds relative to the power of capital to divide and conquer.

Capital is capable of appealing to the interests of particular demographics while oppressing others. Led by Jeff Bezos, capitalists are responding with a "new era" of capitalism that moves beyond shareholder value, with Amazon's Climate Pledge a shining example of corporations attempting to solve problems they created.[26] This renewed platform could easily co-opt current tech movements into a superficially benevolent capitalism. Currently, the majority of tech organizing orbits *accountability*: for example, ensuring corporations divest from fossil fuels and set standards for carbon emissions, establish better protocol around sexual harassment and gender-based discrimination, or limit the development of technology for the surveillance of marginalized people. This does not fundamentally challenge the power relations of society. It plays back into the hands of capital, reinforcing the legitimacy of corporations and the capitalist class as *the* agents of transformative change who now, at the least, must bargain with organized but still fragmented collectives of workers. Tech workers may accept this bargain, giving up a project of emancipation rooted in deeper solidarity with broader layers of the working class for the benefits tech capital can continue to bestow upon the aristocracy, encapsulating them in the bubble once again.

Another trajectory is possible. Halfway across the United States from Seattle's headquarters, workers have been protesting Amazon's inhumane working conditions in warehouses in Minneapolis. In late January 2019, a vicious cold spell hit the upper Midwest, sending workers home without pay. During a later protest, Amazon Employees for Climate Justice reached out to warehouse workers, and wrote in a statement of solidarity, "We cannot create a sustainable, long-term approach to addressing the climate crisis without addressing structural racial and economic inequities that are part of our system of extraction—of energy, material, and human labor—that have caused the crisis."[27] The Tech Workers Coalition was founded to demonstrate solidarity with unionizing 'tech-adjacent' workers on tech campuses. These projects, while meaningful and important points of leverage for unionizing workers, have not consolidated into new organizational forms such as a broader tech-workers union where interests align and demands are shared. This trajectory is a *political* project dependent on the *organization* of the working class into formations capable of advancing a politics around their shared self-interest. What must emerge is a politics of solidarity; for the true power of the working class stems from its ability to express compassion and care through empathy, therefore building unity in a shared moral and ethical commitment to an emancipatory political project.

To address the crucial problems of our age, the movement must weaken capital and corporate control over the future of working-class communities and workplaces.[28] The movement must aim to put more social wealth under democratic or national control, while articulating a strong moral and ethical commitment to our shared humanity and collective flourishing. This looks like funnelling investment away from self-driving cars into public mass transit; moving app design away from producing impulsive consumerism towards facilitating meaningful connection; shifting the work of economists away from exploiting tax loopholes into long-term industrial planning; developing robotics that free the working class from work rather than furthering their impoverishment, and radically empowering skilled and technical workers to work in conjunction with communities to design eco-friendly and liveable cities.

A transformation of this magnitude will require power, including new class organizations along the *economic* terrain of struggle through tech-industry unions and new *political* formations capable of producing a ruling and governing bloc. The working class, united across skill, must develop a shared vision, and a shared organizing bloc, to move us toward a more just world and towards new political formations capable of challenging the meaningless and cruel rule of capital.

NOTES

1. Maya Kosoff, "One Amazon Employee's 'Human Error' May Have Cost the Economy Millions" *Vanity Fair*, March 3, 2017, www.vanityfair.com/

news/2017/03/one-amazon-employees-human-error-may-have-cost-the-economy-millions. Accessed December 1, 2019.
2. David Harvey, *The Condition of Postmodernity* (Oxford: Blackwell Publishers, 1990).
3. David Autor, "Polanyi's Paradox and the Shape of Employment Growth," *NBER Working Paper No. 20485*, September 2014, www.nber.org/papers/w20485.pdf. Accessed September 1, 2019.
4. James Galbraith, *Inequality and Instability: A Study of the World Economy Just Before the Great Crisis* (New York: Oxford University Press, 2012).
5. David H. Autor, Lawrence Katz, and Richard Murnane, "The Skill Content of Recent Technological Change: An Empirical Exploration," *Quarterly Journal of Economics* 118 (2003): 1279–1333.
6. Christophe Lécuyer, *Making Silicon Valley: Innovation and the Growth of High Tech, 1930–1970* (Boston, MA: The MIT Press, 2005).
7. Vladimir Lenin, *Imperialism: The Highest Stage of Capitalism* (New York: International Publishers, 1939).
8. Richard Barbrook and Andy Cameron, "The California Ideology," *Science as Culture* 6(1) (1996): 44–72.
9. Nancy Fraser, "From Progressive Neoliberalism to Trump—and Beyond," *American Affairs* I(4) (2017), https://americanaffairsjournal.org/2017/11/progressive-neoliberalism-trump-beyond/. Accessed September 2019.
10. Ibid., original emphasis.
11. Siva Vaidhyanathan, "Was Obama Silicon Valley's President?," *The Nation*, December 13, 2016, www.thenation.com/article/was-obama-silicon-valleys-president/. Accessed September 1, 2019.
12. Joanna Perlstein, "It's True: Tech Workers Overwhelmingly Support Democrats in 2018," *Wired*, October 26, 2018, www.wired.com/story/tech-workers-overwhelmingly-support-democrats/. Accessed September 1, 2019.
13. Robert G. Valletta, "Recent Flattening in the Higher Education Wage Premium: Polarization, Skill Downgrading, or Both?" *NBER Working Paper 22935*, December 2016.
14. Moira Weigel, "Coders of the World Unite: Can Silicon Valley Workers Curb the Power of Big Tech?," *The Guardian*, October 31, 2017, https://tinyurl.com/yccb6p2b. Accessed September 1, 2019.
15. Joseph Stiglitz and Bruce Greenwald, *Creating a Learning Economy* (New York: Columbia University Press, 2014).
16. Nellie Bowles, "Silicon Valley Goes to Therapy," *New York Times*, September 20, 2019, www.nytimes.com/2019/09/20/business/silicon-valley-therapy-anxiety.html. Accessed September 1, 2019.
17. Emily Chang, *Brotopia: Breaking up the Boys' Club of Silicon Valley* (New York: Penguin, 2019).
18. This is quoted from an upcoming "Sexism in Tech" shareholder resolution at Amazon.

19. Alison Wynn, "Why Tech's Approach to Fixing Its Gender Inequality Isn't Working," *Harvard Business Review*, October 11, 2019, https://hbr.org/2019/10/why-techs-approach-to-fixing-its-gender-inequality-isnt-working. Accessed December 1, 2019.
20. Julie Carrie Wong, "Segregated Valley: The Ugly Truth About Google and Diversity in Tech" *The Guardian*, August 7, 2017, https://tinyurl.com/y9ygs2qd. Accessed December 1, 2019.
21. Ben Tarnoff and Moira Weigel, "Why Silicon Valley Can't Fix Itself," *The Guardian*, May 3, 2018, https://tinyurl.com/y8bkk6ld. Accessed September 1, 2019.
22. Kenneth Andrews, Neal Caren, and Alyssa Browne "Protesting Trump," *Mobilization: An International Quarterly* 23(4) (2018).
23. The pledge can be found at https://neveragain.tech/.
24. Gretchen Roers, "'Solidarity Forever,' Maciej Ceglowski from Tech Solidarity," *Logic Magazine*, June 9, 2017, https://logicmag.io/tech-against-trump/maciej-ceg%C5%82owski-tech-solidarity/. Accessed December 1, 2019.
25. Nitasha Tiku, "Three Years of Misery Inside Google, the Happiest Company in Tech," *Wired*, August 13, 2019, www.wired.com/story/inside-google-three-years-misery-happiest-company-tech/. Accessed September 1, 2019.
26. Richard Henderson and Patrick Temple-West, "Group of US Corporate Leaders Ditches Shareholder-first Mantra," *Financial Times*, August 19, 2019, www.ft.com/content/e21a9fac-c1f5-11e9-a8e9-296ca66511c9. Accessed September 1, 2019).
27. Amazon Employees for Climate Justice, "Quotes of Solidarity for Striking Amazon Warehouse Workers" *Medium*, July 12, 2019, https://tinyurl.com/uh69m4u. Accessed September 1, 2019.
28. Spencer Cox and Nantina Vgontzas, "Amazon's Bullshit Environmentalism," *The Nation*, December 12, 2019, www.thenation.com/article/amazons-bullshit-environmentalism/. Accessed December 19, 2019.

15
The CEO Has No Clothes: Worker Leadership and Amazon's Failures During COVID-19

Dania Rajendra

The COVID-19 pandemic and concurrent economic crisis have put a global spotlight on the ruthlessness of Amazon's business model—in particular a total commitment to profit, market share acquisition, and a subsequent reliance on "spin" to paper over the company's near-total disregard for human health.

Athena, a coalition of worker, community, policy, and other non-governmental organizations was launched in November 2019, only six months before the COVID-19 crisis took hold in the United States.[1] From our inception, we have consistently focused on both the physical and political dangers, to workers, their neighbors, and democracies as a whole. With most upper- and middle-class members of almost all societies sheltering at home, demand for Amazon grew into levels described as "unprecedented."[2] In the midst of a cratering stock market—as well as a crash in the real economy—Amazon's stock continued to rise. Jeff Bezos, despite selling off US$3.4 billion in stock in March and April 2020,[3] became $24 billion richer by the middle of April.[4] With independent and community businesses shuttered, Amazon became, too often, the sole source for essential and non-essential goods. The result? Tightening control over markets, public officials, and customers, despite the promise of the HQ2 pushback. The one place we may have begun to loosen some of Amazon's control, as of this writing, is the workplace.

LABOR SHORTAGES, RISK, AND EXPOSURE

A month into the COVID-19 crisis, Amazon appeared to be facing a severe labor shortage in the face of up to 25 percent in increased demand. The corporation announced hiring as many as 175,000 new workers in the U.S. alone,[5] raising the base wage by $2 to $17 in the U.S. (and the equivalent two units in pounds and euros) and offering double-time for overtime hours worked.[6] One would think in this employment situation—where in late March and early April some 22 million people[7] filed for unemployment—the pay raises would be enough to keep the packages moving. It appeared not.

Workers reported massive absences[8] by people who feared exposing themselves, their families, and neighbors to the virus. Working-class communities, especially communities of color, bore the brunt of the pandemic: exposure, illness, and mortality follow the same socio-economic disadvantages they faced before the crisis. Those include disproportionately suffering from underlying conditions like diabetes, asthma, and heart disease generally due to deprivation of health care, healthy food, and—especially—clean air.[9] The latter has long been the grounds of a prolonged fight with Amazon in Southern California[10] and outside of Chicago,[11] where the trucks and trains that move the goods[12] choke the air with particulate matter.

COVID-19—both the pandemic and the economic crash it unleashed—revealed these deep connections between workers, families, neighbors, and consumers, who found new ways to demonstrate and unite against the threat to public health that Amazon posed. Phillip Ruiz, who worked at JFK8, told Athena leaders that he was as worried about being someone who "brought COVID-19 to my block" as he was about his own health.[13] Similarly, workers distinguished between the relative social benefit of risking their own health and the health of loved ones to deliver truly essential items, with what they often found themselves packing.[14] Throughout the corporation and the geographies it inhabits, workers were vocal about their simultaneous identity as family and community members in talking about their work for Amazon, and Amazon's treatment of them. Their solidarity and public-spiritedness was a dramatic counterpoint to the singular focus of corporate executives: keeping operations going to meet demand, no matter the worker, community, or even public health costs.[15]

With the news in March 2020 that the virus was viable on non-porous surfaces up to 72 hours and on cardboard up to 24, workers focused their attention on the corporation's failure to keep the facilities clean[16] and to change its punitive "time off task" regime, which means workers lack the time—in the unlikely event they have the supplies—to wash their hands. Strikes and walkouts began over just those concerns—and the repeated allegations that the company hid[17] the number of COVID-19 cases among Amazon workers, which prevented people from making meaningful risk analyses about whether to come to work. "I'm scared and feeling like they're trying to hide health risks from the workers. And we're not being kept in the loop about our safety," Terrell Worm, a worker at Amazon's Staten Island warehouse who participated in our April demonstrations told CBS News. According to Worm, after workers were informed that someone had tested positive on Tuesday, the building continued operating as usual: "It was just business as normal."[18] Amazon offered the entire United States—and in particular, the elite media—a real-time lesson in corporate propaganda.[19] As the company continued to tout its two weeks of pay in the case of diagnosis or quarantine, workers reported that, even with documentation, their claims were rejected.[20] Because of overwhelming first-hand worker pushback, Amazon chief spokesperson Jay Carney came under fire on Twitter[21] and on air[22] from journalists about the credibility of his statements. This invited much-needed public light to be cast over Amazon's vast private power.

In France, where, as in many other places, Amazon promised to stop shipping non-essential goods (but, according to workers, didn't), a French court mandated the company to do so—leading to Amazon shutting down all French operations (with full pay for workers).[23] In a much smaller example, the governor of the state of Kentucky, Andy Beshear,[24] ordered the shutdown of a non-essential facility after a COVID-19 outbreak. Unfortunately, the shutdown lasted only for a week, and upon re-opening, the company announced additional exposure.[25]

Overall, the company failed to account for the consequence of its own policy decisions. Workers began to track the COVID-19 exposures—and rumors—on their own, furnishing journalists and the public with facts the corporation should have revealed. Hence the widespread absences, and a new, even more punitive approach to labor relations, including high-profile firings of four workers who had been outspoken about the company's failure to protect worker and public health alike. More firings were expected even as workers creatively collaborated to make up for the corporation's own failures with maps, counts, news searches, and private communications—another example of workers checking in on one another as the corporations and top management failed to do so.

As workers demanded protection for not only themselves but their family members, and via Athena's efforts and others, tens of thousands of people backed their demands in the ensuing weeks. The firings, occasionally, caused federal and state officials to react with approbation, and, at least in New York, an investigation was initiated. Workers not only appealed to the public at large. In California,[26] in Minnesota,[27] and in Pennsylvania,[28] workers filed charges with both worker and public health authorities about Amazon's failure to protect their own and public health. While in some places, local officials publicly decried Amazon's lack of transparency, for local officials like Staten Island Borough President James Oddo, a high-profile backer of projects like the Amazon facility there, support included championing public financing and tax breaks for Amazon.[29] This left Oddo and similar political figures beholden to Amazon and with little leverage over needed information, let alone the will or support for political actions that would protect public health. As the pandemic continued to spread unevenly across the United States, there was simply not enough information for advocates and public officials to know whether the corporation was a vector of the disease.

Though Amazon is a data company, it refused to divulge comprehensive or even aggregated information. In a recent CNN interview, Jay Carney himself stated he didn't know how many people had contracted COVID-19—a claim difficult to believe on its face from a company that prides itself on its commitment to tracking every minute aspect of its operations. Forty-some years of neoliberal governance, including the curtailment of state and federal regulatory capacity and authority, meant that stressed public systems struggled to meet the additional pressure of Amazon's inaction or compliance failure. Amazon reaped all the profits, while its workers and the broader public were left holding all the risk.

This is one reason the Amazon workers' protests and whistleblowing electrified the United States. To tell the truth, to tell it baldly, to tell it with a clear view of the consequences and to do it anyway—was a shocking and thrilling development in an otherwise deeply anti-democratic moment. But the truth is, low-wage workers in America were exceptionally attuned to burgeoning authoritarianism, living through a version—and not only at Amazon—each and every day. After all, it is they who live under the constant surveillance, the blatant disregard for well-being, the Animal Farm-style pronouncements, and the corporate despotism, so that they can make ends meet. Amazon's employment regime was already especially punishing throughout the corporation, including white-collar workers.[30] The algorithmic management was already severely taxing workers' physical and mental health.[31]

The Cost of Free Shipping

WORKERS' RESISTANCE AMIDST THE PANDEMIC

During the pandemic, Amazon executives smeared whistleblower Chris Smalls[32] with racist insinuations and incendiary language. For his part, Smalls, a member of Make the Road New York and New York Communities for Change, remained unbowed. Inside the facilities, executives announced they'd further automate the surveillance of the workers, promising disciplinary procedures—up to and including firing—for anyone caught violating newly mandated social distancing rules.[33] This followed new policies mandating temperature checks. People who failed were sent home without pay, until journalists covered the scandal. Even after that, workers were now promised only part of a shift's pay.[34] As late as the week before, the company had still been text messaging workers to encourage them to "try" to stay up to three feet apart. Fulfillment and distribution facilities are busy places, full of people—especially as they come in and out during breaks and shift changes.

Worker protests—especially by workers like Chris Smalls and Jana Jumpp,[35] who were open about their previous success and satisfaction in their Amazon employment—shifted the national conversation. Before COVID-19, there had been a reflexive trust in the company. One poll showed it was among the most trusted institutions in American life.[36] That trust clearly began to shatter as the reality of Amazon became all the more apparent, as workers, backed by their families, friends, neighbors, and communities spoke up. Nonetheless, it did feel like a race against the clock.

Amazon continued to grow—particularly into "essential" infrastructure, expanding deals with the U.K. government from use of National Health Service (NHS) data to providing COVID-19 testing,[37] and inking new agreements in Canada to deliver medical supplies.[38] As the economy cratered, the American political establishment failed to provide even the most threadbare safety net for working people—there were simply no provisions or protections for workers at the largest firms. Similarly, small business relief was anemic at best. The "relief" that was passed had already been distributed (as of this writing in mid-April 2020), with hedge fund managers[39] first at the trough. Meanwhile, small businesses with little cushion have already been closing down permanently across the United States.

The vision that haunts Athena members isn't only the preventable exposure, illness, and death—it is also the way that Amazon exemplifies a neoliberal economy's fundamental incompatibility with democracy. The way Amazon treats the people who work there is important unto itself. It's also important because it provides the best view into their governance philosophy. As Athena leader Stacy Mitchell, co-director of the Institute of Local Self Reliance says, "If we don't regulate Amazon, we are effectively allowing it to regulate us."[40]

In addition to the workplaces, another site where Amazon has dominated less powerful people is on their marketplace. For example, Amazon's big, international pronouncements that it would "slow" or "suspend" the shipping of non-essential goods,[41] ostensibly to protect workers, seem far more focused on market share and control. French inspectors, American workers, and others all said, simply, it didn't happen. Non-essential goods continued to move. What *did* happen was that Amazon has arbitrarily changed the rules about what shipments they would accept from third parties[42]—cutting off the ability of those people to get their goods to market, because their goods are "fulfilled by Amazon." After yet another investigation,[43] the company walked back the change, reinstating the previous policy.[44] Much like the dangers to workers (though of course, much less dramatic), the sellers' damages from delay, disruption, and uncertainty, however—were unacknowledged and uncompensated.

THINKING BIGGER, TOGETHER

The intricacies of the rest of the Amazon business model—including Amazon Web Services (AWS), the corporation's cash cow—are too far afield for this chapter, but suffice to say Amazon appeared to be refusing to reduce fees[45] and costs[46] to other, smaller businesses throughout its operations, despite their pleas, as the COVID-19 crisis intensified worldwide. In February 2020, Bloomberg reported that Amazon's HQ2 negotiating strategy was "internally summarized" as "Fuck you, we're Amazon."[47] That strategy seems to still be in evidence as it relates to the needs of smaller or less powerful partners—from workers, to sellers, to customers—and arguably, government institutions themselves.

As Amazon is further embedded into public-private partnerships of providing essential services, calls to regulate and oversee the infrastructure, including a suggestion from antitrust scholars K. Sabeel Rahman (director of Athena member Demos) and Zephyr Teachout to borrow the public-utility model for addressing Amazon's role in contemporary commerce and society, become more commonplace. As Rahman and Teachout argued in a paper pre-dating COVID-19, platform corporations, including Amazon "should be viewed as essential infrastructure and regulated as public utilities."[48] Those aspects of the corporation that might serve the public good should perhaps do so more directly. More assertive calls for nationalization dated back at least to the HQ2 fights, for the obvious reason that public dollars should be for public needs, not private gain. On a press call in April, Athena member For Us Not Amazon in Northern Virginia made the point that had Virginia not "donated" $803 million to Amazon, they'd have that money to address residents' community health, economic, and other needs. They demanded Amazon forgo the cash.

In 2018, journalist Sarah Jaffe called for nationalizing Amazon in a piece in *The Outline* which condensed the problems of private power succinctly: "Amazon gets to do basically whatever it wants because the fact is Amazon doesn't have competition."[49] In the pages of *The Nation*, Mike Davis made a similar pitch, especially around saving the U.S. Postal Service, to which Amazon poses a particular threat.[50]

As the fifty-plus organizations that make up Athena begin to chart demands and a strategy for the moment beyond the first crisis, we'll be relying on the fact that the people who best know what they need are the ones directly harmed by the company—at work, at home, online, and in our communities. That's, quite frankly, most of us. What COVID-19 made evident is that we truly are in this together—workers, neighbors, customers—everyone but executives. The pandemic and the economic crash created a moment in which it was a necessity to practice solidarity and we had permission, in a way, to rethink so much about how our economy, society, and health intersect. It was an invitation to think bigger, together. Surely we can have moratoriums on abusive data regimes, robust public utilities, and an economy oriented around a democracy, instead of the other way around. Everyone's health depends on it.

NOTES

1. David Streitfeld, David. "Activists Build a Grass-Roots Alliance Against Amazon," *New York Times*, November 26, 2019, www.nytimes.com/2019/11/26 technology/amazon-grass-roots-activists.html. Accessed April 20, 2020.

2. Lauren Feiner, "Amazon Stock Hits a New All-Time High as it sees Unprecedented Demand," *CNBC*, April 14, 2020, www.cnbc.com/2020/04/14/amazon-stock-hits-a-new-all-time-high.html. Accessed April 20, 2020.
3. Susan Pullian, Coulter Jones and Andrea Fuller, "Amazon's Bezos, Other Corporate Executives Sold Shares Just in Time," *Wall Street Journal*, March 24, 2020, www.wsj.com/articles/bezos-other-corporate-executives-sold-shares-just-in-time-11585042204. Accessed April 20, 2020.
4. Isobel Asher Hamilton, "Jeff Bezos is Wealthier by $24 Billion in 2020, as Amazon Reports at Least 74 COVID-19 US Warehouse Cases and its First Death," *Business Insider*, April 15, 2020, www.businessinsider.com/jeff-bezos-net-worth-jumps-23-billion-during-coronavirus-crisis-2020-4. Accessed April 20, 2020.
5. Mike Snider, "Amazon Hiring an Additional 75,000 Workers to Meet Demand During Coronavirus Pandemic," *USA Today*, April 13, 2020, www.usatoday.com/story/money/business/2020/04/13/amazon-jobs-75-000-more-workers-needed-amid-coronavirus-pandemic/2981902001/. Accessed April 20, 2020.
6. Jessica Guynn, "Coronavirus: Amazon Gives Warehouse Workers Temporary Overtime Pay Raise." *USA Today*, March 21, 2020, www.usatoday.com/story/tech/2020/03/21/amazon-gives-warehouse-workers-temporary-covid-19-overtime-pay-raise/2891603001/. Accessed April 20, 2020.
7. Anneken Tappe and Tami Luhby, "22 Million Americans Have Filed for Unemployment Benefits in the Last Four Weeks," *CNN Business*, April 16, 2020, www.cnn.com/2020/04/16/economy/unemployment-benefits-coronavirus/index.html. Accessed April 20, 2020.
8. Casey Newton, "Amazon's Poor Treatment of Workers is Catching up to it During the Coronavirus Crisis," *The Verge*, April 1, 2020, www.theverge.com/interface/2020/4/1/21201162/amazon-delivery-delays-coronavirus-worker-strikes. Accessed April 20, 2020.
9. Lisa Friedman, "New Research Links Air Pollution to Higher Coronavirus Death Rates," *New York Times*, April 7, 2020, www.nytimes.com/2020/04/07/climate/air-pollution-coronavirus-covid.html. Accessed April 20, 2020.
10. Yvette Cabrera, "As Amazon Speeds Up, a Warehouse Community Braces for a Deadly Combo: Air Pollution and Coronavirus," *Grist*, March 21, 2020, https://grist.org/justice/as-amazon-speeds-up-a-warehouse-community-braces-for-a-deadly-combo-air-pollution-and-coronavirus/. Accessed April 20, 2020.
11. Sophie Yeo, "How Chicago's Mexican Immigrants are Fighting Toxic Air Pollution," *PS Mag*, April 9, 2018, https://psmag.com/environment/chicagos-mexican-immigrants-are-fighting-toxic-air-pollution-again. Accessed April 20, 2020.
12. Maya Shwayder, "Amazon's Airport Ambitions Might Be Squashed by a Tiny Group of Activists," *Digital Trends*, January 29, 2002, www.digitaltrends.com/news/amazon-san-bernardino-airport-air-pollution-environmental-impact/. Accessed April 20, 2020.

13. Michelle Chen, "Your Rent or Your Life," *The Nation*, April 3, 2020, www.thenation.com/article/economy/workers-labor-coronavirus/. Accessed April 20, 2020.
14. Jennifer Mas, "John Oliver Rips Amazon's Treatment of Essential Workers: 'Risking Your Life to Get Someone a Sex Toy Probably Doesn't Feel Fair'," *The Wrap*, April 13, 2020, www.thewrap.com/john-oliver-amazon-essential-workers-coronavirus-warehouse-sex-toys-dildos-sick-leave-policy-jeff-bezos-last-week-tonight-video/
15. David Lee and Patricia Nilsson, "Amazon Faces Protests in US, France, and Italy Over Allegations of Normal Shifts Continuing Despite COVID-19 Cases; Includes Company Comments," *Financial Times (via Business-humanrights.org)*, March 20, 2020, www.business-humanrights.org/en/amazon-faces-protests-in-us-france-italy-over-allegations-of-normal-shifts-continuing-despite-covid-19-cases-includes-company-comments. Accessed April 20, 2020.
16. Louise Matsakis, "9 Amazon Workers Describe the Daily Risks They Face in the Pandemic," *Wired*, April 10, 2020. www.wired.com/story/amazon-workers-pandemic-risks-own-words/. Accessed April 20, 2020.
17. John Dzieza, "Amazon Warehouse Workers are Outraged After a Coworker Tested Positive for COVID-19 and They Weren't Notified," *The Verge*, March 26, 2020, www.theverge.com/2020/3/26/21194739/amazon-warehouse-workers-coronavirus-covid-19-outraged-informed. Accessed April 20, 2020.
18. Irina Ivanova, "Amazon Workers Worry About Catching Coronavirus on the Job," *CBS News*, March 26, 2020. www.cbsnews.com/news/coronavirus-amazon-workers-protection/. Accessed April 20, 2020.
19. Louise Matsakis, "Amazon Workers Face High Risks and Few Options," *Wired*, March 27, 2020, www.wired.com/story/coronavirus-amazon-warehouse-workers-risks-few-options/. Accessed April 20, 2020.
20. Annie Palmer, "'Amazon is not taking care of us': Warehouse Workers Say They're Struggling to Get Paid Despite Sick Leave Policy," *CNBC*, April 8, 2020, www.cnbc.com/2020/04/08/amazon-warehouse-workers-say-they-struggle-to-get-paid-despite-sick-leave-policy.html. Accessed April 20, 2020.
21. Twitter.com. https://twitter.com/noamscheiber/status/1245538008562008064?s=19. Accessed April 20, 2020.
22. Twitter.com. https://twitter.com/CNNnewsroom/status/1251243631714893824. Accessed April 20, 2020.
23. Alex Hern, "Amazon Closes French Warehouses After Court Ruling on Coronavirus," *The Guardian*, April 16, 2020, www.theguardian.com/technology/2020/apr/15/amazon-to-close-french-warehouses-over-coronavirus-concerns Accessed April 20, 2020.
24. Matt Day, "Amazon Says Kentucky Governor Ordered Idling of Returns Facility," *Bloomberg*, March 26, 2020, www.bloomberg.com/news/articles/2020-03-26/amazon-says-kentucky-governor-ordered-idling-of-returns-facility. Accessed April 20, 2020.

25. Billy Kobin, "New COVID-19 Cases Reported at Amazon's Shepherdsville and Jeffersonville Facilities." *The Courier-Journal*, April 3, 2020, www.courier-journal.com/story/news/2020/04/03/coronavirus-new-cases-reported-shepherdsvillekentucky-jeffersonville-indiana-warehouses/2938577001/. Accessed April 20, 2020.
26. Sam Dean, "Fearful of COVID-19, Amazon Workers ask for State Probe of Working Conditions," *Los Angeles Times*, April 9, 2020, www.latimes.com/business/technology/story/2020-04-09/fearful-of-covid-19-amazon-workers-ask-for-state-probe-of-working-conditions. Accessed April 20, 2020.
27. Kabita Kumar, "Workers Group Files OSHA Complaint Against Amazon After Doctor Tells Shakopee Employee to Self-quarantine," *The Star Tribune*, April 10, 2020, www.startribune.com/workers-group-files-osha-complaint-against-amazon-after-doctor-tells-shakopee-employee-to-self-quarantine/569555992/. Accessed April 20, 2020.
28. Spencer Soper and Matt Day. "OSHA is Probing Amazon Warehouse Over Coronavirus Concerns," *Bloomberg*, April 8, 2020, www.bloomberg.com/news/articles/2020-04-08/osha-is-investigating-amazon-warehouse-over-coronavirus-concerns. Accessed April 20, 2020.
29. The Real Deal Staff, "Amazon Inks Massive Lease for Staten Island Warehouse," *The Real Deal*, January 28, 2020, https://therealdeal.com/2020/01/28/amazon-inks-massive-lease-for-staten-island-warehouse/. Accessed April 20, 2020.
30. Jodi Kantor and David Streitfeld, "Inside Amazon: Wrestling Big Ideas in a Bruising Workplace," *New York Times*, August 15, 2015, www.nytimes.com/2015/08/16/technology/inside-amazon-wrestling-big-ideas-in-a-bruising-workplace.html. Accessed April 20, 2020.
31. Shirin Ghaffary, "Robots Aren't Taking Warehouse Employee's Jobs, They're Making Their Work Harder," *Vox Recode*, October 22, 2018, www.vox.com/recode/2019/10/22/20925894/robots-warehouse-jobs-automation-replace-workers-amazon-report-university-illinois. Accessed April 20, 2020.
32. Paul Blest, "Leaked Amazon Memo Details Plan to Smear Fired Warehouse Organizer: 'He's Not Smart or Articulate'" *Vice News*, April 2, 2020, www.vice.com/en_us/article/5dm8bx/leaked-amazon-memo-details-plan-to-smear-fired-warehouse-organizer-hes-not-smart-or-articulate. Accessed April 20, 2020.
33. Donna Fascaldo, "Amazon Might Fire Workers Who Break Social Distancing Rules," *Nasdaq.com*, April 7, 2020, www.nasdaq.com/articles/amazon-might-fire-workers-who-break-social-distancing-rules-2020-04-07. Accessed April 20, 2020.
34. Caroline O'Donavan, "Amazon Will Give Partial Pay to Employees it Sends Home with Fevers During the Coronavirus Pandemic," *Buzzfeed*, April 8, 2020, www.buzzfeednews.com/article/carolineodonovan/amazon-employees-with-fever-5-hours-pay. Accessed April 20, 2020.

35. Noel King, "Can Amazon meet Customer Demand and Keep its Workforce Safe?" *National Public Radio*, March 27, 2020, www.npr.org/2020/03/27/822383402/can-amazon-meet-customer-demand-and-keep-its-workforce-safe. Accessed April 20, 2020.
36. Kaitlyn Tiffany, "In Amazon We Trust—But Why?" *Vox*, October 25, 2018, www.vox.com/the-goods/2018/10/25/18022956/amazon-trust-survey-american-institutions-ranked-georgetown. Accessed April 20, 2020.
37. Lucy Ingham, "Coronavirus Home Test Delivery Gives Amazon Key Move Towards UK Healthcare Dominance," *Verdict*, March 27, 2020, www.verdict.co.uk/coronavirus-home-test-delivery/. Accessed April 20, 2020.
38. Kelsey Johnson, "Canada Signs Agreement with Amazon Canada to Manage Distribution of Medical Equipment," *Reuters*, April 3, 2020, www.reuters.com/article/us-health-cornavirus-canada-amazon/canada-signs-agreement-with-amazon-canada-to-manage-distribution-of-medical-equipment-idUSKBN21L2MO. Accessed April 20, 2020.
39. Katherine Burton and Joshua Fineman, "Hedge Fund Managers Claiming Bailouts as Small Businesses," *Bloomberg*, April 14, 2020, www.bloomberg.com/news/articles/2020-04-14/hedge-fund-managers-are-claiming-bailouts-as-small-businesses. Accessed April 20, 2020.
40. David Streitfeld, "As Amazon Rises, So Does the Opposition," *New York Times*, April 18, 2020, www.nytimes.com/2020/04/18/technology/athena-mitchell-amazon.html. Accessed April 20, 2020.
41. Nicholas Vega, "Amazon Suspends Shipments of Non-essential Products to Warehouses Amid Coronavirus-driven Shortages," *New York Post*, March 17, 2020, nypost.com/2020/03/17/amazon-suspends-shipments-of-non-essential-products-to-warehouses-amid-coronavirus-driven-shortages/. Accessed April 20, 2020.
42. Louise Matsakis, "Amazon's New 'Essential Items' Policy is Devastating Sellers," *Wired*, March 24, 2020, www.wired.com/story/amazon-essential-items-policy-devastating-sellers/. Accessed April 20, 2020.
43. Maddy Varner, "Amazon's Shifting Definition of What is 'Essential,'" *The Markup*, April 7, 2002. https://themarkup.org/coronavirus/2020/04/07/amazons-shifting-definition-of-what-is-essential. Accessed April 20, 2020.
44. Dana Mattioli, "Amazon to expand Shipments of Nonessential Items, Continue Adding Staff," *Wall Street Journal*, April 13, 2020, www.wsj.com/articles/amazon-seeks-to-hire-another-75-000-workers-11586789365. Accessed April 20, 2020.
45. Tae Kim, "Amazon Squeezes Affiliates When They Can Least Afford It," *Bloomberg*, April 16, 2014, www.bloomberg.com/opinion/articles/2020-04-16/coronavirus-amazon-s-struggle-with-demand-costs-some-partners. Accessed April 20, 2020.
46. Kevin McLaughlin and Amir Efrati, "AWS Holds the Line on Cloud Bills As Customers Ask for Relief," *The Information*, April 17, 2020, www.theinformation.

com/articles/aws-holds-the-line-on-cloud-bills-as-customers-ask-for-relief. Accessed April 20, 2020.
47. Spencer Soper, Matt Day, and Henry Goldman. "Behind Amazon's HQ2 fiasco: Jeff Bezos was Jealous of Elon Musk," *Bloomberg*, February 3, 2020, www.bloomberg.com/news/articles/2020-02-03/amazon-s-hq2-fiasco-was-driven-by-bezos-envy-of-elon-musk. Accessed April 20, 2020.
48. K. Sabeel Rahman and Zephyr Teachout, "From Private Bads to Public Goods: Adapting Public Utility Regulation for Informational Infrastructure," *Knight First Amendment Institute*, February 4, 2020, https://knightcolumbia.org/content/from-private-bads-to-public-goods-adapting-public-utility-regulation-for-informational-infrastructure. Accessed April 20, 2020.
49. Sarah Jaffe, "Nationalize Amazon," *The Outline*, November 15, 2018. https://theoutline.com/post/6587/nationalize-amazon-make-bezos-our-bitch?zd=1&zi=sbhapfjg. Accessed April 20, 2020.
50. Mike Davis, "How to Save the Postal Service," *The Nation*, April 6, 2020, www.thenation.com/article/politics/usps-profiteering-nationalize-amazon/. Accessed April 20, 2020.

16
Think Big: Organizing a Successful Amazon Workers' Movement in the United States by Combining the Strengths of the Left and Organized Labor

Peter Olney and Rand Wilson

Amazon is truly the twenty-first-century equivalent of the *Octopus*, a many-armed monster, vividly portrayed by Frank Norris in his fabled 1901 novel of the same name.[1] The many tentacles (which included politicians and the police) of the Southern Pacific Railroad monopoly, the *Octopus*, squeezed the life out of wheat farmers in California who relied on the giant railroad to get their product to market. Like Norris's Octopus, Amazon's oppressive working conditions and impact on local, regional, and even national labor markets are already well documented.[2] While these conditions are familiar to regular working-class folks, the fact that so many people have engaged Amazon as online customers helps to amplify the outrage and greatly enlarges public support for what is now a growing number of Amazon workers' uprisings.[3] It's not just the back-breaking work in warehouses that has provoked workers to rebel. Increasingly, the highly skilled tech workers who program the algorithms that drive Amazon's just-in-time, next-day delivery systems are also engaged in high-visibility social protests.

In this chapter, we explore the prospects for U.S. workers at Amazon to unite in unions, transform their jobs through collective bargaining, and win the good-paying jobs with healthcare and retirement benefits that all workers deserve. How could a substantially weakened U.S. labor movement support such an ambitious effort? What role could the growing number of American socialists play? And what is the potential of these two groups—labor and the left—to work together on this project and how might that collaboration result in success? We believe that if the labor movement ever hopes to exercise significant influence over the U.S. economy, success at Amazon is critical. There needs to be a concerted effort by organized labor with a large investment of resources to help Amazon workers organize. Clearly not an easy task, but a necessary one. Further, Amazon workers themselves must be the agents of any successful workplace organization. And if that is both necessary and desired, it will require a large number of socialists to deliberately enter the tech, warehouse, and delivery workforce. These deliberate workplace organizers must be backed up by the latent power, expertise, and resources of the labor movement. This is hardly new: most large-scale labor organizing in U.S. history has involved a combination of left-wing activism in the workplace and support from the union hierarchy, a melding of political idealism with the strategic chops of union veterans.

Today, organizing at Amazon needs to similarly be conceptualized as finding a way to weld these two forces together in a creative dynamic—determined to actually win prosperity, security and justice for workers and their communities across the American landscape and around the world. Already much has been written on the structure of the company's operations and its vulnerabilities to community and workplace power.[4] Our contribution, based on our experience in workplace organizing and working for powerful supply chain unions, is to further an understanding of the process of melding youthful left-wing enthusiasm with the needs of the existing membership of unions and their elected leaders.[5]

THE CHALLENGES

Amazon's retail model is based on managing logistics in the supply chain better than any other company, and overwhelming competitors with its size and reach. But its high profile and influence brings new vulnerabilities that can be broken down into two categories. First, the public face of Amazon makes the company sensitive to public pressure on many fronts. This vulnerability lends itself to a "metropolitan strategy" involving community, religious, and civic organizations and elected officials. The battle over citing a second headquarters in Queens, New York City in 2019 demonstrated that political and community mobilizations can be very effective (see Chapter

13 in this volume).[6] Further, on Election Day in November 2019, Amazon's attempt at further dominating the Seattle City Council was rebuffed when six out of seven candidates opposed by Amazon were elected—even after the company dumped $1.5 million into the campaign.[7]

Beyond the pressure of public opinion and consumer choices, Amazon's second vulnerability is its supply chain management. The company's business model is based on the sophisticated coordination of product inventory and transportation logistics. That makes it highly susceptible to strategic action by workers—whether in its vast warehouse and sortation centers, shipping its products, or on the technology side. There's really nothing new here: traditional retail has always been susceptible to strikes by delivery drivers bringing merchandise from warehouses to stores.[8] Similarly, manufacturing has been susceptible to work stoppages on an assembly line or at supplier plants that are relied upon for just-in-time delivery of parts to assembly plants.

Amazon is a logistics giant directly supplying the consumer needs of millions worldwide. Its retail home delivery business is guided by the information technology functions of ordering and locating customers, and by immediate delivery from warehouses sited in or near major metropolitan areas. The warehouses rely on the stocking of inventory from far-flung supply chains using air, truck, and water-borne cargo transport. The company employs a complicated system of fulfillment centers, sortation centers, delivery stations, and hubs using over-the-road delivery services ranging from United Parcel Service, FedEx, the U.S. Postal Service, third-party small and medium carriers, and their own Amazon drivers. Since 2013, the company is increasingly using its own delivery services and USPS for the last mile as well.[9] To dominate the supply and delivery of a wide array of products, Amazon is also moving to garner business and capacity on its air and ocean supply routes. Amazon recently bought a cargo airline company,[10] and gained a license as a Non-Vessel Operating Ocean Carrier (NVOOC) to handle ocean-bound freight to a large fleet of trucks, warehouses, and sortation centers close to urban hubs. It may even buy some ships soon.[11]

Amazon's business model is highly reliant on information technology, but is still wedded to human capital. These linkages in the logistics chain offer opportunities for smart strategic organizing. Amazon cannot withstand even short interruptions in service or delays in deliveries. In the auto industry in the 1930s, there were key production facilities crucial to operating the assembly lines. Today, there are junctures in Amazon's system, like its urban-based sortation centers, that have the potential to effectively interrupt the whole flow of product to the end user. The company's own promotions highlight how its sortation centers are crucial to the "everyday and Sunday deliveries that customers love so much."[12]

LEARNING FROM EXPERIENCE AT WALMART

What is the labor movement's recent experience taking on giant retailers? In 2010, Walmart was viewed as the new "Ford"[13] and an imperative for labor to organize. The United Food and Commercial Workers' Union (UFCW)[14] represents tens of thousands of grocery and retail workers whose pay and working conditions were endangered by Walmart's low-wage, no-benefits, business model. UFCW's strategy against Walmart had been to use its local political clout to deny Walmart entry to its unionized markets. As that strategy began to fail, the union stepped up and funded a plan to organisze the competition. UFCW enlisted union strategists with experience in the Service Employees International Union's (SEIU's) successful Justice for Janitors campaign to create an organizing plan for the giant retailer.[15] It embraced a strategy to build an alternative union model—the Organization United for Respect at Walmart (OUR Walmart).[16] OUR Walmart made significant strides spotlighting the company's negative business and employment practices. However, despite spending tens of millions of dollars, it never gained sufficient traction with enough workers for a sustainable on-the-ground organizing force. One major weakness of the campaign was that it never fully engaged UFCW's own membership. Instead, the effort was basically contracted out to OUR Walmart and its team of mostly SEIU-trained organizers.[17] However, organizers missed an important opportunity by never attempting to build support at Walmart's proprietary warehouses, a lynchpin in the company's operations. These warehouses are direct employers because the company recognizes their strategic value and the importance of cultivating stable and loyal employees. Although located far from urban centers, and in that respect more difficult to find workers receptive to forming a union, the effort would have been more strategic.

The campaign did enlist the aid of warehouse worker organizations in both Southern California and Chicago to target third-party logistics providers like Schneider and Excel which handled Walmart products, which led to various successful legal complaints and hefty fines for the companies involved, and new state regulations aimed at protecting warehouse workers. There were work stoppages with community support that briefly gummed up the operations.[18] But the campaign principally relied on low-participation public relations strikes at Walmart stores, designed to tarnish the company's reputation. The campaign overly relied on social media as the principal way to spread the organizing message, with limited effect.[19] If the membership of a union is asked to bankroll a massive campaign, but is not informed, consulted, and organized to support it, then it is only a matter of time before a few leaders and members say, "Why are we spending millions on this quixotic external adventure when we cannot successfully defend our own members?" Ultimately, OUR Walmart fell victim to the UFCW's internal politics, and a new union administration defunded the campaign.[20]

A DIFFERENT ORGANIZING ENVIRONMENT?

Today, Amazon confronts its workers and union organizers with a dilemma very similar to Walmart: a company with massive market and political power—and committed to being "union free." How can Amazon workers, even if supported by seasoned organizers, even dream of success? Yet only a few years removed from the failed Walmart campaign, we are in a new historic moment. Bernie Sanders, running as an open socialist in the 2016 election garnered 13 million votes in the Democratic presidential primaries. Inspired by his campaign and his identification as a democratic socialist, tens of thousands of young idealists swelled the ranks of Democratic Socialists of America (DSA),[21] and many thousands more now identify themselves as socialists. Even old socialists emerged from under the "progressive" label, joined DSA, and carried a red banner for the first time since the '70s. This would not be the first surge in the growth of U.S. socialism. Two major waves occurred in the early 1900s and then again in the '30s. The first led to a new vision of industrial unionism, the second to a new wave of organizing and collective bargaining. We emphatically believe that the distinct challenges and opportunities at Amazon will lead to new organizational innovations of comparable magnitude.

WORKPLACE ORGANIZING GAINING GROUND

In 2019, a thousand Amazon tech workers walked out in Seattle to demand the company do more on climate change. Some of them had previously flown to Minnesota to show their solidarity with warehouse workers who walked out during the company's "Prime Day" sales blast in mid-July. Amazon warehouse workers in Chicago and Sacramento who don't have a formal union have banded together under the banner of local "Amazonians United" groups. Through petitions and marches on the boss, they forced the e-commerce giant to pay them when the warehouse shut down during a heat wave, improved health and safety, and got fired workers unfired. The inside cadre is enhanced by the growing sophistication of a broader movement seeking to challenge Amazon's impact on small businesses, housing, and the environment. On Prime Day in July 2019 in eight cities, there were community labor protests against Amazon for its collaboration with Immigration Control Enforcement (ICE) and the deportation and detention of undocumented immigrants.[22] There is even a movement to break up the company by applying anti-trust laws.[23] Clearly, Amazon affords new organizing opportunities at both the tech and warehouse level that go well beyond collective bargaining.

Most impressive has been the organizing by Amazon workers to pressure the company to support stepped-up action on climate change. Amazon Tech workers have been challenging Amazon with job actions over the environment.[24] On April 10, 2019, 8,215 Amazon employees signed a letter proposing that "Amazon has the resources and scale to spark the world's imagination and redefine what is possible and necessary to address the climate crisis. We believe this is a historic opportunity for Amazon to stand with employees and signal to the world that we're ready to be a climate leader." While the shareholders rejected their proposal, such a large group of tech employees stepping forward on these issues shows the strong potential for internal organizing at Amazon.[25] Later that year, activists got over 900 Amazon employees to sign an open letter with a commitment to walk off the job in support of the worldwide climate change strike on September 20, 2019. These employees were organized under the rubric of "Amazon Employees for Climate Justice" and demanded that the company get to zero emissions by 2030.[26] The internal movement to get the company to address climate change culminated in CEO Jeff Bezos pledging Amazon to reach net-zero carbon emissions by 2040, a decade before the international target date set by the Paris Agreement. Actions over climate and immigration demonstrate the power of employees to influence broader social questions because of the company's vulnerable public profile, but the question for labor organizers is what will it take to bring Amazon workers together in order for them to take action for each other?

THE LEFT AND LABOR: SALTING AND AMAZON

There is a long tradition on the American left of socialists going to work in large-scale enterprises to organize workers. Often called "salting," the origins of the term are ascribed to two metaphors: "pouring salt into the wounds to bring out the festering sores of capitalism," or "salting the mine to surface valuable ores." There is no more powerful organizer than the embedded class-conscious worker who identifies other leaders in the workforce and agitates with their comrades about their on-the-job injustices.[27] Without question, the presence of organized leftists whether from the Communist Party (CP), the Socialist Workers Party, or other ideologically left formations had a significant effect on the successful union organization of mass industries in the 1930s.

Labor historian Joe Richard has chronicled the left influence in labor formations:

> In Detroit, the CP [Communist Party] had been building up strength in auto plants across the city since 1927, with 350 party members working in 12 shop units. In Milwaukee, a CP unit worked for years to unionize the massive Allis-Chalmers works—first by taking over a company union and making forceful demands on the company, then by forming AFL craft unions, then amalgamating them together into a factory-wide Federal Labor Union (FLU), and finally winning affiliation with the new United Auto Workers (UAW). In St Louis, a CP concentration unit in the unorganized electrical appliance manufacturer shops would lead to the creation of District 8 of the United Electrical Workers. A similar pattern prevailed in many of the newly created unions.[28]

A more contemporary example is in the Teamsters union from 1992 to 1998 when it was led by Ron Carey. His election, and subsequent administration, was formed through a center-left coalition with the reform caucus Teamsters for a Democratic Union (TDU). During Carey's two terms, thousands of left-leaning rank-and-file members helped lead five national strikes and dozens of major organizing campaigns.

The 1997 UPS strike was a near-perfect example of what an organized left working with progressive union leadership can accomplish with a large employer. The strike lasted 15 days and involved 185,000 workers who carried signs proclaiming: "Part Time America Won't Work." The strike victory forced UPS to create 10,000 new full-time jobs by combining part-time positions, improve safety and job security for full timers, and drop its concessionary pension demands. It captured extensive support from a broader American public by relating to workers' growing sense of insecurity from the threat of contracted-out, part-time, and temporary labor.[29] The contract campaign and strike never would have been successful without the Carey administration controlling the vast resources of the International Union.

Another important difference between Amazon and Walmart is that either by choice or necessity, there is a growing cadre of socialists working at Amazon and Whole Foods. There are nearly limitless opportunities for young and idealistic organizers to work in the warehouses and sort centers that Amazon relies on. This work can be back-breaking and mind-numbing, but such internal organizing is fundamental to any large-scale plan to organize Amazon.

Salting can be romanticized by doting on glorious histories, but it is a tough road without networks of cadres supporting each other. That is the glue that DSA and other supportive outside groups can provide. But while salting by leftists is necessary, it's also insufficient. Meaningful organization will not take place without the resources and guidance that experienced trade union leaders and organizers can provide. Of course, this is not a new feature of the labor movement. It will be precisely this collaboration between left forces within trade union leadership working closely with Amazon salts that could lead to successful organization of workers at Amazon.

WHAT'S ALREADY WORKING

There already are some successful organizing models at Amazon. The Awood Center, founded by a partnership between the Council on American-Islamic Relations' Minnesota Chapter (a civil rights advocacy organization) and SEIU organizers in Minnesota's Minneapolis-Saint Paul region is a good example. There, Somali community organizers organically connected Somali Amazon workers with the larger immigrant community to conduct the first U.S. work stoppages at Amazon. These stoppages, and sustained protest activity, have led to an array of shop-floor improvements; including worker-community-management negotiations in November 2018 over respect for Muslim prayer rights and other working conditions. The SEIU-CAIR-MN initiative emerged from the progressive leadership of a Twin Cities building services with a large Somali membership. This approach, a "metro" strategy, uses the resources of unions and community groups to wield broad-based support for worker organizing. Ilhan Omar, one of two Muslim women in the U.S. House of Representatives, has been a speaker at their Amazon job actions.

Organizers in the Twin Cities have skillfully framed the struggle around East African community issues and built a fight to make immediate improvements for these workers. This is a base-building model that could be replicated in other areas where local unions see their self-interest in aligning with Amazon workers. It is also a good example of a strategy that acknowledges local conditions; whether it be divisions in the ruling class, the composition of the workforce, and the willingness of particular unions to fund and support Amazon organizing. Inevitably, there will be uneven development in local metro campaigns. Strategies must take different forms in different areas, dictating different tactics. SEIU's national Fight for $15 is an example of a campaign knitting together a wide variety of local struggles into a national consensus for increasing the minimum wage. Under that banner, the campaign adapted its tactics and objectives to very different local conditions. The same opportunity exists to forge a consensus for major improvements in the working lives of Amazon employees.

Direct action at the workplace—coupled with broad community support—is the formula for advancing the Amazon project. If these initiatives are supported and funded by a national union (as in the Twin Cities), the chances of success grow and the skepticism of the broader labor movement and sympathetic foundations diminishes. Inspired by the indigenous activity of the workforce and left-wing supporters, union resources can provide essential support to sustain good organizing both in the short term and over the long haul. SEIU's modest "seed funding" of the Awood Center helped raise an additional $250,000 in funds with significant support from the Teamsters union and several foundations. It set the stage for multiple union funders to share the "risk" of investing in a local Amazon campaign.

Multiple sources of funding also ensure that the campaign won't fall prey to the internal politics of one union.

By nesting worker centers in both the community and the workplace, the model of Minneapolis could be replicated in different areas around the country. If more efforts like the Awood Center blossom, we will see labor's commitment to organizing grow—especially with unions like the Teamsters, SEIU and UFCW that have sufficient resources to support a national effort. The recent formation of Athena holds out the possibility of spreading the lessons and practice of the Awood Center. Over forty community-based organizations including Awood and other immigrant rights coalitions and worker centers came together in November 2019 to launch this ambitious effort.

IS THERE A ROLE FOR INTERNATIONALISM?

There have been inspiring moments on the international front. A strike in Italy at a giant distribution center on Black Friday in 2017 was conducted by the main Italian labor federation, the Confederazione Generale Italiana del Lavoro (CGIL). On Prime Days, July 15–16, 2019, Ver.di, the German industrial union federation, led a two-day strike by 2,000 warehouse workers across seven facilities (see also Chapters 8–10, this volume).[30] Much can be learned from these and other exciting examples to inspire workers everywhere. Certainly, mutual aid and solidarity on every level will always be needed. Such solidarity must certainly extend beyond warehouse workers to the delivery drivers and software engineers worldwide. Just as the labor movement has been successful in organizing on the waterfront by employing internationalist strategies to slow the flow of marine cargo, similar strategies can block or delay the flow of Amazon deliveries.[31] However, and most importantly, any strategy to win at Amazon must focus on the "Belly of the Beast"—the corporation's home country, where the bulk of its workforce is employed.

A LONG VIEW NEEDED

There won't be any quick fixes or easy victories at Amazon. The road to successful organizing and workers' power will inevitably be long and hard. If we are serious about the Amazon organizing project, we should create benchmarks and prepare to measure success (or failure) accordingly. For example: how many supportive community-based workers' centers are in place? How many worker committees have formed at sort centers? How many work stoppages and strike actions occurred this year versus last year? Future technological change in warehouse and delivery logistics may also have important implications for any long-term organizing strategy. The automation of warehouse jobs, driverless vehicles, and drone delivery could put workers on a very different organizing terrain. At the same time, increased automation could magnify the power of the remaining workforce—but only if organized to do so through collective bargaining.[32]

By its very nature, the eventual success of organizing Amazon is inexorably linked to achieving wider political and labor law reforms. The immense structural and political obstacles that Bezos and company throw at worker organizing and empowerment are legion: use of temps, contracting out, automation, and anti-union repression. These obstacles will be overcome by smart base building and organizing—but legal and political reforms will be needed too. While the future is unpredictable, a vibrant political movement has created dramatic shifts in the electoral arena that show real promise. As Luke Elliott-Negri recently wrote, "We need an open-minded approach to developing left labor strategy commensurate with the new moment and the new conjuncture."[33] With the support of Senator Bernie Sanders and former Communication Workers of America (CWA) President Larry Cohen, new, more radical visions of labor law reform are being proposed that embrace sectoral organizing and bargaining approaches.[34, 35] If other mainstream Democrats embrace this approach, it could make for a very different organizing terrain. What's imperative now is to have organizers in strategic Amazon workplaces prepared to seize opportunities as they arise. Finally, organizing at Amazon will help build broader support for winning these much-needed reforms in labor and employment law. Conversely, if reforms are achieved, they would change the nature of the struggle and the likely success of workers at Amazon. The more the project is embraced and supported by the left and institutional labor, the more it will lead to a movement for workers' power at Amazon. Because of the size and scale of Amazon, it would, in turn, be a key part of any movement for systemic reform or political revolution.

Amazonians United is one of several worker-led groups that has organized at Amazon's delivery stations. In July, a group of workers in Chicago came forward demanding healthcare benefits and air conditioning on site. In Eagan, Minnesota, workers walked out over demands related to time off. And Amazon workers in Sacramento campaigned to get two colleagues rehired after they were fired for taking more unpaid time off than allowed. "We're doing back-breaking warehouse work," said a delivery station worker in Chicago:

> So whether it's someone working 40 hours a week who gets injured or somebody working 24 hours a week, it doesn't matter. We just wanted to be treated equally as all of Amazon's other part-time workers. This is what the economy is, part-time work is all we can get. This is the reality of our economy, and we deserve paid time off.[36]

"The fact is that Amazon is a trillion-dollar company run by the richest man in the world," the Sacramento workers wrote in a public petition, "and they intentionally give workers less benefits than regular part-time workers so that they grow the company at our expense. We've had enough."

Inspiring strikes and protests over pay and working conditions, particularly among part-timers at the deliver stations close to urban areas, are occurring somewhere in Amazon almost daily. With support from unions and a broad network of socialists in the workplace, each action at the local, national, or international level is more likely to succeed. As the level of militancy and organization grows, our challenge is to make sure that each action strengthens the movement and builds workers' confidence in the power of collective action.

NOTES

1. Frank Norris, *The Project Gutenberg EBook of The Octopus: A Story of California* (Doubleday, Page & Company, 2008 [1901]). www.gutenberg.org/files/268/268-h/268-h.htm. Accessed April 19, 2020.
2. David Dayen, "How Amazon Is Taking Over Our Lives," *In These Times*, July 2019; James Bloodworth, *Hired: Six Months Undercover in Low Wage Britain* (London: Atlantic Books, 2018).
3. See the Athena coalition's broad membership of community, labor, small business and pro-democracy groups working to win corporate reforms at Amazon: https://athenaforall.org/.

4. Spencer Cox, "Amazon Corporate Profile: Labor Process and the Logistics Supply Chain," *Labor Research Action Network*, February 2017 (unpublished internal report, accessed via personal correspondence).
5. See Peter Olney and Rand Wilson's respective experience at the ILWU and the Teamsters in author biographies.
6. J. David Goodman, "Amazon Pulls Out of Planned New York City Headquarters," *New York Times*, February 14, 2019, www.nytimes.com/2019/02/14/nyregion/amazon-hq2-queens.html. Accessed April 19, 2020.
7. Hannah Knowles, "Amazon spent $1.5 Million on Seattle City Council Races. The Socialist it Opposed has Won." *Washington Post*, November 10, 2019, www.washingtonpost.com/nation/2019/11/10/amazon-spent-million-seattle-city-council-races-socialist-it-opposed-has-won/. Accessed April 19, 2020.
8. Peter Olney, "Beyond the Waterfront: Maintaining and Expanding Worker Power in the Maritime Supply Chain," in Jake Alimahomed-Wilson and Immanuel Ness (eds.), *Choke Points: Logistics Workers Disrupting the Global Supply Chain* (London: Pluto Press, 2018).
9. Brittany Chang, "From Electric Vans to Autonomous Robots, Here are All the Vehicles Amazon has and will use to Deliver Packages to Your Doorstep," *Business Insider*, September 19, 2019, www.businessinsider.com/amazon-vehicles-used-deliver-packages-2019-7; Also see, Chapter 4 in this volume.
10. Amazon Air, https://en.wikipedia.org/wiki/Amazon_Air. Accessed April 19, 2020.
11. Journal of Commerce Staff, "Amazon gets OK to Operate as NVOCC from China to US," *Journal of Commerce*, January14 , 2016, www.joc.com/maritime-news/amazon-gets-ok-operate-nvocc-china-us_20160114.html. Accessed April 19, 2020; A Non-Vessel Operating Common Carrier (NVOCC) is an ocean carrier that transports goods under its own House Bill of Lading, or equivalent documentation, without operating ocean transportation vessels. Rather, an NVOCC leases space from another ocean carrier, or Vessel Operating Common Carrier (VOCC), that they sell to their own customers. An NVOCC can be described as a shipper to carriers and a carrier to shippers. While NVOCCs do not usually own their own warehouses, many own their own fleet of containers. In certain circumstances, a NVOCC may also operate as a freight forwarder. www.flexport.com/glossary/non-vessel-operating-common-carrier. Accessed April 19, 2020.
12. Amazon, "Fulfillment in Our Buildings," www.aboutamazon.com/amazon-fulfillment/our-fulfillment-centers/fulfillment-in-our-buildings/. Accessed April 19, 2020.
13. Ford Motors Company represented a paradigm of American industry in the 1930s.
14. United Food and Commercial Workers Union: www.ufcw.org.
15. Peter Olney and Rand Wilson, "Justice for Janitors: A Misunderstood Success," *The Stansbury Forum*, May 13, 2015, https://stansburyforum.com/2015/05/13/justice-for-janitors-a-misunderstood-success. Accessed April 20, 2020.

16. United for Respect: https://united4respect.org/campaigns/walmart/.
17. For more on Our Wal-Mart visit: https://united4respect.org/.
18. Juan De Lara Juan, Ellen Reese, and Jason Struna, "Organizing Temporary, Subcontracted, and Immigrant Workers: Lessons from Change to Win's Warehouse Worker United Campaign," *Labor Studies* 41(4) (2016): 309–332.
19. Peter Olney, "Where Did the OUR Wal-Mart Campaign Go Wrong?," *Working In These Times*, December 14, 2015, https://inthesetimes.com/working/entry/18692/our-walmart-union-ufcw-black-friday. Accessed April 19, 2020.
20. Ibid.
21. Marc Tracy, "'Bernie or Bust' the Future of the Left? The Democratic Socialists of America Figure Out What it Means to Oppose Donald Trump," *New York Times*, August 6, 2019, www.nytimes.com/2019/08/06/us/politics/bernie-sanders-democratic-socialists-america.html. Accessed April 19, 2020.
22. Hannah Denham, "'No Tech for ICE': Protesters Demand Amazon cut ties with Federal Immigration Enforcement," *Washington Post*, July 12, 2019, www.washingtonpost.com/business/2019/07/12/no-tech-ice-protesters-demand-amazon-cut-ties-with-federal-immigration-enforcement. Accessed April 19, 2020.
23. David Daven, "Some on the Left want to Nationalize Amazon. Breaking it up is a Safer Bet," *In These Times*, July 22, 2019, http://inthesetimes.com/article/21948/break-up-amazon-monopoly-antitrust-nationalize-warren-sanders. April 19, 2020.
24. Rand Wilson and Peter Olney, "Socialists Can Seize the Moment at Amazon," *Jacobin Magazine*, October 4, 2018, www.jacobinmag.com/2018/10/salt-amazon-union-logistics-organizing-socialists. Accessed April 19, 2020.
25. Amazon Employees for Climate Justice, "Open Letter to Jeff Bezos and the Amazon Board of Directors" *Medium*, April 10, 2019, https://medium.com/@amazonemployeesclimatejustice/public-letter-to-jeff-bezos-and-the-amazon-board-of-directors-82a8405f5e38. Accessed April 19, 2020; James Ellsmoor, "Meet the Amazon Employees Challenging Jeff Bezos On Climate Change," *Forbes*, May 29, 2019, www.forbes.com/sites/jamesellsmoor/2019/05/29/meet-the-amazon-employees-challenging-jeff-bezos-on-climate-change/#17fc93da28be. Accessed April 19, 2020.
26. Rob Thubron, "Amazon Workers to Strike Over Company's Climate Change Inaction," *Techspot*, September 10, 2019, www.techspot.com/news/81828-amazon-workers-strike-over-company-climate-change-inaction.html. Accessed April 19, 2020.
27. Carey Dall and Jonathan Cohen, "Salting the Earth: Organizing for the Long Haul," *New Labor Forum* 10 (2002): 36–41, www.jstor.org/stable/40342338?seq=1#page_scan_tab_contents. Accessed April 19, 2020.
28. Joe Richard, "Hunters and Dogs: What Today's Labor Radicals can Learn from the Socialists Who Helped Build the CIO in the 1930s," *Jacobin Magazine*,

October 28, 2016, www.jacobinmag.com/2016/10/cio-unions-communist-party-socialist-party-afl/. Accessed April 19, 2020.
29. David Levin, "The 1997 UPS Strike: Beating Big Business & Business Unionism," *Labor Notes*, August 15, 2017, www.labornotes.org/2017/08/1997-ups-strike-beating-big-business-business-unionism. Accessed April 19, 2020.
30. Joe DeManuelle-Hall, "Prime Day for Amazon Protests," *Labor Notes*, July 17, 2019, www.labornotes.org/2019/07/prime-day-amazon-protests
31. For much more information on international strategies, see: "Strike the Giant! Transnational Organization against Amazon," *Transnational Social Strike Platform*, November 11, 2019, www.transnational-strike.info/2019/11/29/pdf-strike-the-giant-transnational-organization-against-amazon-tss-journal/. Accessed April 19, 2020.
32. Beth Gutelius and Nik Theodore "The Future of Warehouse Work: Technological Change in the U.S. Logistics Industry," *UC Berkeley Labor Center; Working Partnerships USA*, October 2019, http://laborcenter.berkeley.edu/future-of-warehouse-work/. Accessed April 19, 2020.
33. Luke Elliott-Negri "A Strategy to Build Labor Power," *Jacobin Magazine*, August 26, 2019, https://jacobinmag.com/2019/08/rank-and-file-strategy-dsa-labor. Accessed April 19, 2020.
34. "The Workplace Democracy Plan," *Sanders Campaign*, https://berniesanders.com/issues/the-workplace-democracy-plan/. Accessed April 19, 2020. Shaun Richman,"Bernie Sanders' Labor Plan Could Put a Union in Every Workplace in America," *In These Times*, August 22, 2019, https://inthesetimes.com/working/entry/22024/bernie_sanders_labor_plan_wage_boards_just_cause.
35. Larry Cohen, "The Time Has Come for Sectoral Bargaining," *New Labor Forum*, June 2018, https://newlaborforum.cuny.edu/2018/06/22/the-time-has-come-for-sectoral-bargaining/. Accessed April 19, 2020; "The Workplace Democracy Plan," *Sanders Campaign*, https://berniesanders.com/issues/the-workplace-democracy-plan/. Accessed April 19, 2020.
36. Shirin Ghaffary, "Amazon Warehouse Workers Doing "Back-breaking" Work Walked Off the Job in Protest," *Recode by Vox*, December 23, 2019, www.vox.com/platform/amp/recode/2019/12/10/21005098/amazon-warehouse-workers-sacramento. Accessed April 19, 2020.

17
Amazonians United! An Interview with DCH1 (Chicago) Amazonians United

DCH1 Amazonians United

This interview was conducted via email on April 19, 2020 by Jake Alimahomed-Wilson and Ellen Reese with ten Amazon warehouse workers from Chicago, Illinois. All of the workers featured in this interview are core members of DCH1 Amazonians United.

Introduction by DCH1 Amazonians United

This chapter was conducted in the same way we confront our bosses: collectively. We wrote this in the midst of the COVID-19 pandemic, and at the beginning of our international anti-retaliation campaign against Amazon. Our ancestors descend from five continents and yet we met through the process of building our union while waging struggle within the belly of the largest capitalist beast. We honor the legacy of those who came before us by organizing within Amazon and in the process rebuilding an international labor movement.

Interviewers: What is Amazonians United and when did it start?

Response #1: Amazonians United is an organizing worker-based movement, fighting for workers' rights, and improvement of working conditions in our workplaces. We started in 2019 after we won our first organized action: the water demand. Those of us who participated realized the power we had as workers.

Response #2: Amazonians United is a movement of workers organizing to protect ourselves, democratize our workplaces, and advance the interests of all working people.

Response #3: Six of us came together in April of 2019 because we were fed up with so many things at Amazon. Our pay was low, we were talked to like children, we didn't have health insurance. DCH1 was filthy and we didn't have regular access to clean water. The water issue was actually not the issue we were most pissed about, but it was the most ridiculous issue and the one we thought most coworkers would support. The issue is that the 5-gallon water stations were often left open to the dusty air without a 5-gallon water jug. They were never cleaned, there were never any cups, and there was only one water fountain that was either broken or had the "replace the filter" light on. We decided to do a petition about it … Doing an online petition was good because then we got our coworkers' phone numbers or became Facebook friends, but only about 30 co-workers actually signed it … We were nervous about going around the break room collecting signatures, but got over our nervousness once we started talking with co-workers because they all agreed and would talk about how ridiculous it is that we have to do a petition to get some water. It took us a few weeks to get to 150 signatures, but that felt like a good number so we decided to turn it in. We decided that we would type out all the petition signatures into a Word document and print it out with our demands at the top so that we could keep the original petition sheets. We decided to turn the petition in during stand-up, which is the time when every worker, about 120 on that day, is circled around the manager which is leading us in stretches, telling us we need to get our scan rates up, and asking questions like "what's the safety tip?" and "what's the standard work tip?"

We went in having decided that one person would turn the petition in, and multiple others would vocalize their support in some kind of way. When the manager asked for a safety tip, the designated person spoke up and said "I have a safety tip. In fact 150 of us do. We need water! And we have our petition right here." The manager said: "I'll take care of it," then another co-worker said, "When are you going to take care of it? We need it now," and the manager exclaimed "I'll take it care of it right away." The manager tried to move on to another subject, the "standard work tip" and a co-worker raised his hand and said: "My standard work tip is we need water." The manager, exasperated, said "I'll take care of it right away." He quickly ended stand-up and was frantically texting someone and flipping through the petition signatures. Then, within two hours, Ambassadors (which acted like supervisors even though they're Tier 1 workers like everyone else) came around giving everyone bottled water which the manager had gone out to buy from the local grocery store. It had never felt so good to drink water! And everyone saw that when we do something together we can make things happen. After this, six of us (there were some new co-workers that showed up and some that didn't show up) met up again to talk about how things had gone and we decided that we needed to address other issues. But we figured that we should name ourselves ... that was how DCH1 Amazonians United was born.

Interviewers: Can you describe the working conditions at DCH1?

Response #1: In general, Amazon's working conditions are like most other jobs. If you're good at your job, most management and associates who think they can, move up, if they "yes, man it up." They will try to work you into the ground without giving you anything of value in return. Favoritism is rampant. Management spreads misinformation as well as targets co-workers and the most prevalent issue is general incompetence on management's part. Currently, the biggest issue is the lack of care for human life [by] the management (the lives of our fellow co-workers, the lives of our drivers, and the lives of innocent customers) via an unclean facility, improper distancing, and withholding of coronavirus cases within said facility.

Response #2: Since my first day, I was able to tell how much professionalism and organizational skills some leads and managers lack. From cursing with employees to playing favorites. The warehouse itself needs to be more organized physically and with more adequate managers.

Response #3: The working conditions at DCH1 can be quite harsh. It's warehouse work that requires intense physical labor, extended hours on your feet, and working in close contact with others. Also the work culture is far from being professional ... A large number of those in management and people who aspire to become management seem to lack professionalism in dealing with issues at the job. I have witnessed a learning Ambassador cursing out an employee because the woman moved her cart because it was in the way ... Even I had an experience with an Ambassador in my early days at the company. I was still learning the job. I had been sent to an area for an advanced worker to handle. She did get me some help, but the matter in which she told me to hurry up, I felt disrespected and felt the problem could have been handled better.

Response #4: Working too close even before the pandemic. During pick and stage it can be up to seven people in a cell picking. Some cells ... need to be reset to allow more space in them. With several workers, bags, and boxes, it's really tight.

Response #5: During or before the [COVID-19] pandemic? Because before the pandemic was even here, we fought for PTO [Paid Time Off] at the time and that was I believe during peak season. The warehouse was already falling apart. There was a lot of things not being handled like not having enough working scanners for stowers, issues with the boxes coming down the conveyor belts because of unknown leakages that stopped them from coming down, actual leakages from the ceiling parts of the warehouse during and also after it rained/snowed, etc. ... There's still a lot of toxic management from Peak season there to make our lives a living hell.

Response #6: One of the main ongoing issues that I've noticed also is the amount of VTO [Voluntary Time Off] they give out before the shift has even started. When that happens, the people that do show up to work get swamped with having to work at a faster pace to cover being short staffed and later on in the night having to do another job assignment because of the same reason of not having enough people. Another issue is the whole conversion process from a white badge to a blue badge (temporary to permanent employee). They keep giving the runaround on when this conversion will be possible.

Response #7: I've seen plenty of co-workers face issues with co-workers on the same level as them with the fear of management taking the wrong side based on favoritism. I think the biggest issue in our facility is our site leader; under his care this culture of favoritism, targeting, and incompetence has festered ... He targets any associates trying to fight for their rights, care for themselves or their co-workers, and most recently, the safety of the general public. He incompetently handles associates fighting for what's rightfully theirs. He does this by lying to us for what we're entitled to, withholding information, or when all else fails, by threatening us, while stating we're more than welcome to take his statements as threats.

Interviewers: Describe the workforce at DCH1

Response #1: The workforce at DCH1 is majority African American and Hispanic/Latino. The age of employees here range from early 20s and we have employees that are as old as their early 70s.

Response #2: At DCH1 there's a variety with [*sic*] race, age, gender and sexual preferences.

Interviewers: What are some of the things Amazon workers can do to improve their working conditions?

Response #1: Get together with their co-workers, have conversations about what needs to change at work, and fight together against the management to get those needs fulfilled. Fighting can look like signing and presenting petitions to management, coordinating and agreeing not to work at unsafe rates, walking out, striking, and much more. A lot of good ideas can come from just getting together with your co-workers and talking about what to do.

Response #2: Standing together as a unit is the only way to improve our work conditions. For some reason there's a bevy of associates who don't realize that without them Amazon would lose a facility. Without us, the richest man in the world would be out of his riches. As such we should show him what we're capable of beyond our stow rates.

Interviewers: What have you won so far and how?

Response #1: So far, we've won:

- Clean drinking water
- Pay when the warehouse was too hot to work in safely
- Pay when the lights went off in the warehouse

- Pay when the volume of goods was too low and management tried to force people to take unpaid time off
- Paid time off (PTO) for every part-time worker in the U.S.
- Some COVID-19 safety measures like masks and cleaning supplies (not adequate though)
- Full-time jobs
- Health care
- Retraining Ambassadors
- Changed disrespectful behavior from managers

We won these things by talking with our co-workers; building relationships, community, and unity; coming together on issues using petitions; taking action; marching on our bosses, and going on strike.

Interviewers: What do you think is the key to building worker power at Amazon?

Response #1: The key is building a team of solid people at every Amazon facility that gets together, talks regularly through some sort of messaging app, has meetings in person and/or virtually, talks about workplace issues together, decides on what the biggest issue is that would resonate with the most people, writes out a demand together with the small crew, and makes a plan for taking action on that demand in a way that involves other co-workers and in a way that seems reasonable to other co-workers. Most important is that our co-workers see what we're doing and agree that we're in the right. It's key to not seem like crazy unreasonable people, because if you do, then co-workers won't support you and the boss can divide and conquer your teams until it's destroyed. These teams usually start small, and with solid people ... It takes consistency and perseverance ... Once these Amazonians United teams form, they connect with Amazonians United at other Amazon sites and continue growing the movement together ....

Response #2: Standing strong in our convictions, management will attempt to divide whenever possible. However, supporting our own facility as well as others across the globe will prove our wins are consistent. It starts at our own facilities, being educated on our rights and standing strong together.

Amazonians United!

Interviewers: What are some of the biggest challenges you and your fellow workers face? What have you done to try to overcome those challenges?

Response #1: What makes this tough is the constant nitpicking and nagging the management engages within the warehouse. Throughout the entire shift, we have this sense of paranoia and urgency combined. I feel like I've done my best by maintaining a solidarity standpoint and mutual acquaintanceship among some of my co-workers on my shift. We work together to get through our shifts.

Response #2: Most in charge don't care for our well-being, the well-being of drivers/cleaners or our customers. During this pandemic, we've been shown a management that claims to care, prefers their paycheck versus our safety or the safety of others.

Response #4: Our biggest challenges are capitalism, structural racism, and the resulting poverty that denies our freedom of self-determination including our freedom to control our own lives, bodies, and labor. To overcome these challenges, we have built community and solidarity with our co-workers to organize and build our power to transform our workplace and society.

Response #5: Management constantly tries to individualize and atomize us, to keep us weak, divided, and at each other's throats. We counter these efforts by management by getting more organized, extending solidarity to co-workers who are mistreated, explaining that we share common interests as opposed to management's interests. Management is tyrannical and highly organized. We need to be democratic and highly organized to counter them.

Response #6: Amazon manages us through stress. They individualize us, put us at odds with each other, and do everything they can to prevent us from socializing. We do everything we can to build community. For several months, we were organizing a potluck during lunch every Monday. Sharing food does a lot to build community! We make an effort to look our co-workers in the eye and have real conversation, laugh at management's ridiculousness with our co-workers, seek to understand who our co-workers really are, share ourselves with our co-workers, and build meaningful bonds of trust and friendship. We give each other rides, throw kickbacks, go bowling, go to marches, create group texts, form Facebook groups, organize cookouts and sometimes just hang out to talk about whatever is on our mind. We overcome management's structural attempts to divide us by building community between us, and it's fun!

Interviewers: Can Amazonians United help lay the foundation to finally unionize Amazon in the United States or beyond?

Response #1: Yes, and we're working hard to form a worker-run organization in the United States. We also know that there are workers outside of Amazon who are interested in the types of struggles and victories that we've had, and hope to engage them as well. Beyond our borders, we know that Amazon workers have already been organizing and taking action together and we have been working with them to form an international organization of workers.

Response #2: Our workplace organizing committees are the foundation, and Amazonians United is our union. Amazonians United is the organizational manifestation of our unity and collective struggle within and between Amazon workplaces. We don't need the recognition of our bosses or government to be a union. We don't need to file for a union election with the NLRB [National Labor Relations Board] to be a union. We don't need to have a collective bargaining agreement to be a union. We determine, through our solidarity, strategy, and action, if we are a union. We are a true union of workers, by workers, and for workers. We exercise our power to get what we need, and it works. We are unionizing Amazon every time a fellow worker decides to form a workplace organizing committee which drives issue campaigns with the broad support of their co-workers. That is Amazonians United.

Interviewers: All around the world, Amazon warehouse workers are resisting. In Germany, Poland, Italy, Spain, and the United Kingdom, and all over the United States, Amazon's warehouse workers are organizing for better wages and working conditions. How can workers build power across regions, cities, and borders to take on Amazon?

Response #1: In order to take on Amazon, we need to get together, build relationships, and coordinate with one another so that when workers in one region/state/country take action, workers elsewhere take action in solidarity with them. This is absolutely necessary because without that solidarity, Amazon will be able to break actions in any given area by rerouting goods through adjacent areas.

Response #2: As a team not just in our facilities but across the world, unified we have power that management could only hope to replicate.

Response #3: In March 2020, unknowingly flying into one of the centers of the pandemic, we joined Amazon workers in Spain for a transnational convening of workers from Poland, France, Germany, Spain and the U.S. As our plane was descending to the Madrid Airport, we learned that Trump was closing the borders of the U.S. to Europe. Already in Madrid and unable to return, we headed to our international convening and spent three days discussing how we can build international solidarity and organize coordinated campaigns. The situation in each of our countries is unique, because each has its own history and its own legal framework, but the soul-sucking experience of working at Amazon is largely the same. At this tenth international convening, we decided to name our rank-and-file network: Amazon Workers International. We build power by growing organizing committees with our co-workers at every workplace, and then connecting our struggles regionally, nationally, and internationally. It is through our joint struggles that we build solidarity, and it is through this international solidarity between all workers, Amazon and non-Amazon, that we can take on any boss.

Interviewers: How can those not working for Amazon best support the struggle of Amazon workers?

Response #1: Get a job at Amazon and start organizing together with us! Those not working for Amazon can best support the struggle of Amazon workers by keeping an eye out for opportunities to act in solidarity, like showing up to an action when a call is put out and following the lead of the workers; donating funds for workers (make sure that you're actually donating to workers though); and finally, organizing with your co-workers and communities to build up strong, independent mass movements that can link up with ours. That last one is the most important because it's hard to support our struggle unless you also have some organized power yourself. Business unions, NGOs, and politicians have all been unwilling to support workers where there aren't easy dues for them to collect from us, wealthy donors that they can show us off to, or photo-ops for themselves. None of them are coming to save us. We're all that we've got. Without mass movements, we will run into the limits of what is possible within the workplace and stagnate. With mass movements, together, we can create a better world for all of us, one in which the dignity of each and every human being is respected.

Contact DCH1 Amazonians United at: dch1united@gmail.com / www.facebook.com/dch1united.

Conclusion
Resisting Amazon Capitalism

Jake Alimahomed-Wilson and Ellen Reese

The fight against Amazon isn't just about one company. It is a fight for the soul of our democracy and the future of our economy. Will it work for the richest man in the world or will it work for all of us? I believe that we will prevail if we stick together.—Christy Hoffman, General Secretary of UNI Global[1]

Amazon is the new corporate symbol of global capitalism. As the 2020 global coronavirus pandemic ushered in the latest iteration of capitalist crisis around the world, Amazon's power and market dominance expanded.[2] As millions of people stayed home during COVID-19 lockdowns around the world, e-commerce orders spiked, straining Amazon's logistics operations as the corporation processed upwards of 40 percent more packages more than normal.[3] As the death toll climbed ... so did Amazon's profits. Amazon Web Services (AWS), for example, saw a massive boost in business—AWS remains one of Amazon's most profitable operations—and emerged among one of the few "corporate winners" from the coronavirus pandemic. As offices and store closures pushed more activity online, the data cloud storage of Amazon and other big tech firms became an essential link for the world's major corporations.[4]

For Amazon's blue-collar workers in warehousing and delivery, the coronavirus pandemic exacerbated other pre-existing challenges as Amazon's "extreme high churn model"—described as the continual replacement of workers in order to sustain the corporation's dangerous and gruelling workpace demands[5]—carried on throughout its global warehousing operations. Amazon hired an additional 175,000 warehouse and delivery workers[6] in the United States in order to meet what Amazon executives described as an unprecedented backlog of orders due to an increased surge of online purchases.[7] As the COVID-19 pandemic peaked in the United States, Amazon warehouse workers engaged in wildcat strikes and protests while Whole Foods grocery workers called for a global sick-out over workplace safety issues and pay.[8] In turn, Amazon was accused of retaliation after some protesting workers were fired.[9] Across Europe, Amazon's warehouse workers also went on strike over labor conditions related to COVID-19 in Italy, Spain, Poland, and France.[10] While some of the worker rebellions were spotlighted during the crisis, these worker actions were part of a growing wave of popular resistance to Amazon capitalism around the world which was already building momentum.

WE ARE NOT ROBOTS! THE EMERGENCE OF A GLOBAL MOVEMENT AGAINST AMAZON

In 2018, thousands of European Amazon warehouse workers, coordinated by UNI Global Union and other unions, went on strike on Black Friday across the United Kingdom, Italy, Germany, Poland, and Spain, united under the rallying cry of "We are not robots!"[11] Formal worker resistance to Amazon in Europe began years earlier beginning in 2013, when 1,100 German Amazon warehouse workers went on strike in Bad Hersfeld, representing the first labor stoppage in the notoriously anti-union company's history.[12] Since then, the struggle to unionize Amazon's fulfillment centers has become transnational. According to Boewe and Schulten, Amazon employs about 27,500 workers in the United Kingdom, the vast majority of whom work in its 17 fulfillment centers. In the U.K., the General, Municipal, Boilermakers and Allied Trade Union (GMB) has been trying to organize Amazon workers for years and has several hundred members. However, Amazon's union-busting efforts have so far remained effective and workers still receive poor wages.[13] To date, Amazon has not recognized a trade union representing its U.K. workforce, and unionization campaigns are still ongoing in other European nations, including in Eastern Europe.

In other European nations, especially where unions are more institutionalized, worker strikes at Amazon fulfillment centers have been substantial. In June 2014, three major French unions called for the first industrial actions in France against Amazon to start talks over wages, working conditions, and respect for unionization efforts. In the years since, there have been numerous strikes and walkouts, resulting in annual pay increases in 2018 for workers and securing a €500 bonus for French Amazon workers.[14] In addition to growing worker unrest in France, Amazon even became a target of France's Yellow Vest Movement, a popular rebellion which quickly morphed from an anti-tax campaign into a general revolt against neoliberalism, wealth inequality, politicians, and corporations.[15] In Poland, about 400 Amazon workers have joined a grassroots union, *Inicjatwa Pracownicza* (Workers' Initiative). The union, formed in 2014, is made up and run by rank-and-file worker volunteers. The workers have engaged in various actions, including several petition drives and a work slow-down in support of striking Amazon workers in Germany. Meanwhile, in Germany—Amazon's second largest market outside the U.S.—Amazon workers organized through the Ver.di union and have engaged in various short-term strikes, in order to pressure Amazon to sign a bargaining contract with them.[16] In December 2019, about 1,200 German Amazon warehouse workers went on strike over pay and working conditions.[17] Spanish Amazon workers and unions have also been organizing since 2012, after Amazon opened its first warehouse near Madrid. Workers in Spain have engaged in strikes, including on Amazon Prime day, once again over better wages and working conditions. Italy has also been an active site of resistance. Amazon entered Italy in 2011, when it built its first fulfillment center outside Milan. In 2018, a workplace collective agreement that regulated work on the weekend was negotiated at the Piacenza fulfillment center.[18] That same year Italian unions organized a strike of outsourced delivery drivers for Amazon that resulted in negotiations over working conditions.[19]

As European workers and labor activists organized, they also built transnational alliances through joint meetings and a series of internationally coordinated strikes and actions. Many of these were organized by Transnational Social Strike (TSS), a transnational organization that is working collectively to build unity and solidarity among Amazon workers across Europe. By doing so, labor activists sought to maximize their influence, especially as Amazon expanded across Europe and strategically moved its warehouses across borders in an effort to avoid and undercut organized workers. In 2019, "Strike the Giant!" was the call put out by the TSS, which by then involved workers and activists from Europe as well as the United States.[20]

Similar to Europe, resistance to Amazon was already rising rapidly in the United States prior to coronavirus. For example, efforts to organize Amazon warehouse employees emerged in Minnesota, Seattle, Chicago, New Jersey, Portland, Sacramento, Southern California, and New York among other places. Many of these organized Amazon warehouse workers are uniting through Amazonians United, which is not a formal union but rather an autonomous network of warehouse worker-organized local chapters around the U.S., concentrating mostly on various local worker initiatives, some of which have been under way for years.[21] In December 2018, Amazon warehouse employees in Shakopee, Minnesota made history when they protested outside an Amazon's fulfillment center. Local activists, Amazon warehouse workers, and politicians attended the protest, which ended with about 250 people marching on the building's main entrance. The action was organized in part by the Awood Center ("awood" is Somali for "power"), a relatively new worker center representing East African workers in the Minneapolis area. Many Amazon warehouse workers are Somali Muslims who claim that productivity rates infringe upon their need for bathroom breaks as well as their religious freedoms, and their ability to pray. Protesters also advocated for improved working conditions, racial justice, and independent review boards for human resources complaints.[22] In Robinson, New Jersey, Amazon workers and supporters, organized by Warehouse Workers Stand Up, held a protest in December 2018 following a workplace accident in which a warehouse robot broke a can of bear repellent and exposed at least 78 workers to toxic gas. The protesters demanded safer and more humane working conditions, including higher pay, "full-time and predictable work schedules, and health care with paid sick days."[23] Meanwhile, Amazon workers organized by the Retail, Wholesale and Department Store Union in Staten Island, New York pushed to unionize in 2019, and voiced opposition to exhaustion from being over-worked, and unreasonable productivity standards.[24] In March 2019, about 30 warehouse workers in Shakopee, Minnesota carried out an impromptu work stoppage in response to a work speed-up; they demanded more reasonable work rates and other workplace safety measures. At that time, stowers were expected to carry out 240–250 tasks per hour and to only have one error per 2,200 items, compared to one error per 1,000 items in 2017.[25] Early labor actions such as these, along with eye-opening investigative reporting on low wages and deplorable working conditions at Amazon, bore fruit, providing U.S. Amazon warehouse workers with wage gains, and various other improvements in working conditions, even in the absence of unionization.[26]

Conclusion: Resisting Amazon Capitalism

Local worker actions, along with the series of protests that erupted across the U.S. and Europe during Amazon's Prime Day and Cyber Monday in 2019, inspired Amazon warehouse workers in both continents to take further action during the pandemic. Along with a wave of strikes and actions by workers in Europe, many of which were already unionized, U.S. workers, not yet unionized, were taking bold action. For example, in March 2020, a group of Chicago warehouse workers calling themselves DCH1 Amazonians United, organized in order to get paid time off for part-time warehouse workers. This particular group of Chicago workers, led by women of color workers, was fed up with the company failing to provide paid time off (PTO) or vacation time that it had promised to part-time warehouse workers: "They organized, Amazon resisted—and at last, the coronavirus acted as tiebreaker."[27] Such victories by workers, along with workers' growing concerns over working conditions and the corporation's failure to protect workers' health and safety during the pandemic, inspired Amazon warehouse worker organizing to further spread and become more visible in 2020 across the United States as well as Europe.

High-tech employees have also joined the growing labor resistance to Amazon. In September 2019, Amazon Employees for Climate Justice (AECJ) gathered more than 8,000 signatures from Amazon software engineers, designers, and other workers to sign onto an open letter to CEO Jeff Bezos that demanded the corporation to adopt a comprehensive climate action plan; this action was one of the largest employee-driven environmental initiatives in history.[28] About 1,000 Amazon employees in Seattle even walked out of their jobs during the global climate strike. In response, Amazon pledged to become carbon neutral by 2040 and to purchase electric vehicles.[29]

Indeed, the growing revolt against Amazon has reached far outside the workplace. Amazon became the target of a series of class action lawsuits and legal complaints to government regulatory agencies in the Global North related to antitrust, equal opportunity, and labor laws. Community protests against Amazon, especially dramatic in New York, also emerged. In February 2019, Amazon canceled plans to build its second headquarters (HQ2) in Long Island City, New York in response to fierce resistance from a broad, informal coalition of community activists, union leaders, policy makers, and residents; opponents of the HQ2 plan raised concerns about the lack of protections for workers and residents as well as to the nearly US$3 billion worth of government incentives being promised to the e-commerce giant. This public backlash against Amazon occurred at the end of a yearlong and well-publicized competition through which 238 U.S., Canadian, and Mexican cities competed to be the site of Amazon's new headquarters by offering the corporation costly tax breaks and other incentives.[30] When Amazon decided to move its new HQ2 facility to Virginia, they met with protests there too by members of Virginia Educators United, who decried lawmakers' decision to offer a "bountiful set of tax breaks" for Amazon rather than investing in public education.[31] Joining the chorus of opposition, public officials around the nation and even prominent academics, including Harvard's Edward Glaeser and Princeton's Alan Krueger, made public statements and signed petitions against the provision of lavish corporate welfare and tax giveaways to companies such as Amazon.[32] Meanwhile, grassroots community and labor activists in other cities where Amazon was located, such as San Bernardino and Seattle, mounted protests and called on the corporation to do more to pay its fair share of public taxes (e.g., Seattle's "head tax" campaign), as well as to protect clean air, improve working conditions, and address other pressing community concerns.[33]

On Amazon Prime Day in 2019, a growing coalition of community and labor activists coordinated a series of actions across the nation protesting Amazon Web Services' practice of contracting with Immigration and Customs Enforcement (ICE) and other repressive state and law enforcement agencies. In San Bernardino, for example, workers organized by the Warehouse Worker Resource Center held banners and marched against ICE calling for #NoTechforIce.[34] High-tech workers along with immigrant rights activists and even hundreds of musicians also publicly opposed Amazon's role in promoting surveillance technology used to target immigrants and other groups through statements, threats to break ties from Amazon, and other protest activities.[35] Finally, in November 2019, Athena, a growing national network of over 40 community and labor organizations, was launched.[36] Athena helped to coordinate a series of lively protests across U.S. cities from coast to coast by workers as well as environmental, housing, immigrant rights, racial justice, faith-based, anti-monopoly, and other community activists on Amazon's Cyber Monday in 2019. In 2020, it launched petitions and fund drives in support of actions by Amazon warehouse workers.

Conclusion: Resisting Amazon Capitalism

Resistance to Amazon is also emerging in the Global South. For example, in January 2020, the Confederation of All-India Traders, representing 70 million traders and about 40,000 trade associations, organized a series of sit-in protests and rallies in 300 cities across India, with the largest demonstration in New Delhi, during Jeff Bezos's trip to their nation; calling Jeff Bezos an "economic terrorist," they protested the online discounts and other exclusive and predatory pricing practices of Amazon, along with other e-commerce giants, such as Walmart's Flipkart, that threaten their small, local businesses.[37] India's anti-trust regulator ordered a formal probe of complaints that pricing practices by Amazon and Flipkart violated Indian trade laws, including requirements that e-commerce businesses provide neutral marketplaces.[38]

Amazon's immense scale and power make it a tangible site and target to build a global coalitional resistance movement to challenge the many social ills inherent in capitalism. As this book demonstrates, Amazon's detrimental impact on workers, consumers, the environment, communities, cities, and entire economies has been profound and continues to spread globally. But so has the momentum of a growing coalition of movements confronting the corporate giant, offering new opportunities and possibilities to build a global movement—bridging multiple social justice struggles, workforces, and locations—that have the potential to challenge the destructive economic, cultural, political, and social maladies of contemporary capitalism even as they build solidarity and transformative visions for the future.

NOTES

1. Christy Hoffman, "Preface," in Jörn Boewe and Johannes Schulten (eds.), *The Long Struggle of Amazon Employees: Laboratories of Resistance* (2nd edition) (Brussels: Rosa Luxemburg Stiftung), December 10, 2019, www.rosalux.eu/en/article/1557.the-long-struggle-of-the-amazon-employees.html. Accessed April 11, 2020.
2. Maureen Callahan, "Coronavirus is Only Making Jeff Bezos and Amazon More Powerful." *NY Post*, March 31, 2020, nypost.com/2020/03/31/coronavirus-is-only-making-jeff-bezos-and-amazon-more-powerful/. Accessed April 9, 2020.
3. Dana Mattioli and Sebastian Herrera, "Amazon Struggles to Find Coronavirus Footing: 'It's a Time of Great Stress,'" *Wall Street Journal*, March 31, 2020, www.wsj.com/articles/amazon-struggles-to-find-its-coronavirus-footing-its-a-time-of-great-stress-11585664987?mod=hp_lead_pos5. Accessed April 9, 2020.

4. Aaron Tilley, "One Business Winner Amid Coronavirus Lockdowns: The Cloud," *Wall Street Journal*, March 27, 2020, www.wsj.com/articles/one-business-winner-amid-coronavirus-lockdowns-the-cloud-11585327905?mod=article_inline. Accessed April 9, 2020.
5. Iren Tung and Deborah Berkowitz, "Amazon's Disposable Workers: High Injury and Turnover Rates at Fulfillment Centers in California." *National Law Employment Project*, March 6, 2020, https://s27147.pcdn.co/wp-content/uploads/Data-Brief-Amazon-Disposable-Workers-Injury-Turnover-Rates-California-Fulfillment-Centers3-20.pdf. Accessed April 19, 2020.
6. Dana Mattioli, "Amazon to Expand Shipments of Nonessential Items, Continue Adding Staff," *Wall Street Journal*, April 13, 2020, www.wsj.com/articles/amazon-seeks-to-hire-another-75-000-workers-11586789365. Accessed April 9, 2020.
7. Jonathan Capriel, "Amazon's Coronavirus Plan: Hire 100,000 Displaced Workers, Raise Pay," *BizJournals*, March 17, 2020, www.bizjournals.com/phoenix/news/2020/03/17/amazons-coronavirus-plan-hire-100-000-displaced.html. Accessed April 11, 2020.
8. Mike Snider, "Work Strikes at Amazon, Instacart and Whole Foods Show Essential Workers' Safety Concerns," *USA Today*, March 30, 2020, www.usatoday.com/story/money/business/2020/03/30/coronavirus-safety-drives-strikes-amazon-instacart-and-whole-foods/5086135002/. Accessed April 9, 2020.
9. Sebastian Herrera, "Fired Amazon Warehouse Workers Accuse Company of Retaliation, Which it Denies," *Wall Street Journal*, April 14, 2020, www.wsj.com/articles/fired-amazon-warehouse-workers-accuse-company-of-retaliation-which-it-denies-11586891334. Accessed April 19, 2020.
10. Melissa Heikkilä, "Amazon Workers in France, Italy, Spain, and Poland Strike Over Labour Conditions During COVID-19 Pandemic," *Business-Human Rights*, March 31, 2020, www.business-humanrights.org/en/amazon-workers-in-france-italy-spain-poland-strike-over-labour-conditions-during-covid-19-pandemic. Accessed April 19, 2020.
11. Cale Guthrie Weissman, "Thousands of Amazon Workers in Europe Stage Black Friday Strike," *FastCompany*, November 23, 2018, www.fastcompany.com/90271926/thousands-of-amazon-workers-in-europe-stage-black-friday-strike. Accessed April 11, 2020.
12. Boewe and Schulten, *The Long Struggle of Amazon Employees*. Accessed April 11, 2020.
13. Ibid.
14. Ibid.
15. Reuters, "French Police Fire Tear Gas as Latest 'Yellow Vest' Protests Turn Violent," *Reuters*, February 16, 2019, www.reuters.com/article/us-france-protests/french-police-fire-tear-gas-as-latest-yellow-vest-protests-turn-violent-idUSKCN1Q50GD. Accessed April 19, 2020.

16. Amazon Workers and Supporters, "Stop Treating Us Like Dogs! Workers Organizing Resistance at Amazon in Poland," in Alimahomed-Wilson and Ness (eds.), *Choke Points*.
17. Michelle Martin and Elke Ahlswede, "German Union Extends Strike at Amazon's Leipzig Warehouse Until December 24," *Reuters*, December 20, 2019, www.reuters.com/article/us-amazon-germany-strike/german-union-extends-strike-at-amazons-leipzig-warehouse-until-december-24-idUSKBN1YO1KI. Accessed April 11, 2020.
18. Transnational Social Strike Platform, *Strike the Giant! Transnational Organization Against Amazon*, Fall 2019 Journal. Available at: www.transnational-strike.info/wp-content/uploads/Strike-the-Giant_TSS-Journal.pdf. Accessed April 19, 2020.
19. See Francesco Massimo's Chapter 8, this volume.
20. Transnational Social Strike Platform.
21. See DCH1 Amazonians United, Chapter 17 in this volume.
22. Joe DeManuelle-Hall, "Minnesota Amazon Workers Walk Off the Job Over Speed-Up," *Labor Notes*, March 22, 2019, www.labornotes.org/2019/03/minnesota-amazon-workers-walk-job-over-speed. Accessed April 19, 2020; Bryan Menegus, "Hundreds March on Amazon Fulfillment Center in Minnesota." *Gizmodo*, December 16, 2018, https://portside.org/2018-12-16/hundreds-march-amazon-fulfillment-center-minnesota. Accessed February 28, 2019.
23. Michelle Chen, "Is This the Turning Point in the Fight Against Amazon," *The Nation*, December 21, 2019, www.thenation.com/article/amazon-workers-labor-prime/. Accessed April 19, 2020.
24. Michael Sainato, "'We Are Not Robots': Amazon Warehouse Employees Push to Unionize," *The Guardian*, January 1, 2019, https://portside.org/2019-01-01/we-are-not-robots-amazon-warehouse-employees-push-unionize. Accessed February 28, 2019
25. DeManuelle-Hall, "Minnesota Amazon Workers Walk Off the Job."
26. Joe DeManuelle-Hall, "The Hard Fight at Amazon." *Labor Notes*, November 27, 2019, https://labornotes.org/blogs/2019/11/hard-fight-amazon. Accessed April 19, 2020. See also Transnational Social Strike Platform, *Strike the Giant! Transnational Organization Against Amazon*, Fall 2019 Journal, www.transnational-strike.info/wp-content/uploads/Strike-the-Giant_TSS-Journal.pdf. Accessed April 19, 2020.
27. Devin Coldewey, "Amazon Warehouse Workers Organized to Demand PTO, and Coronavirus Clinched It," *TechCrunch*, March 24, 2020, https://techcrunch.com/2020/03/24/amazon-warehouse-workers-organized-to-demand-pto-and-coronavirus-clinched-it/. Accessed April 19, 2020.
28. Monica Nickelsburg, "Thousands of Tech Workers Fighting for Climate Action Descend on Amazon HQ," *GeekWire*, September 20, 2019, www.

geekwire.com/2019/thousands-tech-workers-fighting-climate-action-descend-amazon-hq/. Accessed April 11, 2020.
29. DeManuelle-Hall, "The Hard Fight at Amazon."
30. See Chapter 10 this volume.
31. Rachel M. Cohen, "Coming off LA Strike Victory, A New Wave of Teacher Protests Takes Hold," *The Intercept*, January 29, 2019, https://portside.org/node/19252/printable/print. Accessed February 28, 2019.
32. Prashant Gopal, "A Backlash is Mounting in Cities Bidding for Amazon's HQ2," *Bloomberg News*, February 16, 2018, https://portside.org/2018-02-10/backlash-mounting-cities-bidding-amazons-hq2. Accessed February 24, 2019.
33. See Chapters 9, 11, and 12 in this volume.
34. Warehouse Worker Resource Center. "#NoTechforICE, WWRC Demands at Amazon Warehouse in San Bernardino," *Warehouse Worker Resource Center*, July 24, 2019, www.warehouseworkers.org/notechforice-wwrc-protests-at-amazon-warehouse-in-san-bernardino/. Accessed April 11, 2020.
35. Hannah Denham, 'No Tech for ICE': Protesters Demand Amazon Ties with Federal Immigration Enforcement," *Seattle Times*, July 12, 2019, www.seattletimes.com/business/amazon/no-tech-for-ice-protesters-demand-amazon-cut-ties-with-federal-immigration-enforcement/. Accessed April 11, 2020; Andrew Flanagan, "Hundreds of Musicians Pledge to Cut Ties with Amazon," *NPR*, October 24, 2019, www.npr.org/2019/10/24/773121764/hundreds-of-musicians-pledge-to-cut-ties-with-amazon-in-no-music-for-ice-letter. Accessed April 19, 2020; Drew Harwell, "Amazon Met With ICE Officials Over Facial Recognition System That Could Identify Immigrants," *Washington Post*, October 23, 2018, www.washingtonpost.com/technology/2018/10/23/amazon-met-with-ice-officials-over-facial-recognition-system-that-could-identify-immigrants/. Accessed April 19, 2020.
36. See Rajendra's Chapter 15 in this volume.
37. Saritha Rai, "Amazon's Bezos to Face Unprecedented Protests During India Trip," Bloomberg.com News, January 12, 2020, www.bloomberg.com/news/articles/2020-01-13/amazon-s-bezos-faces-unprecedented-protests-during-india-trip; Tyler Sonnebaker, "Indian business owners are furious about Amazon's $1 billion expansion into their country and are calling Jeff Bezos an 'economic terrorist,'" *Business Insider*, January 15, 2020, www.businessinsider.com/indian-shop-owners-protesting-amazon-call-bezos-economic-terrorist-2020-1. Accessed April 19, 2020.
38. Ravi Agrawal and Kathryn Salam, "Why India is Greeting the World's Richest Person with Protests and an Antitrust Case," *Foreign Policy*, January 14, 2020, https://foreignpolicy.com/2020/01/14/india-amazon-jeff-bezos-ecommerce-protests-antitrust-lawsuit-flipkart-walmart-economy/. Accessed April 19, 2020.

About the Authors

Jake Alimahomed-Wilson is Professor of Sociology at California State University, Long Beach. His research focuses on race, gender, labor, logistics, and global workers' struggles. He is the co-editor (with Immanuel Ness) of *Choke Points: Logistics Workers Disrupting the Global Supply Chain* (Pluto Press, 2018), author of *Solidarity Forever? Race, Gender, and Unionism in the Ports of Southern California* (Lexington Books, 2016), and co-author (with Edna Bonacich) of *Getting the Goods: Ports, Labor, and the Logistics Revolution* (Cornell University Press, 2008).

Juliann Allison is Associate Professor and Chair of Gender and Sexuality Studies at UC Riverside. Her current research examines the sustainability of Southern California's warehousing industry, gender and transitions to renewable energy sources, the ethics and politics of access to rock-climbing venues, and ecological grief and resilience. Her work has appeared in *Energy Research and Social Science*, *Journal of Labor and Society*, *Collabra*, *Journal of Poverty*, *Journal of Public Scholarship in Higher Education Collaborative Anthropologies*, *Global Environmental Politics*, and *The International Feminist Journal of Politics*, among other publications.

Jörn Boewe is a politologist and journalist specializing in labor issues and questions of trade union organizing. He and Johannes Schulten have been working together for years as a team, and run a Berlin-based journalist's office called "Work in Progress."

Spencer Cox is a doctoral candidate in the Geography, Environment and Society Department at the University of Minnesota. His research and activism seeks to further worker- and community-led movements based in a project of social emancipation and economic democracy. His writings concerning Amazon can be found at *The Nation* and *The Guardian*.

DCH1 Amazonians United is a union of workers based in the Chicago, Illinois region that is fighting for the respect, dignity, and decent working conditions that Amazon management denies them.

Sheheryar Kaoosji is the Founder and Executive Director of the Warehouse Worker Resource Center. He worked as a research analyst and strategist in support of efforts to organize workers in the supply chains of major global manufacturers, retailers, and food companies. He has a Master's Degree in Public Policy from UCLA and a B.A. from University of California Santa Cruz.

Steve Lang is Professor of Sociology at LaGuardia Community College in New York City, where he teaches courses in urban and environmental sociology. His research and writing focus on urban waterfront redevelopment and public space issues, as well as the politics of urban sustainability and resiliency.

Francesco S. Massimo is a doctoral student in Sociology at Sciences Po Paris, Center of Sociology of Organizations. He previously lived and studied in Italy, Spain, and the U.S. For the last three years, he has been studying work and management inside Amazon facilities in France and Italy, cooperating with workers and union members. He is also a founding editor of *Jacobin Italia*.

Ruth Milkman is Distinguished Professor at the City University of New York's (CUNY) Graduate Center. She is a sociologist of labor and labor movements and has written on a variety of topics involving work and organized labor in the United States, past and present. She is the author of numerous books, including her most recent book *Unfinished Business: Paid Family Leave in California and the Future of U.S. Work-Family Policy* (Cornell University Press, 2013), co-authored with Eileen Appelbaum. Milkman's prize-winning book *Gender at Work: The Dynamics of Job Segregation by Sex during World War II* (1987) is still widely read and cited. She has also written extensively about low-wage immigrant workers in the United States, analyzing their employment conditions as well as the dynamics of immigrant labor organizing.

Kim Moody was a founder of *Labor Notes* in the U.S. and the author of several books on labor and politics. His most recent is *On New Terrain: How Capital is Reshaping the Battleground of Class War* (Haymarket Books, 2017). He is currently a Visiting Scholar at the Centre for the Study of the Production of the Built Environment of the University of Westminster in

About the Authors

London, and a member of the National Union of Journalists, University and College Union, the British Universities Industrial Relations Association, the Labor and Working Class History Association, and the Working Class Studies Association.

Peter Olney is the retired Organizing Director for the International Longshore and Warehouse Union (ILWU). Active in the labor movement for over 45 years, he has worked as an organizer and negotiator for the International Ladies Garment Workers Union (ILGWU), the United Furniture Workers and SEIU's Justice for Janitors campaign. Since coming to California in 1983, he has mainly focused on building organization with immigrant workers. From 2001 until 2004, Olney was Associate Director at University of California Berkeley's Institute for Labor and Employment. Currently Olney trains organizers with the Building Trades Academy at Michigan State. Olney has an M.B.A. from University of California Los Angeles and frequently contributes to the *Stansbury Forum* and resides in San Francisco.

Dania Rajendra directs the coalition Athena, dedicated to delivering democracy by removing Amazon as an impediment to a democracy that finally represents us all and an economy that benefits everyone.

Ellen Reese is Professor of Sociology and Chair of the Labor Studies program at University of California Riverside. Her research focuses on gender, race, and class, public policy, and social movements. She is author of *They Say Cutback; We Say Fightback! Welfare Activism in an Era of Retrenchment* (American Sociological Association's Rose Series, 2011) and *Backlash Against Welfare Mothers: Past and Present* (University of California Press, 2005). She is co-editor of *The Wages of Empire: Neoliberal Policies, Repression, and Women's Poverty* (Paradigm Publishers, 2007) and co-author of *The World Social Forums and the Challenges of Global Democracy*, 2nd Edition (Paradigm Publishers, 2014).

Sreerekha Sathi is an Assistant Professor in Gender and Political Economy at the International Institute of Social Studies of Erasmus University in the Hague, Netherlands. She previously taught at the University of Virginia in its Global Studies Program, and at the Department for Women's Studies at Jamia Millia Islamia in New Delhi, India. She is author of *State Without Honour* (Oxford University Press, 2017).

Johannes Schulten is a journalist and Ph.D. student in Sociology at Friedrich-Schiller-University Jena. His doctoral thesis examines strategic trade union responses to structural change in the retail sector. He and Jörn Boewe have been working together for years and run a Berlin-based journalist's office called "Work in Progress."

Jeb Sprague is a Research Associate at the Institute for Research on World-Systems at the University of California Riverside. He has taught sociology at the University of Virginia, the University of California Santa Barbara, and in East Asia and the Caribbean. He is the author of *Globalizing the Caribbean: Political Economy, Social Change, and the Transnational Capitalist Class* (Temple University Press, 2019), *Paramilitarism and the Assault on Democracy in Haiti* (Monthly Review Press, 2012), and is the editor of *Globalization and Transnational Capitalism in Asia and Oceania* (Routledge, 2016).

Filip Stabrowski is Associate Professor of Anthropology at LaGuardia Community College at the City University of New York (CUNY). He has written about immigration, housing, and gentrification in New York City. His work has appeared in *Antipode*, *International Journal of Urban and Regional Research*, *Cambridge Journal of Regions, Economy, and Society*, and the *American Journal of Economics and Sociology*, among other publications.

Jason Struna is Assistant Professor of Sociology and Anthropology at the University of Puget Sound in Tacoma, Washington State. His research focuses on transnational class formation, and the labor processes that make contemporary capitalist globalization possible. His work appears in *Globalizations*, *Perspectives on Global Development and Technology*, *Labor Studies Journal*, and *The Journal of Labor and Society*. He is currently writing a book on shop-floor social life within Southern California's warehouse and logistics industry.

Nantina Vgontzas is a postdoctoral researcher at the AI Now Institute at New York University (NYU). Their research is focused on the sociology of labor, climate, and party politics in the United States and Europe. Previously they were a fellow at the Center for Engaged Scholarship and Urban Democracy Lab at NYU.

About the Authors

Dana M. Williams is an Associate Professor of Sociology at California State University, Chico, with interests in social movements, social inequalities (i.e., class, gender, and race), public sociology, and socio-political trust. Scholarship has appeared in *Contemporary Justice Review, Critical Sociology, Working USA: The Journal of Labor and Society, Social Science Journal, Race, Ethnicity, & Education, Teaching Sociology*, and many others. Williams is the author of *Black Flags and Social Movements: A Sociological Analysis of Movement Anarchism* (Manchester University Press, 2017) and co-author of *Anarchy & Society: Reflections on Anarchist Sociology* (Brill, 2013).

Katie Wilson is a co-founder and the General Secretary of the Transit Riders Union (TRU) in Seattle. TRU is a democratic organization of working and poor people building power to fight for public transit, affordable housing, progressive taxation, and other quality-of-life issues in the Emerald City. TRU coordinated the Housing for All Coalition, which championed a big business tax that was passed and then swiftly repealed under pressure from Amazon in 2018. Katie was also a member of the Progressive Revenue Task Force on Housing and Homelessness convened by the Seattle City Council to make recommendations for the tax measure.

Rand Wilson has worked as a union organizer and labor communicator for nearly forty years and is currently Chief of Staff for SEIU Local 888 in Boston. Wilson was the founding director of Massachusetts Jobs with Justice. Active in electoral politics, he ran for state auditor in a campaign to win cross-endorsement (or fusion) voting reform and establish a Massachusetts Working Families Party. In 2016, he was elected as a Sanders delegate to the Democratic National Convention. Wilson is president of the Center for Labor Education and Research, and is on the board of directors of the ICA Group, the Local Enterprise Assistance Fund and the Center for the Study of Public Policy. He also serves as a trustee for the Somerville Job Creation and Retention Trust.

Index

Adani Group 52
air pollution *see* environment
Alexa xii, 8, 9, 26, 41–42
algorithms xii, 7, 86, 133
Alibaba (China) 3, 30, 54, 55
Alliance for a Greater New York (ALIGN) 165, 167, 168
Amazon (corporation)
  book business 37
  capital-intensive facilities of 30, 91
  competitors of 30–31
  control of workforce by 129–130, 135, 141
  corporate clients of 39
  credit card sales and debt 57
  food delivery services 58
  "Friends and Favorites" 36
  global expansion of 25, 26
  growth of xi, 1, 37, 210–211, 220
  hostility to unions 137, 139, 210
  impact on global economy 2–3
  income from sales 3, 5–6, 22, 71, 72
  investigation into by EU 37
  investment in property by 22
  lawsuits and legal complaints against 74, 104, 113, 139, 143n16, 186, 202, 279, 281
  links to law enforcement agencies 44
  links to CIA 5, 27, 36, 40, 41
  links to ICE 5, 36, 41, 167–168, 232, 255, 280
  links to US government agencies 5, 38, 40, 232
  lobbying by 38
  logistical structure of 21, 25, 129, 252
  logo of 35
  management of staff consent by 133–137
  move into banking by 6
  "Pay to Quit" program 97, 112, 137
  political donations by 5, 38, 40, 149, 153, 155
  resistance to 46, 277–281
  response to COVID-19 xi, xiii, 1, 10, 238–243, 275–276
  sale of health care products by 37
  self-presentation to workers by 132–133
  Shipping with Amazon 75
  slogan "work hard, have fun, make history" 135, 137
  staff training by 133–134, 136
  and surveillance technology 4–5
  symbolism of name of 37
  tax avoidance by 3, 22, 38–39, 148
  tax breaks for xii, 161, 162, 165, 184, 280
  and vertical integration 37
  vulnerability of 171–172, 251
  see also France, India, Seattle, etc.; fulfillment centers, warehouses, etc.
Amazon Air 9
Amazon Alliance movement xii, 219–220
Amazon Campus program 7
"Amazon capitalism" xi, 2, 4, 12
Amazon Care 58
Amazon Climate Pledge 181, 186, 234
Amazon Connection 136–137
Amazon Delivery Service Partners 8, 9
Amazon Delivery Service Provider 69

Index

Amazon Employees for Climate Justice 232, 234–235, 255, 279
Amazon Flex 8–9, 27, 69, 73, 74, 75, 76
Amazon Go stores 6
Amazon HQ2 xiii, 152, 161–162, 164, 279
  competition for 171
  opposition to 165–173, 280
Amazon Logistics 27
Amazon Pay 6, 37
Amazon Political Action Committee (CAC) 38, 40
Amazon Prime xii, 6, 7, 81, 82
  US members of xii, 7, 82
Amazon Prime Day 81, 82
  protests on 41, 219, 220, 255, 259, 279, 280
Amazon Prime Now 26
Amazon Prime Video 37
Amazon Publishing 37
Amazon Studio 37
Amazon Web Services division (AWS) 6, 22, 26, 36, 39–40, 43, 225, 243, 275
  and links to CIA 27, 36, 40
  and links to ICE 41, 280
Amazon Workers International 273
Amazonians United (organization) 255, 260–261, 265, 272, 278
American Civil Liberties Union 43
American Legislative Exchange Council (ALEC) 38
Anita Borg Institute 231
anti-trust laws 6, 37–38
Apple 1
  Siri speakers 42
Athena (organization) xiii, 238, 242, 243, 244, 259, 280
Atlantic, The 27
Australia 3, 4
automation 10, 85, 96–98, 120, 181, 182–183, 225
  recruitment and hiring by 90–91
  workforce fears of replacement by 96–97, 98
  see also warehouses
Autor, David 226
Awood Center 113, 257, 258, 259, 278
  see also Muslim workers, Somali workers

Bad Hersfeld 123, 124, 210, 212, 213–214, 220
Ballmer, Steve 148
Basic Care (company) 37
Berman, Ray 75
Bezos, Jeff xi, 11, 21, 25, 38, 50, 102, 148, 152, 161, 255, 281
  personal wealth of 1, 39, 147, 238
Bharatiya Janata Party (BJP) 52
"big box" retailers 35, 69, 70, 72, 75
"big data" 36, 40
Black Employee Network 231
Black Friday, strikes on 219, 220, 276
  strikes in Italy on 139, 217–218, 259, 277
Black workers 9, 81, 88–89, 102–104, 113, 231, 269
Bloomberg News 243
Bloomington, California 185
blue-collar workers 9–10, 85, 90, 93, 102–103, 105, 108, 275
Blue Origin (rocket company) 38
bookstores 37
Borders (bookstore) 37
Botwinick, Howard 30
Brandt, Richard *One Click* 11
Braverman, Harry *Labor and Monopoly Capital* 130
Brazil 3–4
brick-and-mortar retail xi, 3, 6, 7, 8, 9, 25
Britain *see* United Kingdom
Burawoy, Michael 130, 134
Burning Man (festival) 227
"buy-box" 7

291

California, sales tax in 184
  see also Inland Southern California; Riverside; San Bernardino
California Ideology 227–228
Canonical Corporation 46
capitalism 1–2, 12, 45, 55, 225, 234
  variegated capitalism 7
Carey, Ron 256
Carney, Jay 38, 240, 241
Carrefour 29
CartonWrap packaging system 183
caste system, in Indian workforce 59
Castel San Giovanni, strikes in 217
Center for Community Action and Environmental Justice (CCAEJ) 181, 184, 185, 186
Center for Investigative Reporting 28
Center for Responsive Politics 38
Central Cottage Industries Emporium (CCIE) 58
Central Intelligence Agency (CIA)
  links with Amazon 5, 27, 36, 40, 41
China 3, 22–23, 50
choke points 117, 119, 120, 121
City University of New York (CUNY) 164
Civic Alliance for a Sound Economy (CASE) 149, 155
civil rights, violation of 5
Clinton, Bill 228
Clinton, Hillary 148, 228
cloud computing xi, 3, 5, 6, 39, 40, 167
Cohen, Larry 260
Color of Change (organization) 38
Communist Party (US) 256
Confederación General de Trabajo (CGT) 218
Confederación Sindical de Comisiones Obreras (CCOO) 218
Confederation of All India Trades (CAIT) 50, 52, 281
Confédération Autonome du Travail (CAT) 138, 139
Confédération Française Démocratique du Travail (CFDT) 138
Confédération General du Travail (CGT) 134, 138, 216, 217
Confederazione Generale Italiana del Lavora (CGIL) 140, 141, 217, 218, 259
Confederazione Italiana Sindicati Lavatori (CISL) 217
consumerism 4, 35, 72
corporate personhood 36–37, 39
corporations 1–2, 50, 156
"cost of obstruction" 30
Costa Rica 4
Council on American-Islamic Relations 257
COVID-19 xi, xiii, 1, 10, 238–242, 275–276
Cox, Kate 73
Crowley, Joseph 169
Cuomo, Andrew 161, 165, 169
customers
  Amazon Prime members xii, 7, 82
  collection of data on 35–36
  satisfaction of 133–4
  surveillance of xii, 4–5, 42
  violations of privacy of 5, 41–45
Cyber Monday, protests on 279, 280
Czech Republic 211

Dalit workers 60
Daraz Group 54
data centers 23–24, 26–27, 29
data collection 35–36
  audio data 41–42
Datacenters.com 26
Davis, Mike 244
de Blasio, Bill 161, 165, 168
deindustrialization, consequences of 116–117, 131
delivery
  logistical systems for 23, 69–72
  subcontracting of 73, 74

Index

delivery centers 76
  location of 179–180
  vulnerability of 119
delivery drivers 8, 70–71, 74, 76–81
  demographics of 77, 80–81
  employment status of 27–28, 73–4
  surveillance of 72, 77
Democratic Socialists of America (DSA) 169, 254
Desis Rising Up and Moving (DRUM) 168
DHL 23, 72
Diaper.com 7
Dijon, strikes in 216
distribution centers 24, 177
dot.com boom 22
drivers *see* delivery drivers
Duhigg, Charles 5–6
Durkan, Jenny 149, 150, 153

Eastern Europe 211
Eastgate Air Cargo Logistics Center 185–186
Eastvale Fulfillment Center 181
e-commerce 4, 50, 51–53, 54, 60–61, 69–70, 71, 75
Echo speakers 6, 41–42, 56
Economic Times, The (India) 55
Economist, The 180
Edwards, Richard 85
El Prat fulfillment center, strikes in 218
Electronic Data Interchange (EDI) 23
Electronic Frontier Foundation 43, 44
Electronic Privacy Information Center 42
Elliott-Negri, Luke 260
encryption platforms 43–44
environment, pollution of xii, 180–181, 184–185
Equal Employment Opportunities Commission 113
Europe 129
  strikes in 276–277
  trade unions 141–142, 210–211
  see also Eastern Europe; Western Europe
European Union, investigation into Amazon by 37
European Works Council 220

FAANG (US tech companies) 225, 229
facial recognition platforms 43, 233
families, work-related problems of 104, 111–112, 113
Federation of Indian Chambers of Commerce and Industry (FICCI) 58
FedEx 23, 27, 72, 73, 75, 177
"first-mile" delivery 27
Flipkart 52, 54–55, 56, 59, 281
"flywheel" business strategy 6
food delivery services xi, 58–59
For Us Not Amazon (organization) 244
Force Ouvrière (trade union) 216
Ford Motors 120–121
  "Fordism" 130, 134, 137
FoxConn 226
France 131, 138, 142, 276–277
  and COVID-19 240
  reform of labor laws 216–217
  strikes in 134, 139, 216–217, 219
  trade unions 138, 139
Fraser, Nancy 227
freight, value of 23
Fulfillment By Amazon (FBA) 8, 27
fulfillment centers xi, 3, 26, 76, 117, 118–119, 126, 130, 177
  location of 179–180
Fulfillment Operating System 119, 120

Galloway, Scott 21
gamification xii, 135, 136
Gates, Bill 147
gender, division of labor by 103–110, 113, 230, 233
  see also male workers, warehouse workers, women workers

General Motors 120–121
German Works Constitution Act 212
Germany 118, 138, 209, 211–213, 219
   Nazi period 232
   strikes 117, 123–4, 210, 212–213, 220, 259, 276, 277
   trade unions 118, 121–123, 209, 220
   warehouses in 123–125
   works councils in 209, 212
   see also Bad Hersfeld
Ghosh, Jayati 55
Gianaris, Michael 165, 168–169, 170, 171, 173
"gig" workers 8–9, 73–74
Gilets Jaunes *see* Yellow Vest movement
Glaeser, Edward 280
Global Financial Crisis *see* Great Recession
Global North 3, 9, 116
Global South 3, 50, 55, 58, 60, 116, 281
GMB (UK trade union) 216, 276
Goldman Sachs 170
Google 1, 3, 4, 29, 170
   slogan "Do no Evil" 35, 227
   workers' protest movements 233
GPS (global positioning system) 23
Graphical Paper and Media Union, UK (GPMU) 215, 216
Great Recession (2008) 117, 184
GrubHub (food delivery service) 58
Guardian, The 28

Hillwood Enterprises 185
Hindutva (Hindu nationalist movement) 52
Hirschman, Albert O. *Exit Voice and Loyalty* 135, 137
Hoffman, Christy 275
Hollande, François 216
Housing for All (Seattle organization) 149, 150, 151
Hudson Yards 172, 173
Hunger Games, The (film) 162, 173

Husing, John 181–182
hybrid retail 75

IBM 232
immigrant workers 40–41, 77, 81, 102, 104, 110, 124, 211, 257–258
Immigration and Customs Enforcement (ICE)
   links with Amazon 5, 36, 41, 167–168, 232, 255, 280
India 3, 4, 50–51, 54–61
   commercialisation of festivals 55–56
   composition of workforce 59–60
   food delivery services in 58–59
   military links to Amazon 57
   multiple language services via Alexa 56
   and neoliberalism 51–52
information and communication technologies 226, 229, 231
Inland Coalition for Immigrant Justice (IC4IJ) 185
Inland Congregations United for Change (ICUC) 185
Inland Empire Labor Council 185
Inland Southern California (ISC) 85, 102–103, 176–179, 182
   fulfillment centers in 177
   protest movements in 185–186
   warehouses in 176, 179, 181
   see also Riverside; San Bernardino
Institute of Local Self Reliance 243
Italy 131, 138, 142, 218, 219
   strikes in 139, 141, 217–218, 259, 277
   trade unions 140, 217
Izquierda Unida (political party) 218

Jaffe, Sarah 244
Jameson, Greg *Amazon's Dirty Little Secret* 11
Japan 3, 24
J.B. Hunt 23
JD.com 30, 54

Index

Joint Enterprise Defense Infrastructure (JEDI) 40
Jumpp, Jana 242
"just-in-time" (inventory system) 22, 24, 28, 29

Kapruka.com 54
Kiva robots 91, 96, 120
Kogan.com 4
Krueger, Alan 280

labor market, division of 131–132
labor process
  decoupling of 119–120, 124
  dispersal of 120, 121, 124–125
  dissociation from skills 130
  fragmentation of 130
labor relations 121
Labor Revitalization Studies (LRS) 213
LaGuardia Community College 164, 169–70
"last mile" delivery xi–xii, 27, 69, 71, 72–73, 75, 81, 119, 177
Latin America 3–4
Latinx workers 9, 79, 85, 90, 102–103, 105, 113, 182, 269
law enforcement agencies, use of Amazon technology by 44
lead-time 24
LeCavalier, Jesse 23
Lega Nord (political party) 218
Leipzig, strikes in 123, 125
Lille, strikes in 216
lobbying 38
logistical delivery systems 69–72
logistics companies 8, 23, 176
logistics complexes
  infrastructure of 21–22, 23, 24, 25, 69–72
  location of 9, 177
  vulnerability of 28–29
Long Island City xiii, 161–162, 164, 166, 279
  opposition to HQ2 165–171

Los Angeles, deliveries in 70–71, 75, 76

McKinsey Report (2018) 152
Macron, Emmanuel 217
"make rate" 10, 93
Make the Road New York 165, 166, 168, 242
male workers 103, 104–106, 108
March for Science 232, 233
Marcus, James *Amazonia* 11
Marx, Karl, on production process 24, 25
Mary's Place (organization) 149
Mechanical Turk (crowd-sourcing system) 9
Mellow, Gail 169
Mercado Libre (Argentina) 3
Mexico 3–4
Microsoft 3, 40, 147
Middle Eastern workers 111
military-industrial complex 40, 233
Minneapolis xii–xiii, 113, 234
Minnesota 278, 257–8
Mint operating system 46
Mira Loma, California 184–5, 186
Mitchell, Stacy 37, 243
Modi, Narendra 52
monitoring, of warehouse workers 10, 86, 91–95, 136
Montélimar, strikes in 216
Moody, Kim 117
Morning in America (political campaign) 154
Morris, Pat 181
Mosqueda, Teresa 155
Mother Jones (magazine) 28
MPower Change (organization) 168
Muslim workers xiii, 111, 113, 278
  see also Awood Center

Nation, The 244
National Football League (NFL) 40

Nature Conservancy, The (TNC, India) 52, 53
neoliberalism 156, 225–6
   progressive neoliberalism 227–228, 232
network redundancy 117, 119, 120
Never Again (movement) 41, 232
"New Democrats" 228
New York City xiii, 61, 161–2, 172
   Community Advisory Committee (CAC) 161, 169, 170–171, 172
New York Communities for Change 165, 242
New York Daily News 170
New Yorker, The 5–6
Newman, Penny 181
Norris, Frank *Octopus* 250

Obama, Barack 228
Ocasio-Cortez, Alexandria 169, 173
Oddo, James 241
Omar, Ilhan 258
"One Belt One Road" initiative 23
"one-click" consumerism 4, 7, 11, 35
online shopping platforms 6–7
Organization United for Respect at Walmart (OUR Walmart) 253, 254
Orléans, France, strikes in 216
Outline, The 244
OZZ inicjatywa Pracownicza (IP) 214, 215, 277

Pakistan 54
Pantry Fresh Food 26
Patchett, James 163–164
Patterson, California 184
Peerless Research Group 183
Piacenza, strikes in 217–8
Pillpack Inc. 37
Poland 123, 125, 138, 211, 213–215, 277
   strikes in 214
   trade unions 214, 215, 277

police forces, use of Amazon technology by 44
pollution *see* environment
Poznán, strikes in 213, 214
predatory pricing 7
privacy, violations of 5, 41–45
production processes 120–121, 225
   Marx on 25
progressive neoliberalism 227–228, 232
Project Connected Home over IP 45
protest movements, organization of 157

Queens Democratic Socialists of America 169
Queens Neighbourhood United 166, 168
Queensbridge Houses 164, 169, 170

"Rabbit" delivery device 77–78, 80
racialization of labor 70, 80–81, 88–89, 103–105, 107, 110–111, 113, 230, 231
   see also black workers; Latinx workers, etc.
racism 103, 107, 110–111
   see also black workers; Latinx workers, etc
Rahman, K. Sabeel 243–244
Rakuten (Japan) 3
Rao, Narasimha 51
refugee workers 220–221
Rekognition (facial recognition system) 5, 41
   links to government agencies 43
Reliance Ltd 52
retail trade 9, 75, 252
   see also brick-and-mortar; big box
Retail Wholesale and Department Store Union (RWDSU) 165, 166, 167, 278
Reveal (website) 28
Richard, Joe 256

Ring home surveillance system 5, 39, 41, 44
Riverside, California 85, 86, 102
robots 10, 91, 96, 120, 183
Ruiz, Phillip 239
Ryder delivery service 23

"salting" (union organizing) 256, 257
San Bernardino 86, 87, 102, 103, 111, 177, 184, 185, 280
San Bernardino Generation Now (SBGN) 185
San Fernando de Henares, Spain 218, 219
San Francisco, business tax in 156
Sand Hill Road 227
Sanders, Bernie 148, 254, 260
Saran, France, strikes in 216
Sarsour, Linda 168
Sawant, Kshama 151, 152, 155
scanners 10, 91
Schneider Logistics 23, 253
Seattle 147–150, 151–152, 155, 226, 280
  Amazon threat of capital strike 152
  homelessness in 149–150, 152
  radical history of 148
  tax laws 147, 155
  "Trump-Proof Seattle" 149
Seattle City Council 166–167, 252
  opposition to tax increases 153–155
  proposed tax increases 149–150, 151, 153
Seattle Metropolitan Chamber of Commerce 150, 152–153
Seattle Times 153, 155
second machine age 50, 53
Service Employees International Union (SEIU) 185, 253, 258, 259
  SEIU Healthcare 149–150
sexism 103–113, 233
  see also male workers; women workers
Shaikh, Anwar 30

Sheffi, Yossi 23, 29
shopping centers 9
ShoppingBag.pk 54
ShoppingExpress.pk 54
Sierra Club 185, 186
Silicon Valley 226, 227
Siminoff, Jamie 44
Simpson, April 169, 170
Singapore 54
Singh, Manmohan 51
Smalls, Chris 242
smartphones, retail transactions from 72
Smith, Cooper 180
Smith, Noah 178–179
socialism and socialists 251, 254, 256
Socialist Workers Party 256
Solidaires Unitaires Démocratiques 138, 216
Solidarność 214, 215
Somali workers xiii, 113, 257, 278
  see also Awood Center
sortation centers 26, 59, 76
South Asia 51, 54, 55, 60
South Coast Air Quality Management District (SCAQMD) 186
South East Asia 3
Southern Pacific Railroad 250
Spain 138, 218–219, 277
spatial inequality 178–180, 182, 225
Spector, Robert *Get Big Fast* 11
Sri Lanka 54
state surveillance 27
State University of New York (SUNY) 164
state-corporate nexus 5, 35, 41
Staten Island fulfillment center 167, 240, 278
Stone, Brad *The Everything Store* 11
supply-chain risk management (SCRM) 28–30
supply chains
  disruption to 29

logistics of 27, 251, 252
management of 69–71
vulnerability of 28–30, 81, 252
surveillance 5, 36, 98
 of customers xii, 4–5, 42
 of delivery drivers 72, 77
 of workers 5, 86, 92
 see also monitoring; warehouse workers
"surveillance as a service" 42
surveillance capitalism 4–5, 11, 36, 41, 98
Swiggy (food delivery service) 58

Target Corporation 29
Tata Group 52, 55
Tax Cuts and Jobs Act (2017) 39
Taylor, Bishop Michael 169, 170
Taylorism 130, 135
Teachout, Zephyr 243–244
Teamsters 1932 (trade union) 185
Teamsters for a Democratic Union 256, 259
tech industry 229–231, 232
"Tech Left" 233
Tech Solidarity 232
tech workers 225, 226, 279, 280
 demographics of 230
 privileged status of 226–227, 228–229
 protest movements by xiii, 232–233, 250, 254–255, 279
 social class aspects of 228, 231, 234
Tech Workers Coalition 232, 235
TED Talks 227
Tencent Holdings Ltd 54, 55
Third Party Logistics (3PL) companies 23, 253
third-party sellers 4, 7, 27
Time-Based Competition 24
"time off task" 10, 239
time-space compression 53
Trade Union Share Owners (TUSO) 216

trade unions 121–122, 134, 137, 213, 219
 international networking by 210, 213, 219–220
 shop-floor activism 221
 see also France; Germany, etc.
Trades Union Congress UK (TUC) 216
Transit Riders Union (TRU) 148, 149, 154
transnational capitalist class (TCC) 54, 58
transnational corporations 50, 53
Transnational Social Strike (TSS) 277
Transport Topics (journal) 21, 23
transportation 22–23, 25, 27–28, 252
 by air 9, 22, 23, 252
 by rail 22
 by sea 22
 impact on environment of xii, 180–181, 184–185
 value of freight 23
Trump, Donald 40, 148, 149, 228, 232
Twin Cities, Minnesota 258
Twitch Prime video streaming service 36, 39

Ubuntu operating system 46
UNI Commerce 219
UNI Global Union 218, 276
Uniform Land Use Review Process (ULURP) 162–163, 166
Unione Generale del Lavoro (UGL) 140
unions *see* trade unions
Unione Italiana del Lavoro (UIL) 217
Unite (trade union) 215, 216
United Food and Commercial Workers Union (UFCW) xii, 253, 254, 259
United Kingdom 210, 215–216, 242, 276
United States
 government agency links to Amazon 5, 38, 40, 232
 US Federal Trade Commission 37

Index

US Postal Service (USPS) 8, 9, 26, 27, 72, 73, 244
US Securities and Exchange Commission (SEC) 27, 30
United Trade Service Union (Ver.di) 118, 122–123, 125, 209, 212, 213, 218, 221, 259
UPS 23, 27, 72, 73, 75, 177
   strike by workers 257
Urban Upbound (organization) 170

Van Bramer, Jimmy 165, 166, 168–169, 170
venture capital companies 22, 227
Ver.di *see* United Trade Service Union
Victoria, Anthony 182
Vietnam 27, 54
Virginia 27, 244, 280
Virginia Educators United 280

Walmart xi, xii, 8, 22, 24, 29, 30, 50, 55, 71
   campaign against 253–254, 257
warehouse workers
   "associates" 10, 90, 93, 137
   break times for 95
   demographics of 9, 87–90, 102–104, 112–113, 182
   disciplining of 92–94
   fears of replacement by automation 96–97, 98
   gender discrimination of jobs for 102–110, 112–113
   injuries to 10, 28, 94, 97
   loneliness of 95
   monitoring of 91–95, 97
   pay of xi, 9, 182
   problem solvers 108, 120
   racial discrimination of 104, 107, 110–111, 113
   strikes by xii–xiii
   surveillance of 5, 86, 92
   working conditions of xi, 10, 28, 234, 266–267

Warehouse Workers for Justice 105
Warehouse Workers Resource Center (WWRC) 185, 280
Warehouse Workers Stand Up 278
warehouses xi, 23
   automation in 10, 85, 91, 94, 96–98, 120, 182–183, 120
   cross-dock 24
   impact on environment of 180–181, 184–185
   location of 9, 117, 179–180
   resistance to 184–185
   robots in 10, 91, 96, 120, 183
   size of 177
   working conditions in xi, 9–10, 28, 129, 234, 266–267
Washington Post, The 38, 40, 172
Washington State, tax laws 147, 148
Washington Technology Industry Association 148
Weill Cornell Medicine 170
West, Emily 42
Western Europe xii, 3, 210–211
   strikes in 138
   trade unions xii, 137–138
#WeWontBuildIt (protest movement) 232–233, 250
white workers 104–105, 108, 182, 230
Whole Foods Inc. 172, 257, 276
   acquisition by Amazon xi, 3, 6, 25, 26, 75, 65, 82
Wired (magazine) 227, 228
women workers 103, 108, 110, 113
   favoritism shown to 108
   gender discrimination for jobs of 104, 105–107
   gender harassment of 109–110
   pregnancy discrimination towards 113
   see also families
Womxns' March 232, 233
workers
   control of 129–130, 135, 141

demographics of 81, 88–89, 102–104, 182, 269
deskilling of 130–131, 132
employment status of 124
fostering of competition between 136
harassment of 104, 106
organizing of 221, 251, 253–254, 256–260
pay of xi, 9, 182
permanent workers 132
as producers of value 25
reserve army of 131–132
surveillance of 5, 86, 92
temporary workers 131–132, 136, 182, 182
"zero-hours" contracts for 216
see also Black workers, blue-collar workers, Dalit workers, delivery drivers, Latinx workers, male workers, Middle Eastern workers, racism, racialization of labor, Somali workers, tech workers; warehouse workers; women workers
works councils 121, 123, 209, 212
World Bank 22, 54
Worm, Terrell 240
Wrocław, strikes in 214

xenophobia 110, 113
XPO 23

Yellow Vest movement 139, 217, 277
Yuan, Quan 180

Zappos.com 7
"zero-hours" contracts 216
Zomato (food delivery service) 58
Zuboff, Shoshana 36, 98

Thanks to our Patreon Subscribers:

Abdul Alkalimat
Andrew Perry

Who have shown their generosity and comradeship in difficult times.

Check out the other perks you get by subscribing to our Patreon – visit patreon.com/plutopress. Subscriptions start from £3 a month.

The Pluto Press Newsletter

Hello friend of Pluto!

Want to stay on top of the best radical books we publish?

Then sign up to be the first to hear about our new books, as well as special events, podcasts and videos.

You'll also get 50% off your first order with us when you sign up.

Come and join us!

Go to bit.ly/PlutoNewsletter